International Law and Economics

More information about this series at http://www.springer.com/series/13428

Luis Tomás Montilla Fernández

Large-Scale Land Investments in Least Developed Countries

Legal Conflicts Between Investment and Human Rights Protection

Springer

Luis Tomás Montilla Fernández
Institute of Law and Economics
University of Hamburg
Hamburg, Germany

ISSN 2364-1851 ISSN 2364-186X (electronic)
International Law and Economics
ISBN 978-3-319-65279-5 ISBN 978-3-319-65280-1 (eBook)
DOI 10.1007/978-3-319-65280-1

Library of Congress Control Number: 2017951454

Printed on acid-free paper

This Springer imprint is published by Springer Nature
The registered company is Springer International Publishing AG
The registered company address is: Gewerbestrasse 11, 6330 Cham, Switzerland

To my Parents,
for their Support

Acknowledgments

I doubt I would have been able to finalise this book without the support of the following persons and institutions:

Professor Anne van Aaken was more than a supervisor in the mere sense of the word. Her dedication and enthusiasm supported me throughout each step of the investigation. My co-supervisor Professor Hans-Bernd Schäffer always had the time to discuss the smallest details and to inspire me with new ideas.

Dr. Christian Häberli and Professor Christian Kirchner also provided invaluable comments and constructive criticism during the early stage of this project.

The unconditional support provided by my parents, family, and friends is the greatest gift anyone has ever given me. I would also like to thank my colleagues from the Institute of Law and Economics in Hamburg for our numerous interesting discussions, their scholarly input and willingness to correct my English, and their reassuring support in times of self-doubt.

The financial contributions of the German Research Foundation (*Deutsche Forschungsgemeinschaft*), the Institute of Development Studies at the University of Sussex, and the Dispute Settlement in Trade: Training in Law and Economics (DISSETTLE) enabled me to conduct field research in Ghana and to pursue further research at the University of Accra, UC Berkeley, Columbia University, and the University of St. Gallen. I am grateful to all these institutions for their support.

October 2015 Luis Tomás Montilla Fernández
Munich, Germany

Contents

Acronyms

ACHPR	African Commission on Human and Peoples' Rights
ADB	African Development Bank
ARSIWA	Articles on Responsibility of States for Internationally Wrongful Acts
Banjul Charter	African Charter on Human and Peoples' Rights
BIT	Bilateral Investment Treaty
CAT	Committee Against Torture
CEDAW	Convention to Eliminate All Forms of Discrimination Against Women
CERD	Committee on the Elimination of All Forms of Racial Discrimination
CESCR	Committee on Economic, Social and Cultural Rights
CIL	Customary International Law
CMW	Convention on the Protection of the Rights of All Migrant Workers and Members of Their Families
CRC	Convention on the Rights of the Child
CRPD	Convention on the Rights of Persons with Disabilities
CT	Contract Theory
CWFS	Committee on World Food Security
EACJ	East African Court of Justice
EC	European Commission
ECHR	European Convention on Human Rights
ECtHR	European Court of Human Rights
ECOWAS	Economic Community of West African States
EU	European Union
FAO	Food and Agricultural Organisation
FDI	Foreign Direct Investment
FET	Fair and Equitable Treatment
FIAS	Foreign Investment Advisory Service

GDP	Gross Domestic Product
HR Committee	Human Rights Committee
HRC	Human Rights Council
HRL	Human Rights Law
HRs	Human Rights
ICARRD	International Conference on Agrarian Reform and Rural Development
ICC	International Criminal Court
ICCPR	International Covenant on Civil and Political Rights
ICESCR	International Covenant on Economic, Social and Cultural Rights
IACHR	Inter-American Court of Human Rights
ICJ	International Court of Justice
ICSID	International Centre for Settlement of Investment Disputes
IFC	International Finance Corporation
IFPRI	International Food Policy Research Institute
IGO	Inter-governmental Organisation
IIA	International Investment Agreement
IIL	International Investment Law
IL	International Law
ILC	International Law Commission
ILO	International Labour Organisation
IMF	International Monetary Fund
IO	International Organisation
ISO	International Organization for Standardization
LCIA	London Court of International Arbitration
L&E	Law and Economics
LDCs	Least Developed Countries
LSLI	Large-scale Land Investment
MAI	Multilateral Agreement on Investment
MIA	Multilateral Investment Agreement
MFN	Most Favoured Nation
NAFTA	North American Free Trade Agreement
NCP	National Contact Points
NGO	Non-governmental Organisation
NHRI	National Human Rights Institutions
NIE	New Institutional Economics
NPM	Non-precluded Measures
NT	National Treatment
OHCHR	Office of the United Nations High Commissioner for Human Rights
PAT	Principal-agent Theory
PCA	Permanent Court of Arbitration
PPT	Positive Political Theory
RC	Rational Choice

SADC	Southern African Development Community
TTIP	Transatlantic Trade and Investment Partnership
UDHR	The Universal Declaration of Human Rights
UN	United Nations
UNCAC	United Nations Convention Against Corruption
UNCAT	Convention Against Torture
UNCTAD	United Nations Conference on Trade and Development
UNCITRAL	United Nations Commission on International Trade Law
UNHCR	United Nations High Commissioner for Refugees
VCLT	Vienna Convention on the Law of the Treaties
WFP	World Food Programme
WTO	World Trade Organisation

List of Figure

List of Tables

Chapter 1
Introductory Part

1.1 Relevance of This Book

The rationale for this book is based on the increasing relevance of agricultural Foreign Direct Investment (FDI) as a political priority for the global investment agenda since 2008. FDI has been promoted by the international community as a tool to improve food security and the production of biofuels. It is also expected that agricultural FDI will have positive effects on poverty reduction and development. Repercussions of expanded agricultural FDI include conflicts in the area of international law (IL).

This study is also motivated by the existing problems of land governance in some least developed countries (LDCs) created by the lack of proper protection of property rights. The study offers an in-depth Law and Economics (L&E) analysis that elucidates to what extent IL can incentivise relevant stakeholders to mitigate associated negative effects.[1] Agricultural FDIs often involve a changeover in the ownership of land. This is a sensitive economic and social issue in some African countries as more than 60% of the population are small-scale farmers who depend on the land for their livelihoods. Land tenure is linked to access to food, and also represents social privilege.[2] Aside from the highly polarised discussions surrounding large-scale land investments (LSLIs) by foreign investors in LDCs, there is a persistent concern in academia about the lack of knowledge and expertise in the area of agricultural FDI. One explanation may be that the scarcity of land investment in the previous decades made it a less pertinent issue.[3] While other disciplines

[1]On the weak situation of property rights in Africa see: Heltberg (2002), p. 189; Framework and Guidelines on Land Policy in Africa and also Amanor (2012).

[2]Source: The World Bank (2016).

[3]Moran (2011) broadly analyses diverse types of FDI, however specific agricultural FDI are not considered. See: Food and Agriculture Organization of the United Nations, *Contract Farming* (FAO 2001), p. 1. See additionally: United Nations Conference on Trade and Development, *World*

L.T. Montilla Fernández, *Large-Scale Land Investments in Least Developed Countries*, International Law and Economics, DOI 10.1007/978-3-319-65280-1_1

have seen more in-depth LSLI research, legal scholars have paid less attention to these questions and their implications for land governance, IL, and legal fragmentation.[4]

To ensure good governance, it is extremely important to guarantee patterns of broad-based development. Hence, participation and consensus, effectiveness and efficiency, transparency and accountability, lack of corruption, rule of law, equality, stability, and freedom are considered fundamental to this process.[5] Social scientists have concluded that the lack of a minimum level of governance and legitimacy produces discontent within the population affected by agricultural FDI.[6] Such a situation frequently leads to civil unrest in which the affected population may seek government intervention to address the problems of food security, undernourishment, unemployment, or other negative consequences of the investments that interfere with their fundamental rights, such as the right to education, work, and housing.[7] Some opinions highlight the risks associated with LSLIs mainly because of how they operate.[8] In some cases LSLIs entail a prohibitive social cost when the particularities of the projects are not addressed in the national investment framework. Studies on other kinds of FDI have shown that foreign investments can be positive, but in addition to FDI, the domestic institutional framework may need to be reconsidered in order to achieve the proposed developmental goals of host countries.[9]

The international dimension of LSLIs also motivates this research project. There is a transnational element to investments involving public and private economic actors that are frequently protected by international investment law (IIL) through international investment agreements (IIAs). Thus in some cases, violations of the right to property and food are related to the performance of LSLIs. This occurs, for instance, in contexts where traditional rights systems have been affected by *de facto* expropriations without appropriate, or any, compensation. Some NGOs have become specialists in the area of LSLIs and have illustrated this phenomenon by reporting, for example, that 22,000 people were displaced in Uganda after their land

Investment Report 2009. Transnational Corporations, Agricultural Production and Development (World Investment Report 2009, 2009); Vermeulen and Cotula (2010), p. 13.

[4]Probably the only legal scholar that has developed a research agenda on LSLIs is Lorenzo Cotula. Here are some of his contributions: Cotula et al. (2009); Cotula (2010a); Vermeulen and Cotula (2010). Cotula has also analysed the instruments used to perform the investments: Cotula (2011).

[5]Deininger et al. (2011), p. 95. Governance is seen as one of important requirements to achieve the expected social and development goals of NGOs. See i.e.: Pinstrup-Andersen and Watson (2011), p. 246.

[6]Seminally, see the following publication: Williamson (1996). For more concrete literature focussing on LSLIs investment we refer to: Deininger et al. (2011), p. xxvii.

[7]See i.e. some of the media reports: The Economist; The Guardian; Bach (2010). See also this article that refers to the opinion of Nigerian Parliament.

[8]von Braun and Meinzen-Dick (2009); De Schutter (2011), p. 249; Borras et al. (2011), p. 209.

[9]For a study on the effects of NGOs on different economic sectors see the seminal contributions by: Moran (2006, 2011).

was sold to a British company for timber production.[10] Locals have also been displaced in the Gambella region of Ethiopia.[11] Similar cases have also been reported in other African countries such as Tanzania,[12] Sierra Leone,[13] and Zambia.[14]

Agricultural FDI has been promoted at the domestic and international level as a panacea for poverty-related problems, which is the most prominent cause of hunger in LDCs. It has taken centre stage in political discourse in recent years.[15] This line of argument has contributed to the international community's tolerance for wrongful acts, including human rights (HRs) violations justified under the pretext of development and global food security. In this sense this topic is relevant since it appears that neither national law nor IL have been able to provide appropriate remedies when such rights infringements occur.

1.2 The Problems Approached in This Book

1.2.1 Overview

This study analyses LSLIs made by foreign investors for agricultural purposes in Africa's LDCs from a L&E perspective.[16] It examines the protective mechanisms that IL provides to hold investors accountable when HRs of third parties are violated. More specifically it is about an explicit kind of FDI (large-scale acquisitions of land with agricultural purposes) and their relationship with Human Rights Law (HRL), which is functionally analysed through the lens of L&E methodology. The very reason that this study focuses on this topic is because IL is fragmented and is frequently unable to hold investors accountable.

[10] Al Jazeera.

[11] The Oakland Institute (2011a).

[12] The Oakland Institute (2011b).

[13] The Oakland Institute (2011a).

[14] The Oakland Institute (2011c).

[15] See, for example, the Ethiopian government's invitation to investors from India to invest in Ethiopia: Varadarajan (2011).

[16] We rely on the UN's definition of LDCs, low-income countries suffering from the most severe structural impediments to sustainable development. These handicaps are manifested in a low level of human resource development and a high level of structural economic vulnerability. The criteria for defining a country as a LDCs can be found at: United Nations (2016).

1.2.2 International Legal Conflicts Related to LSLIs: State of the Art

A rapid increase of LSLI began to be reported by NGOs and International Organisations (IOs) in 2008.[17] The reports considered this increase to be a reaction to the food and financial crises dominating global markets during 2008 and 2009.[18] Land markets were stimulated by national policies bringing about a process whereby host states, most of them LDCs, transmitted property rights by selling or leasing land for long periods (up to 99 years) to private and public investors.[19] These policies aimed at increasing the production of food commodities for global markets and obtaining raw materials for the production of biofuels. In economic terms these policies entail, in some cases, the creation, stimulation, or reactivation of land markets in LDCs in order to offer attractive development opportunities. Development opportunities predominantly arose in four areas: infrastructure, jobs, technology, and knowledge. All factors led to higher agricultural efficiency and thus increased overall food security.[20] Ideally investors would reclaim fallow or underused land at low prices. The local population would benefit through both direct and indirect effects, such as new jobs, food security, and better infrastructure. Such a win–win situation would improve the condition of all affected parties.

The stimulation of land markets that entails the transmission of property rights is, from an economic point of view, highly welcome. Under free market conditions it makes possible the efficient allocation of resources and therefore an increase in productivity. From a narrow contractual point of view, it supposes a relationship between the sovereign state and the investor with expected positive effects for third parties. This approach assumes that the local population might benefit from a redefinition of property rights, the improvement of domestic food security, and the increase in the supply of global food and energy markets. This means that governments, as representatives or social delegates, sign contracts with foreign investors that might directly benefit the local population and, indirectly, also the population abroad. In many LDCs where agricultural activities are the most important economic sector, such investment contracts are considered to be the most important instruments to promote development at the household level. Local governments consider these investments to be a unique opportunity to achieve high levels of economic development since the land that is being used for this purpose was underused by previous tenants or was non-productive state property. IOs like the World Bank and the Food and Agricultural Organisation (FAO) see these types of investment as a way to incentivise local economies and promote development.[21]

---

[17] The first relevant report written on this issue was: GRAIN (2008).

[18] De Schutter (2011), p. 249; von Braun (2010), p. 299; OECD (2008).

[19] A more detailed description of the deals at Sect. 2.3.

[20] Häberli (2012).

[21] FAO (2008) at para 2; Deininger et al. (2011), 34 ff.

IIAs[22] play a predominant role as a mechanism designed to balance risks that are virtually omnipresent in negotiations involving LDCs. IIAs are inter-state treaties especially designed to mitigate political risks. They provide investors coming from both signatory states with a higher level of legal security because[23] they have great variance, but they typically guarantee the principle of non-discrimination, Fair and Equitable Treatment (FET), protection against expropriation, and a neutral forum for adjudication in the event of such matters arising. Domestic courts are excluded in the vast majority of cases. IIAs can be considered a means of activating IL without exhausting domestic remedies.

In well-functioning states the transmission of property rights, for instance as a result of LSLI, is protected by legal institutions. These institutions create incentives for contracting parties to reduce the negative effects for third parties while simultaneously incentivising third parties to enforce their rights when they are infringed upon.[24] Nevertheless in some jurisdictions the institutional environment is not able to create such incentives for third parties to enforce their rights against the unexpected or unwilled effects of investments. If effective institutions are perhaps missing in national law, IL is expected to provide institutions that allow states to prevent investments from affecting the rights of third parties, or to provide remedies where the existence of damages can be shown.

This is all happening in the context of a worldwide process of economic integration in which legal and economic actors are interacting with asymmetric information and, therefore, asymmetric bargaining power. In some exceptional cases, it seems to be problematic that neither national law nor IL are able to create appropriate incentives for LSLIs to generate the expected results. Even though the differences between the actors involved in the global market are well known, the fact that they are carrying out transactions demanding land, which is an essential good for the subsistence of populations in LDCs, has produced a wave of strong reactions. This issue can be illustrated by two examples. The first example is drawn from a jurisdiction in which private property rights are protected, the second where there is no protection of property rights.

In 1990 the Ugandan government began a series of land reforms to increase productivity and reduce national poverty. This project was monitored by FoodFirst

[22]In the framework of this book the term IIAs follows the approach of the UNCTAD that denotes that: 'Professional Trade and Investment Agreements (PTIAs) refer to a variety of different international arrangements, including free trade agreements, regional trade agreements, economic framework agreements, economic partnership agreements, new-age partnership agreements, economic complementation agreements, agreements for establishing a free trade area and closer economic partnership arrangements. PTIAs, however, do not include BITs. The term 'International Investment Arrangements' (IIAs) includes both PTIAs and BIT.' FAO (2012).

[23]This statement is made under the premise that IIAs were signed between developed and developing countries. IIAs offer better legal security to investors investing in developing countries.

[24]On the role on institutions in creating incentives in order to achieve proposed goals see the seminal work by: North (1990).

Information and Action Network (FIAN), which released its first report in 2009.[25] The restructuring project included legal reforms such as the Investment Code of 1991, which was adopted by the Investment Authority and designed to comply with the demands set by the International Monetary Fund (IMF) and the World Bank.[26] In 2000 the government initiated a 'Poverty Eradication Plan', which was the foundation for a new state agricultural policy. The government chose specific regions to initiate the plan and entered into negotiations with foreign investors. Even though national law imposed a ban on selling land to foreign investors, the expropriation of property from nationals was sometimes followed by the granting of long-term rent contracts to foreign companies on the same properties. The most recent report on this project was made in 2009.[27] It informs us that most of those evicted are still living on the periphery of the plantations, and it remains uncertain whether they will be allowed to stay there. No compensation has been made to the locals for their loss of livelihood, and no political will demonstrated to give them back their land. The government has not recognised the protection of their traditional land despite existing legal provisions and regulations in the Land Act 1998 that recognises traditional ownership and the duty of the government to properly compensate in expropriations.[28] The Act also regulates cases in which illegal occupations take place. In these cases the statute of limitations is set at 12 years for initiating any legal action. The prescription of the term of 12 years gives the occupants the right not to be unwillingly displaced because occupants are *bona fide* occupants in such cases. Cases have been reported where 2% of displaced locals received compensation. Nevertheless it has often been the case that they were allocated less land than they held in the past.

A second scenario given for consideration is set in Ethiopia, where the state is the owner of the land. This was reaffirmed by the constitutional reform carried out in 1994.[29] It included the right of farmers to obtain free land, gave protection from eviction, gave rights to pastoralists, and provided for compensation in the case of expropriation. The Federal Rural Land Administration and Land Use Proclamation 89/1997 grants power to local governments to manage their lands.[30] Even though the

---

[25]Graham et al. (2008).

[26]This in the framework of the so-called 'Washington Consensus' that as explained by John Williamson describe a set of policy prescriptions that constituted the 'standard' reform package promoted for crisis-wracked developing countries by Washington D.C.-based institutions such as the International Monetary Fund, World Bank and the US Treasury Department. Source: Williamson.

[27]Graham et al. (2008), p. 34.

[28]Uganda Land Act (No. 16 of 1998) An Act to provide for the tenure, ownership and management of land; to amend and consolidate the law relating to tenure, ownership and management of land; and to provide for other related or incidental matters. Uganda Gazette No. 41, 2 July, 1998, Acts Supplement No. 11, pp. 1–83.

[29]Constitution of Ethiopia LEX-FAOC129684 [1994] art 40.3.

[30]Federal Democratic Republic of Ethiopia Rural Land Administration and Land Use Proclamation (No. 456/2005) art 5.

land is owned by the state, the terms expropriation and compensation are used and applied where tenants had acquired rights through their possession of the land.[31] The history of resettlement and villagisation in Ethiopia gains new relevance with the introduction of new investments. This is not the first time Ethiopia has dealt with these issues. It seems, however, that the dimensions of these new investments are much broader than in the past. To take just one example of a widespread occurrence, indigenous landowners in the region of Gambella were evicted and now face the problem of a lack of food. In almost every case, the occupancy of land is not supported by any kind of documentation or cadastre, making it difficult to prove or demonstrate any rights locals may have acquired during the period of time they occupied or made use of the land. Compensation—one relevant issue that has been reported in Ethiopia—may be provided in cases of forced displacement. According to information provided by the Ethiopian government, however, this has never taken place.[32] Moreover, rules on compensation are based on the condition that affected farmers should be able to prove, by way of legal title, their rights to the land. Even though at a constitutional level the right to land is ensured even if land titles do not exist, the procedures of expropriation and compensation apply only if a legal title exists. Thus in most cases in which indigenous peoples are affected, the expectation to be compensated is, in fact, very low. Since land registration is almost non-existent in Ethiopia, the state has enormous discretionary power to distribute and redistribute land.

A common denominator in these examples is the fact that affected people are unable to enforce their rights. Only two examples were given in order to draw a general picture and make the issue more comprehensible in terms of what the specialised literature means when it refers to the phenomenon of 'land grabbing'. The aim of this research project will not be to provide a proper definition of land grabbing. The literature uses this term in a rather opaque and unclear way that could bias a well-intentioned academic approach. Beyond this opacity the broad, complex, and far-reaching scope of the issue would probably lead us to fail. It is sufficient for us to mention some of the most common occurrences of the phenomenon. This will facilitate the construction of a solid starting point for this research project.

In a first category of cases, conflicts arise due to uncompensated expropriations, development-induced displacements, as well as the impossibility of demonstrating the ownership of land due to the lack of a cadastre. In a second category of cases, governments sell land that, even though it formally belongs to the state, has been in the possession of individuals and communities for many years (in this case land possessors are not considered owners). In a third category of cases, conflicts arise when investments lead to a change in the use of land. In most cases land that was used to produce food is converted to land used for the production of biofuels.[33]

---

[31]Ibid.

[32]Tekle; The Oakland Institute (2011b); Fisseha (2012).

[33]See for example the selection of following articles that make reference on these issues: Bundesministerium für Wirtschaftliche Zusammenarbeit und Entwicklung, *Entwicklungspolitische Positionierung zum Thema: Großlchige Landkäufe und - pachten in Entwicklungsländern - "Land*

Aside from the costs associated with the transmission of property rights, the main problem seems to be that affected individuals are unable to enforce their rights.

Prima facie the growth of LSLIs by foreign investors may not be a bad idea. After all, the process of privatisation is not an uncommon state policy and has been successful in other places. In many sectors privatisation is implemented in order to remedy efficiency problems that arise when services are run by the state. There are states in which public services such as water, gas, electricity, public transportation, road tolls, and infrastructure projects are allocated to private actors with the expectation of better services and increased access to these services. Privatisation, however, can increase the complexity of certain situations. When private actors are bound to provide services that are essential for a well-functioning state and for the fulfilment of the state's pre-established obligations at the international level, the relationship between the state and private actors is blurred. As an example, although privatisation agendas are not necessarily introduced as a means to fulfil international HRs obligations, in many cases this role cannot be avoided.[34] The private sector contributes to the fulfilment of HRs obligations. This means that states tacitly delegate the fulfilment of their HRs responsibilities to private hands.[35] From a legal point of view this creates a stronger relationship between the different legal jurisdictions and legal regimes at the domestic and international levels as they become increasingly interdependent. This interdependence occurs because the fulfilment of HRs obligations that are initially given to states in the framework of HRL in fact now depend on private actors. Even though private actors are required to fulfil HRs obligations traditionally given to states, there is no extra-contractual mechanism to enforce HRs that were infringed by investors since they are governed by a different legal regime, namely that of IIL. It can be expected, therefore, that in well-functioning states governments need to create coordination mechanisms to garner the economic benefits from investment while also fulfilling their HRs obligations. If investments produce unexpected externalities, questions regarding the applicability of appropriate national law or IL might arise since investors are not accountable under the international HRL framework.[36]

At the international level, this can lead to a conflict between the norms of these two jurisdictions. The analysis of the conflict between these norms and the

---

Grabbing" (2009), p. 8; von Braun and Meinzen-Dick (2009); von Braun (2010), p. 299; GRAIN; Graham et al. (2011); Deng (2011).

[34]This statement is an implication of the obligations states have regarding the protection and promotion of human rights. With regard to states' obligations and the role of transnational corporations see: Stiglitz (2007), p. 451; as well as Human Rights Council (2011a). For the same line of argumentation see Human Rights Council, *Report of the Special Representative of the Secretary-General on the issue of human rights and transnational corporations and other business enterprises* (A/HRC/8/5/Add2, 2011).

[35]For a similar view see: Principles for Responsible Agricultural Investment that Respects Rights, Livelihoods and Resources [2010] available <http://siteresources.worldbank.org/INTARD/214574-1111138388661/22453321/Principles_Extended.pdf> accessed 25 December 2013.

[36]On the responsibility of multinational enterprises see at footnote: 34.

potentially detrimental effects is not novel in IL.[37] Conflict between the positive norms of different legal jurisdictions has been identified and analysed in the legal literature under the theoretical framework of legal fragmentation.[38] In light of this, legal scholars have been analysing the relationship and potential conflicts between IIL and other legal areas in order to find a way to offer balanced legal security between the protections offered by IIL and other legal jurisdictions, such as HRs or environmental law.[39]

In well-functioning states investment contracts have specific norms that, in addition to guaranteeing investors' rights, ensure that certain HRs-related goals are also fulfilled. However, there is increased complexity in investor-LDC relationships due to the weak institutional environment that affects contractual design, which in turn produces high enforcement costs in the case of non-performance. A weak institutional framework makes possible the misallocation of contractual incentives to achieve pre-established goals and ensures that promises and extra-contractual obligations remain unfulfilled.[40] Even though it is not expected, nor even conceivable, that contractual parties foresee all future events affecting the contractual relationship, ignored negative effects that were either foreseeable or strategically planned by the contractual parties are highly problematic. They become even more problematic due to the regulatory restrictions of states from IIAs. If investment contracts do not create proper incentives to achieve pre-established HRs-related goals, a host of legal conflicts may arise if investors infringe a third party's rights that are protected by a different legal jurisdiction, and enforcement for affected legal subjects is prohibitively costly.[41] Investment contracts may produce negative side effects for third parties. When negative side effects occur, governments frequently do not have the incentive to take the necessary steps to protect third parties under their jurisdiction. This leads to the question of whether the affected third parties can or should intervene in the contractual relationship so that damages can be avoided or repaired. In order to clarify this introductory question and lay a more detailed foundation for the introduction of our

---

[37]As we will show in this book, this issue has been broadly covered by the ILC in its study about the fragmentation of International Law. Simma and Kill (2009). For a study approaching the norm conflicts and its effects on governance: ILC (2006).

[38]The most relevant contribution regarding fragmentation of international law was made by the ILC. The Commission proposed ways to avoid the further fragmentation and to deal with cases where fragmentation is relevant. See: ILC (2006); Pauwelyn (2003).

[39]Some of the most relevant contributions dealing with fragmentation in the law and economic literature are: ILC (2006); van Aaken (2006); Benvenisti and Downs (2007), p. 595; Trachtman (2008); Pauwelyn (2003); van Aaken (2009), p. 483; Pauwelyn.

[40]For a contribution reviewing the economic literature on the relationship between corruption, agrarian policies and development see: United Nations Conference on Trade and Development, *Intellectual Property Provisions in International Investment Arrangements* (UNCTAD/WEB/ITE/IIA/2007/1 2007). For a theorisation of the role of institutions for development see: Bardhan (1997), p. 1320; Raeschke-Kessler and Gottwald (2008), p. 588.

[41]The report of the ILC offers an explanation about the source of legal conflicts arising due to the existence of legal fragmentation. See footnote: 37.

research topic, we offer a brief analysis of how third-party enforcement works at the national and international level.

1.2.2.1 Framing a Legal Mechanism for Third-Party Enforcement

The first issue that needs to be examined in order to elucidate to what extent affected individuals can enforce presumably infringed rights is the legal link between the affected third party and the contractual parties. This is necessary in order to establish a legal interest and activate legal mechanisms that make it possible to build a legal claim. The legal link is given by the fact that the contractual relationship between the state and the investor facilitates the infringement of the protected rights of third parties. This problem is by no means exclusive to IIL. It also happens frequently in everyday contractual relationships.[42] Samuel Williston affirmed this in his study published in the Harvard Law Review (1902) with such conclusiveness that one of the most discussed issues in contract law in national jurisdictions is whether a third party has any rights in a contract that is signed by others but benefits them.[43] One cannot always consider LSLI contracts to be beneficial to third parties because specific promises of effects for third parties are missing. It is this point that causes problems, at least from the point of view of the adjudication of property rights.[44] The conflict of interest arises from the simultaneous transmission of rights and duties while the property rights in question belong to a person who is not a party to the original contract.

The consequences of the contract for the third party could be positive or negative. Where they are positive, the effects of the contract benefit the third party. In economics literature negative consequences are known as negative externalities, and the human behaviour or activity that allows such effects to arise is known as opportunism. Ergo, there might be a relationship between opportunism and negative externalities.[45] When the third party is harmed, it is expected that legal institutions provide protection to ensure that the third party can enforce their infringed property rights. The legal protection of these rights does not emanate from contract law (because the third party is not part of the contract) but stems from the fact that property rights are protected by special national law. Therefore, the legal actions available to a third party to uphold their property rights and the contractual effects of such legal action are marginal. Third parties have *standi* because property rights have been infringed, not because a contract has been signed.

---

[42]Concerning the problematic of third-party enforcement and the potential inclusion of counter-claim clauses in international treaties see: ILC (2006).

[43]Williston (1902), p. 101.

[44]Even though Williston exemplified the problems by using the transmission of property rights, it does not exclude its applicability in other legal areas and the conflicts with other protected rights.

[45]On opportunism see *infra* at: 4.3.

The discussion offered by Williston addresses the literature in two different ways. First it focuses on the recognition of third parties as legitimate subjects who can intervene in a contractual relationship. Second it sets out the necessary legal policies that need to be implemented so that the gap between the dogmatic and the legal policy aspects can be minimised. At the domestic level, the historical treatment of these discussions has been different, varying from legal system to legal system. Nevertheless, civil and common law systems have a unified criteria for the legitimation of a third party to exercise legal actions when a contract has a negative impact on their property rights.[46] At the international level, the discussion about prosecution structures allowing possible enforcement through third parties has gained relevance. These models are seen as part of the construct to strengthen the link between governance and enforcement. It has also produced competence between adjudicating institutions and 'traditional' mechanisms existing beyond arbitrators, as well as between the different arbitration institutions themselves.[47]

Third parties have *standi* when their legal personality and their right to property are recognised.[48] In a well-functioning legal system harmed third parties are endowed with the ability to enforce their rights. Therefore, contracting parties will have incentives to take these considerations into account during the negotiation process so that they minimise the risk of producing damages, at least up to the point where they cannot internalise them. This means that contractual parties will be willing to internalise potential damages (i.e. through compensation) but only up to a level where the difference between the gains and losses is zero.

At the international level enforceability for individuals is very costly because access to judicial remedies is limited. Individuals are considered legal subjects only in exceptional cases and therefore their right to initiate legal disputes is restricted. Therefore, when such a situation arises it is difficult to fulfil the minimal requirements for legal adjudication. IIL does not recognise individuals to be legitimately able to enforce their rights. Consequently, infringements are almost unenforceable. One could argue that parties assume that national jurisdictions of the contracting state will be accessible to those actors affected by the investment activity. This point of view is not wrong, since national constitutions and laws protect such rights. However, problems arise if national laws fail, as oftentimes happens in LDCs. In

[46]Williamson (1985); Williston (1902), p. 101, 773.

[47]See, i.e., the contribution of Dammann and Hansmann that makes an analysis on the institutional competence between the two system and highlights the difficulties that courts in weak jurisdictions have given the fact that they have the tendency to be corrupt, slow and inept. The possibility that the parties can turn to a stronger jurisdiction contributes to the stimulation of markets that allow actors to access the principled adjudication mechanism needed to support contractual relations. Dammann and Hansmann (2006). See also: Bayer (1995).

[48]The considerations made here concerning a contract for the benefit of a third person are offered in a general way. It is not our intention offer an in-depth discussion about this institution. It is used in a more descriptive way to explain the legal link between a contract and third parties. Our intention is to show how legal institutions at the national level might work when the property rights of a third person are affected through the signature of a contract.

spite of this, the law must resolve failures that arise when contractual parties cause damage to third parties. Seemingly, however, there is no legal structure in place to make contractual parties accountable in third-party HRs violations.[49]

Let us consider the following illustrative example. State *S* and investor *I* are negotiating an investment contract.[50] The object of the contract is the sale of land for agricultural purposes. For reasons of liquidity, it is impossible for *S* to compensate the actual landowners who will eventually be evicted. Therefore, *S* and *I* agree that *I* will compensate the displaced people immediately after signing the investment contract. *S* and *I* close the negotiation, sign the contract, the land is expropriated, and the people are displaced; but *I* does not fulfil its obligation to compensate them.

Applying the described considerations, at the domestic level the harmed third parties would be able to enforce their property rights and make the reparation of damages enforceable. If one looks at the jurisdiction of IIL, even though it is applicable to the regulation of the investment activity of *I* in *S*, third-party individuals cannot enforce their property rights because they do not fulfil the requirements. In this case they are not recognised as legal subjects. Therefore, IIL appears to structurally fail as it allows a completely legal economic activity to produce *de facto* damages, which can be proven but not enforced. This implies that IIL is not able to create the proper incentives for the contractual parties to behave correctly or repair the damages incurred when infringements arise. Those affected by the contract, however, have the option of exercising legal remedies at the domestic level and, after exhausting those remedies, would have access to international HRL. However, there are many cost-based problems in exercising these legal mechanisms. Not only is it difficult to gain access to HRL, its enforcement is costly. Both access and cost are obstacles to enforcing rights that have been infringed upon at the national and international level. Another issue is that the judicial system of the LDCs fails regularly because of internal problems associated with weak institutions.[51]

Although this failure of IIL has been pointed out in academic research, a practical solution is still lacking.[52] This case has particular relevance because the increase in investment activity in the agricultural sector (which is protected by IIL through IIAs) is seen as the most effective way to realise the right to food in LDCs,

---

[49]The consideration here is made with regard to the missing solid structure in IIL that would make it possible for affected third individuals to intervene in arbitration procedures. However, this absolutely neglected possibility is slowly changing, probably as a consequence of the increasing competition between the arbitration courts, as well as the mechanisms existing beyond the existing procedures. See the broad legal evolutionary approach dealing with the enforcement mechanisms, although in commercial arbitration by: Dammann and Hansmann (2006). See also: Cafaggi (2012).

[50]The existence of an IIA between *S* and the State where *I* is domiciled is assumed.

[51]Many researchers, NGOs and think tanks have been trying to find the way to make investors or traders accountable for human rights violations. For a well-developed study see: Dammann and Hansmann (2006). For a well-developed paper dealing with the Ruggie's understanding of complicity in general as well as complicity in particular see: Weschka (2006); Narula (2006), p. 691; Sunga (1992).

[52]Wettstein (2013), p. 243; Ellickson (1993).

as well as to promote economic development. In the next section we will introduce IIAs and their relevance to the agricultural investment agenda.

1.2.2.2 Explaining Why IIAs Are Relevant in Liberalising Land and Agricultural Markets

There are some aspects of IIAs that make them relevant the moment the agricultural sector is liberalised. Currently more than 3000 IIAs regulating bilateral and regional investment relationships are in force.[53] Although the literature has not completely demonstrated the effect of IIAs on agricultural FDI flows,[54] we do know that IIAs offer a high level of protection to investors. This protection limits the ability of the state to exercise its sovereign powers, e.g. the introduction of measures to regulate economic areas. Due to the expectation that IIAs will create an investor-friendly environment, potential host countries use this legal instrument to signal their willingness to attract agricultural investors. For instance, in 2013 the sub-Saharan Africa region showed a high level of activity by creating new free trade areas and regionalising investment and trade negotiations.[55] IIAs are thought to stimulate FDI by mitigating the political risks that are common in LDCs.[56] They can be seen as mechanisms that balance high levels of risks investors face vis-à-vis potential hostilities in the host states due to the nature of the investment activity, their status as foreigners, and the institutional environment governing host countries. The long-term element of most FDI makes the investment activity risky *per se*; all in all there is no FDI without risk. Risk encompasses, among other things, a long payback time, high temptation for state opportunism, technological innovation that could make the investment less profitable, changes in regulatory preferences over time due to governmental ideology, subsidies, competition policies, and also how projects are performed.[57]

[53]United Nations Conference on Trade and Development, *World Investment Report 2013* (World Investment Report 2013, 2014) 101.

[54]The question whether IIAs attract FDI has been treated in previous empirical studies that have not provided consistent results. We go into more details in Chap. 2 of this study.

[55]United Nations Conference on Trade and Development, World Investment Report 2013 (World Investment Report 2013, 2014) 101.

[56]Regarding the definition of IIA, see footnote: 22. For a classical view in economics see: MacDougall (1960), p. 13; Blomström and Kokko (1999); Moran (2006). And, now in the legal literature see: Moran (2011). See also Dolzer and Stevens (1995).

[57]Peter Muchlinski approaches policy issues and risks concerning NGOs in a nice way. Regarding the change of governments' preferences because ideological issues. Muchlinski (2008). Guzman also refers to aspects regarding the risks in FDI. Guzman (1998), p. 639.

1.2.2.3 FDI and IIA: Relationship, Relevance, and the Changing Map

In 2006 in the sub-Saharan Africa region, investment flows accounted for approximately USD 22 billion, rising to USD 30 billion in 2007, and then reaching USD 72 billion in 2008.[58] Although FDI inflows to Africa decreased to an estimated USD 56.3 billion in 2013, if one compares the figures for 2006–2013, this decrease still represents a considerable increase in FDI.[59] One product of globalisation and the proliferation of IIAs is an unavoidable increase in global economic integration and interdependence between countries. In this environment the developing world has gained significance. Studies point to the fact that more than one-third of FDI flows to developing economies originate from other developing economies.[60] This changes the classical structure of FDI in which a developed country invests in a developing country. According to the 2012 World Investment Report, inward flows of FDI worldwide rose 16% in 2011; this increase surpassed the level achieved before the economic crisis in 2008.[61] In real numbers this means that FDI reached USD 1.5 trillion. FDI flows to developed countries grew in 2013 and reached USD 566 billion, which represents only 60% of their average before the 2008 economic crisis.[62] Developing countries continued to account for more than half of global FDI as they reached USD 777 billion. This was a new high for developing countries, representing 54% of global inflows.[63] In recent decades inward inflows have continuously increased. The exception was 2008, when foreign investments were affected by the global financial crisis, as was the case with other sectors.[64] This upward trend in FDI, described in the literature as an 'explosion', can be associated with an increase in privatisation projects promoted by IOs in diverse countries. Increasing FDI in developing countries was driven by a 10% rise in Asia and 16% in Latin America.[65] The poorest countries remained in a FDI recession, with flows to LDCs contracting by 11% to USD 15 billion.[66] FDI in agriculture began to rise as a result, and according to the UNCTAD went from an average of USD 600 million annually in the 1990s to an average of USD 3 billion in the period between 2005 and 2007.[67]

---

[58]United Nations Conference on Trade and Development, World Investment Report 2013 (World Investment Report 2013, 2014), p. 104.

[59]United Nations Conference on Trade and Development, *World Investment Report. Investing in a Low-Carbon Economy* (20 edn, United Nations 2010), p. 33.

[60]United Nations Conference on Trade and Development, *Global FDI Rose By 11%; Developed Economies are Trapped in a Historically Low Share* (UNCTAD, N 15 January 2014, 2014), p. 7.

[61]United Nations Conference on Trade and Development, *World Investment Report 2014* (World Investment Report 2014, 2015), p. xvii.

[62]Ibid.

[63]Ibid.

[64]United Nations Conference on Trade and Development, *World Investment Report 2012* (World Investment Report 2012, 2013), p. xiii.

[65]Ibid.

[66]Ibid xiv.

[67]Ibid.

The main reason for the promotion of FDI is the hope that they will stimulate economic cooperation and development.[68] They are widely considered a potential instrument for poverty reduction in LDCs. It is axiomatic that countries need economic success to raise their populations out of poverty and to reduce the number of people earning less than USD 1 per day. In Africa the effort to increase cooperation and regional integration has been intensified through the creation of regional economic organisations. With the rapid increase in economic growth in the last decades, cross-border operations originating in other African countries have increased by up to 18% between 2009 and 2013, up from around 10% in the period between 2003 and 2008.[69] Developing countries have undergone a market liberalisation process; however, in most cases this has not resulted in the kind of poverty reduction and development effects that were expected.

In more recent years, in addition to entering into IIAs, most LDCs have demonstrated efforts to improve their national investment environment with the aim of attracting FDI. Examples of such efforts include tax law reforms, constitutional reforms, and the creation of investment promotion agencies.[70] In recent times 80% of investment flows in LDCs went to resource-rich economies in Africa.[71] This resulted in an increase in natural resources investments, which are known as non-traditional investment activities.[72] Since agriculture is the principal economic sector in most sub-Saharan countries, high FDI flows might have direct repercussions on land use and the commercialisation of agricultural and non-agricultural activities. They might also have repercussions on interactions between the national and local governments, and between investors and the local population. Agricultural FDI also brings interested heterogeneous groups of actors together and makes it necessary for them to be involved in negotiations. These groups consist of foreign investors, state representatives (which include investment agencies, ministries, and local authorities), NGOs, and members of the local population. Suppliers, insurers, and contractors are also commonly involved in agricultural investment activity. NGOs that are frequently present in LDCs are renowned for promoting the interaction of these actors to expand fair trade and investment, as well as local development.

---

[68]In most of the IIAs the wording include aspects related to development. For example the BIT between Ethiopia and Germany states that parties desire to 'intensify economic co-operation between both states'. Treaty Between the Federal Republic of Germany and the Federal Democratic Republic of Ethiopia Concerning the Encouragement and Reciprocal Protection of Investments (Ethiopia Germany) [2004]. In the case of the BIT between the government of the United Kingdom of Great Britain and the Government of the Republic of Sierra Leone parties include the term 'prosperity in both States' as the conductive goal of the reciprocal protection under the BIT. Agreement between the Government of the United Kingdom of Great Britain and Northern Ireland and the Government of the Republic of Sierra Leone (Great Britain-Sierra Leone) [2000] available at <http://investmentpolicyhub.unctad.org/IIA/country/221/treaty/2903> accessed 15 September 2015.

[69]United Nations Conference on Trade and Development, World Investment Report 2014 (World Investment Report 2014, 2015), p. 40.

[70]Sharma and Aykut (2003), p. 149.

[71]United Nations Conference on Trade and Development (2011), p. 7.

[72]Ibid.

Growing investment activities in sub-Saharan Africa poses a challenge to both investors and states to integrate these economic activities into the institutional framework at the local level. There is a need to coordinate all of the relevant interest groups, given the highly sensitivity nature of land ownership and the deep changes that the liberalisation of FDI represents. On the one hand, decisions concerning agriculture in LDCs are a highly sensitive issue for the host state, as in some cases this sector represents over 30% of the host state's GDP.[73] On the other hand, market liberalisation involves a profound process of reforms and adaptations that touch upon many aspects of local culture with potentially far-reaching consequences. In LDCs common property rights are often the customary norm and their transmission is made verbally without access to a centralised property registration authority.[74] In many states where LSLIs take place, up to 90% of the population live in rural areas.[75] They are subsistence farmers,[76] and for the vast majority of these people land is seen as more than a simple factor of production: it has political, religious, social, economic, and cultural value. Land is considered a factor of social stability, a privilege.[77] Additionally, the gap between written legal protection and its enforcement are of great relevance here, since in most LDCs cadastre registers are absent.[78] Of course these characteristics differ in their intensity from one African sub-region to another. What remains constant, however, is the notion that the liberalisation of FDI in LDCs requires property rights that are sufficiently well defined and enforceable to attract foreign investors. Notwithstanding, this transformation can make the investment process more complex and time consuming. IIAs might be seen as a vehicle to achieve FDI goals without having, *prima facie*, to undertake substantial institutional changes. IIAs offer a set of guarantees to investors and a set of limitations on states that produce high costs in the case of contractual breach. IIAs result in a state relinquishing sovereignty to incentivise investors. This becomes relevant if, *ex post,* states are forced to introduce regulatory measures to offset the social costs that may arise as a result of LSLIs.

---

[73]Ibid.

[74]For an analysis about the benefits of land registration and the respective problematic situation in sub-Saharan Africa see: Atwood, p. 659. On harmonisation of customary land tenure systems see: Lavigne.

[75]This is based on data compiled by the World Bank that can be found at: The World Bank (2016).

[76]Wehrmann (2008) and Behnassi and Yaya (2011).

[77]An introduction to the relevance of land tenure and sub-Saharan Africa and the conflicts associated with land tenure see: Bernstein (2005).

[78]With regard to enforcement, we follow the notion that enforcement includes judicial and non-judicial measures. That enforcement includes either public or private measures that lead the legal subject to comply with *ex ante* commitments. It also includes different types of adjudication procedures that are designed either privately, by states or IOs, including self-enforcing systems. Issacharoff (2010). Enforcement represents a strategic juncture for the effectiveness and legitimacy of the economic activity of foreign investors, see: Katz (1995). This is contrary to the notion that affirms enforcement promoted by the private sector is outside of the sphere of enforcement and belongs specifically to the social sphere. See i.e.: Bernstein (2005), 68 ff. administrative and also private enforcement measures.

1.3 Research Context

The negative effects of LSLIs by foreign investors on host countries' local populations and the apparent failure of IL to create incentives to offset them frame the scope of this paper. To the best understanding of the author of this study, approaching LSLIs from a L&E perspective has not yet been attempted. This short section aims to draw a general picture of how academia has engaged with this issue to date. Legal contributions that are considered in greater depth in the next chapters are introduced here, as well policy proposals to ameliorate the negative effects of LSLIs. It also introduces legal instruments at the international level that could be applied to improve the protection of locals' rights in the context of LSLIs.

Most of the insights relating to the inside elements of LSLIs come from NGOs. The organisation GRAIN initiated the discussion on land grabbing in 2008 by presenting the results of a study conducted in sub-Saharan Africa.[79] This publication was further updated in 2016.[80] The research highlights the detrimental effects of LSLIs in diverse regions of the world. Apart from GRAIN, the Land Coalition and the Oakland Institute have arguably conducted the most well-known studies.[81] They initiated research projects in an attempt to disclose information about LSLI projects and the direct impact these projects have on the local population in Zambia, Tanzania, and Ethiopia.[82] Very few legal scholars have addressed the question of agricultural FDI and LSLI. Some examples are Cotula et al. (2008, 2009), Cotula (2011, 2015), De Schutter (2011), and Borras et al. (2011). These analyses examine certain aspects of this issue, such as the existing legal institutions and policies, in an effort to identify the best approach to protect the right to food of minorities. Cotula (2011) specifically emphasises contractual design as a mechanism to improve the situation.[83] Cotula (2015) offers an analysis of the interface between land rights and Bilateral Investment Treaties (BITs). His analysis focuses on the fact that a better understanding of that interface will help to rethink land policies and investment treaties.[84] From an economic point of view, the World Bank published the most relevant studies.[85] They investigate whether LSLIs are able to yield sustainable equitable benefits. In this controversial report, the World Bank exposes land grabs and reveals that they tend to

---

[79]The study that opened the discussion on Land Grabbing was: GRAIN (2008). Two additional seminal studies have been published that focus on finance actors and their role in expanding LSLIs. See: GRAIN; GRAIN.

[80]GRAIN (2016).

[81]GRAIN is an international non-profit organisation that works to support small farmers on food production issues. The Oakland Institute is a policy think tank dedicated to advancing public participation and fair debate on critical social, economic, and environmental issues.

[82]For a detailed resume on organisations that have published articles on Land Grabbing we refer to: Palmer (2011).

[83]A legal contractual analysis of LSLIs: Cotula (2010b).

[84]Cotula (2015).

[85]Deininger et al. (2011). See also: Rabah et al. (2011).

occur in regions where corruption and institutional failures dominate the local environment. The same report, however, considers opportunities to 'yield gaps' where productive investment can make use of arable land to produce rations.[86]

From a policy point of view, IOs or NGOs have developed regulatory instruments in the framework of soft law that seek to impose some discipline on investment activities. Apparently according to some NGOs, the translation of the stated good intentions of some foreign investors into concrete action has been hard to perceive. The suggestions made to date concentrate on developing a stronger regulatory framework for land markets. Land investment is seen as the solution to the problem of food shortages, which currently affects about one billion people in the world, and also a catalyst for the further development of energy markets.[87] IOs believe that FDI in agriculture will contribute towards guaranteeing global and local food security and also stimulate depressed sub-Saharan economies.[88]

IIAs are the primary source of the legal content contained in the corpus of IIL. Yet in these agreements, no specific consideration is given to agricultural markets and the potential problems arising from agricultural investments. Nor do these agreements consider the inclusion of HRs and labour rights. If we look more specifically at HRs law, environmental law, and labour law, the opposite is true where continuous legal development has taken place in the last decades. From a substantive point of view, these developments provide greater protection for HRs, albeit in many cases these rights are still unenforceable.[89] In this regard the most applicable research, and indeed the most relevant contribution to the substantive development of HRs regulation in general, is the work of John Ruggie, Special Representative of the Secretary-General on the Issue of Human Rights and Transnational Corporations and Other Business Enterprises.[90] He has authored two reports that offer a new approach to dealing with corporations that are HRs violators.[91] On the one hand, it is stated that private actors are not considered in

---

[86]For comments on the study of the World Bank see: Borras et al. (2011), p. 209.

[87]Borras and Franco (2009), p. 50; Meinzen-Dick and Markelova (2009).

[88]See for example the reports by the FAO: von Grebmer et al. (2012); FAO and OECD (2010); FAO Rome Declaration on World Food Security. Food World Forum Summit [1996] WSFS 2009/2; FAO (2008); FAO Declaration of the World Summit on Food Security [2009] WSFS 2009/2; FAO, WFP and IFAD (2012). As well as the researches ran by the World Bank: FAO (2012); Rabah et al. 2011. However, the same president of the World Bank recognises some risks of LSLIs by stating: 'The World Bank Group shares these concerns about the risks associated with large-scale land acquisitions'. Source: 'Access to Land is Critical for the Poor' *The World Bank Group*.

[89]Pringle (2011).

[90]For a broad discussion about the work of Prof. Ruggie in his role as Secretary-General on the Issue of Human Rights and Transnational Corporations and Other Business Enterprises we recommend the edited following edited book: Ruggie.

[91]The reports were submitted in 2006 and 2007 and in 2008. He proposed a framework to 'Protect, Respect and Remedy' human rights. Deva and Bilchitz (2013). In the 2008 report he developed legal policies to think in potentials actions to make the first report realizable. Human Rights Council (1998).

HRs mechanisms as potential HRs violators.[92] On the other hand, the report underlines the prevalence of such actors in their role as HRs violators. The contribution of these reports to the creation of new laws is still being realised. What is clearly recognisable is that these reports have brought the issue of the relevance of private actors in the HRs arena, and the necessity to make them accountable for their actions, to the discussion table.

This contribution examines the interface between HRs protection and investment activities by looking at how investment activities affect local people's rights.[93] Increased investment in agricultural land has been a central factor in increasing claims of HRs violations, especially violations of the right to property and the right to food. Nevertheless, further academic research in this regard is still needed.[94]

The problem arising from the rapid increase of land acquisitions, which received extensive media coverage through 2011, seems to have been forgotten. Neither the academic community nor IOs are following the development of this phenomenon in the affected countries. While some states and corporations were held responsible for the effects of LSLIs, like the increase in quotas for the production of biocombustibles and manipulation of the land market, the level of responsibility required of states and corporations lost its significance. However, the HRs issue is still latent in affected regions, specifically in countries where agricultural policies based on large-scale investment were introduced.[95]

1.4 Research Questions

This research study provides a systematic L&E analysis of LSLIs. It examines whether IL has mechanisms to address HRs violations in the presence of LSLIs. To that end, the general question that forms the core of this investigation is this: can IL provide legal remedies to adequately deter HRs violations in LSLIs in LDCs? Of course this general question raises a string of other questions.

1. Although we already offered some specifications and examples to set up the kinds of investments that are being referred to, it is considered necessary to answer the following questions: what are LSLIs? Why are LSLIs categorised as land grabbing? Why are new land and agrarian policies needed in sub-Saharan Africa? Who are the actors involved in negotiations for LSLIs? What legal instruments are used to perform the economic agricultural activity? What

[92]Human Rights Council (2007), para 35.

[93]Human Rights Council (2011b).

[94]The most relevant publications dealing with the negative effects of LSLIs are the followings: Sornarajah (2010); De Schutter (2009); Schonecke and Kurzke-Maasmeier (2009).

[95]For example, in 2014, the World Bank explicitly recognised the failures of its projects in Ethiopia; which rather than producing the developing oriented effects as expected, produced forced displacement of indigenous people. See the document of the World Bank recognising its failures at: The Inspection Panel (2014).

potential benefits are associated with LSLI contracts? Are the expected effects congruent with the known effects? Are the employed contractual instruments adequate for the desired investments?

2. To address the question of how the rights to property and food are protected by IL, we will examine the mechanisms in HRL at the universal, regional, and domestic levels to protect the rights to property and food of sub-Saharan Africans. What enforcement mechanisms are offered by HRL? What mechanisms are offered by IIL at the international and domestic levels to protect the rights to property and to food? What are the differences between the protection offered by IL in the contexts of HRL and IIL regimes?
3. After analysing the problem from a legal perspective, we will turn to the social sciences to analyse whether IL can properly allocate incentives to mitigate what we consider opportunistic behaviour. First, we introduce a theoretical economic perspective to test whether the economic concept of opportunistic behaviour can be applied as a lens to help analyse the issue of concern here. Having passed the test, we will build a theoretical model in an effort to provide potential solutions. We therefore apply social science to answer the questions: what is opportunism? What are the sources of opportunism in LSLI contracts? What form does opportunism take? What kind of incentives does IL offer to mitigate opportunistic behaviour? How can the problem of opportunism, which arises in the presence of principal-agent problems and incomplete contracts, be solved?
4. This research then looks at the legal mechanisms and potential remedies that might counter opportunism. Without pretending to offer a panacea, this project maps strategies which are considered to be a comprehensive set of potential solutions to the problems arising from LSLIs in LDCs. We will map these strategies by first of all determining the control mechanisms that already exist or might be developed in IL to tackle opportunism, and identifying stakeholders who might have the potential to curtail opportunistic behaviour. Further, we will proceed by describing the regulatory power of states when confronted with food emergencies.

1.5 Research Tools for Theorizing LSLIs from a Law and Economic Perspective

In this section we will present a general overview of our methodological approach. Each subsequent chapter will further develop this approach. This research uses L&E methodology for an analysis of LSLIs made by foreign investors in LDCs. It may also be seen as a contribution to the agricultural investment and HRL research agenda that has already been categorised as essential by specialised literature in this area.[96] We particularly consider LSLIs made by foreign investors as a legal issue

[96] van Aaken (2013), p. 27 <http://investmentpolicyhub.unctad.org/Blog/Index/22der> accessed 12 July 2015; Häberli (2012); Cotula (2015), p. 49.

that needs investigation by identifying the relevant legal actors and their challenges in getting desirable effects from these transactions. From the IL point of view, the legal failures leading to the undesirable effects produced by LSLIs are considered a product of the misallocation of incentives, leading to the violation of pre-existing HRs obligations. Based on this observation we intend to provide a set of potential solutions to solve these legal conflicts. To this end we will analyse whether IL has the appropriate instruments to strike a balance between promoting FDI flows and preventing the HRs violations of the local population of a host state. Enforcement mechanisms play a central role as potential solutions in this research.[97]

This research will conduct a functional analysis through the lens of economic theory.[98] We will consider rational choice (RC)[99] assumptions by applying a theory of institutions known as new institutional economics (NIE). To achieve this goal we will apply contract theory (CT) and principal-agent theory (PAT).[100] As conceived by North, NIE incorporates 'a theory of institutions into economics. It builds on, modifies, and extends neoclassical theory. It retains and builds on the fundamental assumption of scarcity and hence competition—the basis of the choice theoretic approach that underlies microeconomics.'[101] NIE includes work in transaction costs, moral hazard, political economy, property rights, hierarchy and organisation, and public choice. The main goal of NIE, and its contribution to this research project, is 'to explain what institutions are, how they arise, what purposes they serve, how they change and how they should be reformed'.[102] The most relevant advantage we see from applying NIE is that it allows us to analyse an economic phenomenon at the ground level. The fact that the model proposed by NIE relaxes and includes new variables (in comparison to the neoclassical approach) allows us to achieve a better approximation and therefore a more complete perception of

[97]On the relevance of enforcement in international law referring to LSLIs see: Cotula (2012); a general approach: Scott and Stephan (2006).

[98]Some scholars have use the term 'L&E' and 'functional analysis' as synonyms. We also apply both terms to refer the analysis of legal problems applying economic theories. For the same use of this term see: Reinier et al. (2009); van Aaken (2010); van Aaken (2014), p. 827.

[99]The model developed by RC theory has been traditionally used to elaborate law and economic approaches. There are other models proposed by constructivists that suppose collectivism, contrary to relying on methodological individualism as we do. In such models the rational considerations of economic actors as conceived by methodological individualism is rejected because it fails by neglecting the formative influence of ideas, norms and values on behaviour. And, because rational choice does not consider the effect that a system has on economic actors. See i.e. Checkel (1998), pp. 325 ff.; Finnemore and Sikkink (2001). For an overview see: Wendt (2000), p. 165.

Rational Choice assumptions have been commonly applied in the field of L&E. As stated by van Aaken 'Rational choice assumptions are the cornerstone of positive economics and economic analysis of law, which applies economic methods to analyse law' See: van Aaken. For a deep study on the application of Rational Choice in Legal Theory see: van Aaken (2003), Pauwelyn (2006) and Guzman (2008).

[100]See Chap. 4 of this research that offers a deep analysis of both theories.

[101]North (1992), p. 1.

[102]Ibid.

actual phenomena. NIE takes existent methodologies of other disciplines and applies them to concrete problems.

NIE was developed based on a notion of rationality classically defined by Becker as the following: 'All human behaviour can be viewed as involving participants who maximize their utility from a stable set of preferences and accumulate an optional amount of information and other inputs in a variety of markets.'[103] Rational actors are characterised by two main elements: (1) they are self-interested utility maximisers, and (2) they are able to pursue their own interest by making decisions. NIE assumes—in opposition to neoclassical economics—that economic actors do not have complete information. As a result, transactions have a cost that is influenced by the information possessed by economic actors and the effort expended in acquiring new information.[104] Coase introduced the definition of this cost, namely the transaction cost, when developing his theory on the nature of the firm. The notion of transaction costs is broadly accepted and even used in the analysis of non-market activities; for example, to assess the costs of political transactions[105] or international relations.[106]

The first characteristic of rational actors, namely being self-interested utility maximisers, is approached through the theoretical framework of methodological individualism.[107] This theory requires a contractual approach[108] to clarify social events arising from the interaction of individual actors. It assumes that the preferences and aims of individuals impact not only their immediate surroundings, but determine the actions of large-scale or macro social phenomena. As a result, larger collectives like political parties, the state, or society are seen not as autonomous entities but as brought about through the interaction of individuals.[109] The theory considers each individual as a profit maximiser of their own utility function; social choice is a consequence of individual interactions.[110] Economic actors are rational and self-interested. Through the interaction of economic actors, efficiency based on the 'Paretian criterion' gains a maximum of relevance. Put simply, methodological individualism emphasises that people are diverse, with varied goals, purposes, and ideas.

The second element is the locus of decision making. When investigating the introduction of new policies it is necessary to know who has the power to make decisions, under what conditions decisions are made or redesigned, when to terminate the contractual relationship, and what kind of control mechanisms are needed to achieve specific goals. A theory of domestic policymaking is needed to model

---

[103]Becker (1976), p. 14.

[104]Ibid.

[105]Coase (1937), p. 386. See also: Mueller (2008).

[106]Snidal (2002), p. 73.

[107]Udehn and Heath.

[108]This statement, which is supported in this study, was elaborated by: Dunoff and Trachtman (1999), p. 1, 27.

[109]van Aaken (2003), p. 56.

[110]Dunoff and Trachtman (1999), p. 1, 11.

such elements. We therefore apply political economy and public choice theory. Political economy theory and the Putnamian two-levels-game approach allow us to analyse the behaviour and preferences of states at the domestic and international level.[111] This theory attempts to explain bargaining outcomes at the international level by modelling the strategic implications of the negotiations between the state representatives (politicians) and their domestic constituents.[112] In this regard our study sees singular relevance in domestic special interest groups to explain the motivation of politicians to enter into negotiations and sign agreements, as well as to explain the way that voters can induce increased governmental involvement in LSLIs. Theories of public choice and political economy assume that individuals (politicians, negotiators, or decision makers) cooperate only when they are sure that such a negotiation will make them better off.[113] This means that they maximise their utility function in light of given informational boundaries. The political economy approach of Grossman and Helpman explains the relevance of special interest groups in the decision-making process at the domestic level.[114] As a result, we assume that political decisions made by individuals or homogeneous groups of individuals (for example, members of the same political party) are influenced by interest groups that guarantee the decision maker's political stability. This makes the politician better off. Furthermore, we assume that the international effects of national policies are taken into account because they are also guarantors of a decision maker's political stability.[115]

An implication of our assumption of incomplete and asymmetric information between actors is that when individuals interact, they try to optimise their information in order to maximise their own utility. On the one hand, the more information a party has the more profitable the transaction will potentially be, as there is less uncertainty involved. On the other hand, the party will be reluctant to provide information to the other party, as withholding one's own knowledge makes the maximisation of gains possible. This implies that the party with more information will find a more efficient way to achieve a proposed goal. In the absence of incentives (e.g. enforceable legal rules, market sanctions, reputational costs), self-interested actors will not be motivated to prevent negative externalities

[111]The theoretical approach developed and applied by Grossman and Helpman is the most relevant for this research. Grossman and Helpman (1994), p. 833; Grossman (1995), p. 667; Grossman and Helpman (2001). We recommend a short review on the contribution of Grossman: Baron (2002), p. 1221; van Aaken and Trachtman (2016).

[112]Putnam (1988), pp. 427 and 437. The application of a two-levels game has taken relevance in the field of politic economic as well as in L&E. The approach consists in demonstrating that the behaviour of traders on an international level reflects their national behaviour so that they can achieve proposed goals.

[113]For the seminal contributions, see: Downs and Rocke (1995), p. 24. For an introduction in public choice for lawyers see: Farber and Frickey (1991).

[114]See footnote: 111.

[115]This approach that has be enriched by the contributions of: Putnam (1988), p. 427; Grossman (1995), p. 667; Downs and Rocke (1995), p. 24; and also Milner (1997).

(e.g. violation of third parties' rights or infringement of environmental regulations), since such an infringement does not increase the cost of achieving a proposed goal. This kind of behaviour, which can be considered a superlative expression of self-interest, is what Williamson defined as opportunism.[116]

1.6 Overview and Structure of This Book

This book is divided into six chapters. Chapter 1, which you have just read, provides introductory remarks explaining the raison d'etre of this research study and a foundational overview of the research topic. Chapter 2 is a positive analysis that gives a detailed description of the research topic, LSLIs. Here we make a critical distinction between LSLIs and 'land grabbing'. We also look at relevant legal and historical aspects concerning land policies in sub-Saharan Africa. Chapter 2 is subdivided into three main chapters. Section 2.1 provides an overview, Sect. 2.2 is entitled 'Framing Land Grabbing', and contains three sections. Section 2.2.1 provides a definition of land grabbing and contrasts it with LSLIs. Section 2.2.2 deals with the actors involved in the negotiation process. It is followed by the analysis of investment contracts (Sect. 2.2.3). Chapter 2 concludes by offering an intermediate result that highlights the impact of LSLIs on local populations' property rights and right to food.

Following the positive analysis, Chap. 3 lays out the international legal contexts in which LSLIs are performed, and also explores the question of the protection of the right to property and the right to food. After an overview (Sect. 3.1), the following sections are pillars that allow us to construct a legal analysis oriented towards elucidating the protection mechanisms IL offers in cases where the performance of LSLIs infringes upon the right to property and the right to food. Section 3.2 approaches the relevance of considering IL as a unified whole, Sect. 3.3 offers an analysis of legal fragmentation, and Sect. 3.4 introduces the concept of soft law and explains its development in the framework of LSLI. Issues that are related to soft law will be addressed in more detail in later sections of this study. These sections will focus on the ability of soft law to protect the right to property and the right to food. Sections 3.5 through 3.8 concentrate on the mechanisms in IL to protect the rights of locals and the rights of investors. Section 3.5 concentrates on local populations' rights to property and food; Sect. 3.6 focuses on the protection of foreign investors' rights to property in the context of IL and IIL, including investments with and without an investment contract and investments under IIAs; Sect. 3.7 compares the mechanisms of protection in HRs and IIL regimes. This comparative analysis leads us to our preliminary results (Sect. 3.8) concerning the asymmetric level of protection

[116]Williamson (1985), p. 47; Williamson (1979), p. 233, 234.

offered by the respective regimes and their ability to incentivise opportunistic behaviour. This result constitutes the cornerstone of our discussion in Chap. 3.

Chapter 4 applies a social science approach to opportunism in LSLIs, which might arise from two different sources: agency problems and incomplete contracts. Following an overview (Sect. 4.1), Sect. 4.2 justifies the application of the theoretical framework of NIE in this book. Section 4.3 defines opportunism and its sources. Section 4.4 then applies PAT to identify opportunism in relationships concerning delegation activities and offers some solutions to the problems that arise from opportunism. Section 4.5 applies CT to the same end when opportunism arises from insufficiently complete investment contracts. Section 4.6, presents the preliminary result, namely that control mechanisms are needed in order to tackle opportunistic behaviour of economic actors in the presence of LSLIs.

Chapter 5 approaches the control mechanisms that might apply in the framework of IL to tackle opportunistic behaviour. We consider unilateral control mechanisms applicable by states and investors in Sect. 5.2, contract-based control mechanisms in Sect. 5.3, arbitration in Sect. 5.4, and Sect. 5.5 analyses external international actors as control mechanisms. After understanding how control mechanisms work in IL, we will have a framework that allows us to determine how states can introduce and analyse the potential outcomes of these mechanisms during the performance stage of the contract, especially in cases where states face food shortages. To make this determination, we construct a hypothetical scenario in which, due to food shortages, a state introduces regulatory measures that could be considered a breach of an investment contract or IIA.

References

Agreement between the Government of the United Kingdom of Great Britain and Northern Ireland and the Government of the Republic of Sierra Leone (Great Britain-Sierra Leone) [2000] available at http://investmentpolicyhub.unctad.org/IIA/country/221/treaty/2903. Accessed 15 September 2015.

Amanor, K. (2012). *Land governance in Africa* (Vol. 1). International Land Coalition.

Atwood, D. (n.d.). Land registration in Africa: The impact on agricultural production. *World Development, 18*, 659.

Bach, S. (2010). Die Gier nach Fremdem Land: Lebensmittel, Investment, Biosprit. *N-TV* (13.11.2010), http://www.n-tv.de/politik/dossier/Die-Gier-nach-fremdem-Land-article1913411.html. Accessed 24 March 2010.

Bardhan, P. (1997). Corruption and development: A review of issues. *American Economic Association, 35*, 1320.

Baron, D. (2002). Review of Grossman and Helpman's special interest politics. *Journal of Economic Literature, XL*, 1221.

Bayer, W. (1995). *Der Vertrag Zugunsten Dritter: Neuere Dogmengeschichte, Anwendungsbereich, Dogmatische Strukturen*. Mohr.

Becker, G. (1976). *The economic approach to human behavior*. University of Chicago Press.

Behnassi, M., & Yaya, S. (2011). Land resource governance from a sustainability and rural development perspective: Sustainable agricultural development. In M. Behnassi, S. A. Shahid, & J. D'Silva (Eds.), *Sustainable agricultural development*. Springer.

Benvenisti, E., & Downs, G. (2007). The empires new clothes: Political economy and the fragmentation of international law. *Stanford Law Review, 60*, 595.

Bernstein, H. (2005). Rural land and land conflicts in Sub-Saharan Africa. In S. Moyo & P. Moyos (Eds.), *Reclaming the land the resurgence of rural movements in Africa, Asia and Latin America*. Zed Books.

Blomström, M., & Kokko, A. (1999). *How foreign investment affects host countries*. The World Bank.

Borras, S., & Franco, J. (2009). From threat to opportunity? Problems with the idea of a "Code of Conduct" for land grabbing. *Yale Human Rights & Development Law Journal, 13*, 507.

Borras, S., Hall, R., Scoones, I., Ben, W., & Wendy, W. (2011). Towards a better understanding of global land grabbing: An editorial introduction. *Journal of Peasant Studies, 37*, 209.

Bundesministerium für Wirtschaftliche Zusammenarbeit und Entwicklung. (2009). *Entwicklungspolitische Positionierung zum Thema: Großlchige Landkäufe und -pachten in Entwicklungsländern - "Land Grabbing"*.

Cafaggi, F. (2012). Introduction: The transformation of transnational private regulation: Enforcement gaps and governance design. In F. Cafaggi (Ed.), *Enforcement of transnational regulation*. Edward Elgar.

Checkel, J. (1998). The constructivist turn in international relations theory. *World Politics, 47*.

Coase, R. (1937). The nature of the firm. *Economica, 4*(16), 386.

Constitution of Ethiopia LEX-FAOC129684 [1994].

Cotula, L., Dyer, N., & Vermeulen S. (2008). Fuelling exclusion? The biofuels boom and poor people's access to land (The outlook of farmland acquisitions 2008). London: IIED.

Cotula, L., Vermeulen, S., Leonard, R., & Keeley, J. (2009). *Land grab or development opportunity? Agricultural investment and international land deals in Africa*. London: FAO/IIED/IFAD.

Cotula, L. (2010a). Deals can be good news when not made behind closed doors. *Guardiancouk*. London, 03 July 2010, http://www.guardian.co.uk/environment/2010/mar/07/africa-land-grab-food-water/print. Accessed 03 July 2010.

Cotula, L. (2010b). Investment contracts and sustainable development: How to make contracts for fairer and more sustainable natural resource investments. *Natural Resource Issues, 20*.

Cotula, L. (2011). *Land deals in Africa: What is in the contracts?* International Institute for Environment and Development.

Cotula, L. (2012). The international political economy of the global land rush: A critical appraisal of trends, scale, geography and drivers. *Journal of Peasant Studies, 39*.

Cotula, L. (2015). *Land rights and investment treaties: Exploring the interface*. International Institute for Environment and Development.

Dammann, J., & Hansmann, H. (2006). Globalizing commercial litigation. *California Law Review, 94*.

De Schutter, O. (2009). *Report of the Special Rapporteur on the right to food. Agribusiness and the right to food* (A/HRC/13/33).

De Schutter, O. (2011). How not to think of land-grabbing: Three critiques of large-scale investments in farmland. *Journal of Peasant Studies, 37*, 249.

Deininger, K., Byerlee, D., Lindsay, J., Norton, A., & Selod, H. (2011). *Rising global interest in farmland. Can it yield sustainable equitable benefits?* World Bank.

Deng, D. K. (2011). "Land Belongs to the Community" demystifying the "Global Land Grab" in Southern Sudan. Global Land Grabbing, 6–8 April 2011. University of Sussex.

Deva, S., & Bilchitz, D. (Eds.). (2013). *Human rights obligations of business*. Cambridge.

Dolzer, R., & Stevens, M. (1995). *Bilateral investment treaties*. M. Nijhoff.

Downs, G., & Rocke, D. (1995). *Optimal imperfection? Domestic uncertainty and institutions in international relations*. Princeton University Press.

Dunoff, J., & Trachtman, J. (1999). Economic analysis of international law. *Yale Journal of International Law, 24*, 1.

Ellickson, R. (1993). Property in land. Faculty Scholarship Series Paper 1314.

FAO. (2008). *Soaring food prices: Facts, perspectives, impacts and actions required* (HLC/08/INF1).

FAO. (2012). *The state of food and agriculture*. FAO.

FAO and OECD. (2010). *Agricultural outlook 2010–2019*.

FAO Declaration of the World Summit on Food Security [2009] WSFS 2009/2.

FAO Rome Declaration on World Food Security. Food World Forum Summit [1996] WSFS 2009/2.

FAO, WFP and IFAD. (2012). *The state of food insecurity in the world: Economic growth is necessary but not sufficient to accelerate reduction of hunger and malnutrition*. FAO.

Farber, D., & Frickey, P. (1991). *Law and public choice: A critical introduction*. University of Chicago Press.

Finnemore, M., & Sikkink, K. (2001). Taking stock: The constructivist research program in international relations and comparative politics. *Annual Review of Political Science, 4*.

Fisseha, M. (2012). *A case study of the Bachera agricultural development project, Ethiopia*. International Land Coalition; Cirad.

Food and Agriculture Organization of the United Nations. (2001). *Contract farming*. FAO.

Graham, A., Aubry, S., Künnemann, R., & Suárez, S. M. (2008). *Land grab study*. FIAN.

Graham, A., Aubry, S., Künnemann, R., & Suárez, S. M. (2011). The role of the EU in land grabbing in Africa - CSO monitoring 2009–2010 "Advancing African Agriculture" (AAA): The impact of Europe's policies and practices on African agriculture and food security. Paper presented at the International Conference on Global Land Grabbing, 6–8 April 2011.

GRAIN. (2008). *Seized! The 2008 land grab for food and financial security*.

GRAIN. (2016). *El Acaparamiento Global de Tierras 2016*.

GRAIN. Fondos de Pensiones: Actores Claves en el Acaparamiento Mundial de Tierras Agrícolas. Accessed 20 June 2011.

GRAIN. Land grabbing for biofuels must stop: EU biofuel policies are displacing communities and starving the planet, http://www.grain.org/article/entries/4653-land-grabbing-for-biofuels-must-stop. Accessed 10 July 2014.

Grossman, G. (1995). The politics of free-trade agreements. *American Economic Review, 85*, 667.

Grossman, G., & Helpman, E. (1994). Protection for sale. *American Economic Review, 84*, 833.

Grossman, G., & Helpman, E. (2001). *Special interest politics*. Cambridge.

Guzman, A. T. (1998). Why LDCs sign treaties that hurt them: Explaining the popularity of bilateral investment treaties. *Virginia Journal of International Law, 38*, 639.

Guzman, A. T. (2008). *How international law works: A rational choice theory*. Oxford University Press.

Häberli, C. (2012). Foreign direct investment in agriculture: Land grab or food security improvement? *Third Biennial Global Conference Society International Economic Law*.

Heath, J. *The methodological individualism*, http://plato.stanford.edu/entries/methodological-individualism/. Accessed 17 July 2015.

Heltberg, R. (2002). Property rights and natural resource management in developing countries [Blackwell Publishers Ltd]. *Journal of Economic Surveys, 16*, 189.

Human Rights Council. (1998). *Promotion and protection of all human rights, civil, political, economic, social and cultural rights, including the right to development. Protect respect and remedy: A framework for business and human rights* (Human Rights Council A/HRC/8/5).

Human Rights Council. (2007). *Business and human rights: Mapping international standards of responsibility and accountability for corporate acts* (Report of the Special Representative of the Secretary-General (SRSG) on the Issue of Human Rights and Transnational Corporations and Other Business Enterprises [2007] A/HRC/4/035).

Human Rights Council. (2011a). *Report of the special representative of the Secretary General on the issue of human rights and transnational corporations and other business enterprises. Piloting principles for effective company/stakeholder grievance mechanisms: A report of lessons learned* (A/HRC/17/31/Add1).

Human Rights Council. (2011b). *Report of the special representative of the Secretary-General on the issue of human rights and transnational corporations and other business enterprises. Guiding principles on business and human rights: Implementing the United Nations "Protect, Respect and Remedy" Framework* (A/HRC/17/31).
ILC. (2006). *Fragmentation of international law: Difficulties arising from the diversification and expansion of international law* (A/CN4/L682).
Issacharoff, S. (2010). *Principles of the law of aggregate litigation*. The American Law Institute.
Jazeera, A. Oxfam sounds Uganda land-grab warning. *Al Jazeera*, http://www.aljazeera.com/video/africa/2011/09/2011922111515150690.html. Accessed 16 August 2014.
Katz, A. (1995). Taking private ordering seriously. *University of Pennsylvania Law Review, 144*.
Lavigne, P. Harmonising formal law and customary land rights in French-speaking West Africa. In *Evolving land rights, policy and tenure in Africa, DFID/IIED/NRI*, http://www.gret.org/ressource/pdf/harmonising.pdf. Accessed 03 September 2011.
MacDougall, G. D. A. (1960). The benefits and costs of private investment from abroad: A theoretical approach. *Economic Record, 36*, 13.
Meinzen-Dick, R., & Markelova, H. (2009). Necessary nuance: Toward a code of conduct in foreign land deals. In M. Kugelman & S. L. Levenstein (Eds.), *Land grab? The race for the world's farmland*. Woodrow Wilson International Center for Scholars.
Milner, H. (1997). *Interests, institutions, and information: Domestic politics and international relations*. Princeton, NJ: Princeton University Press.
Moran, T. (2006). *Harnessing foreign direct investment for development*. Center For Global Development.
Moran, T. (2011). *Foreign direct investment and development*. Peterson Institute for International Economics.
Muchlinski, P. (2008). Policy issues. In P. Muchlinski, F. Ortino, & C. Schreuer (Eds.), *The Oxford handbook of international investment law*. Oxford University Press.
Mueller, D. (2008). *Public choice III*. Cambridge University Press.
Narula, S. (2006). The right to food: Holding global actors accountable under international law. *Columbia Journal of Transnational Law, 44*, 691.
Nigerian Parliament Condemns Land Grab by Chinese Firms. *Premium Times* (Abuja) http://www.premiumtimesng.com/news/top-news/216665-nigerian-parliament-condemns-land-grab-chinese-firms.html. Accessed 20 March 2017.
North, D. (1990). *Institutions, institutional change and economic performance*. Cambridge University Press.
North, D. (1992). *The new institutional economics and development*. Washington University.
OECD. (2008). *Rising food prices: Causes and consequences*. OECD.
Palmer, R. (2011). *A new annotated guide to bibliographies on biofuels, and land rights in Africa, and global land grabbing*. September 2011, http://www.mokoro.co.uk/publications. Accessed 15 July 2015.
Pauwelyn, J. (2003). *Conflict of norms in public international law*. Cambridge University Press.
Pauwelyn, J. (2006). *Optimal protection of international law*. Cambridge.
Pauwelyn, J. *Fragmentation of international law*. Max Planck Encyclopedia of Public International Law, http://opil.ouplaw.com/view/10.1093/law:epil/9780199231690/law-9780199231690-e1406?rskey=0dMLs5&result=1&prd=EPIL. Accessed 18 August 2015.
Pinstrup-Andersen, P., & Watson, D. (2011). *Food policy for developing countries: The role of government in global, national, and local food systems*. Cornell University Press.
Principles for Responsible Agricultural Investment that Respects Rights, Livehoods and Resources [2010] available http://siteresources.worldbank.org/INTARD/214574-1111138388661/22453321/Principles_Extended.pdf. Accessed 25 December 2013.
Pringle, J. (2011). Land grabs and the World Bank. *Worldpressorg* (16.11.2011), http://worldpress.org/print_article.cfm?article_id=4134&dont=yes.
Putnam, R. (1988). Diplomacy and domestic politics: The logic of two-level games. *International Organization, 42*, 427.

Rabah, S., Klaus, D., & Harris, S. (2011). *What drives the global land rush?* The World Bank, Development Research Group, Agriculture and Rural Development Team Policy Research Working Paper 5864, http://elibrary.worldbank.org/content/workingpaper/10.1596/1813-9450-5864. Accessed 25 June 2012.

Raeschke-Kessler, H., & Gottwald, D. (2008). Corruption. In P. Muchlinski, F. Ortino, & C. Schreuer (Eds.), *The Oxford handbook of international investment law*. Oxford University Press.

Reinier, K., et al. (Eds.). (2009). *The anatomy of corporate law: A comparative and functional approach* (2nd ed.). Oxford University Press.

Ruggie, J. *Obstacles to justice and redress for victims of corporate human rights abuse*, http://ohrh.law.ox.ac.uk/about/opbp/. Accessed 17 July 2015.

Schonecke, W., & Kurzke-Maasmeier, S. (2009). *Das Menschenrecht auf Nahrung im Kontext des Land Grabbing: Normative und Politische Implikationen.*

Scott, R., & Stephan, P. (2006). *The limits of Leviathan. Contract theory and the enforcement of international law*. Cambridge University Press.

Sharma, R., & Aykut, D. (2003). South-South FDI flows: How big are they? *Transnational Corporations, 13*, 149.

Simma, B., & Kill, T. (2009). Harmonizing investment protection and international human rights: First steps towards a methodology. In A. Reinisch & U. Kriebaum (Eds.), *International investment law for the 21st century essays in honour of Christoph Schreuer*. Oxford.

Snidal, D. (2002). Rational choice and international relations. In W. Carlsnaes, B. Simmons, & T. Risse (Eds.), *Handbook of international relations*. Sage.

Sornarajah, M. (2010). *The international law on foreign investment* (3rd ed.). Cambridge University Press.

Stiglitz, J. (2007). Regulating multinational corporations: Towards principles of cross-border legal frameworks in a globalized world balancing rights with responsibilities. *American University International Law Review, 23*, 451.

Sunga, L. (1992). *Individual responsibility in international law for serious human rights violations* (1st ed.). Springer.

The Economist. The surge in land deals. When others are grabbing their land: Evidence is piling up against acquisitions of farmland in poor countries, http://www.economist.com/node/18648855. Accessed 12 May 2011.

The Inspection Panel. (2014). *Ethiopia: Promoting Basic Services Phase 3 Project.*

The Oakland Institute. (2011a). *Understanding land investment deals in Africa: Addax & Oryx Group Bioenergy Investment in Sierra Leone.*

The Oakland Institute. (2011b). *Understanding land investment deals in Africa: Country report: Ethiopia.*

The Oakland Institute. (2011c). *Understanding land investment deals in Africa: Country report: Zambia.*

The World Bank. (2016). *Working for a world free of poverty*. The World Bank, http://data.worldbank.org. Accessed 14 January 2016.

Trachtman, J. (2008). *The economic structure of international law*. Harvard University Press.

Treaty Between the Federal Republic of Germany and the Federal Democratic Republic of Ethiopia Concerning the Encouragement and Reciprocal Protection of Investments (Ethiopia Germany) [2004].

Udehn, L. *Methodological individualism*. Oxford Bibliographies, http://www.oxfordbibliographies.com/view/document/obo-9780199756384/obo-9780199756384-0092.xml?rskey=KMaAxz&result=1&q=methodological individualism-firstMatch. Accessed 19 August 2013.

Uganda Land Act (No. 16 of 1998) An Act to provide for the tenure, ownership and management of land; to amend and consolidate the law relating to tenure, ownership and management of land; and to provide for other related or incidental matters. Uganda Gazette No. 41, 2 July, 1998, Acts Supplement No. 11, pp. 1–83.

Unied Nations. (2016). *Development policy and analysis division*. UN, http://www.un.org/en/development/desa/policy/cdp/ldc/ldc_criteria.shtml. Accessed 13 August 2016.

United Nations. (2010). *Minority rights: International standards and guidance for implementation* (HR/PUB/10/3).

United Nations Conference on Trade. (2007). *Intellectual property provisions in international investment arrangements* (UNCTAD/WEB/ITE/IIA/2007/1).

United Nations Conference on Trade. (2009). *World investment report 2009. Transnational corporations, agricultural production and development*. World Investment Report 2009, 2009.

United Nations Conference on Trade. (2011). *Foreign direct investment in LDCs: Lessons learned from the decade 2001–2010 and the way forward.*

United Nations Conference on Trade. *World investment report 2012*. World Investment Report 2012, 2013.

United Nations Conference on Trade. (2014). *Global FDI rose by 11%; Developed economies are trapped in a historically low share*. UNCTAD, N 15 January 2014.

United Nations Conference on Trade. *World investment report 2013*. World Investment Report 2013, 2014.

United Nations Conference on Trade. *World investment report 2014*. World Investment Report 2014, 2015.

van Aaken, A. (2003). *"Rational Choice" in der Rechtswissenschaft: Zum Stellenwert der Ökonomischen Theorie im Recht*. Nomos.

van Aaken, A. (2006). Fragmentation of international law: The case of international investment law. In J. Klabbers & K. Creutz (Eds.), *Finnish yearbook of international law* (Vol. 17). Martinus Nijhoff Publishers.

van Aaken, A. (2010). Primary and secondary remedies in international investment law and national state liability: A functional and comparative view. In S. Schill (Ed.), *International investment law and comparative public law*. Oxford.

van Aaken, A. (2013). *Large scale agricultural investment and international investment law*. UNCTAD, http://investmentpolicyhub.unctad.org/Blog/Index/22 der. Accessed 12 July 2015.

van Aaken, A. (2014). Smart flexibility clauses in international investment treaties and sustainable development: A functional view. *Journal of World Investment and Trade, 15*, 827.

van Aaken, A. *Rational choice theory*, available at http://www.oxfordbibliographiescom/view/document/obo-9780199796953/obo-9780199796953-0051xml?rskey=qyeNms&result=21&q=. Accessed 26 November 2013.

van Aaken, A., & Trachtman, J. (2016). Political economy of international law: Towards a holistic model of state behavior. In A. Fabbricotti (Ed.), *The political economy of international law a European perspective*. Elgar.

Varadarajan, S. (2011). *Come and farm our virgin lands, Ethiopia tells India*. The Hindu (26.05.2011), http://www.thehindu.com/news/national/article2048964.ece?css=print. Accessed 10 June 2013.

Vermeulen, S., & Cotula, L. (2010). *Making the most of agricultural investment: A survey of business models that provide opportunities for smallholders*. IIED, FAO, IFAD, SDC.

von Braun, J. (2010). Land grabbing. Ursachen und Konsequenzen internationaler Landakquirierung in Entwicklungsländern. *ZAS, 3*, 299.

von Braun, J., & Meinzen-Dick, R. (2009). "Land Grabbing" by foreign investors in developing countries: Risks and opportunities. *International Food Policy Research Institute Policy Brief, 13*, 1.

von Grebmer, K., Ringler, C., Rosegrant, M., Olofinbiyi, T., Wiesmann, D., Fritschel, H., et al. (2012). *Global hunger index. The challenge of hunger: Ensuring sustainable food security under land, water and energy stresses.*

Wehrmann, B. (2008). *Land conflicts: A practical guide to dealing with land disputes*. GTZ.

Wendt, A. (2000). On the via media: A response to the critics. *Review of International Studies, 26*, 165.

Weschka, M. (2006). Human rights and multinational enterprises: How can multinational enterprises be held responsible for human rights violations commited abroad? *ZaöRV, 66*.

Wettstein, F. (2013). Making noise about silent complicity. In S. Deva & D. Bilchitz (Eds.), *Human rights obligtions of business*. Cambridge.

Williamson, J. *The Washington consensus as policy prescription for development*, http://www.iie.com/publications/papers/williamson0204.pdf. Accessed 19 July 2015.

Williamson, O. (1979). Transaction-cost economics: The governance of contractual relations. *Journal of Law and Economics, 22*, 233.

Williamson, O. (1985). *The economic institutions of capitalism: Firms, markets, relational contracting*. Collier Macmillan Publishers.

Williamson, O. (1996). *The mechanisms of governance*. Oxford University Press.

Williston, S. (1902). Contracts for the benefit of a third person. *Harvard Law Review, XV*, 101.

Chapter 2
What Is 'Land Grabbing'

2.1 Overview

This chapter offers a positive analysis of the research subject, LSLIs, in order to elucidate its most relevant characteristics. We will include descriptive elements that allow us to understand the incentives for economic actors who invest in land.[1] There are two main parts in this section. The first part offers an expanded and more comprehensive definition of land grabbing, which was briefly introduced in the last section. It is necessary for us to be able to clearly distinguish between the concepts of LSLI and land grabbing. Although the main focus of the analysis is legal aspects, additional elements must be considered in order to develop a broad understanding of the phenomenon and to elaborate a functional analysis. To this purpose we briefly analyse the historical aspects of land interests in sub-Saharan Africa. This analysis encompasses a comparison, at a macro level, of the land situation before and after sub-Saharan independence. Of course it is not possible to cover all the specific land policy issues of every country in the region; our goal is to give a general overview. Our emphasis is on: (1) policies concerning property rights to land; (2) the design of new competition structures through the creation or restructuring of land markets; and (3) the relevance of land policies in which IOs have played an important role. Based on these aspects we justify the need for new agrarian policies. The section concludes by analysing the bargaining power and level of participation of the local population in the design and performance of agrarian policies, which are seen as essential elements to relieving poverty and promoting development.

The second part of this chapter discusses the formal aspects of LSLIs, including the relevant actors and contracts. Contracts are the drivers of LSLIs and the primary source of substantive law, both in terms of the negotiation process and the potential benefits and negative impacts. Using a variety of sources of information, we will

[1]For an study about positive analysis in L&E see: van Aaken (2003), p. 45.

L.T. Montilla Fernández, *Large-Scale Land Investments in Least Developed Countries*, International Law and Economics, DOI 10.1007/978-3-319-65280-1_2

provide a detailed analysis of LSLI contracts. Data was collected from diverse contracts as well as from the reports of NGOs and the Land Matrix.[2] The negative impacts arising from LSLIs are highly relevant as they constitute the essential link between elaborating the legal argumentation and developing this study further. These effects are related to the violation of HRs. We will close this chapter with a third section that analyses the impact of LSLIs under certain circumstances and how this constitutes a violation of national and international positive HRL. A later chapter explores the international legal system in order to determine the mechanisms in IL to avoid the negative effects associated with some LSLIs. After having developed this chapter, the research will go a step further to erect a legal approach and show to what extent IL can ameliorate the negative effects arising from the performance of LSLIs.

2.2 Framing 'Land Grabbing'

2.2.1 General Aspects

In the following chapter we will offer a detailed description of what we understand to fall under the concept of land grabbing.

2.2.1.1 Definition

Large-scale acquisition of land for agricultural purposes is the legal term for the phenomenon widely, albeit from a legal point of view incorrectly, known as land grabbing.[3] Nowadays it is a standardised term used in academic research and by IOs and NGOs.[4] Large-scale acquisition of land for agricultural purposes will be referred to as large-scale land investment (LSLI) in this paper. LSLIs take the legal form of lease or purchase contracts, and usually aim to produce agricultural

[2]The Land Matrix is a global and independent land monitoring initiative. The information collected by the Land Matrix is an open source tool considered as a Global Observatory for collecting and visualising information about LSLI. Its goal is to facilitate an open development community of citizens, researchers, policy-makers and technology specialists to promote transparency and accountability in decisions over land and investment. Source: International Land Coalition (2011).

[3]For a similar definition see: Häberli (2012), p. 1. For an overview of studies employing the term of land grabbing see: Palmer (2011). Borras Jr. et al. consider the phrase land grab as a 'catch-all to describe and analyse the current explosion of large scale (trans)national commercial land transactions. Borras et al. (2011), pp. 209, 210.

[4]This term has been strongly criticised by some authors and politicians. For example Häberli (2012) describe this term as: 'the impolite and incorrect word for large-scale land acquisitions by foreigners.' For an overview of studies employing the term land grabbing see: Palmer (2011) and Cotula et al. (2009).

commodities. From the literature it can be seen that the negative connotations of land grabbing include the involuntary nature of the transfer of land from locals, as well as the detrimental effects of LSLIs on locals.[5] In some cases LSLIs are linked to the violation of HRs, including the distortion of traditional structures, an increase in food insecurity, and the infringement of traditional systems of property rights.[6]

For our purposes LSLI projects are considered land grabbing when they lead to a HRs violation, specifically the basic human right to food and property.[7] A further condition is that the contracting parties in the LSLI project include a state and either another state, a private investor, or a semi-private investor.[8]

One relevant aspect of LSLIs is the change in the use of land related to the performance of LSLIs. Although the principal motivation for the introduction of LSLIs in LDCs was to increase food production, the data available shows that LSLIs are much more frequently concerned with non-food crops than with food crops. Data published by the Land Matrix covering countries on all continents shows that only 18% of the deals aim to produce food crops, 29% non-food crops (i.e. biofuels), 27% flex crops, and 26% of the deals are negotiated with multiple uses in mind.[9] Data specific to the African continent shows that 25% of the deals are for food crops, 27% for non-food crops, 17% for flex crops, and 31% for multiple uses. Multiple uses include several crops in different categories.[10] Due to the fact

[5]See seminally on the effects of LSLIs: Deininger et al. (2011).

[6]For our objectives, the expression of Human Rights is reduced to two examples namely: the right to food and the right to property. This delimitation is only made for methodological reasons and natural limitations of this project. It does not mean that the legal architecture as developed in this research cannot be applied in the context of other human rights infringements.

[7]For the motivation and justification about the focus on these two rights see in this book Sect. 1.3.

[8]Even though the phenomenon of land grabbing has been characterised by the heterogeneity of actors, this research is limited to investment activities in which one party is the state or a public entity and on the other side a foreign investor.

[9]The Land Matrix is a global and independent land monitoring initiative that promotes transparency and accountability in decisions over land and investment. Due to the nature of the negotiations, the data of the Land Matrix relies extensively on unofficial sources. Data errors may arise if the information provided by the source is inaccurate. As the information source is provided, the user may decide the extent to which they determine the source to be trustworthy. Errors may also arise from mistakes in entering the data. The new database management system accompanying the June 2013 upgrade contains safeguards to detect likely mistakes, but these are impossible to eliminate. Furthermore, errors may arise from the information going out of date; we rely on our networks in different countries and users of the website to provide updates. In this light, the dataset is inherently unreliable but it is almost the only data that is able to provide a picture of LSLIs. Over time it is expected that it will become more accurate. Land deals are notoriously un-transparent. In many countries, established procedures for decision-making on land deals do not exist, and negotiations and decisions do not take place in the public realm. Furthermore, a range of government agencies and levels of government are usually responsible for approving different kinds of land deals. Even official data sources in the same country can therefore vary, and none may actually reflect reality on the ground. Decisions are often changed, and this may or may not be communicated publically. International Land Coalition (2011).

[10]Ibid.

that LSLIs result in a variety of different uses for the land, it is important for us to examine how this impacts the status quo. We will go into more detail in the next part, which also explains the motivation of investors and states to enter into LSLI contracts. At this point it is important to highlight two different trends, namely land deals that result in the production of non-food-oriented agricultural products, and deals that result in the production of food-oriented agricultural products.

2.2.1.2 Historical Aspects of the Land Interest (Rush) in Sub-Saharan Africa

The use of LSLIs in sub-Saharan Africa was a relatively simple matter during colonial times, as local governments or authorities did not play an important role in the decision-making processes. Land was not considered *per se* a *res commercium*, and its distribution was decided in a centralised manner.[11] The *General Act of the Berlin Conference on West Africa* (hereafter the *Berlin Act*), a treaty promoted by the German chancellor Otto von Bismarck in 1884, gives us some information about the first formal land distribution in sub-Saharan Africa.[12] Thirteen European states and the United States of America signed the treaty.[13] With this treaty, the signatories settled the political apportionment of Africa. Several changes occurred some thirty-five years later after the First World War. One of the changes concerned the four colonies belonging to Germany. These colonies came under the control of the League of Nations, which introduced special administrative rules.[14]

The *Berlin Act* was a legal institution designed to reduce coordination costs between colonial powers. It might be considered the first official land rush in Africa, making colonial powers the official owners of African land.[15] This act distributed land between the colonial powers and created geopolitical obligations for the signatories to inform their fellow signatories of expansionist intensions.[16] In addition, the signatory powers recognised their obligation to ensure the

[11]Bernstein (2005), p. 73 ff.

[12]General Act of the Berlin Conference on West Africa [1885] available at http://africanhistory.about.com/od/eracolonialism/l/n_BerlinAct1885.htm. Accessed 15 July 2015; Crowe (1970).

[13]**Great Britain**, Austria-Hungary, Belgium, Denmark, **France**, **Germany**, Italy, The Netherlands, **Portugal**, Russia, Spain, Sweden and Norway, Turkey and the United States. The **Bold** were the most important contracting parties due to the size of dominated territory.

[14]Crowe (1970).

[15]Potts (2013), p. 17.

[16]Art 34 Berlin Act stated: Any Power which henceforth takes possession of a tract of land on the coasts of the African continent outside of its present possessions, or which, being hitherto without such possessions, shall acquire them, as well as the Power which assumes a Protectorate there, shall accompany the respective act with a notification thereof, addressed to the other Signatory Powers of the present Act, in order to enable them, if need be, to make good any claims of their own. General Act of the Berlin Conference on West Africa [1885] available at http://africanhistory.about.com/od/eracolonialism/l/n_BerlinAct1885.htm. Accessed 15 July 2015.

establishment of a centralised authority in occupied regions to enforce their rights. 'Their rights' referred to the colonial powers' rights and not the rights of local inhabitants.[17] The goal of this treaty was to coordinate the economic interests of the signatory parties. Each colonial power extended their domestic form of government to the colonised territory. Economic programmes in the colonies centred on the production of agricultural commodities that were brought to Europe for the manufacturing of final products. Obviously the result of this policy was that European industry reaped a large portion of the benefits.[18] It should be mentioned that Europe was in an economic crisis at the time, and so it was thought that investments in agricultural commodities in Africa might help to stimulate local markets. The *Berlin Act* also incentivised European economic actors to increase productivity and reactivate internal markets, further reducing production costs.

The wording of the *Berlin Act* makes it apparent that the signatories did not consider at any point that the local population already owned the land they were distributing. As referred to in paragraphs 6 and 34, the colonial powers assumed the responsibility of controlling the occupied regions. The only mention in the *Berlin Act* to the local population was related to the promotion of religion and scientific or charitable institutions.[19]

The European powers also overhauled or reformed existing African structures. They were the only powers authorised to recognise property, which had to be proved by way of land titles, permits, or concessions.[20] In later years new laws allowed locals to participate in negotiations and agricultural production, but such concessions were only made to elites who were already participants in trade. In some cases property was recognised as belonging to local chiefs, as a result of which small portions of land were demarcated for use by natives. These policies

---

[17]Art 35 Berlin Act stated: The Signatory Powers of the present Act recognise the obligation to insure the establishment of authority in the regions occupied by them on the coasts of the African continent sufficient to protect existing rights, and, as the case may be, freedom of trade and of transit under the conditions agreed upon.

[18]Potts (2013), p. 17.

[19]Art. 6 Berlin Act: All the Powers exercising sovereign rights or influence in the aforesaid territories bind themselves to watch over the preservation of the native tribes, and to care for the improvement of the conditions of their moral and material well-being, and to help in suppressing slavery, and especially the slave trade. They shall, without distinction of creed or nation, protect and favour all religious, scientific or charitable institutions and undertakings created and organised for the above ends, or which aim at instructing the natives and bringing home to them the blessings of civilisation. Christian missionaries, scientists and explorers, with their followers, property and collections, shall likewise be the objects of especial protection. Freedom of conscience and religious toleration are expressly guaranteed to the natives, no less than to subjects and to foreigners. The free and public exercise of all forms of divine worship, and the right to build edifices for religious purposes, and to organise religious missions belonging to all creeds, shall not be limited or fettered in any way whatsoever. General Act of the Berlin Conference on West Africa [1885] available at http://africanhistory.about.com/od/eracolonialism/l/n_BerlinAct1885.htm. Accessed 15 July 2015.

[20]Wily (2013), p. 18.

were introduced following pressure from reactionary movements, which in turn were a product of the repression imposed by Europeans.[21]

The most well-known reactionary movements came into being after the First World War, when force was used to control the rebellions caused by the global economic depression.[22] Since European markets were depressed, production in their colonies declined and the size of the labour force decreased, creating extreme poverty in the local population. As the global economy recovered from the economic depression, big European companies started to do business in Africa, and export-oriented production emerged. As a result new land restrictions for the local populations came to pass. New agrarian models were implemented in the 1930s, but forced labour and other inhumane practices continued to be a part of production processes.[23] After the Second World War new land policies were introduced. Some land entitlement policies were implemented that took the *de jure* and *de facto* owners into consideration when they were introduced. As Wily (2013) puts it, '[t]he plan was that this should speedily give way to individual English freehold entitlements, to be engineered through compulsory adjudication and titling of smallholders' farms.'[24]

After the independence processes the UN implemented specific programmes to promote further modernisation.[25] However, the policies of newly formed states affected investment activity.[26] Nationalisation processes, as part of socialist movements in Africa, gave rise to a high level of protectionism and created an unfavourable environment for investors. In many instances legal changes were introduced by the state, subsequent to which non-nationals were prohibited from owning land. On the producers' side, new institutional frameworks were developed. Investors developed new systems that allocated production to local firms, allowing investors to remain within the process of transformation and elaboration of commercial products. This model made agricultural activity more attractive because investors were able to diversify risk and increase profit.[27]

These types of production structures were highly profitable. In the agricultural value chain economic risks are traditionally concentrated in primary production, while processing and distribution take most of the profits. These high-value activities were traditionally carried out by the colonial power in the mother country. Activities carried out by the colonisers included the promotion of their own operations through advantageous labour conditions and the introduction of special

[21] Ibid.

[22] Ibid.

[23] Amanor (2012), p. 23.

[24] Wily (2013), p. 18.

[25] For a brief review of the development programmes promoted by the UN see: Jolly (2010) and Deininger (2003).

[26] Wily (2013), p. 18.

[27] Selby (2009).

subsidies that facilitated the internalisation of market distortions. These value chains ensured high gains for the coloniser from the commercialisation of products.

After colonised territories gained their independence, foreign investors based in Europe, North America, and Japan continued to monopolise high-value activities. The increase and volatility of basic food prices after decolonisation raised the opportunity for profit making in primary production and shifted the risk upstream to the more price-sensitive secondary production. This incentivised agribusinesses to vertically integrate and rationalise LSLIs.[28] Investors designed long-term investment projects for the supply of non-processed products. Investors were mostly interested in developing transformation technologies, know-how, machinery, and improvements in seed quality and distribution mechanisms. Examples of such projects are well known in banana farming, for instance.[29]

Up until 2008 investments in agriculture in sub-Saharan Africa were considered to be an unattractive economic activity. In the 1980s very restrictive investment policies were in place in sub-Saharan Africa. These polices primarily affected the agricultural sector. Exchange rates were overvalued, high export taxes were in place, and public expenditure in agriculture fell below 4% of government spending.[30] All of these factors created an unattractive investment environment and impacted the development of infrastructure, the implementation of new technologies, and research.[31] In the 1990s trade liberalisation was initiated, more attractive taxes were introduced, and a decrease in inflation rates made the agricultural sector more attractive to investors. Additionally, entitlement policies were introduced in some countries at this time.[32] However, policy failures led to the non-realisation of many projects that had already been started, i.e. the implementation and enforcement of anti-corruption laws and entitlement campaigns.

The new trend in agricultural contracting differs from past practice in terms of its impact, proportions, and high international acceptance. The proliferation of LSLIs, especially in sub-Saharan Africa, is seen to be mutually beneficial to the investor and the host country, in line with the theory of what FDI should do.[33] Today such agrarian policies are considered to be part of the public policies of host and home countries. Recipient states view such investments as public policies and see the possibility of job creation, improved national infrastructure, increased food production, and hence an increase in their own food security as well. In order to bring this about, investor states create incentives to invest in agriculture abroad through subsidies for the production of biocombustibles and food, for example. On the recipient side, countries also create special conditions to attract investors. These conditions include systems of preferential taxes, entering into IIAs, and the

[28]Cotula et al. (2009), p. 57.

[29]See the example of Somalia explained by: Samatar, p. 25.

[30]Deininger et al. (2011), p. 23.

[31]Ibid.

[32]Ibid.

[33]See Sect. 3.5.3 of this investigation.

stimulation of investment through the creation of investment agencies. Nowadays the vast majority of African countries have investment agencies whose purpose is to establish bilateral investment relationships and promote regionalisation.[34] In the past there had been no international element to these relationships as the colonies were considered to be territories of the colonial power, and trade took place in Europe.

2.2.1.2.1 Property Rights Situation Before and After Independence Processes

The *Berlin Act* created a structure to stimulate competition between the markets of colonial powers. Through this mechanism, the local population was formally dispossessed of the land they 'owned'. During the colonial period, various small rebellions such as those of 1899, 1906, and 1910 brought about specific procedures to grant some land concessions to African elites.[35] Laws were promulgated that demarcated special zones in which the local population could exercise their economic activities. Besides such land policies, demarcations were continuously altered depending on the necessities and preferences of the colonial powers.[36]

In the aftermath of the independence processes, new formal structures were created. The local population was no longer subordinate to colonial powers but now answered to the new state. However, notable changes did not occur in the area of property rights. Land rights remained unwritten and in many cases communally based. African constitutions recognised different kinds of property rights and established binding linkages with IL, but these efforts often failed to transform practice at the local level. In many cases these reforms looked good on paper but failed in the implementation phase. For example, the state was still considered to be the owner of non-registered land.[37]

These structures of property rights facilitated processes that continuously reallocated land. Governments coordinated these activities with African elites to determine how colonial land would be distributed,[38] allocating or reallocating land to the elites in privileged zones. In some cases these actions, in which former colonial powers still played a relevant role, produced profound social conflict that resulted in civil war. With some exceptions this process of reallocation dominated the African region from 1965–90, with the result that in the 1990s small farmers had less security of tenure than they had had in colonial times.[39]

---

[34] For an overview of the development of investment agencies in development countries see: OECD (2005).

[35] Some examples are described by: Wily (2011b), p. 96 ff.

[36] See ibid for some examples.

[37] Atwood, p. 659.

[38] Wily (2011b), p. 24.

[39] Wily (2013), p. 20.

Governments designed constitutions that stressed the formal protection of land rights and property rights. In some cases tenants of land became the legal owners. The property rights of minorities such as indigenous peoples, nomad groups, and peasants were guaranteed.[40] This legal modernisation process failed, however, because specific rules needed to formalise and make property rights on land enforceable were not included. Furthermore, international projects promoting the development of a land registry also failed.[41] Although a regulatory process had been undertaken, the risk of losing land had, in fact, grown in practice.[42]

The literature has evaluated processes of land reform in sub-Saharan Africa as a process of land accumulation, rural social differentiation, decentralisation, and centralisation of administration and political alliances.[43] All these structural changes were made under the premise of development and were based on modern agricultural theories that would produce different outcomes. These protectionist policies were introduced under the premise of national interest and the necessity of development.

Even today there are some countries in sub-Saharan Africa where most of the arable land remains unregistered. This situation produces an uncertain legal situation: on the one hand, constitutional provisions and international treaties guarantee the property rights of the people considered to be the possessors, whilst on the other hand, there is no formal title to support this claim.[44] Chains of titles are not officially registered due to high costs, cultural realities, and traditions, or because there is no system of cadastre in a given region. With the exception of Kenya, the common situation is that approximately 10% of the registered arable land is owned by white farmers of South Africa, Namibia, and Zimbabwe.[45] This situation leads to conflict not only between the state and the local community or private actors, but also between different groups at the local level, especially when they are in competition with each other. Vis-à-vis the relationship with the state, the problem is that both the state and the local community claim to be the owners. In fact there are legal regimes that apparently support both views: while the norms applied by the state consider the state to be the owner, under local customary norms the local population is considered to be the owner. Despite this conflict of norms it is the position of the state that has prevailed, as it is the more powerful decision maker. It can displace local occupants of the land and transmit property rights to national or foreign investors in an apparently legal transaction. The transaction between the

[40] In addition to the protection offered to minorities and indigenous people at national level, at international level the UN and ILO promulgated declarations protecting traditional property rights and labour rights respectively. See in this study Sect. 3.6.4.

[41] Atwood, pp. 659, 668.

[42] Wily (2013), p. 20.

[43] Amanor (2012), p. 26.

[44] Davis.

[45] Wily (2013), p. 12.

state and investors appears to be legal because locals are unable either to prove their ownership or to enforce their traditional property right. States Wily (2013):

> [...] The current rush now helps materialise legal dispossession on the ground. As the legal owner, governments are lawfully selling (or mainly leasing) lands from under the feet of their citizens. As Owners, they need not, at a stretch, even consult with the occupants and users ahead of eviction, let alone involve them in contractual negotiations.[46]

African Constitutional Laws broadly recognise different types of property rights. However, the trends in protecting communal property laws are quite different. Wily (2011a) analysed thirty constitutions in sub-Saharan Africa to uncover the various forms of protection for property rights. She shows that out of more than fifty countries, only seven fully recognise customary land holdings to have the force of real property rights.[47] Even though there are some cases in which administrative procedures present legal loopholes, these countries recognise communal property rights even without the formalisation of land titles. A group of nine countries recognise customary property rights, albeit with nuances for certain situations. These situations may include a requirement to register the land, the prohibition against registration by certain groups, and titles that do not allow the owners to fully exercise their property rights. A third group of countries offers very limited protection of customary property rights. These countries have derogated from existing customary community rights and transformed them into state-granted rights.[48] In a last category of countries, Wily (2011b) includes states in which there is no customary property rights protection at all. These countries host a population of 630 million people. In these states local people are, in fact, considered by the state to be tenants of the land, which means that they are considered *de facto* owners.[49] The state is considered to be the *de jure* owner.

In some cases, from the legal point of view, small landholders might be considered both *de facto* and *de jure* owners of the land. They are considered *de facto* owners because they actively cultivate and use the land; they usufruct the land. Further they are considered *de jure* owners because their customary ownership of the land has been legally recognised at the national level by the constitutions of most of the countries in question, and at the regional level through the African Charter on Human and Peoples' Rights (Banjul Charter).[50] Thus the *de facto* ownership provides constitutional protection to small landholders and indigenous peoples. Though international law and national constitutional law protect the

---

[46]Ibid.

[47]Wily (2011a), p. 12. The countries herewith referred are: Ghana, Mozambique, Uganda, Tanzania, South Sudan, Burkina Faso and South Africa.

[48]Ibid.

[49]Wily (2013), p. 13.

[50]Contrary to some studies that assume small farmers, indigenous people and minorities are not owner of their land, we completely refuse such approaches. Internationally, the land posed by such individuals is their land and they are legally recognised owners, even though, property tittles are missed. See our approach on this at Sect. 3.6.4.

traditional property rights of indigenous peoples, the determination of whether a specific group can be considered indigenous is absent. This aspect makes the enforcement of property rights even harder. Again, the local population can enforce these rights only through strong institutions, which are rarely found in LDCs.[51]

However, in order for the state to systematically define what is communally or privately owned land, demarcation or land titles are needed. As a result of their absence, and the failure of efforts to make the ownership of land recognisable, states can freely sell land even though the land is being used or occupied. Although cadastral policies were introduced in some countries, their scope is limited. Advantages accrued from titling include the stimulation of local markets from the incentives that property rights create, increased ability to secure funding for land investments, and the initiation of economic interaction between more efficient users and less efficient land users. In this sense land policies have traditionally included three relevant aspects: (1) smallholder farmers are more efficient than large mechanised estates; (2) an equitable distribution of land secures stable access to land, provides a better foundation for livelihoods and employment, and allows the poor to benefit from broad-based development initiatives; (3) the promotion of democratic rights, local empowerment, and political stability.[52] However, in most of the countries in the region such policies have yet to be implemented. Land titling can be seen as a political instrument to undermine the informal rights of rural people and to convey land to political interest groups.

To conclude, the fact that states deny the recognition of communal or private property rights results in local farmers practically receiving the same treatment as in colonial times. They are tenants of their own land but this land is administered by the state.

2.2.1.2.2 Recent Precedents

Notwithstanding the arrival and proliferation of LSLIs across the sub-Saharan region in recent years, we can see that a similar phenomenon has already been dealt with in a variety of ways, in different periods, under different forms of government, and within different political structures.[53] Over the last 6 years, however, the phenomenon has peaked and gained resonance principally because of its scope, the effects it produces, and the attention paid to it by civil society and NGOs.

Although many LDCs have attempted to formally deal with this issue following their independence, legal policies have failed to solve other problems related to land

---

[51]See: Deininger et al. (2011), p. 28. Cotula makes also the same affirmation in his thesis by explaining the bargaining power of local population deciding on their natural resources, see: Cotula (2012a); as well as Cotula et al. (2003), p. 2.

[52]Amanor (2012), p. 5. Collier and Dercon.

[53]Deininger and Gershon (2001), p. 23.

distribution including productivity, underinvestment, poverty, and the development of infrastructure.[54] In light of the internal problems LDCs are attempting to resolve, LSLIs as a form of FDI are seen as a solution to each of these pre-existing problems because they are deemed to promote development in general.[55] In theory, LSLIs are supposed to produce a win-win situation for the investor, locals, and the government. The idea is that the investment project can coexist with pre-existing local structures and with the requirements of local governments. Apparently these projects have not borne out the theory with sufficiently positive results.[56]

The wave of land acquisitions starting in 2007–2008 was preceded by a time of heightened uncertainty worldwide. The prices of primary foods in particular peaked.[57] Discussions about food sovereignty and food security reached the point where they became central political issues not only in LDCs but also in developed countries. The global financial crisis also contributed to raising the interest cost applied to transactions for investors acquiring agricultural land, especially highly capitalised investors.[58] In this context the purchase of land was used as a catalyst to bring about inflation in many economies. This happened as a result of the mistrust pervading financial markets, increased political instability, and the added value chain offered by land purchases. Food crises and abrupt stimulation of land markets are not new phenomena, especially in sub-Saharan Africa.[59] Both occur repeatedly in the global market. However, these phenomena do not generally appear at the

---

[54]Some examples have been investigated by: Potts (2013), p. 1; Berry (2002), p. 63; Amanor (2012).

[55]As already stated by investment tribunals: 'to protect investments is to protect the general interest of development and of developing countries.' *Amco Asia Co v Republic of Indonesia* [1981] Decision on Jurisdiction ARB/81/1 (ICSID). Moreover, The Standards of due process and good governance (see *infra* at: 3.5) are proposed with the goal that national jurisdictions set new standards and equilibrate the level of protection between foreigners and nationals. Muchlinski et al. (2008), p. VI.

[56]See for example the initiative made by German BMZ Bundesministerium für Wirtschaftliche Zusammenarbeit und Entwicklung (2009); GIZ (2011). The most complete publication of the World Bank also highlights some gaps that lead to produce undesirable effects of investment projects, see: Deininger et al. (2011). Additionally the frequent publications in the media about the negative effects of investment projects has also be considered as evidence, see in form of few examples: The Economist, 'The Surge in Land Deals. When Others are Grabbing their Land: Evidence is Piling up Against Acquisitions of Farmland in Poor Countries' http://www.economist.com/node/18648855. Accessed 12.05.2011; Vidal (2011b); The Guardian (2011); The Guardian, 'Ethiopians Talk of Violent Intimidation as Their Land is Earmarked for Foreign Investors' *Guardiancouk* (London); Vidal (2011a); Lorenz, 'Foreign Firms Drive Cambodians from Farms' *Spiegel Online*, http://www.spiegel.de/international/business/foreign-companies-are-taking-farmlands-away-from-cambodians-a-935801.html. Accessed 01 December 2013; Sharife (2009). See also: 'Nigerian Parliament Condemns Land Grab by Chinese Firms' Premium Times (Abuja), http://www.premiumtimesng.com/news/top-news/216665-nigerian-parliament-condemns-land-grab-chinese-firms.html. Accessed 20 March 2017.

[57]FAO (2008), p. 3.

[58]Deininger et al. (2011), p. 1.

[59]See: Custodis (2013), p. 310 ff.

same time. It was the convergence of both at the same time that gave them greater significance in late 2007 and 2008. While the financial crisis of 2008 contributed to the increase in land deals, the same financial crisis also led to a stagnation of progress in projects due to liquidity problems.[60]

Food prices also soared after the convergence of different market forces.[61] On the supply side, weather-related production shortfalls triggered price hikes against a backdrop of continuously declining production levels in major exporting countries. A gradual reduction in global stock levels after the last price peak in 1995 also decreased buffer supplies.[62] Policy changes leading to the liberalisation of food markets, technological progress leading to less costly risk-management strategies, decreasing transportation costs, and an increasing number of exporting countries were all contributing factors.[63]

Markets can become more competitive under these conditions. Hence, prices can increase as a result of unexpected effects either on the demand or supply side. Higher fuel costs raise fertilizer prices, costs for industrial agriculture, and transportation costs. It is logical that supply-side factors have effects on prices, and can be connected to demand-side issues. The rapid changes brought on by globalisation also contribute to the acceleration of increased land investments. Continuing economic growth, changing diets, growing demand for energy, global financial instability, and increased urbanisation are all pushing the global demand for food and fuel, which are both dependent on agricultural activity.[64]

The most drastic changes in the agricultural market are closely related to the necessity of adapting to new requirements on the demand side.[65] They include structural changes in land use resulting from converting land into a resource used for both food production and non-food production (i.e. the case of biofuels, rubber, or the tourism industry).

Biofuels are heavily subsidised and are becoming a more competitive alternative to fossil fuels as crude oil prices fluctuate.[66] Changes in the diets of growing populations in emerging and developing countries (who are living in an increasingly urbanised environment) have gradually affected the demand structure, but do not explain the sudden peak in prices in 2008. The FAO argues that financial market operations (especially the development of new derivatives in a context of high liquidity and low interest rates) were the consequence, rather than the cause, of this price volatility.[67] Nevertheless, these developments were exacerbated by short-term national policies that sought to protect their respective local populations by

---

[60]Cotula (2012b), p. 666; Shepard and Anuradha (2011).

[61]FAO (2008), p. 4.

[62]Ibid.

[63]Ibid.

[64]Food and Agriculture Organization of the United Nations (2011); FAO (2008), p. 12.

[65]FAO (2008), p. 5.

[66]Ibid.

[67]Ibid.

blocking exports.[68] Exchange rate developments also affected relative prices for agricultural products and changed trade patterns. Most agricultural commodities are traded in USD, and the devaluation of the dollar shifted demand to US-exported commodities.

Food price volatility greatly affects LDCs when they become more dependent on aid programmes. Although the agricultural sector is the most important economic sector for LDCs, its underdevelopment, and in some cases its reliance on the production of a single crop, makes it incapable of meeting the demands of the domestic market. Therefore, LDCs need to import a large portion of the products they consume. In addition, the products exported by LDCs are usually non-processed, while imported products are usually processed and thus have a higher value.

LDCs see FDI in agriculture as a way to improve their domestic situation. This was not possible in the past because investors were confronted with high political risks and hostility and thus lacked an incentive to invest. Nonetheless, the events described above have produced a change in this situation. LDCs may now rapidly introduce agrarian policies involving the transmission of some land rights to investors, many of whom are foreign. Indeed, this process is already underway. In the next section we will offer a deeper justification of the imminent need for new agrarian and food policies in LDCs, especially with regard to sub-Saharan Africa.

2.2.1.3 The Need for New Agrarian Policies

The most important economic sector for LDCs is agriculture.[69] The economies of some LDCs are highly dependent on agricultural exports. Furthermore in some countries, over 50% of inhabitants live in rural areas.[70] These rural inhabitants are directly employed and directly dependent upon agricultural activities, whilst the rest of the population is considered to be indirectly dependent on this sector.[71] Of the 1.2 billion people catalogued by the FAO as living in absolute poverty, around 75% depend on the agricultural sector for their livelihoods.[72] Agricultural development in LDCs is expected to increase the production of agricultural commodities and bring about the stabilisation of food prices. As the world population continues to grow, food consumption is also increasing. Food consumption is expected to increase to 3130 kilocalories per person per day by 2050. Both of these realities will require agricultural production in developing countries to nearly double if global food requirements are to be met.[73]

---

[68]Collier and Dercon, p. 11.

[69]United Nations Office of the High Commissioner for Human Rights (2012).

[70]OECD et al. (2014), p. 24.

[71]The World Bank (2016). See also International Labour Organization (2012).

[72]See the followings reports: OECD et al. (2014), p. 25; Food and Agriculture Organization of the United Nations (2011), p. 14 ff.

[73]The World Economic Forum (2013).

In reality, however, the development of cereal yields in sub-Saharan Africa from 1961 to 2010 fails to show even a 50% increase, rising from 818.73 kg/ha in 1961 to 1301.81 kg/ha in 2010.[74] Compared to worldwide average cereal yields, sub-Saharan Africa produces 2405.19 kg/ha less. Compounding the problem of inadequate increases in yields, during the same time period the regional population grew by a factor of 3.6, or from 235,988,196 to 854,266,626 people.[75] These huge differences highlight the problem of low food production, especially that of non-processed food, and its potentially severe consequences.

In comparison to other geographic areas with similar agroclimatic conditions, sub-Saharan Africa performs particularly poorly. This problem is usually referred to as the 'yield gap'. For example, a yield gap exists 'if appropriate practices, inputs, technologies and knowledge were applied', yet the yield still falls short of what is theoretically possible.[76] The absence of agricultural machinery is a common issue, and most farmers work the land by hand. There were some countries, for example, where a single machine covered 15,750 ha of arable land in 1961.[77] Although by 2006 this ratio had fallen to 3615 ha, it is still remarkably high compared to machine use in agriculture in wealthier countries. It should be noted that during the early 1990s, the figure was as low as 900 ha of arable land per machine. This illustrates certain trends in the adoption of new technologies. While new technology is adopted in some areas, others have little to no exposure to new agricultural techniques and equipment, resulting in their slow and sporadic introduction. While the yield gap is greatest (and still increasing) between sub-Saharan Africa and the rest of the world, the gap between the developed world and both Latin America and South Asia is also noteworthy.[78] Experts agree that the key to the development of sub-Saharan Africa lies in reducing the yield gap. Hence, economies based on agricultural production have a unique opportunity to set the continent on a course for growth.[79]

Consequently, governments concerned with food security have been promoting LSLIs, and investors keen to capitalise on profit-maximising opportunities have been making LSLIs predominantly in LDCs. From an economic point of view, the fact that sub-Saharan agricultural markets are stimulated by FDI is highly welcome. Host countries have benefited from development opportunities provided by FDI. These benefits include improved food security and lower prices as a result of more efficient food production. These developments have also created or modified property rights. Host countries and IOs (at some point) welcomed the increase in FDI because they

[74]Deininger et al. (2011), p. 14.

[75]The World Bank (2016).

[76]Ibid.

[77]As defined by the World Bank, agricultural machinery refers to the number of wheel and crawler tractors in use in agriculture at the end of the calendar year specified or during the first quarter of the following year. This variable is referred in order to approach the access to technology, the investment capacity and therefore its contribution with the augment of land productivity. Source: ibid. For similar approach see: Food and Agriculture Organization of the United Nations (2016).

[78]Deininger et al. (2011), p. 11.

[79]Ibid.

considered it to be a unique opportunity to develop the internal markets of LDCs. Other associated benefits are economic growth, the improvement of infrastructure, the development of technology levels, and improved agricultural know-how.

The introduction of these policies, however, poses a big challenge at the domestic level. One reason for this lies in the inadequacies of institutions in LDCs. Another reason is the drastic change that such policies bring to the everyday lives and social structure of locals. This is the case at least in sub-Saharan countries, where a majority of the rural population are subsistence farmers owning only 2 ha of land on average.[80] Policy changes induced by FDI usually bring about a change from traditional small-farming to mega-farms.[81] To put it more concretely, the best-case scenario is that these policies transform local farmers into employees of newly created mega-farms.

From an economic perspective, the increase in LSLIs that reclaim[82] large areas of idle or underused land appears to be a desirable market reaction to the excess demand for food and other derivatives. Rising prices promise higher profits that attract (often foreign) investment to LDCs. Although the local population already cultivates at least some of the land in question, property rights are often poorly defined in LDCs. Interestingly, large-scale investments serve to define property rights. Well-defined property rights are essential to attracting investors interested in pursuing large-scale food production. Host countries are motivated to increase agricultural production, thereby securing the nourishment of a growing population.[83] Decentralised market interactions between the sellers (lessors) and the buyers (leasers) of land define property rights so that market interactions are incentivised and thus become competitive. In this process a governmental authority registers the land so that its ownership is guaranteed. In economic theory, clearly defined and enforceable property rights provide the essential incentive for investment, or even economic activity in general. Without clearly defined rights to the produced output, nobody would cultivate land in the first place (at least not on a large scale). Once such rights have been defined, investors will provide the necessary capital for long-term economic growth, as assumed by Solow's (1956) and Swan's (1956) neoclassical growth model.[84] Consequently, LSLIs can be seen as a public policy issue in regions where underproduction, accelerated demographic

[80]It has to be highlighted that what constitutes a 'small' farmer varies from region to region. While in Malawi for example small farmers belong until less than one-fourth of a hectare in other region small farmers have between 1 and 4 ha. The World Economic Forum (2013), p. 26.

[81]Pinstrup-Andersen and Watson (2011), p. 192.

[82]With the term 'reclamation' we refer in our analysis to the preparation of land for large-scale agricultural exploitation. We do not refer to the preparation necessary for small-scale agriculture. As we argue below, land that is already in use by small-scale farmers usually needs less reclamation than idle land.

[83]Some relevant studies on the definition of property rights and the abolishment of poverty specially emphasised on sub-Saharan Africa: Deininger et al. (2011), p. 4; Arthur (2008), p. 69; Knack and Philip (1995), p. 207 and also Daron et al. (2001).

[84]Solow (1956), p. 65; Swan (1956), p. 334.

growth, and high levels of undernourishment have prevailed. FDI in agriculture offers attractive development opportunities for LDCs in terms of infrastructure (mainly propagated as the creation of jobs), technology, and knowledge. As these developments result in higher agricultural productive efficiency, they increase overall food security. Ideally investors would reclaim fallow or underused land. In this scenario the local population would not be directly affected but would benefit from indirect effects such as better infrastructure and new jobs. Such a win-win situation would improve the position of all parties involved (states, investors, and local people).[85] Investing in the agricultural sector is attractive because this sector carries enormous socio-economic importance in LDCs in particular. Moreover, new land policies might succeed where previous legislation aiming to promote small farmers' production as a proven way to tackle poverty has failed. Since small farmers in LDCs are a heterogeneous and fragmented group, coordination activities among them are very costly. By contrast, LSLIs require lower coordination costs and present lower risk because potential losses can be internalised more easily by large investors.

2.2.1.4 Property Rights and Bargaining Power: Investors Vis-à-Vis Locals and Politicians

One of the main challenges posed by the introduction of new land policy is the disparate negotiating power of economic actors, which results from the large informational asymmetries between the parties involved in a negotiation.[86] Bargaining power plays a central role in this regard. Its relevance increases when decisions must be agreed upon by groups of landowners or tenants.[87] When rights are weakly defined, governance is weak, or those affected lack voice, the investments can carry high risks for the parties involved.[88] If we consider that each group of actors engaging in a negotiation has particular interests, conflict between these interests may arise. If a government promotes policies leading to the reallocation of property rights, the bargaining power of the actors involved might be indispensable

[85]Research made by Knack (2001), p. 1152 stated as well the possibilities of development that such projects offer. They reported that: 'investments can provide benefits through four channels: (i) supporting social infrastructure, often through community development funds using land compensation; (ii) generating employment; (iii) providing access to markets and technology for local producers; and (iv) higher local or national tax revenue'.

[86]In the land grabbing literature the issue concerning lack of participation and transparency in the negotiation is almost omnipresent. We approach this issue in the apart using some elements provided by the political economy literature. These elements are explained as part of our research tools for theorizing LSLIs from a L& perspective in Sect. 1.5.

[87]Seminal contribution on interest groups and lobbying is offered by: Mueller (2008), p. 472.

[88]Principles for Responsible Agricultural Investment that Respects Rights, Livehoods and Resources [2010] available http://siteresources.worldbank.org/INTARD/214574-1111138388661/22453321/Principles_Extended.pdf. Accessed 25 December 2013, p. 1.

for the performance of such a policy, as well as for its sustainable implementation. Following our methodological assumptions,[89] freely negotiating parties will only cooperate if they believe that non-cooperation is less favourable than cooperation. This means that locals will cooperate with investors and governments only if they receive a surplus in benefit from the negotiation.[90] Difficulties might arise if actors have a range of preferences. In such cases the level of coordination required to settle and align diverse interests can carry very high costs that might be ultimately prohibitive.[91] This is a significant characteristic of the group of local producers. They are a very heterogeneous, fragmented, and large group with great differences in preferences *inter se,* and have limited access to information compared to the other groups taking part in the negotiations, namely the government and investors. These characteristics, in addition to the problem of poorly defined property rights, give rise to a situation where landowners find themselves in a weaker position than the other parties involved in the negotiation.

In addition, landowners can be differentiated from investors exerting coercive or persuasive power in negotiations. Investors have access to capital, new forms of technology and know-how, a broader range of information, leverage in public decision-making and social relations, as well as a more defined and internalised perception of the relative productivity of competing forms of natural resource use.[92] All of these advantages in bargaining power give investors a large degree of control over land and crops and, therefore, significant influence across the value chain. Without efficient institutions to check the power of politicians, they can negotiate and misrepresent weak interest groups whose bargaining power, as we have already seen, is *per se* limited.[93] State representatives and investors commonly engage in reprisals and disproportionate exercises of power to ensure that an investment can be made.[94] Consultancy processes are unnecessary in such scenarios because the lack of legitimacy is not an impediment to the investment, at least not in the short run.

The game becomes even more complex when political actors become involved in the negotiation process and their interests also need to be taken into account.[95] Politicians, who might be seen as profit maximisers, adapt public policies in order to confer benefits upon specific groups of individuals in exchange for political support.[96]

---

[89]See Sect. 1.5 of this study.

[90]Cooter and Ulen (2012), p. 101.

[91]Amanor (2012), p. 33. See also Mueller (2008), p. 473.

[92]Mueller (2008), p. 472. For the case of LSLIs see: von Braun and Meinzen-Dick (2009), pp. 1, 2.

[93]Cotula (2012b), p. 665.

[94]The World Economic Forum (2013), p. 43; Vidal (2011a), p. 172.

[95]Models of interest groups in politics are detailed explained by: Mueller (2008), p. 475, especially interesting is the interpretation of campaign as explained by 'political man theory' in which candidates after having preselected their positions, interest groups contribute to the candidate whose position on the issues comes closes to their favoured position.

[96]This under the rational the FDI increase the probabilities for politicians to remain in the power because they satisfy the necessities of interest groups. For a similar view, see: Broadly: Thomas (2014), p. 1.

At the same time, investors want to maximise the efficiency of their investment so that profits and productivity increase with relatively low expenditures. In states with weak democratic institutions and high levels of corruption, specific interest groups might behave in an opportunistic manner to achieve their goals. In order to be able to internalise the risks associated with agricultural economic activity, only massive investors are able to undertake LSLIs in the agricultural sector of LDCs. In some instances the investors are more powerful than the LDCs themselves.[97] Therefore, the presence of investors in a specific country can directly impact political stability. The effects of this power imbalance play out via unilaterally stipulated compensation mechanisms and the manipulation of price and market structures. Although affected individuals receive some compensation, field studies have shown that this neither represents reparation of the actual damages, nor the real market value of the acquired land.[98]

The problem of bargaining power—especially of LDCs—has been recognised internationally. IOs and NGOs have created programmes to encourage the involvement of the local population. These programmes range from attempts to reduce information asymmetry by eliciting relevant information from the local population to monitoring the governance process before LSLIs are finalised so that the local population can participate in the negotiation process. These campaigns have frequently been affected by reprisals from state authorities, and in some cases by reprisals from private investors against local leaders and rights defenders. The United Nations (UN) has paid special attention to individuals who collaborate with potentially affected populations and seek to strengthen local bargaining power. Such individuals are officially called 'human rights defenders'. In many cases HRs defenders have suffered irreparable damages because of the delicate programmes they are involved with, mostly in LDCs. Therefore, the UN adopted a declaration promoting the protection of HRs defenders.[99] Furthermore, in 2013 the Human Rights Council (HRC) adopted a resolution that called upon states to ensure that all legal provisions affecting HRs defenders were clearly defined, determinable, and non-retroactive in order to avoid potential abuse.

---

[97]The following contributions deal with the problems arising in such situations in which investors can have even more power than the host state: Wettstein (2007); Koeltz (2010), p. 43.

[98]To gain a better understanding of individual cases see the following reports: Häberli (2012); Bach (2010); Holdinghausen. The aspect of compensation has played a relevant role in the recommendations and principles developed by IOs, see i.e.: Fritz (2008).

[99]De Schutter (2009b). Elaboration of the Declaration on HR defenders began in 1984 and ended with the adoption of the text by the General Assembly in 1998, on the occasion of the fiftieth anniversary of the UDHR. A collective effort by a number of human rights NGOs and some State delegations helped to ensure that the final result was a strong, very useful and pragmatic text. Perhaps most importantly, the Declaration is addressed not just to States and to human rights defenders, but to everyone. It tells us that we all have a role to fulfil as human rights defenders and emphasises that there is a global human rights movement that involves us all. Source: General Assembly (UN) A/53/625/Add.2 Declaration on the Right and Responsibility of Individuals, Groups and Organs of Society to Promote and Protect Universally Recognized Human Rights and Fundamental Freedoms [1998] A/RES/53/144.

At the regional level, there are treaties that promote local participation in decision-making processes. One example is the Aarhus Convention on Access to Information, Public Participation in Decision-Making and Access to Justice in Environmental Matters.[100] This is a binding convention that aims to contribute to the protection of the right of every person of present and future generations to live in an environment adequate to his or her health and well-being, with each party guaranteeing the right of access to information, public participation in decision-making, and access to justice in environmental matters in accordance with the provisions of the convention. However, the scope is restricted to Europe and transitional economies in Central Asia.[101]

Moreover, soft law instruments that were developed to encourage discipline in the implementation of LSLIs frequently seek to strengthen the participation of locals. The Voluntary Guidelines on the Responsible Governance of Tenure of Land, Fisheries and Forests in the Context of National Food Security make specific reference to the participation of local populations as one of the principles needed for a fruitful implementation of LSLI.[102] This instrument demands that states be consistent in their principles of consultation and participation in order to legitimise the implementation of land policies. States should prevent corruption with regard to tenure rights and stimulate participation, rule of law, transparency and accountability.[103] Moreover, non-discriminatory and gender sensitive assistance might be provided to landowners to offer access to the services of implementing agencies and judicial authorities, or to participate in a process that can affect the *status quo* of land rights.[104] Some additional examples of instruments considering participation to be a key issue when implementing LSLIs are CFS, Principles for Responsible Investment in Agriculture and Food Systems,[105] OECD-FAO Guidance for Responsible Agricultural Supply Chains,[106] Land Policy Initiative (AUC-AfDB-UNECA), Guiding Principles on Large Scale Land Based Investments in Africa,[107] and United Nations Principles for Responsible Contracts.[108]

In principles 1 and 10 of the 1992 Rio Declaration on Environment and Development, a reference is made to the need for cooperation between states to avoid environmental damage resulting from the introduction of new policies. In addition,

---

[100]Convention on Access to Information, Public Participation in Decision-Making and Access to Justice in Environmental Matters [2001] No. 37770 available on http://www.unece.org/env/pp/treatytext.html. Accessed 15 July 2015.

[101]United Nations (2004).

[102]Voluntary Guidelines on the Responsible Governance of Tenure of Land, Fisheries and Forests in the Context of National Food Security [2013] CL 144/9 C 2013/20, p. 4.

[103]Ibid.

[104]Ibid.

[105]Principles for Responsible Investment in Agriculture and Food Systems [2014] available http://www.fao.org/3/a-au866e.pdf. Accessed 18 August 2015.

[106]OECD-FAO (2016).

[107]African Union (2014).

[108]Human Rights Council (2011).

there is an obligation to take into account the effect of new measures on the local population so that a higher quality of life for all is guaranteed. More precisely, in principle 10 the declaration states the essential aspects concerning the integration of the local population into decision-making processes.[109]

Such instruments, recognised internationally, play an important role in the effort to increase the bargaining power of small farmers. Protection offered by IL to HRs defenders has made it possible for representatives of civil society organisations to make contact with potentially affected landowners and offer their consultancy services. The result of these activities manifests in the context of land acquisitions.[110] The access to information offered by external actors, in this case HRs defenders, might be seen as a contribution to the contractual governance needed to balance conflicting interests of parties. To guarantee the sustainable performance of LSLIs, it is necessary to strike a delicate balance between the interests of people directly affected but indirectly involved in the project, and those of the wider public.

Following our definition of land grabbing and our justification of the need for new land policies in the framework of new agrarian strategies to reduce poverty and promote development in LDCs, we now turn to the analysis of the negotiations *per se*. In the next section we will focus on the actors involved in negotiations, the instruments, the performance of the projects, and the impacts that they produce.

2.2.2 *Relevant Actors: States and Foreign Investors*

Most LSLI agreements are formally concluded bilaterally; they take the form of bilateral synallagmatic contracts. On one side there are recipient countries and on the other side there are states, enterprises (public or semi-public), or private investors. The vast majority of land is acquired by private actors, although some of them are publicly owned by the investor's home country.[111] Joint ventures between agricultural firms and financial companies also undertake LSLIs. Even though there are diverse contractual structures, the focus of our research is on cross-national relationships in which at least one of the parties is a state acting as a sovereign entity, not as a private entity. Ergo, the implications of states' measures have to be analysed differently given the principles of sovereignty and immunity for public officers.[112] Lastly, we do not consider local owners to be actors in the investment negotiations. The property of local owners has in most cases been

[109] General Assembly (UN) Rio Declaration on Environment and Development [1992] A/CONF.151/26 (Vol. I).

[110] For some actions taken by the HRC see: European Center for Constitutional And Human Rights (2015).

[111] Deininger et al. (2011), p. XXXIII.

[112] For a law and economic analysis about the differences and implications of states acting as sovereign or private actors given the legal problems that arise due to the principle of state immunity see: von Braun and Meinzen-Dick (2009), p. 1; van Aaken (2013).

expropriated and the land is *de facto* owned by the host state. We consider such actors in a later part by analysing the effects of the contracts and their enforcement.

Until 2014 the vast majority of LSLIs were made by high-income countries, most of them OECD members (OECD countries represent 63% of the 963 documented LSLI agreements).[113] Lower middle-income countries account for 292 deals (21%) and upper middle-income countries for 200 deals (15%).[114] As reported by the Land Matrix in the second semester of 2014, the USA, Great Britain, and the Netherlands are the most active countries in the area of LSLIs. In addition, there are groups of investors from small states with strong financial sectors such as Singapore and Hong Kong. Moreover, there are investors from populous emerging economies such as Malaysia, India, and South Korea.[115] The regions from which investments originate are characterised by economic liquidity, a continuously increasing demand for food, energy crops, and forage plants, and high or relatively high demographic density. In addition, some of these countries struggle with scarred or poor soil and limited access to quality water. While most developing countries focus on food security, developed countries have a broader focus and are also interested in oil crops, maize, and sugar cane with the goal of obtaining safe and secure energy production in the future. Actors from these developed countries are mainly located on the European continent.[116] In countries such as Nigeria, Sudan, Cambodia, and Mozambique, many investments are made by locally based corporations using capital gathered from abroad.[117]

Host countries are countries with a high potential for agricultural development and vast areas of underdeveloped and low-cost land.[118] The most active countries receiving investments are South Sudan, Papua New Guinea, Indonesia, Democratic Republic of the Congo, Sudan, Mozambique, Ethiopia, Liberia, Sierra Leone, and Madagascar.[119] Recipient countries are, in most cases, LDCs where economic improvement is needed in order to stimulate local markets and promote policies to decrease staggering levels of poverty. Since agricultural activity is the most relevant sector for the national economy of host countries, the stimulation of this sector could cause repercussions at the national level. In addition to a high level of poverty, common characteristics of these countries include the necessity for the creation of new sources of employment, growth and revenue, as well as the necessity of introducing policies to guarantee local food security. Moreover, host countries are characterised by a weak legal institutional structure with high degrees

[113]Source: International Land Coalition (2011).

[114]Source: ibid.

[115]Source: ibid.

[116]Holt-Gimnez et al. (2011), p. 1.

[117]Anseeuw et al. (2012), p. 19.

[118]About the levels of production in sub-Saharan Africa see Sect. 2.2.2. For literature about highlighting the necessity of increase the productivity see: Cotula (2012b); von Braun and Meinzen-Dick (2009), p. 1.

[119]Anseeuw et al. (2012), p. 53; See also: International Land Coalition (2011).

of corruption and weak democratic institutions.[120] Most of the countries witnessing an increase in land investments have introduced liberalisation policies in recent years hoping that this legislation would enable them to attract foreign investors.[121] Even though the cost associated with political risk is still high,[122] national investment policies have brought about an increase in revenue improving the investment climate.[123]

Due to the secrecy governing land investments, it is difficult to identify the origin of the investing company on the one hand, and the origin of the resources funding the projects on the other. While there are states that openly invest in land, as is the case with China and Saudi Arabia, other countries and multinational enterprises offer indirect incentives to promote investments.

2.2.3 Legal Instruments: Contracts

2.2.3.1 Overview

This section has two primary goals. First, we will offer a brief description of the most relevant elements of LSLI contracts in order to provide a complete picture of this phenomenon. Second, we will concentrate on figuring out why contracting parties choose to agree to the contracts and the terms therein. Although investment contracts can contribute to the development of LDCs, they often create challenges for domestic institutions that lack well-oriented policies to account for pre-existing domestic and international legal obligations. Therefore, we expect local governments to be concerned with the inclusion of pertinent contractual clauses so that the expected outcomes can be achieved. In order to evaluate LSLI, it is crucial to figure out to what extent the design of investment instruments might progressively contribute to the achievement of the goals of agricultural FDI in LDCs.

Before we begin an analysis of the legal instruments of LSLIs, we need to highlight how difficult it is to access information about these instruments. The expectation that research can be conducted by gathering a considerable number of contracts for an empirical examination of this phenomenon is illusory. In reality,

---

[120] Anseeuw et al. (2012), p. 5 refer to the problem of legitimation during the negotiation process.

[121] As reported by UNCTAD the domestic measures improving the liberalisation of investment activity continues increasing. Cotula (2012b), p. 670. For empirical approaches confirming the positive relationship between weak institutions (corruption) and NGOs see: Anyanwu (2012), p. 425.

[122] Political risk includes three basic types of events or situations generally accepted as comprising 'political risk': (1) Confiscation, expropriation, or nationalisation of an investment; (2) Currency inconvertibility, (3) Damage from political violence from war or civil disturbance and (4) default on obligations, including breach of contract. United Nations Conference on Trade and Development, World Investment Report 2012 (World Investment Report 2012, 2013), p. 78.

[123] Nadakavukaren (2013), p. 509; Cotula et al. (2009), p. 58.

contracts are negotiated in secret, most of the time they are neither registered nor published, and public access is difficult. Even though examples of these contracts were found whilst conducting this research, they do not facilitate the drawing of a general picture of this issue. Furthermore, most of the found and examined contracts are incomplete. The contracts are missing appendices, allowing only for a tentative analysis or explanation of the issues. For this reason, this research project also relies on information compiled for other studies. In order to undertake this cross-referential analysis, the most significant sources of information are the study conducted by Cotula in 2011,[124] a series of publications by the Oakland Institute in 2011,[125] data provided by the Land Matrix,[126] as well as the online repository of open land contracts published by the Columbia Center on Sustainable Investment and the World Bank in 2015.[127]

To achieve the two primary goals of this section, both a legal and a political economic theoretical framework must be applied. This two-pronged analysis will allow us to better understand both the outcomes (by outcomes we mean the final contracts produced after the completion of negotiations) and the design of investment policies. From this understanding, we will be able to offer suggestions as to the correct design of legal measures that can be undertaken at national and international levels to improve the structure of new contracts and increase the levels of governance in contracts that have already been concluded.

2.2.3.2 The Contracts

Investment contracts mainly take one of two forms in LSLI negotiations: either (1) long-time leases or (2) purchases. While lease contracts are significantly more detailed than purchase contracts, the short-term and long-term effects of either type of contract are essentially the same.[128] Of course, from a very narrow legal point of view one cannot make this affirmation, given the fundamentally different natures of these two legal situations. What can be said is that in both cases local populations lose access to their land. The nature and content of LSLI contracts are very heterogeneous depending on the country, legal system, and type of specific agricultural investment.

---

[124]World Bank Group (2009).

[125]Regarding the Oakland Institute: The Oakland Institute (2011b); The Oakland Institute (2011a); The Oakland Institute (2011c); The Oakland Institute (2011d).

[126]Regarding the Land Matrix See *supra* footnote 2 in this chapter.

[127]Columbia Center on Sustainable Investment and World Bank Group (2015).

[128]The fact that some countries have controls to sale the land to foreigners has a historical background, however since there is not limits to other forms of contract, lease long run lease contracts seem to be an attractive solution to promote investments in land.

2.2.3.3 Contractual Anatomy

The structure of contracts differs drastically from state to state. In some cases, state agencies follow a contractual template that creates different degrees of regulatory quality and varying distributions of rights and duties between the parties.[129] Due to the lack of access to such contracts, a more detailed analysis cannot be developed. This does not mean, however, that a more detailed picture of the contracts cannot be drawn. Previous studies, for example, make reference to the size of these contracts, which varies from 3 to 56 pages.[130] The literature also highlights various degrees of regulatory quality that impact contractual terms.[131] Cotula (2011), for example, refers to contracts that regulate the distribution of revenues, sophisticated partnerships, the level of specificity in demarcating land that is subject to investment, specific investment commitments regarding jobs and education, processing issues, and environmental safeguards. Case studies conducted by the Oakland Institute stress that investment contracts lack both regulatory measures and publicity surrounding the land negotiations specific to their study.[132]

In Ethiopia, for example, government agencies draw up land investment contracts by following a template designed at the national level. In countries like Liberia, Tanzania, Sierra Leone, South Sudan, Mozambique, and Zambia, contracts are individually designed. In these countries, unlike Ethiopia, different government agencies are involved in designing and negotiating contracts at different stages of the process. The publicly accessible Ethiopian government template includes several relevant aspects.[133] In a first section, the parties are identified. Following the allocation of land, terms and payment for the lease contract are specified. For the lessee, the template includes an obligation to manage and develop the acquired land for production, and to decide what is to be produced on the land. The lessee is also responsible for the development of infrastructure. Infrastructure development includes but is not limited to irrigation systems, roads, bridges, houses, and other structures that might be beneficial to the successful operation of the lease agreement. The lessee is obliged to begin working on the leased landholding immediately after the contract is signed, to pay the royalty required by local authorities, and to provide information to the lessor if a dispute arises with a third party or parties regarding the lease agreement. The lessee must preserve the integrity and natural balance of the landholding until the lease expires. This may involve protecting it from soil erosion by applying terraced farming and creating windbreaks. The lessee

[129] Cotula (2010). He compares three different contract models, see pages 23 and ff.

[130] Cotula (2011a), p. 20.

[131] We had access to 24 Contracts between Ethiopia and private investors. 85% of the contracts follow a template and the rest 15% are individually designed.

[132] The Oakland Institute (2011b), p. 38.

[133] The website of the Oakland Institute offers the most relevant links to access such templates. The information can also be confirmed by using the data offered by Land Matrix. See footnote: 2 in this chapter.

must also maintain the ecological balance of the area by conducting studies and obtaining the necessary permits before expanding any work on the landholding. The lessee is also obliged to return the landholding or renew the lease agreement upon expiration or cancellation of the term.

The rights and responsibilities of the lessor are also stipulated in the contract. The most relevant duties of the lessor include the following:

- to deliver the correct acreage of the landholding as specified in the lease agreement
- to guarantee the resolution of any conflict that may arise as a result of the interference of third parties pertaining to the allocation of the landholding to the lessee so that the lessee shall make good use of the landholding leased
- to control and evaluate the landholding leased without affecting the operational activities of the lessee

In addition, the template states some rules regarding the delivery of products and the potential transfer of the lease to other investors. Moreover, the lessee has the responsibility to repair and maintain the landholding leased for agricultural production. The contract includes specific considerations that address annulments. The lessee has the right to an early termination of performance of the contract by notifying the Rural Development Office at least 6 months in advance. The contract can be terminated in case of non-fulfilment of the obligation of payment or if public purpose necessitates it.[134]

One of the most relevant aspects of land investment contracts is their level of specification. While many governance structures are generally in place, in reality these structures are often difficult to enforce. Certain contractual commitments may be difficult to enforce, such as the prevention of soil erosion, the specific start date of the project, and the development of unspecified infrastructure. In Ethiopia, contracting parties agree that the government will grant the peaceful use of the specified land to the investor. It is stated that the government may solve all conflicts that arise with third persons obstructing the execution of the investments.

In addition to the contract model described above, the literature refers to the existence of contracting structures in the form of concessions, production sharing agreements, and joint ventures. These types of contracts, however, are more relevant for extractive industries than for agricultural activities.[135]

---

[134] The information about this template is publically accessible in: The Oakland Institute (2011c) The Oakland Institute (2011b).

[135] See i.e.: Cotula (2010) as well as Food and Agriculture Organization of the United Nations (2001) and Agrawal (1999), p. 293.

2.2.3.4 Timing, Size, and Distribution of Rights and Duties

There is no underlying rationale behind the time periods specified for leases in LSLI contracts. In the contracts we were able to access, the time periods varied from 25 to 50 years. Cases reviewed by Cotula (2011) refer to contracts of periods up to 99 years.[136] The amount of land specified in predominantly agricultural contracts range from 431 ha to 150,000 ha, and the leasing rates vary from USD 0 to USD 12.38 (median USD .54), respectively from Ethiopian Birr (ETB)158 to ETB 712.61 (median ETB 158)[137] per hectare per month. In not a single contract could we find specific regulations binding either the host governments or the investors to achieve the goals promised to the local people. The same applies to compensation clauses for development-oriented displacements that, according to some studies, took place in order to free up the land for investors.[138] Based on the contracts examined, neither compensation nor the history of ownership of the land is sufficiently outlined in the contracts. Only ten of the accessed contracts promised to create jobs (from 42 to 4500 for the largest 150,000 ha project, with a median of 577). However, specifications pertaining to the quality of the jobs and the timeline for their creation are completely absent.[139] Cotula (2011a) refers to some contracts in which specifications regarding job creation and the improvement of infrastructure have been made.[140] The reports compiled by the Oakland Institute, however, highlight the lack of appropriate regulations necessary to achieve social goals.[141]

Timelines regulating the starting time of projects are not clearly specified. When projects are delayed, arable land often lies idle.[142] It is not clear whether or in what way local people can be integrated into projects, meaning their job security is not guaranteed. If smallholders are not provided with market access and the necessary

[136]The Oakland Institute (2011c), p. 11. See also Robertson and Pinstrup-Andersen (2010), pp. 271, 276.

[137]In June 2012, ETB1 was worth US$.0565. This would mean prices from US$8.927 to US$40.26 per Ha per month. However, the ETB depreciated significantly (about 50%) against the US$ in the last 10 years. This is why we provide the values in ETB in the text. See: International Land Coalition (2011).

[138]Deininger et al. (2011), p. 17.

[139]In more detail, the numbers of jobs (project size) were 42 (10,000); 84 (10,000); 300 (10,000); 577 (73,513); 577 (73,513); 628 (21,500); 670 (6214); 2200 (6141); 4500 (150,000) (one contract for a 30,000 ha project gave no number for the promised jobs). The relative numbers of jobs per ha are 0.004; 0.008; 0.008; 0.008; 0.029; 0.03; 0.03; 0.108; 0.358 (rounded after the third decimal place). For a broad analysis about the inclusion of social clauses in large-scale investment contracts see: The Oakland Institute (2011b).

[140]Such cases are concentrated in Liberia where interested groups are involved in the negotiations and they have professional assistance, some of them have expert to design finance projects. In such cases development agencies work in close to such groups and they are the bridge between locals and investors. See: Montilla (2012), p. 78.

[141]See the impact of the projects in Zambia for example: Cotula (2011a), p. 2.

[142]This phenomenon of acquiring land for nothing has been well documented by The Oakland Institute (2011c), p. 26.

means to buy food for themselves, a worst-case scenario sees not enough food being produced locally for the smallholders and puts their food security at risk. Furthermore, people may not be guaranteed sufficient amounts of water, accommodation, access to education, health care, or social services, which are the most attractive promises made by host governments.

In addition, essential contractual arrangements to guarantee the proper execution of projects are missing. Even though there are some clauses that allow the host country to 'follow up' on the realisation of the project, the procedures and obligations of the investor to disclose relevant information are not outlined. Contracts do not clearly specify conditions for production or for a planned capital contribution. The potential extent of the social and environmental impact of the project is rarely included. It has also been noted that even the geographic coordinates of the investments are not part of the contract. In such cases it is not possible to enforce the contract since there is no delimitation of the contractual object. Even when regular monitoring mechanisms are included in the contracts, specific procedures regarding the evaluation of progress and the contribution of the investment to the development of local communities are absent. In most cases, HRs impact assessments are also completely absent from the contracts. The anatomy of the contracts makes it possible to highlight the asymmetric distribution of risks, costs, and benefits between the contracting parties and the affected third parties. Such omissions are highly problematic and affect future access to water and local food security. Access to water and food security depend on the investors since they are the only ones who have been officially granted access to the water and land.

From a policy design point of view, the contractual structure demonstrates the host states' official capacity to deal with large-scale negotiations. States seem to lack the necessary institutions to properly implement these deals, making the process more difficult and costly.[143] In scenarios where uncompensated or inadequately compensated expropriations take place, tenure, land security, and social stability are affected.[144] States appear unwilling to act to prevent the negative consequences arising from ill-designed LSLI contracts, including the impact they have locally and the cost that future implementation of new policies could represent. Renegotiation clauses are often not included. Long-term investment contracts require these types of clauses so that the contracting parties can adapt the contractual relationship to new situations.

The fact that these contracts do not explicitly mention smallholder interests might be because these interests are implicitly protected by international HRs agreements or national laws. Thus, these interests do not require specification in the contracts. We will neither confirm nor refute this hypothesis here but return to it in a later section, and test its validity with a political economic approach.

---

[143]This is because of the social costs related to the performance of the contract if the local population disagrees with the implementation of new investment policies.

[144]The Oakland Institute (2011c), p. 26.

2.2.3.5 Objective of Contracting

Having reviewed the most relevant aspects of the structure of these contracts, we now turn to explaining the objective of contracting. Our main goal is to elucidate the extent to which contractual design can be thought of as an instrument to achieve security and development. For practical reasons, as we announced before, we will divide the objectives of the contracts into two categories, namely the guarantee of food security through improved and expanded agricultural production, and the promise of development opportunities through the production of non-food oriented agricultural products. These two objectives have a strong political background based on the necessity to reduce poverty and promote development in LDCs. By evaluating the objective of contracting, our research project will be able to determine whether the content of a contract can, in fact, lead to the realisation of a political agenda that promotes LSLIs.

2.2.3.5.1 Guarantee of Food Security

Food security is a sensitive issue in developing nations, and is used by governments to justify entering into LSLI contracts. NGOs, IOs, and governmental agencies approach the guarantee of food security from different angles. LSLI contracts are promoted and supported by IOs for their potential to guarantee access to food for the local population, thereby improving food security. IOs also support projects aiming to produce more food in an effort to control price volatility and to fight the alarming levels of undernourishment in regions like sub-Saharan Africa.[145] Policies and projects designed to fight hunger and poverty easily gain support. While levels of undernourishment have decreased worldwide in recent years, those in sub-Saharan Africa are the lowest reported.[146] Particularly affected are malnourished children and people suffering from micronutrient deficiencies.[147] The potential of LSLIs to guarantee food security and reduce poverty are probably their most influential drivers. This has been affirmed by the FAO (2012):

> Agricultural growth is particularly effective in reducing hunger and malnutrition. Most of the extreme poor depend on agriculture and related activities for a significant part of their livelihoods. Agricultural growth involving smallholders, especially women, will be most

[145]Even though sub-Saharan Africa has improved the levels of undernourishment it development has been less rapidly than in all other regions in the world. In Western Asia, he prevalence of undernourishment was increasing before 2007 and continued its upward trend. In sub-Saharan Africa, the modest progress achieved during 2002–05 was reversed, with hunger rates rising by % per year since 2007. In Latin America and the Caribbean, from an average annual rate of reduction of 1.9% per year in 2002–05 to 0.9% per year in 2006–09. Source: International Land Coalition (2011).

[146]FAO, WFP and IFAD (2012), p. 9.

[147]Ibid.

effective in reducing extreme poverty and hunger when it increases returns to labour and generates employment for the poor.[148]

Many states in sub-Saharan Africa must invest abroad in order to guarantee their own food security and to address problems associated with soil fertility, overpopulation, and climate change. Consequently, food security plays a role not only for LDCs, but also for industrialised countries. Moreover, FDI in agriculture is sold as a mechanism to ensure global food security by increasing the supply of agricultural products. In this sense, the argument in favour of FDI is based on the necessity to guarantee global food security. Promoting FDI should reduce the problem of local food security. However, it does not always work this way. A rising tide doesn't necessarily raise all boats. Due to their extreme poverty, local farmers in LDCs do not have access to international food markets, neither as sellers nor as buyers. Therefore, although the supply of food could be secured globally, the demand side would not, in some cases, have access to such products.

We have already discussed the increasing need in sub-Saharan Africa to produce more food for local demand. We have shown that demographic development in this region is the opposite of the development of food production. Therefore, the introduction of policies aimed at increasing food production is an unavoidable necessity. The continuing rise in food prices constitutes an incentive that stimulates such investments. From an economic point of view, the food crisis of 2008 and the high price volatility of the successive years are the most important factors contributing to the increase in land investment. However, investment and increased food production have not translated into a decrease in food prices in the host countries. In spite of the introduction of political measures intended to stabilise food prices, experts predict continuing food price inflation.

Other factors also contribute to the uncertainty over food security. Soil degradation caused by agriculture and related activities is a cause for concern. The quality of water is deteriorating continuously due to soil degradation and contamination. It is expected that climate change will accelerate the process of land degradation and water scarcity in some areas, while causing flooding in others. Both phenomena are already altering the traditional planting and harvesting cycles and are impacting agricultural productivity. As a result, small farmers lose their seeds for future plantings and are confronted with an increase in production costs.[149] Some studies have shown that the increased food-price volatility has led firms to vertically integrate primary production.[150]

In addition, political actors and investors are concerned about the ever-growing global population and migration to urban areas. These changes imply new dietary requirements associated with the consumption of new products. As poverty continues to decrease worldwide (however, not as fast as expected), more food must be

[148]Ibid.

[149]Subsistence farmers are normally not able to internalise the cost that would mean the acquisition of seeds to start new plantation cycles.

[150]Anseeuw et al. (2012), p. 26.

produced to satisfy the appetite of the growing middle class. This is especially true for Middle Eastern countries, but also for countries in the African region.[151]

2.2.3.5.2 Non-Food Oriented Agricultural Products: The Case of Biofuels

The production of biofuels as a non-food-oriented agricultural product has been a key incentive to land investment.[152] Natural resource constraints and competing demands, especially the production of biofuels, present a considerable challenge for agriculture worldwide, especially in those countries where land is easy to acquire.[153] Government policies setting mandatory targets for the use of biofuels are creating new and certain markets, and increasing global demand. In order to carry out such policies, regional legislation (for example in the EU) has been promoted.[154] Moreover, financial aid and subsidies have been implemented. If such public policies continue to be implemented, experts predict that the demand for biofuels will be inelastic to oil prices in a decade or so, and the production of biofuels derived from cellulosic materials will become viable.[155] Biofuels represent a highly profitable sector due to their promise of energy security, their contribution to rural development, and the export development that they might provide.[156] The production of biofuels has, however, led to changes in land use that seems to affect local food security.[157] The biofuels sector has developed investment networks with other industrial sectors that rely on the acquisition of land to ensure their investments are profitable and realisable.[158]

A cross-referenced study provided by the Land Matrix shows that over 40% of land negotiations are driven by the production of biofuels, while only 15.5% of

[151]The analysis of dietary changes See FAO, WFP and IFAD (2012), p. 17 ff.

[152]A concrete study on biofuels has been made by: Robertson and Pinstrup-Andersen (2010), p. 271.

[153]FAO, WFP and IFAD (2012), p. 30.

[154]The so-called Renewable Energy Directive of the EU establishes an overall policy for the production and promotion of energy from renewable sources in the EU. It requires the EU to fulfil at least 20% of its total energy needs with renewables by 2020—to be achieved through the attainment of individual national targets. All EU countries must also ensure that at least 10% of their transport fuels come from renewable sources by 2020. Directive 2009/28/EC European Parliament and of the Council on the promotion of the use of energy from renewable sources and amending and subsequently repealing Directives 2001/77/EC and 2003/30/EC [2009] OJ L 140 p. 16.

[155]Deininger et al. (2011), p. 15.

[156]Dufey et al. (2007).

[157]As a respond to the accelerated change of land use, a new directive emanated from the European Commission with the purpose of promote the production of biofuels but also the control the change of land use. Directive (EU) 2015/1513 European Parliament and of the Council amending Directive 98/70/EC relating to the quality of petrol and diesel fuels and amending Directive 2009/28/EC on the promotion of the use of energy from renewable sources [2015] OJ L 239 pp. 1–29.

[158]Borras et al. (2011), p. 209.

negotiations are driven by food production.[159] A closer look at these percentages reveals that 64% of negotiations dealing with food production proposals occur in Europe. Other regions have dramatically lower percentages, Africa with 16%, followed by Asia with 12%, and America and Oceania with 2%.[160] Predictions of the increment of crop use for the elaboration of biodiesel and bioethanol suggest that their production will continue to increase.[161] General equilibrium models that allow for trade, crop substitution, and land use conversion suggest that the emergence of new biofuel policies will produce large indirect effects on land-use change, particularly the conversion of pasture and forests to land that can be used for the production of biofuels.[162] European governments promote the consumption of biofuels, while African governments promote their production.

The biofuel sector, however, is rife with volatility. Several biofuel production projects have run into financial difficulties.[163] Incentives designed to increase biofuel production have potential consequences affecting energy security (especially in the developed world), rural development, and export development. In many cases, biofuels projects encounter such severe financial difficulties that they would not be able to launch without incentives. Most of the problems are associated with liquidity, technology, and access to capital. Such cases have been reported in Mozambique, Madagascar, and Congo.[164] In addition to financial problems, some projects are troubled by permanent conflict with communities on the ground.

Other markets have also seen the potential for benefits from land acquisitions. Societies in which wealth is increasing require agricultural commodities not necessarily associated with food, such as cotton and rubber. In this sector, China reports high levels of activity and is considered the investment leader. Raw materials are necessary for the further transformation and commercialisation of products. This fact not only affects enormous land areas, but is also reminiscent of old colonial relationships. Even after countries became independent, in many cases old colonial masters were simply given new concessions to extract minerals and oil.[165] Timber and carbon markets are also driving this trend of using land for the production of raw materials rather than food production. International companies are now acquiring forested land not to transform it into arable land for biofuels, but to satisfy the constantly increasing demand for timber and carbon.[166] The cost of renting land in Africa allows for the acquisition of large areas of land with minimal investment commitments.[167] LSLIs are also

[159] Cotula (2012b), p. 63.

[160] International Land Coalition (2011).

[161] Cotula et al. (2008).

[162] Deininger et al. (2011), p. 163.

[163] Cotula (2012b), p. 663.

[164] Deininger et al. (2011), p. 67.

[165] Anseeuw et al. (2012), p. 37.

[166] Ibid.

[167] For a broad explanation about carbon-oriented large-scale acquisitions see: Cotula (2011a, 2012b).

motivated by the potential future value of the land. This fact creates incentives for investors to buy land as an object of speculation. This speculative behaviour involves many other actors, including pensions and hedge funds. Although some studies report an increase in specifically speculative activity, concrete information is not available.

2.2.3.6 Conclusion of Investment Contracts

The way in which investment projects are introduced differs between countries and production sectors. Reasons for this include highly fragmented land tenure systems and domestic legal institutions. The process of concluding LSLI contracts is crucial to achieving the proposed goals. LSLI contracts are introduced as part of agrarian reforms passed by governments to attract foreign investment. In some cases, they are also justified on the basis that the land being acquired by the foreign investor is 'unproductive' or 'underused'.[168] However, procedures determining whether land is in fact unproductive or underused are not public and differ from case to case.[169] In an ideal scenario, the land that is the object of investment is neither used nor claimed by the local population. Such land can be bought directly from the host government. Contracts are mostly negotiated and signed by investors and state representatives.

In cases of purchase—which are more sporadic than rentals—the new owners proceed to register the land in their own name. In the case of land rental, the relevant local agency registers the land and rents it to the investors.[170] The registration allows them to use the land more freely. Given the difference in property rights throughout the region, the details of the purchase are particular to each country and each negotiation. Sometimes investors deal directly with the possessors of the land. In other cases host countries have agencies tasked with renting the land. Either they register and rent the land in the name of the possessor, or in their own name. In some cases a local chief has the competence to decide how land on which families live and work will be distributed. In other cases neither the chief nor the local people have property titles to the land that they usufruct. In such

[168]von Braun and Meinzen-Dick (2009), p. 2 refer to the failures by determining whether a specific land is or is not to be considered underuse or underproductive. The inexistence of administrative procedures at local level generates a grey zone in which decision makers can in a case-by-case system decide whether the land can be used for new investments or not.

[169]In some cases the procedure is lacking of transparency and affected communities have knowledge about the negotiation when they are already being displaced, i.e.: Cotula et al. (2009), p. 66; Vidal, 'Ugandan Farmer: My Land Gave me Everything. Now I'm one of the Poorest' *Guardiancouk* (London) http://www.guardian.co.uk/environment/2011/sep/22/uganda-farmer-land-gave-me-everything. Accessed 21 January 2013; The Guardian (2011). In other cases although some kind of consultancy is made, local population are not able to enforce their rights in cases of not fulfilment of political promises. The Oakland Institute (2011b); The Guardian, 'Indian Land Grabs in Ethiopia Show Dark Side of South-South Co-operation' Guardiancouk (London).

[170]In all of the available contracts register numbers of the land acquired by the state is included, however, the previous owners are not specified so that the tradition of the land could be followed.

cases it is common for the state's agencies to intervene. As can be seen, a high number of permutations can be present during the negotiations.[171] However, a characteristic common to all of them is that the participation of owners (*de facto* and *de jure*) is not necessarily a requirement to deciding whether investment should take place or not.

Finally, the local agencies or foreign investors proceed to 'clean' the land. If smallholders inhabit the land they have to be reallocated. In 2013 Human Rights Watch reported how this is done in Ethiopia. In Gambella, Human Rights Watch found evidence of forced relocations and villagers being moved from fertile to infertile areas.[172] People sent to the new villages frequently have to clear the land and build their own huts under military supervision, while the promised services (schools, clinics, water pumps) often have not yet been put in place. In addition, the report states that:

> In south Omo *(Ethiopia)* around 200,000 indigenous peoples are being relocated and their land expropriated to make way for state-run plantations. Residents reported being moved by force, seeing their grazing lands flooded or ploughed up, and their access to the Omo River, essential for their survival and way of life curtailed.[173]

Their former accommodation and precarious agricultural infrastructure were destroyed. Unless the projects provide for the coexistence of small and large scale farming, including out-grower schemes, or focus on crops which do not necessitate large-scale mechanisation (all of which we found to be more the exception than the rule), traditional knowledge of small-scale farming will disappear. Along with this knowledge, cultural heritage fundamental to indigenous peoples' identities will also disappear. One could argue that this is not problematic as long as local people are adequately compensated. In that case people would voluntarily agree to give up parts of an identity and culture for which they have less need in their new lives. However, the complete lack of transparency and consultancy at the household level makes it impossible for affected communities to take part in the negotiations.[174]

While LSLIs are often touted as a means to stimulate local markets and to promote development in LDCs, the existing procedures for the implementation of such projects have been strongly criticised as inappropriate for the achievement of the proposed goals.[175] These procedural failures increase the lack of transparency

---

[171]In countries like Ghana where the land is owned in a 90% by the state and the local political power is exercised under chieftainships, the role that chiefs play at the moment of close the negotiation is very high. In such cases the state is officially an intermediary between chief and investor. For documented cases see: Cotula (2011b), p. 19. On the role of chiefs in Ghana see: Brobbey (2008).

[172]The Oakland Institute (2011b), p. 35.

[173]Human Rights Watch (2013), p. 118.

[174]We will show in a next part that although local population perceive the negative effects of the investment the prohibitive coordination costs they have to internalise to intervene in the negotiation process limit their capacity to make a public choice.

[175]See i.e.: Human Rights Watch (2013), p. 118.

and encourage corruption. Further, they incentivise opportunistic behaviour not only on behalf of investors but also on behalf of governments and negotiators, as their own investments could suffer from such dubious procedures.

One important element observed in various studies is that fully negotiated and concluded investment projects are not being carried out. This phenomenon is associated with the consequences of the financial crash of 2008. Studies in Mozambique, Tanzania, and Zambia have shown that it is hard to identify projects in which work had actually commenced (most of them are biofuels projects).[176] We achieved the same results based on direct observation in the north of Ghana. Of ten projects visited in the region of Tamale (in the north of Ghana), only one had been commenced. The local population informed us that the other projects had never started because of liquidity problems within the firms.[177] It has also been shown that the inexperience of investors is an additional reason why projects fail. In some cases investors lack the knowledge to carry out production in the region and do not understand the complexity of agricultural operations. Often the state does not require enough information about the intentions and capabilities of the investor during the negotiation process. The biofuels sector has been most affected by liquidity problems leading to the non-commencement of many projects. The causes include *ex ante* miscalculations producing costs that the investors are unable to internalise.[178]

Besides financial and basic structural difficulties in negotiations, previous studies have mentioned the problem of social costs. In some cases investors have delayed planned projects because of local conflicts. Local representatives have been killed, and it is assumed that their death is associated with their political engagement in trying to stop development-oriented enforced displacements.[179] Madagascar is one of the most relevant examples of local conflicts, but there have also been conflicts in Liberia that escalated to the highest political levels.

2.2.3.7 Potential Benefits and Risks of Large-Scale Land Investment

At the most general level LSLIs have been promoted as a means to supply global food markets by 2050. This claim is based on data provided by the FAO stating that developing nations need between USD 83 and 209 billion in annual agricultural investment to achieve this goal.[180] Many expect that developing countries cannot

---

[176] De Schutter (2011a), pp. 249, 262.

[177] Source: Nyari, 'Biofuel Land Grabbing in Northern Ghana' http://biofuelwatch.org.uk/docs/biofuels_ghana.pdf. Accessed 23 August 2015.

[178] Deininger et al. (2011), p. 67 exemplify the 'change of plans' with a case that occur in the Democratic Republic of Congo, where one project shifted its planned 10,000 ha of sugarcane to maize for food consumption, partly in response to government subsidies. It happened the same to China with 3 million ha acquired in Congolese rainforest for oil palm.

[179] Ibid; Shepard and Anuradha (2011), p. 2.

[180] Wehrmann (2008), p. 6; FAO (2009).

finance agricultural development by themselves, and view the potential contribution of LSLIs as a necessity.[181] Furthermore, LDCs would benefit from the improved national food security, access to food markets, and reduced levels of poverty that may result from LSLIs. LSLIs offer potential benefits to LDCs by fulfilling pre-existing HRs obligations.

Investors are optimistic about agricultural FDI. They consider cross-border investment flows produced by land investments to be an opportunity for LDCs, as they stimulate capital inflows and technology transfer leading to innovation and an increase in productivity.[182] LSLIs are seen as an important measure in alleviating poverty in LDCs. One of the most emphasised aspects of LSLIs, as we have already mentioned, is the expectation that they will be able to fill domestic demand for food. From the point of view of property rights, FDI in agriculture can contribute to the definition or redefinition of such rights and therefore to the reactivation of depressed markets. They can provide public goods and improve local public services.[183] In light of the financial constraints of LDCs, well-designed land investment contracts can lead to modernisation and the activation of the local economy. They can be used as a development tool for communities that have been given land for the realisation of specific projects. Projects can also contribute to national tax systems at both a local and a national level.[184]

The performance capability of foreign investors constitutes a benefit for the host country. For investors, land acquisitions present low monetary costs and promise an increase in control over the value chain. Since many sub-Saharan governments tend to underestimate the price of the land, official land fees are not a decisive aspect of a decision over whether or not to invest. Host countries see that expected benefits exceed opportunity costs. Hence for investors it is attractive to lease land for USD 0 or, like in Sudan, for USD 2.[185] Such prices go down well in negotiations and lighten the mood, but the huge problem of corruption and weak institutions, rule of law, and governance are always present.

Some countries have created even more attractive incentives by combining agricultural policies with new tax models and trade policies for investors. These measures have created an investment environment where investors' risks are minimised. Foreign investors have the crucial advantage of IIAs providing better protection *per se* of their investment than national investments. In some cases investors can influence future decisions of the host country because of their great economic power. Since investors are not usually obliged to supply the host country's domestic market, there is an incentive to produce and allocate their products abroad.[186] Investment protection clauses contained in IIAs might

[181]Food and Agriculture Organization of the United Nations (2009).

[182]Robertson and Pinstrup-Andersen (2010), pp. 271, 276.

[183]David Hallam (2009a).

[184]Meinzen-Dick and Markelova (2009), p. 72.

[185]With regard to land prices see Sect. 2.2.3 of this study.

[186]There are some investors that concentrate on cover the domestic food demand of host country.

additionally minimise the risk of host states introducing new investment regulations after having signed the contract. An additional advantage promised by LSLIs is the increase in social benefits through the creation of jobs, indirect occupations, and the development of local infrastructure. Since previous landowners were subsistence farmers, the promise of being a worker for the investment company is often a strong incentive.

The discussion surrounding the risks related to LSLIs is highly polarised. In order to get a general idea of the risks and effects at the ground level, we used the results of a previous media survey concentrating on daily and weekly newspapers.[187] Here we could observe that even established media outlets predominantly report LSLI scandals by highlighting HRs violations. They mostly ignore the possible benefits linked to LSLI contracts.[188] The two negative effects (or potential negative effects) mentioned most frequently are the violation of local property rights and the violation of the human right to food at the local level.[189] Moreover, campaigns by IOs and NGOs intended as a warning to host countries focus on the negative impact of LSLIs on the local population. Such effects may include an increase in food insecurity, violation of property and cultural rights, or a profound negative impact on customary social structures and cultural heritage. These effects are far from the intended effects. Even though protests by the local population have increased and widespread attention has been given to this phenomenon by the media, reliable empirical studies are still lacking.

NGOs have been crucial in releasing information on the impact of LSLIs on locals.[190] While some organisations have published highly polarising and speculative reports, others have followed transactions and been able to evaluate the impact of specific LSLI projects on locals. One of the most solid case studies was conducted by the Oakland Institute, which reported the production of non-food export crops in specific projects in Ethiopia involving Indian firms. This means that these projects will not contribute to solving the perennial problem of food shortages, while tax incentives offered to foreign investors deprive Ethiopia of valuable tax revenue. The Oakland Institute came to similar conclusions analysing investments in Cameroon, Mali, Mozambique, Senegal, Sierra Leone, South Sudan,

---

[187]The media survey, its methodology and precise results were previous published in the following article: Montilla and Schwarze (2013), p. 1223.

[188]Media information regarding the issue of LSLIs might be cautiously treated. While some recognised authors have used them as primary source other also recognised authors have heavily criticised the data coming from such articles. See for example the discussion in the blog of IFPRI in 2009 between Bebohra Brautigam and Ruth Meinzen-Dick. Accessible at: http://www.ifpri.org/blog/land-grabbing-foreign-investors-developing-countries.

[189]In addition to the media survey some additional articles were also consulted: Hallam (2009b), p. 33, von Braun and Meinzen-Dick (2009), Sharife (2009), Schweizer Fernsehen Video Portal (2011); The Guardian (2011); Sale and Iain (2011); Miriri and Hardy (2009).

[190]The seminal work was published by: GRAIN (2008). In addition the county-based contributions by The Oakland Institute, give a more detailed picture of the phenomenon and its effects in a country based level.

Tanzania, and Zambia: promises of job creation remain unfulfilled, as plantation work offers only menial low-paid jobs.[191] Other NGOs such as Oxfam, the International Land Coalition, Amnesty International, and Human Rights Watch corroborate such outcomes and warn of the dramatic effect that LSLIs are producing.

In addition to the expertise gained through the work of NGOs, IOs have also evaluated the high risks associated to the performance of LSLIs. They analysed the effects produced in LDCs in areas such as food security and the protection of local property rights systems. The discussion was led by the UN Special Rapporteur on the human right to food, who developed principles to create a balance between export-oriented investments and the right to food of the local population.[192] The report underlines the way in which new agrarian policies were introduced and denounces the profound social change confronting small farmers because of centralised decision-making procedures. It also criticises the way in which LSLIs have been promoted, and compares LSLI 'land-grabbing' to colonial times. LSLIs are rarely criticised because of the associated opportunity costs for LDCs, and because they are seen as a unique opportunity to achieve development goals. The report states that even if such projects promote development, they should also ensure that HRs are safeguarded.[193] In addition, the report criticises the way in which new systems of property rights are *de facto* developed and vertically introduced while ignoring pre-existing structures that are protected by binding international HRs treaties.[194]

Not only IOs working directly on HRs protection have recommended new investment approaches. The WTO, FAO, IFAD, UNCTAD, and the World Bank Group are also concerned about the negative effects of agrarian policies in LDCs, especially regarding the human right to food and upholding local systems of property rights.[195] They have also called on parties to adhere to international standards and recommendations for the introduction of land policies. These standards recognise local rights and seek to increase local participation (bargaining power) and transparency during the negotiation process. Moreover, governments of developed countries have also acknowledged the impact of some LSLIs on local

---

[191]Human Rights Watch (2013), p. 184.

[192]The Guardian, 'Indian Land Grabs in Ethiopia Show Dark Side of South-South Co-operation' Guardiancouk (London).

[193]De Schutter (2009b).

[194]Ibid.

[195]Ibid. More recent and even relevant are the affirmation of the World Bank in which is recognised that economic improvement is not the solution of the problematic. Access to resources is a key element to achieve higher levels of development. See: Principles for Responsible Agricultural Investment that Respects Rights, Livehoods and Resources [2010] available http://siteresources.worldbank.org/INTARD/214574-1111138388661/22453321/Principles_Extended.pdf. Accessed 25 December 2013. Earlier, the UNCTAD published the annual investment report especially dedicated to agricultural investments and how they might be introduced to promote domestic economic motors for modernisation and diversification of production. See: FAO, WFP and IFAD (2012).

populations. The German Minister for Economic Cooperation and Development recognised the sensitivity of the issue and launched a campaign to promote fair deals that respect locals' rights in LDCs, while at the same time increasing the production of biofuels and crops to ensure food security.[196]

The next section is the last part of this chapter. By explaining why LSLIs are associated with land grabbing, going through the negotiation process, and highlighting the most relevant actors, their interests, and the objectives of contracting, we have elucidated the main benefits and risks associated with LSLIs. In the following section we will examine some of the impacts of LSLIs as well as their success in achieving their proposed goals.

2.3 Intermediate Result: LSLI Impact on Local Populations' Property Rights and the Right to Food

This research project takes seriously the effects produced by LSLIs for third parties, and evaluates potential legal remedies at the international level in light of these effects. As we argued at the beginning of this chapter, it is in our interest to investigate the impact of such contracts on locals, and thus expand our analysis beyond the contractual parties to include third parties.

Infringements of the right to property can be seen in forced displacements and restriction of access, use, or illegal transmission of land.[197] Such measures are frequently reported in regions where projects have been carried out. Land represents more than an economic possession for small farmers. It allows them to produce their own food and in some cases to allocate the excess to the market. This generates an income, enabling farmers to buy what they cannot produce.[198] In regions where agriculture is a subsistence activity, any structural change and political reform is imbued with high risks. Experts have demonstrated the close relationship between land policy, property rights, and local food security in LDCs, which is determined by: (1) the percentage of the population living in rural areas (in some cases 80%) and (2) the importance of the agricultural sector to the state's GDP, which is 30% of the total in some cases.[199] The most problematic potential result of LSLIs is that property rights of small-scale producers are not enforced and they lose access to their land as a result. This is made all the worse by a failure to provide sufficient compensation and a lack of consultation regarding the projects and their effects.[200] These risks are a result

[196]United Nations Conference on Trade and Development (2009), p. 104.

[197]For legal protection of the right to property in HRL see *infra* at: 3.5.

[198]For a complete study about the international regime of development oriented displacement see: Oleschak (2009).

[199]Pinstrup-Andersen and Watson (2011), p. 196.

[200]The same line of argumentation is followed by many authors, here some examples: FAO, WFP and IFAD (2012); Schultheiss (2010); Deng (2011); Matavel et al. (2011); Goldstein and Udry

of the disproportionate allocation of bargaining power between locals, investors, and government agencies, as well as the weak institutional set-up that often characterises LDCs.

The arbitrary distribution of land in sub-Saharan Africa is familiar both from colonial times and the more recent past. The social cost of land investments, including conflict and unrest resulting from displacement, has to be internalised by investors and may become prohibitive. This was demonstrated in Madagascar in 2009, when the enterprise Daewoo Logistics planned to lease half of the country's arable land. Madagascar's citizens were outraged that their government was prepared to give up such an implausibly large amount of land. These actions concerned the country's citizens greatly and provoked demonstrations (backed by the military) which culminated in the overthrow of the government. The deal was denounced frequently in the media and by NGOs, which helped bring this about.[201]

The violation of the human right to food is the second most well-known effect of LSLIs, and it is seen as a result of the violation of the right to property. A violation of the human right to food occurs when land access is limited and affects the access to food production of subsistence farmers.[202] In doing so, LSLIs inhibit the progressive realisation of the pre-existing international legal obligations to implement at HRs standards.

In some cases LSLIs diminish the ability of LDCs to achieve self-sufficiency because there is no guarantee of supply for the domestic market. It leads to an increased dependence of affected people on governments, international aid programmes, and foreign investors. This has been the case in Ethiopia and Sudan where, despite the promise of LSLIs to improve food security, requests for assistance to the World Food Programme (WFP) have not decreased.[203] While a discourse of promoting global food security is used to stimulate liberalisation of agricultural markets and promote LSLIs, their negative effects appear to be a marginal and less considered effect.

Many of the LSLIs are closely tied to—and financially backed by—home country governments. Thus, in times of a food crisis home governments which in most cases have monetary liquidity can be assumed to be able to create economic incentives so that investors shift the production preferentially to export markets and (more specifically, to their home country) instead of leaving the yields in the host country.[204] As a result, LSLIs primarily guarantee food security to investor

(2008), p. 981; Cotula et al. (2004) for anecdotes of Burkina Faso see page 26. In addition reports from IOs and human rights Rapporteurs also reaffirm this line of arguments, some examples: Rabah et al. (2011), p. 5; FAO, WFP and IFAD (2012); De Schutter (2009a), para 5.

201 Andrianirina-Ratsialonana et al. (2011).

202 Some of relevant studies and reports with the same line of argumentation: De Schutter (2011b); OECD (2008); Wodon and Zaman (2008); FAO (2008); von Braun and Meinzen-Dick (2009); High Level Panel of Experts on Food Security and Nutrition of the Committee on World Food Security (2013).

203 See Shepard and Anuradha (2011), p. 49.

204 Meinzen-Dick and Markelova (2009), p. 10.

countries, not to host countries. By infringing the right to property and the right to food, states and foreign investors often produce a situation where affected people have an even more limited access to the markets and are denied an adequate diet as a result.

Reading the stated intentions of politicians in newspapers and official documents, it appears that investments are well-thought-out projects. However, an analysis of the design of investment contracts makes clear that such an aim is achievable only when investors act altruistically. One can affirm that land governance and the definition of property rights in sub-Saharan Africa have not improved greatly since the old colonies became sovereign states. Such domestic failings become relevant when economic activities, especially those performed by foreign investors, infringe upon rights protected at the international level. An aggravating factor is that in addition to the weak institutional framework at the domestic level, LSLIs do not contain substantial provisions to achieve the goals mentioned by politicians to promote this investment policy. In addition, we suspect that the international legal framework protecting the right to property and the right to food fails to provide effective prophylactic mechanisms or legal remedies to ameliorate the described effects. Hitherto we have shown two contradictory scenarios: on the one hand, LSLIs are intended to boost food security in a world producing plenty of food but distributing it poorly. On the other hand, LSLIs exacerbate costs by violating property rights and the human right to food (other effects are also mentioned frequently, but we concentrate on these two for methodological reasons).

In the next chapter we will present a legal analysis of the mechanisms available in IL to protect against HRs violations. Following a detailed description of LSLIs and highlighting the most sensitive aspects associated with the issue, the next chapter will analyse whether IL can fill a contractual gap where third parties' rights are not considered and are therefore affected by the performance of LSLIs. As stated previously, we will not only consider judicial enforcement mechanisms. While most legal approaches focus on international judicial enforcement mechanisms, we will show that they constitute only one of a diverse range of approaches provided by IL to correctly allocate incentives and achieve compliance. In a later chapter we will analyse LSLIs as a public policy through the lens of economic theory. It will allow us to understand, at the domestic and international levels, how interest groups can promote governance and justiciability when positive rights have been violated.

References

African Union. (2014). African Development Bank and Unied Nations Commission for Africa. In *Guiding principles on large scale land based investments in Africa*.

Agrawal, P. (1999). Contractual structure in agriculture. *Journal of Economic Behavior and Organization, 39*, 293.

Amanor, K. (2012). *Land governance in Africa* (Vol. 1). International Land Coalition.
Amco Asia Co v Republic of Indonesia [1981] Decision on Jurisdiction ARB/81/1 (ICSID).
Andrianirina-Ratsialonana, R., Ramarojohn, L., Burnod, P., & Teyssier, A. (2011). *After Daewoo? Current status and perspectives of large-scale land acquisition in Madagascar*. Commercial Pressures on Land.
Anseeuw, W., Wily, A. L., Cotula, L., & Taylor, M. (2012). In T. Bending & D. Wilson (Eds.), *Land rights and the rush for land: Findings of the global commercial pressures on land research project*. International Land Coalition.
Anyanwu, J. (2012). Why does foreign direct investment go where it goes? New evidence from Africa countries. *Annals of Economics and Finance*, 425.
Arthur, G. (2008). Democracy, property rights and economic growth. *Journal of Development Economics, 6*(116), 69.
Atwood, D. (n.d.). Land registration in Africa: The impact on agricultural production. *World Development, 18*, 659.
Bach, S. (2010). Die Gier nach Fremdem Land: Lebensmittel, Investment, Biosprit. *N-TV* (13.11.2010), http://www.n-tv.de/politik/dossier/Die-Gier-nach-fremdem-Land-article1913411.html. Accessed 24 March 2010.
Bernstein, H. (2005). Rural land and land conflicts in Sub-Saharan Africa. In S. Moyo & P. Moyos (Eds.), *Reclaming the land the resurgence of rural movements in Africa, Asia and Latin America*. Zed Books.
Berry, S. (2002). Debating the land question in Africa. *Comparative Studies in Society and History, 44*, 638.
Borras, S., Hall, R., Scoones, I., Ben, W., & Wendy, W. (2011). Towards a better understanding of global land grabbing: An editorial introduction. *Journal of Peasant Studies, 37*, 209.
Brobbey, S. A. (2008). *The law of chieftaincy in Ghana: Incorporating customary arbitration, contempt of court, judicial review*. Advanced Legal Publications.
Bundesministerium für Wirtschaftliche Zusammenarbeit und Entwicklung. (2009). *Entwicklungspolitische Positionierung zum Thema: Großlchige Landkäufe und -pachten in Entwicklungsländern - "Land Grabbing"*.
Collier, P., & Dercon, S. African agriculture in 50 years: Smallholders in a rapidly changing world. In *Expert Meeting on How to Feed the World in 2050*. Rome: Food and Agriculture Organization of the United Nations.
Columbia Center on Sustainable Investment and World Bank Group. (2015). *Openland contracts (Beta)*. Openland, http://www.openlandcontracts.org/about. Accessed 12 July 2015.
Convention on Access to Information, Public Participation in Decision-Making and Access to Justice in Environmental Matters [2001] No. 37770 available on http://www.unece.org/env/pp/treatytext.html. Accessed 15 July 2015.
Cooter, R., & Ulen, T. (2012). In D. Battista (Ed.), *Law & economics* (6th ed.). Pearson Adison Wesley.
Cotula, L. (2010). Investment contracts and sustainable development: How to make contracts for fairer and more sustainable natural resource investments. *Natural Resource Issues, 20*.
Cotula, L. (2011a). *Land deals in Africa: What is in the contracts?* International Institute for Environment and Development.
Cotula, L. (2011b). *The outlook of farmland acquisitions*. International Institute for Environment and Development.
Cotula, L. (2012a). *Human rights, natural resources, and investment law in a globalised world: Shades of grey in the shadow of the law*. Routledge Research in International Economic Law.
Cotula, L. (2012b). The international political economy of the global land rush: A critical appraisal of trends, scale, geography and drivers. *Journal of Peasant Studies, 39*.
Cotula, L., Dyer, N., & Vermeulen, S. (2008). *Fuelling exclusion? The biofuels boom and poor people's access to land*. The Outlook of Farmland Acquisitions.
Cotula, L., Toulmin, C., & Hesse, C. (2004). *Land tenure and administration in Africa: Lessons of experience and emerging issues*. International Institute for Environment and Development.

Cotula, L., Vidar, M., & FAO Legal Office. (2003). *The right to adequate food in emergencies*. Food and Agriculture Organization of the United Nations.

Cotula, L., Vermeulen, S., Leonard, R., & Keeley, J. (2009). *Land grab or development opportunity? Agricultural investment and international land deals in Africa*. London: FAO/IIED/IFAD.

Crowe, S. E. (1970). *The Berlin West African Conference*. Westport: Negro Universities Press.

Custodis, J. (2013). Keep calm and carry on: What we can learn from the three food price crises of the 1940s, 1970s, and 2007–2008. In T. Allan, et al. (Eds.), *Handbook of land and water grabs in Africa: Foreign direct investment and food and water security* (1st ed.). Routledge.

Daron, A., Johnson, S., & Robinson, J. (2001). The colonial origins of comparative development: An empirical investigation. *American Economic Review, 91*.

Davis, M. J. The United Nations Declaration on the Rights of Indigenous Peoples. University of New South Wales Law Research Paper 2008-16, http://papers.ssrn.com/sol3/papers.cfm?abstract_id=1392569. Accessed 14 April 2014.

De Schutter, O. (2009a). *Promotion and protection of all human rights, civil, political, economic, social and cultural rights, including de right to development* (No. A/HRC/10/5).

De Schutter, O. (2009b). *Report of the Special Rapporteur on the right to food* (A/HRC/13/33/add2).

De Schutter, O. (2011a). How not to think of land-grabbing: Three critiques of large-scale investments in farmland. *Journal of Peasant Studies, 37*, 249.

De Schutter, O. (2011b). *Report submitted by the Special Rapporteur on the right to food, Olivier De Schutter. Human Rights Council* (Report No. A/HRC/19/59).

Deininger, K. (2003). *Land policies for growth and poverty reduction: Key issues and challenges ahead* (World Bank Policy Research Report).

Deininger, K., & Gershon, F. (2001). Land institutions and land markets. In E. Roberts & P. Pingali (Eds.), *Handbook of agricultural economics* (Vol. 1). Elseiver.

Deininger, K., Byerlee, D., Lindsay, J., Norton, A., & Selod, H. (2011). *Rising global interest in farmland. Can it yield sustainable equitable benefits?* World Bank.

Deng, D. K. (2011). "Land Belongs to the Community" demystifying the "Global Land Grab" in Southern Sudan. Global Land Grabbing, 6–8 April 2011. University of Sussex.

Directive (EU) 2015/1513 European Parliament and of the Council amending Directive 98/70/EC relating to the quality of petrol and diesel fuels and amending Directive 2009/28/EC on the promotion of the use of energy from renewable sources [2015] OJ L 239 pp. 1–29.

Directive 2009/28/EC European Parliament and of the Council on the promotion of the use of energy from renewable sources and amending and subsequently repealing Directives 2001/77/EC and 2003/30/EC [2009] OJ L 140 p. 16.

Dufey, A., Vermeulen, S., & Vorley, B. (2007). *Biofuels: Strategic choices for commodity dependent developing countries*, http://www.olade.org/realc/documento.php?doc=23559.

European Center for Constitutional And Human Rights. (2015). *Neueste Publikationen*. ECCHR, http://www.ecchr.de. Accessed 05 April 2015.

FAO. (2008). *Soaring food prices: Facts, perspectives, impacts and actions required* (HLC/08/INF1).

FAO. (2009). *From land grab to win-win* (Economic and Social Perspectives Policy Brief 4).

FAO. (2012). *The state of food and agriculture*. FAO.

FAO, WFP and IFAD. (2012). *The state of food insecurity in the world: Economic growth is necessary but not sufficient to accelerate reduction of hunger and malnutrition*. FAO.

Food and Agriculture Organization of the United Nations. (2001). *Contract farming*. FAO.

Food and Agriculture Organization of the United Nations. (2009). On horizon 2050- Billions needed for agriculture. *High-level forum to weigh investment needs*. Rome.

Food and Agriculture Organization of the United Nations. (2011). *The state of food insecurity in the world: How does international price volatility affect domestic economies and food security?* FAO.

Food and Agriculture Organization of the United Nations. (2016). *FAOSTAT*. FAO, http://faostat3.fao.org/browse/I/*/E. Accessed 27 April 2016.

Fritz, T. (2008). *Dem Weltmarkt Misstrauen. Die Nahrungskrise nach dem Crash*. Berlin: FDCL-Verlag.

General Act of the Berlin Conference on West Africa [1885] available at http://africanhistory.about.com/od/eracolonialism/l/n_BerlinAct1885.htm. Accessed 15 July 2015.

General Assembly (UN) A/53/625/Add.2 Declaration on the Right and Responsibility of Individuals, Groups and Organs of Society to Promote and Protect Universally Recognized Human Rights and Fundamental Freedoms [1998] A/RES/53/144.

General Assembly (UN) Rio Declaration on Environment and Development [1992] A/CONF.151/26 (Vol. I).

GIZ. (2011). Bundesministerium für Wirtschaftliche Zusammenarbeit und Entwicklung and German Institute for Human Rights, *Land Grabbing and Human Rights*.

Goldstein, M., & Udry, C. (2008). The profits of power: Land rights and agricultural investment in Ghana. *Journal of Political Economy*, 981.

GRAIN. (2008). *Seized! The 2008 land grab for food and financial security*.

Häberli, C. (2012). Foreign direct investment in agriculture: Land grab or food security improvement? *Third Biennial Global Conference Society International Economic Law*.

Hallam, D. (2009a). International investments in agricultural production. In M. Kugelman & S. Levenstein (Eds.), *Land grab? The race for the world's farmland*. Woodrow Wilson International Center for Scholars, http://www.wilsoncenter.org/sites/default/files/ASIA_090629_LandGrab_rpt.pdf. Accessed 11 November 2013.

Hallam, D. (2009b). International investments in agricultural production. In M. Kugelman & S. L. Levenstein (Eds.), *Land grab? The race for the world's farmland*. Woodrow Wilson International Center for Scholars.

High Level Panel of Experts on Food Security and Nutrition of the Committee on World Food Security. (2013). *Biofuels and food security. A report by the HLPE of the Committee on World Food Security*.

Holdinghausen, H. Auf dem Boden der Tatsachen. *TAZDie Tageszeitung* Schwerpunkt, http://www.taz.de/!105856/. Accessed 21 July 2015.

Holt-Gimnez, E., Wang, Y., & Shattuck, A. (2011). *The urban and northen face of global land grabs*. Global Land Grabbing, 6–8 April 2011, University of Sussex.

Human Rights Council. (2011). *Principles for responsible contracts: Integrating the management of human rights risks into state-investor contract negotiations: Guidance for negotiators* (Human Rights Council A/HRC/17/31/Add3).

Human Rights Watch. (2013). *World Report 2013 Events of 2012*.

International Labour Organization. (2012). *Global employment trends for youth 2012*.

International Land Coalition. (2011). *The land matrix. Beta version 2.0. International Land Coalition*. ILC, http://www.landmatrix.org/en/about/. Accessed 3 April 2015.

Jolly, R. (2010). *UN intellectual history project* (Briefing Note Number 7, May 2010).

Knack, S. (2001). Aid dependence and the quality of governance. *American Journal of Agricultural Economics, 25*, 1152.

Knack, S., & Philip, K. (1995). Institutions and economic performance: Cross-country test using alternative institutional measures. *Economics and Politics, 7*, 207.

Koeltz, K. (2010). *Menschenrechtsverantwortung Multinationaler Unternehmen: Eine Untersuchung "Weicher" Steuerungsinstrumente im Spannungsfeld Wirtschaft und Menschenrechte*. wvb.

Lorenz, A. Foreign firms drive Cambodians from farms. *Spiegel Online*, http://www.spiegel.de/international/business/foreign-companies-are-taking-farmlands-away-from-cambodians-a-935801.html. Accessed 01 December 2013.

Matavel, N., Dolores, S., & Cabanelas, V. (2011). *Lords of the land - Preliminary analysis of the phenomenon of land grabbing in Mozambique*.

Meinzen-Dick, R., & Markelova, H. (2009). Necessary nuance: Toward a code of conduct in foreign land deals. In M. Kugelman & S. L. Levenstein (Eds.), *Land grab? The race for the world's farmland*. Woodrow Wilson International Center for Scholars.

Miriri, D., & Hardy, W. (2009). Interview-Ethiopia sets aside land for foreign investors. *Reuters* (London, 29 July 2009), http://in.reuters.com/article/2009/07/29/ethiopia-farmland-idINLT58431220090729. Accessed 23 August 2015.

Montilla, L. (2012). Land policies and labour markets in Sub-Saharan Africa. *IDS Bulletin, 43*, 78.

Montilla, L., & Schwarze, J. (2013). John Rawls's theory of justice and large-scale land acquisitions: A law and economics analysis of institutional background justice in Sub-Saharan Africa. *Journal of Agricultural and Environmental Ethics, 26*, 1223.

Muchlinski, P., Ortino, F., & Schreuer, C. (Eds.). (2008). *The Oxford handbook of international investment law*. Oxford University Press.

Mueller, D. (2008). *Public choice III*. Cambridge University Press.

Nadakavukaren, K. (2013). *International investment law*. Edward Elgar.

Nigerian Parliament Condemns Land Grab by Chinese Firms. *Premium Times* (Abuja) http://www.premiumtimesng.com/news/top-news/216665-nigerian-parliament-condemns-land-grab-chinese-firms.html. Accessed 20 March 2017.

Nyari, B. Biofuel land grabbing in Northern Ghana, http://biofuelwatch.org.uk/docs/biofuels_ghana.pdf. Accessed 23 August 2015.

OECD. (2005). A policy framework for investment: Investment promotion and facilitation. In *OECD Conference Investment for Development: Making it Happen*, Rio de Janeiro, October 25–27, 2005.

OECD. (2008). *Rising food prices: Causes and consequences*. OECD.

OECD, African Development Bank, United Nations Economic Commission for Africa, & United Nations Development Programme. (2014). *African Economic Outlook 2014*. African Development Bank; Development Centre of the Organisation for Economic Co-operation and Development.

OECD-FAO. (2016). *Guidance for responsible agricultural supply chains*.

Oleschak, R. (2009). *The international law of development-induced displacement*. NiedermannDruck AG.

Palmer, R. (2011). *A new annotated guide to bibliographies on biofuels, and land rights in Africa, and global land grabbing*. September 2011, http://www.mokoro.co.uk/publications. Accessed 15 July 2015.

Pinstrup-Andersen, P., & Watson, D. (2011). *Food policy for developing countries: The role of government in global, national, and local food systems*. Cornell University Press.

Potts, D. (2013). Land alienation under colonial and white settler governments in Southern Africa: Historical land "Grabbing". In T. Allan, et al. (Eds.), *Handbook of land and water grabs in Africa: Foreign direct investment and food and water security* (1st ed.). Routledge.

Principles for Responsible Agricultural Investment that Respects Rights, Livehoods and Resources [2010] available http://siteresources.worldbank.org/INTARD/214574-1111138388661/22453321/Principles_Extended.pdf. Accessed 25 December 2013.

Principles for Responsible Investment in Agriculture and Food Systems [2014] available http://www.fao.org/3/a-au866e.pdf. Accessed 18 August 2015.

Rabah, S., Klaus, D., & Harris, S. (2011). *What drives the global land rush?* The World Bank, Development Research Group, Agriculture and Rural Development Team Policy Research Working Paper 5864, http://elibrary.worldbank.org/content/workingpaper/10.1596/1813-9450-5864. Accessed 25 June 2012.

Robertson, B., & Pinstrup-Andersen, P. (2010). Global land acquisition: Neo-colonialism or development opportunity? *Food Security, 2*, 271.

Sale, P., & Iain, C. (2011). Are we on the brink of a new global food crisis? *Guardiancouk*. London, 06.15.2011.

Samatar, A. I. (n.d.). Structural adjustment as development strategy? Bananas, boom, and poverty in Somalia [Clark University]. *Economic Geography, 69*, 25.

Schultheiss, M. (2010). *Land grabs and the local population's right to property*. Master thesis, Law Faculty of the University of Bern.

Schweizer Fernsehen Video Portal. (2011). *Land-Grabbing: Genfer Firma verärgert Afrikanische Bauern*. Schweizer Fernsehen.

Selby, A. (2009). Institutional investment into agricultural activities: Potential benefits and pitfalls. In *Land governance in support of the MDGS: Responding to new challenges*, Washington, DC, March 09–10, 2009).

Sharife, K. (2009). Land grabs: Africa's new 'resource curse'? *Pambazuka* (Kenya, 11.26.2009).

Shepard, D., & Anuradha, M. (2011). *(Mis)Investment in agriculture: The role of the international finance corporation in global land grabs*. Oakland Institute.

Solow, R. (1956). A contribution to the theory of economic growth. *Quarterly Journal of Economics, 70*, 65.

Swan, T. (1956). Economic growth and capital accumulation. *Economic Record, 32*, 334.

The Economist. The surge in land deals. When others are grabbing their land: Evidence is piling up against acquisitions of farmland in poor countries, http://www.economist.com/node/18648855. Accessed 12 May 2011.

The Guardian. (2011). Small-scale farmers increasingly at risk from "Global Land Grabbing". *Guardiancouk*. London, 05.19.2011, http://www.guardian.co.uk/global-development/poverty-matters/2011/apr/15/risks-over-increasing-global-land-deals/print. Accessed 19 May 2011.

The Oakland Institute. (2011a). *Understanding land investment deals in Africa: Addax & Oryx Group Bioenergy Investment in Sierra Leone*.

The Oakland Institute. (2011b). *Understanding land investment deals in Africa: Country report: Ethiopia*.

The Oakland Institute. (2011c). *Understanding land investment deals in Africa: Country report: Tanzania*.

The Oakland Institute. (2011d). *Understanding land investment deals in Africa: Country report: Zambia*.

The World Bank. (2016). *Working for a world free of poverty*. The World Bank, http://data.worldbank.org. Accessed 14 January 2016.

The World Economic Forum. (2013). *The Africa Competitiveness Report 2013*.

Thomas, C. A. (2014). The uses and abuses of legitimacy in international law. *Oxford Journal of Law and Economics*, 1.

United Nations. (2004). *Human rights defenders: Protecting the right to defend human rights* (Fact Sheet No. 29).

United Nations Conference on Trade. (2009). *World investment report 2009. Transnational corporations, agricultural production and development*. World Investment Report 2009, 2009.

United Nations Conference on Trade. *World investment report 2012*. World Investment Report 2012, 2013.

United Nations Office of the High Commissioner for Human Rights. (2012). *Human rights council adopts nine resolutions and two decisions*. UN, http://www.ohchr.org/en/NewsEvents/Pages/DisplayNews.aspx?NewsID=13167&LangID=E. Accessed 12 July 2015.

van Aaken, A. (2003). *"Rational Choice" in der Rechtswissenschaft: Zum Stellenwert der Ökonomischen Theorie im Recht*. Nomos.

van Aaken, A. (2013). *Blurring boundaries between sovereign acts and commercial activities: A functional view on regulatory immunity and immunity from execution*. University of St Gallen Law and Economics Working Paper Series 2013–17, http://papers.ssrn.com/sol3/papers.cfm?abstract_id=2236767. Accessed 14 April 2014.

Vidal, J. (2011a). Ethiopia at center of global farmland rush. *Guardiancouk* (London, 03.21.2011), http://www.guardian.co.uk/world/2011/mar/21/ethiopia-centre-global-farmland-rush. Accessed 6 June 2013.

Vidal, J. (2011b). Oxfam warns of spiralling land grab in developing countries. *Guardiancouk* (London, 09.22.2011), http://www.guardian.co.uk/environment/2011/sep/22/oxfam-land-grab-developing-countries.

Vidal, J. Ugandan farmer: My land gave me everything. Now I'm one of the poorest. *Guardiancouk* (London), http://www.guardian.co.uk/environment/2011/sep/22/uganda-farmer-land-gave-me-everything. Accessed 21 January 2013.

Voluntary Guidelines on the Responsible Governance of Tenure of Land, Fisheries and Forests in the Context of National Food Security [2013] CL 144/9 C 2013/20.

von Braun, J., & Meinzen-Dick, R. (2009). "Land Grabbing" by foreign investors in developing countries: Risks and opportunities. *International Food Policy Research Institute Policy Brief, 13*, 1.

Wehrmann, B. (2008). *Land conflicts: A practical guide to dealing with land disputes*. GTZ.

Wettstein, F. (2007). *Multinational corporations and global justice: The human rights obligations of a quasi-governmental institution*. Thesis no 3320. DPhil thesis, University St. Gallen.

Wily, A. (2011a). *The tragedy of public lands: The fate of the commons under global commercial pressure*. CIRAD, International Land Coalition.

Wily, A. (2011b). *Whose land is it? The status of customary land tenure in Cameroon*. Centre for Environment and Development.

Wily, A. (2013). Enclosure revisited. Putting the global land rush in historical perspective. In T. Allan, et al. (Eds.), *Handbook of land and water grabs in Africa: Foreign direct investment and food and water security* (1st ed.). Routledge.

Wodon, Q., & Zaman, H. (2008). *Rising food prices in Sub-Saharan Africa*. Policy Responses Research Working Paper 4738, https://openknowledge.worldbank.org/bitstream/handle/10986/6938/WPS4738.pdf?sequence=1. Accessed 14 April 2014.

World Bank Group. (2009). *World Bank Group Agriculture Action Plan: FY2010–2012*. The International Bank for Reconstruction and Development/The World Bank.

Chapter 3
International Law Conundrum

3.1 Overview

The previous chapter describes how LSLIs, under certain circumstances, are not beneficial to local people. In this chapter we will go a step further to outline how LSLIs violate HRs. Our first goal is to map the different protection mechanisms in hard and soft law that IL, as a whole system, offers to protect and enforce the right to food and the right to property. The fact that the right to property is protected by HRL, and that IL contains protection clauses in IIL, leads us to compare the different systems and evaluate whether their scopes of protection differ. If yes, how do these differences impact LSLIs, and are legal subjects able to choose the better option of protection when seeking succour?

The initial challenge we are confronted with in this chapter is that *prima facie* LSLI contracts do not formally lack international legality, even though *de facto* HRs violations occur.[1] For this reason it is necessary to consider the fragmentation of IL as a relevant issue that affects the enforcement of protected rights. Legal fragmentation represents a challenge for IL because of its role in providing legal security and in preserving international public order. In *stricto sensu*, it is a weakness that the fulfilment of investment obligations can lead to HRs violations. So, we make the assumption that IL fails to protect legal subjects under HRL by offering superior property rights protection to foreign investors. We will demonstrate the validity of our hypothesis by showing that IL allocates incentives more efficiently to protect investors and, in effect, allows the violation of HRs. This chapter will attempt to answer the question about the effects of the law rather than

[1]This affirmation has been broadly discussed in the legal literature and has been also considered by the design of development policies. Throughout this chapter we will come back to this aspect and we will discuss it from different angles. Thomas (2014) describes for example how it is possible in IL to make use of different legal regimes to legitimate infringements of other legal regimes. We highly recommend the following book to understand the increment of international regulation and an answer to the question why trade agreements boost HRs. Hafner-Burton (2009).

L.T. Montilla Fernández, *Large-Scale Land Investments in Least Developed Countries*, International Law and Economics, DOI 10.1007/978-3-319-65280-1_3

engaging in a discussion about why the law is as it is. To make this chapter more comprehensive it must be kept in mind that the law is considered as an *explanans*.[2]

For methodological purposes and in order to proceed in a systematic way, this chapter is structured as follows. The starting point is an introduction to IL as a unified whole. We explain its relevance and the relevance of soft law for our research objective. Then, we analyse the issue of legal fragmentation and the potential legal problems arising from it. We then concentrate on elucidating whether legal fragmentation and the potential effects of LSLIs go back to the asymmetric levels of protection IL offers between HRL and IIL. In order to do so we analyse the protection developed by HRL and IIL regimes specific to the rights to property and food. Thereafter, we return to the most relevant aspects of each regime and briefly compare them. By comparing substantive law, standards of protection, access to the judicial system, enforcement mechanisms, and remedies, we will attempt to answer whether there is a link of causality between fragmentation of IL and the effects of LSLIs, and to what extent IL can tackle such effects. In this chapter we will exclude emergency protection mechanisms in IIL and HRL because they are included in a subsequent section (I.G). The chapter will end by highlighting the implications of our findings. In a later chapter we will apply social science methodology to address how failures in this area may be addressed.

3.2 International Law: A Unified Whole

In the unitary whole of IL diverse regimes regulate relationships between legal subjects in order to preserve public order.[3] The legal protection guaranteed by IL may produce incentives among international actors to interact and cooperate, and therefore ultimately seeks to facilitate their coexistence. A simple way to describe the relationship between states and IL is that states willing to cooperate delegate a monitoring power to IL that allocates sanctions when promises are breached.

These promises may be found in multilateral, regional, or bilateral treaties, or any kind of obligation recognised by IL. This classic view of IL changed after the Second World War when a more globalised approach was developed. The unity of IL was supplemented by reinvigorated legal frameworks. This led to a proliferation of legal instruments, as well as adjudicators operating in specialised areas and producing jurisprudence. Consequently, IL continued to develop specific regimes of law in diverse areas allowing states to delegate the function of monitoring their behaviour. Some examples are HRL, IIL, trade law, environmental law, maritime

[2]See in Sect. 1.5 the definition of this variable.

[3]This statement refers to the possibility that the VCLT, in article 31(3)(c), gives tribunals the possibility to apply relevant rules of IL in the framework of a systemic interpretation approach that is based on the fact that IL is a whole. See i.e.: Prost (2012), p. 23 ff.; Dörr and Schmalenbach (2012), p. 560; Dörr (2012), p. 521 ff.

law, and so on. States conforming to IL restrict their sovereignty and thus increase cooperation.[4] Developing more solid or quasi-autonomous jurisdictions does not mean, in theory, a lack of unity in IL, but instead reflects an evolution of IL that should be conducive to increased cooperation between international legal subjects.[5]

There is little doubt that one way for states to promote investment is the provision of legal security to foreigners. Legal security allows foreign investors to amortise investment costs over a given period of time.[6] For investors the fact that a host state might use its power to expropriate or change the rules governing their investments creates relevant risks. These risks are called political risks.[7] Since expropriations are not internationally forbidden and constitute an expression of sovereign power, states use the promise of compensation to guard against this occurrence. By doing so they offer a credible commitment to foreign investors that they will be able to achieve their investment goals. In addition, states usually promise not to discriminate, to offer equal treatment, access to international justice without having exhausted national remedies, and expatriation of capital. The protection, however, varies case by case. Early on, states used diplomatic protection mechanisms to solve investment conflicts. Nevertheless, these mechanisms eventually became obsolete and opened the door to new, more comprehensive and stimulating mechanisms. These mechanisms are often bilaterally or regionally signed in the framework of IIAs.

The same example of coordination between international actors exists in HRL. States delegate the capacity to monitor their HRs-oriented promises to IL. They demonstrate, at least in theory, their shared commitment to promoting cooperation by ratifying human right treaties. In the case of HRL, mechanisms are multilateral.

Occasionally, two or more legal regimes join legal and economic insiders to protect the same legal object. When states are considered international legal subjects that hold concentrated power, the role of legal regimes is to create a balance between states and individuals, or investors controlling the state's exercise of power. In some cases IL creates obligations at a domestic level. In other cases the obligations apply at the international level. In still other cases there is an interaction between international and national laws. Two or more jurisdictions may have joint legal objects but this does not represent a problem in and of itself, as collisions

---

[4]This is clearly expressed, for example, in the Art. 1.3 of the UN Charter that reads: 'The Purposes of the United Nations are: [...] 3. To achieve international cooperation in solving international problems of an economic, social, cultural, or humanitarian character, and in promoting and encouraging respect for human rights and for fundamental freedoms for all without distinction as to race, sex, language, or religion'. Charter of the United Nations [1945] 1 UNTS XVI.

[5]Ibid and see i.e. Fry (2007–2008), p. 77.

[6]On the early recognition of the relevance of protect investors' rights to stimulate markets in Europe see the contribution by Kneer (2013), p. 15.

[7]This concept includes three basic types of events or situations generally accepted as comprising 'political risk': (1) Confiscation, expropriation, or nationalisation of an investment; (2) Currency inconvertibility, (3) Damage from political violence from war or civil disturbance and (4) default on obligations, including breach of contract. Nadakavukaren (2013), p. 509.

between norms of different jurisdictions do occur circumstantially. Both IIL and HRL protect the right to property, for instance. In both cases the law protects the addressees of state interferences.[8] While IIL protects foreign investments, HRL protects the right to property (which might also be an investment) whether the subject is a national or a foreigner. It has been broadly recognised that the protection of the right to property in HRL is an instrument of equality, leading to the achievement of other HRs such as acceptable standards of living, housing, food, and work.[9] This is because HRs cannot be seen in isolation or independently.[10]

While both jurisdictions protect the right to property, their addressees are not identical. Fragmentation gains relevance if normative conflicts between jurisdictions arise and lead to the legal problem of determining which law applies. Though it seems to be only an issue of interpretation, it still represents a challenge for adjudicators when making decisions. As one might presume we will now consider the hypothesis that there exists a normative conflict between HRL and IIL allowing LSLIs to produce the effects considered to be a violation of the right to property and the right to food. Before we introduce the fragmentation of IL we will consider it pertinent to provide a brief overview of soft law since it will be considered as a variable that might alter the outcomes when applying interpretative techniques.

3.3 Emergence of Legal Fragmentation

Even though IL is considered to be a unitary whole, its structure has led to a process of natural fragmentation.[11] This fragmentation occurs in response to the need to settle specific norms, which in turn regulate particular issues such as HRs, environmental law, and trade law.[12] Fragmentation is unproblematic if it doesn't create tensions or conflict between different regimes. However, it seems that the evolution of specific regimes in IL has created tensions and conflicts between these regimes.

---

[8] Kriebaum (2008), p. 31.

[9] See i.e. the approach made by Krause (1999), p. 359.

[10] The World Conference on Human Rights on Human Rights; Vienna Declaration and Programme of Action [1993] available at http://www.ohchr.org/en/professionalinterest/pages/vienna.aspx accessed 11 November 2014 article 5 reads: 'All human rights are universal, indivisible and interdependent and interrelated. The international community must treat human rights globally in a fair and equal manner, on the same footing, and with the same emphasis. While the significance of national and regional particularities and various historical, cultural and religious backgrounds must be borne in mind, it is the duty of States, regardless of their political, economic and cultural systems, to promote and protect all human rights and fundamental freedoms'.

[11] Some approaches dealing with the issue of fragmentation of IL are: Pauwelyn, 'Fragmentation of International Law' Max Planck Encyclopedia of Public International Law http://opil.ouplaw.com/view/10.1093/law:epil/9780199231690/law-9780199231690-e1406?rskey=0dMLs5&result=1&prd=EPIL accessed 18 August 2015; Trachtman (2011), Koskenniemi and Leino (2002), p. 553; van Aaken (2006).

[12] For an overview we refer to: Waibel (2011).

Notwithstanding, this is not a novel issue and has gained considerable relevance over the last years. In the 1980s Brownlie highlighted his disbelief over the effects of fragmentation:

> A related problem is the tendency to fragmentation of the law which characterises the enthusiastic legal literature. The assumption is made that there are discrete subjects, such as 'international human rights law' or 'international law and development'. As a consequence the quality and coherence of international law as a whole are threatened. . .[13]

In 2006 the International Law Commission (ILC) completed a study on this issue in order to analyse how the fragmentation of IL could be dealt with in a sustainable way.[14] Investigating the causes of fragmentation, the ILC believes that it is a result of globalisation.[15] One may observe its development in the continuous increase of specific legal systems that limit the scope of application and produce legal tensions.[16] The issue has an institutional and a substantive side. Institutionally, the proliferation of isolated international tribunals produces jurisprudential deviations and forum shopping. Substantively, 'special laws' create specialised branches in IL that lack a clear relationship to one another[17]; as could be the case with IIL and HRL. Besides substantive fragmentation there exists geographical fragmentation, for instance in regional systems of HRs protection. These various types of fragmentation give rise to tensions between parallel norms in the same issue area.[18]

In the above-mentioned study, the ILC interprets Articles 31, 3 (c) of the Vienna Convention on the Law of the Treaties (VCLT) and 103 of the UN Charter. This analysis refreshes the interpretation and application of the general principles of public IL. Its aim is to determine how the collision of norms can be avoided in order to tackle legal fragmentation. It also seeks to stimulate a harmonisation and legal cooperation between different areas of IL. The ILC's interpretation recognises that it is not possible to slow down the rapid development of public IL. Nevertheless, the ILC is convinced that cooperation between different areas helps to avoid undesirable collisions and contributes to international public order. The ILC states that if norms are absent, legal conflicts might be solved analogically by applying relevant norms of other legal areas. Specifically, '. . .where treaty regimes do not exist or have proved imperative.'[19] With this statement the application of general principles of public IL gains in importance.[20] It means that it is applicable in specific or general cases when norm collisions take place. In other words it

[13]Brownlie (1988), p. 1.

[14]ILC (2006).

[15]Ibid.

[16]Brownlie (1988), p. 15.

[17]ILC (2006) at paras 9 and 483.

[18]Pauwelyn, 'Fragmentation of International Law' Max Planck Encyclopedia of Public International Law, at para 4 http://opil.ouplaw.com/view/10.1093/law:epil/9780199231690/law-9780199231690-e1406?rskey=0dMLs5&result=1&prd=EPIL accessed 18 August 2015.

[19]*Republic of Guinea v Democratic Republic of the Congo* [2007] Preliminary Objections and Judgment, ICJ Report 2017, p 582 (ICJ) at para 88.

[20]Van Aaken (2006), p. 129.

can be applied when arbitrators have to decide contractual breaches, or simply to explain the application of more general rules and principles in specific legal areas.

Some scholars see the fragmentation of IL as a key problem that affects the stability of IL. For Benvenisti and Downs fragmentation 'sabotages the evolution of a more democratic and egalitarian international regulatory system and undermines the normative integrity of IL.'[21] For Trachtman it can be considered descriptively and normatively. It is descriptive in the sense that '. . .an artefact of the existing decentralised structure for making IL - the decentralised nature of global government' is just one of manifold effects of allocation problems. It is normative in the sense that '[f]ragmentation may be understood as a kind of inter-regime externality, dependent in some cases on supra-regime governance to appropriately prioritise across governmental functions.'[22] These externalities depend on how much value is given to legal and political aspects at the decisions-making moment. In other words externalities can be positive or negative; 'claimants get different answers depending on whom they ask.'[23]

The impact of fragmentation appears in the form of tensions between special and general law, between prior and subsequent law, between laws and different hierarchical levels, or in relation to its normative environment more generally.[24] We follow the wide definition of conflict adopted by the ILC that involves two rules or principles for dealing with a problem.[25] This definition contrasts with more narrow definitions in the sense that it not only presumes the existence of a conflict if 'it is possible for a party to two treaties to comply with one rule and therefore fail to comply with the other' (incompatibility), but also when a treaty 'frustrates the goals of another treaty without there being any strict incompatibility between their provisions.'[26]

The fragmentation of IL produces conflicts that are relevant for this study because of the resulting practical difficulty in deciding what law is applicable. Legal failures arising from LSLIs are *per se* an expression of fragmentation due to the conflicts arising between diverse IL regimes. We suggest that LSLIs inhibit the normal development of positive law and that they are also a consequence of the rule-making possibilities that IL subjects can exercise. LSLIs can produce unexpected effects. Not controlling these effects would lead to the continued alteration of the natural development of IL. The existence of negative externalities (for instance, the violation of HRs without possible sanction in investment law) shows that the structure of IL allows specific actions that that infringe protected values even though they are detrimental for other international jurisdictions. Additionally, the legal policies applied in investment law apparently prevent such violated values being taken into account. This is the case because of jurisdictional limitations, access to justice, and the high cost of enforcing HRs.

[21]Benvenisti and Downs (2007), pp. 595, 597.

[22]Trachtman (2011), p. 2.

[23]ILC (2006) at para 483.

[24]Ibid.

[25]Ibid.

[26]ibid., Jenks (1953), pp. 401, 426; ILC (2006) para 24.

Even though we are confronted with many issues arising from the fragmentation of IL, at this stage we will only consider the most important. Perhaps the most important issue caused by fragmentation is its impact on the legal security of individuals. Some legal subjects experience compromised bargaining power. Fragmentation also allows IL to offer more protection to legal subjects who have recourse to investment law vis-à-vis individuals not protected by IIL. Investors' rights are protected in both IIL and HRL, while individuals' rights are only protected through HRL. If a conflict arises caused by a violation of HRs, investors have direct access to IL (among a variety of other potential means of recourse), while individuals (except in the case of *ius cogens* violations) have no access to the justice system through IIL. Due to these imbalances individuals must rely on the will of their home state to enforce HRs and sanction HRs violations. When legal claims are made conflicts between the applicability of different types of special laws might arise. Finally, there is the special case of 'regulatory chill'.[27]

In the next section we will analyse the mechanisms of property and food rights protection in HRs vis-à-vis investment law. This analysis will focus on the substantive and procedural enforcement mechanisms that HRs victims can use to protect their rights. We will also outline a comparative analysis of HRL and IIL regimes to test our assumption concerning the applicable remedies IL offers to third parties who are injured by the performance of investment projects.

3.4 Influence of Soft Law

In this section we will highlight the relevance and effects of soft law in the context of LSLI. Then we will proceed to separately look at soft law instruments designed to protect the human right to property (Sect. 3.5.1) and food (Sect. 3.5.2). Later we will consider how these instruments contribute to promoting discipline in LSLIs.

3.4.1 General Aspects

Although there is no commonly accepted definition of soft law, most legal scholars agree on its effects.[28] Soft law is usually thought of as the commitments, norms, standards, and guidelines that might influence the behaviour of specific groups.[29]

---

[27]The following articles report some empirical findings on the effects of investor-dispute-state dispute settlement on regulatory chill Harten and Scott (2016), p. 92; Janeba (2016).

[28]Desta (2012), p. 50.

[29]See the discussion proposed in the following contribution to understand the meaning of soft law: ibid. See also: Abbott and Snidal (2003), pp. 421, 422, analyses why actors decide to make arrangement based on hard but also in soft law to solve pacifically political governance affecting governance issues.

Thürer defines it as 'norms in the twilight between law and politics.'[30] These norms are recognised as instruments with extra-legal binding effects that contribute to achieving functional cooperation between states to reach international goals.[31] These legal tools, principles, and rules governing international and national relations do not derive from IL sources.[32] Soft law does not produce legal effects since its norms are not binding.[33] While these norms are neither entirely legal nor social, they do influence the behaviour of international actors. Some advantages of soft law are the low cost of negotiation and the information about preferences that it discloses. Soft law may include a group of norms composed of resolutions by IOs, programmes of action, declarations to IOs, and interpretations of conventions. Soft law discloses important information that makes it possible to predict the behaviour of specific actors signing soft law instruments.[34]

There are different opinions on the development and creation of soft law norms, particularly in relation to international soft law. On the one hand it has been stated that soft law facilitates coordination in international relations. On the other hand legal theorists do not welcome the existence of soft law because it can create and modify customary international law (CIL). Soft law makes it possible to transform *lex ferenda* into *lex lata*.[35] A more neutral opinion on soft law suggests that:

1. Soft law should have some constraints so that it codifies rather than modifies CIL.
2. Soft law might crystallise new legal tendencies, persuading those with little or no relevant state practice to participate in developing the norm.
3. Soft law might create precedents and help form new CIL.
4. Soft law might consolidate political opinion around the need for action on a new problem and foster consensus that may lead to treaty negotiations or new soft law.
5. Soft law might fill gaps in existing treaties.
6. Soft law might form part of the subsequent state practice that can be used to interpret treaties.

[30] Daniel Thürer, 'Soft Law' Max Planck Encyclopedia of Public International Law, at A http://www.mpepil.com/subscriber_article?script=yes&id=/epil/entries/law-9780199231690-e1469&recno=1&searchType=Quick&query=soft+law accessed 05 March 2012.

[31] Shelton (2008) 3 http://ssrn.com/abstract=1003387 accessed 11.13.2013.

[32] Thürer, 'Soft Law' Max Planck Encyclopedia of Public International Law, 2 http://www.mpepil.com/subscriber_article?script=yes&id=/epil/entries/law-9780199231690-e1469&recno=1&searchType=Quick&query=soft+law accessed 05 March 2012.

[33] This meaning is expressed by Timothy Meyer by stating that: 'Soft law obligations while not legally binding themselves, are created with the expectation that they will be given some direct or indirect legal effect through related binding obligations under either international or domestic law.' Meyer (2009), p. 890.

[34] This statement is based on the assumptions made in this research that are explained in this study in Sect. 1.5.

[35] Schaffer and Pollack (2011), pp. 1147, 1158.

7. Soft law might provide guidance or a model for domestic laws without international obligation; it might also substitute for legal obligation when ongoing relations make formal treaties too costly and time consuming, or otherwise unnecessary or politically unacceptable.[36]

We already mentioned that soft law can influence the behaviour of specific actors. These actors might be international banks, investment funds, NGOs, or governments. With regard to LSLIs, soft law is probably the most rapidly developing regime offering tools to ameliorate the short-term undesirable effects caused by certain actors in agricultural development. Soft law has been influential in bringing together diverse economic actors with the purpose of creating new codes of conduct. For example, soft law has contributed to the formulation of the principles for responsible investments proposed by the FAO.[37] Voluntary guidelines were developed concerning the responsible governance of land tenure, fisheries, and forests in the context of national food security. UNCTAD adopted the Investment Facilitation Compact.[38] A more general example of the impact of soft law is the growing number of instruments used to influence the reputation of firms whose activities directly affect the precarious situation of HRs in recipient countries. At this moment in time, however, it is not possible to determine whether the initiatives facilitated by soft law will be able to alleviate the negative effects of LSLIs for locals. In spite of the fact that soft law is playing a crucial role in the development of agricultural investments, its importance is still viewed with some scepticism.

3.4.2 Soft Law Instruments Relevant in the Context of LSLIs

In this section we will focus on soft law instruments that are closely related to LSLIs. In a later chapter we will explore soft law mechanisms that protect the human right to property and the human right to food.

---

[36]Shelton (2008) 8 http://ssrn.com/abstract=1003387 accessed 11.13.2013.

[37]Principles for Responsible Agricultural Investment that Respects Rights, Livehoods and Resources [2010] available http://siteresources.worldbank.org/INTARD/214574-1111138388661/22453321/Principles_Extended.pdf accessed 25 December 2013.

[38]United Nations Conference on Trade and Development, 'Investment Facilitation Compact' (*UNCTAD* 2013a) http://unctad.org/en/Pages/DIAE/Investment%20Facilitation%20Compact/Investment-Facilitation-Compact.aspx accessed 12 April 2015.

3.4.2.1 The European Union Land Policy Guidelines to Support Developing Countries

The European Union Land Policy Guidelines to Support Land Policy Design and Land Policy Reform in LDCs focuses on issues specific to rural land. Rural land is considered to be an asset of the greatest importance in many parts of the world.[39] As stated by the EC, this instrument is a 'response to request for support to land policy reforms from developing countries and countries in transition.'[40] It is not a restrictive guideline but rather an instrument that elucidates the mechanism applied by the EU to support land policies reforms where EU donors are involved. The guidelines recognise that land has strong links to social, cultural, and religious values, and is an asset and source of wealth for individuals, families, and entire communities. The support of the EU as stated in the guidelines 'aims to achieve certain objectives relating to the security and distribution of land rights, land use and land management, and access to land, including the forms of tenure in which it is held.'[41] It also aims to ameliorate the conflicts and inefficiencies arising from the frequent contradictions between formal and informal tenure rules and institutions.[42] The guidelines include fourteen key principles that contribute to successful policy design. These include goals to:

1. learn from local land policies to encourage greater equity, environmental sustainability, and long-term processes
2. promote inter-ministerial work with in-depth analysis of the current situation
3. promote a participatory approach to policy making
4. take into account the distance between statutory law and local practice
5. identify key principles and allow for diverse solutions within them
6. take implementation costs into account in the design of land tenure reform measures
7. recognise that the impact of reform depends on changes in practices and not on the legal texts alone

[39]EU Guidelines to Support Land Policy Design and Reform Processes in Developing Countries. Annex to the Communication. Commission Staff Working Paper [2004] SEC(2004)1289 see at introduction. Also related: Commission of the European Communities Guidelines to Support land Policy Design and Reform Processes in Developing Countries. Communication from the Commission to the Council and the European Parliament [2004] COM(2004)686, and: EU Guidelines for Support to Land Policy Design and Land Policy Reform Processes in Developing Countries [2004] available at https://ec.europa.eu/europeaid/sites/devco/files/methodology-eu-land-policy-guidelines-200411_en_2.pdf accessed on 15 July 2015 1.

[40]EU Guidelines to Support Land Policy Design and Reform Processes in Developing Countries. Annex to the Communication. Commission Staff Working Paper [2004] SEC(2004)1289 see at introduction.

[41]Ibid.

[42]Commission of the European Communities Guidelines to Support land Policy Design and Reform Processes in Developing Countries. Communication from the Commission to the Council and the European Parliament [2004] COM(2004)686 2.

8. ensure widespread dissemination of information about the scope and content of the reform as well as on the policy, legislation and procedures, and gender issues needed for a careful approach
9. adequately recognise the rights of minorities and indigenous peoples and land policy has to include sound land-use planning[43]

The guidelines highlight the roles of different stakeholders, the establishment of more democratic forms of governance at national and local levels, and the guarantees that should be offered to the different needs of stakeholders.[44]

One relevant aspect mentioned in the guidelines is transparency. Transparency is considered a necessary part of the entire investment process in order to guarantee the effective administration and governance of land.[45] Transparency is critical during the preliminary phases of the administrative, legislative, and legal procedures accomplishing the voluntary transmission of property rights and overseeing the regulations governing expropriations.[46] It is also relevant for the political environment because of the implications of land rights at the local level. By conducting LSLIs in a transparent manner it may be possible to avoid political manipulation of land investments.[47] Transparency also contributes to legitimising policies and decreasing the social costs involved in land policies.[48] The guidelines consider the host government responsible for providing accountable, transparent, and cost-effective procedures for land administration. Such a system might be oriented towards ensuring the rights of poorer and less powerful groups.[49] The guidelines also highlight that EU member states can assist LDCs by supporting local land reforms and funding policies that guarantee transparency and accountability of property rights' transmission.[50]

The guidelines also emphasise the character of legality that is required to enable the fruitful realisation of land policies. Issues of *de jure* equalities and *de facto* discrimination, apparently omnipresent in LDCs, are directly addressed. It is recognised that although constitutional provisions concede legal protection to all nationals, in many cases minorities still encounter systemic discrimination. The guidelines require EU member states themselves improve interaction with civil society in order to build social and political support for the land reforms, and promote cross-ministerial discussion and coordination. The discussion and support might be oriented towards the correction of historical inequalities and seek to

---

[43]EU Guidelines for Support to Land Policy Design and Land Policy Reform Processes in Developing Countries [2004] available at https://ec.europa.eu/europeaid/sites/devco/files/methodology-eu-land-policy-guidelines-200411_en_2.pdf accessed on 15 July 2015 1.

[44]Ibid.

[45]Ibid.

[46]Ibid.

[47]Ibid.

[48]Ibid.

[49]Ibid.

[50]Ibid.

achieve legality and legitimacy by recognising legitimate informal or customary rights. Other areas of discussion include recognising local administrative systems, improving the level of cash-based land transitions, recognising the need to provide more secure rights for vulnerable groups, and promoting the restitution of native titles.[51]

This instrument recognises the need to link land policies with other policy initiatives in order to achieve desirable goals. The relevant areas included in the guidelines are poverty reduction, gender equality, agricultural development, conflict and post-conflict recovery, local administration and governance, local government and decentralisation, taxation, and environment.[52] The guidelines are complemented by operational guidelines to assess national policies and to design an EU response strategy. The operational guidelines provide a comprehensive methodology for the implementation of specific policies.[53] The implementation requires the participation of governments, civil society, the private sector, and local communities.

Monitoring mechanisms are included in the guidelines to promote compliance. The instrument suggests the inclusion of independent monitoring mechanisms as a measure to ensure transparency and to avoid political manipulation.[54] The private sector, civil society groups, and local communities are seen as stakeholders that play a relevant role in implementing land policies. These stakeholders might participate in monitoring activities by evaluating the performance of new rules, structures, and procedures. This type of independent assessment can ensure proper implementation and improve policy effectiveness.[55] The guidelines also include a regulatory framework with a set of indicators designed to engage monitoring mechanisms. The indicators include tenure security, trends in land market, environmental impact, and natural resource management.

Even though the guidelines are intended to be an instrument 'to be considered by EU donors in the design of their support for intervention on land policy and administration in developing countries',[56] some key elements were completely ignored when drafting the document. The first aspect that has to be criticised is the complete exclusion of HRs. In addition, the guidelines do not include any sanction mechanism if either member states, host states, or the private sector fail to implement the guideline. Implementation of the guidelines is purely voluntary for an EU member state. Whether or not EU member states decide to implement the guidelines is often dependent on the investors.[57]

---

[51]Ibid.

[52]Ibid.

[53]Ibid.

[54]Ibid.

[55]Ibid.

[56]Ibid.

[57]Ibid.

3.4.2.2 The World Bank Group Principles of Responsible Agricultural Investments

The Principles for Responsible Agricultural Investment that Respects Rights, Livelihoods and Resources,[58] drafted in 2010, was influenced by several previous projects. In 2003 the *Land Policy Framework*[59] was published by Oxford University Press. This publication examines LSLIs in the context of agricultural and natural-based applications. The FAO supported and promoted this publication in 2010. In 2009 the International Food Policy Research Institute promoted the publication of a code of conduct intended to support transparency in negotiations, respect existing land rights, include customary and common property rights, share benefits, support environmental sustainability, and adhere to national trade policies.[60] Relevant stakeholders are currently negotiating the contents of Principles for Responsible Agricultural Investments, and they are expected to be endorsed in the near future.[61] The principles being drafted consider empirical evidence from 20 of the most affected countries.[62] This instrument has been discussed since 2010 and includes seven principles dealing with issues related to:

- respecting land and resources
- ensuring food security
- ensuring transparency, good governance, and a proper enabling environment
- consultation and participation
- responsible agro-enterprise investing
- social sustainability
- environmental sustainability

The principles and the guidelines proposed by the EU share a number of elements. Both proposals emphasise the need to maintain a standard of transparency in order to achieve a set of primary goals. The World Bank's principle 3 provides a detailed description of transparency as an essential requirement to reduce conflicts. It states that investments must be negotiated in transparent manner, and that 'stakeholders can benefit from transparent processes in specific way.'[63] The main benefits for local communities are the clarification of their rights and duties vis–àvis investors, and the mechanisms they can use to hold parties accountable for contractual breaches. For investors, transparency contributes to a more realistic

[58]Principles for Responsible Agricultural Investment that Respects Rights, Livehoods and Resources [2010] available http://siteresources.worldbank.org/INTARD/214574-1111138388661/22453321/Principles_Extended.pdf accessed 25 December 2013.

[59]Klaus Deininger and World Bank (2003).

[60]Meinzen-Dick and Markelova (2009).

[61]Principles for Responsible Agricultural Investment that Respects Rights, Livehoods and Resources [2010] available http://siteresources.worldbank.org/INTARD/214574-1111138388661/22453321/Principles_Extended.pdf accessed 25 December 2013 2.

[62]von Braun and Meinzen-Dick (2009), p. 1, 5.

[63]Ibid.

approach for evaluating the viability of projects and a better understanding of enforcement mechanisms.[64] The principles require a standard of legality that includes the recognition and respect for existing land and resources rights.[65] This standard also includes:

- identification of all rights holders
- legal recognition of all rights and uses in combination with options for their demarcation and registration or recording
- negotiation with land holders based on informed and free choice in order to identify the types of rights to be transferred and modalities for doing so
- fair and prompt payment for all acquired rights
- independent access to resolving disputes or grievances.

In addition to addressing the legal framework of negotiations, the principles discuss issues of national land policy, institutional reform, food security, and the environment.

Although the principles are still under discussion, it is expected that they will be transferred into a policy instrument. The realisation of this, however, depends on governments and stakeholders. On the one hand governments are a source of information and are responsible for establishing contact between investors and locals, as well as for the protection of vulnerable regions and minority groups. On the other hand stakeholders are required to run extensive consultation processes that consider all potentially affected groups. The text that has been made available to the public does not include any mechanism to achieve compliance. Notwithstanding, monitoring mechanisms are continuously being proposed in order to verify compliance with the requirements established by the principles.

The principles focus on HRs when considering the responsibilities of investors. Principle 5 suggests that investors should maintain a high standard of business practices and ethical behaviour. Principle 5 also describes responsible investors as those who respect HRs in general. These practices include the protection of workers' rights, high standards of occupational safety, and maintaining the best practices in food safety and health at each step in the supply chain.[66] These HRs obligations are complemented by a shared responsibility between investors and governments to achieve cost-effective processes in order to assess viability and monitor implementation by governments.[67] If the principles are endorsed as they have been discussed, the main problem will be their enforceability in case of non-compliance. Even though the inclusion of monitoring mechanisms should promote compliance, the principles do not provide any sanction mechanisms to incentivise their fulfilment.

[64]Food and Agriculture Organization of the United Nations (2014).

[65]Principles for Responsible Agricultural Investment that Respects Rights, Livehoods and Resources [2010] available http://siteresources.worldbank.org/INTARD/214574-1111138388661/22453321/Principles_Extended.pdf accessed 25 December 2013 principle 1.

[66]Ibid.

[67]Ibid.

3.4.2.3 Voluntary Guidelines FAO-CWFS

The Committee on World Food Security (CWFS) drafted a set of voluntary guidelines focusing on food security goals for land tenure and fisheries. It is important to note that this committee is an organ of the FAO. The committee was reformed in 2009 in order to expand its scope by including stakeholders concerned with the debate on food security at a global level.[68] The CWFS reports to the Economic and Social Council at the UN annually. The voluntary guidelines are global in scope and may be adapted to national legal systems. Since the guidelines are voluntary, their interpretation must comply with previously existent obligations at the national and international level. The guidelines are a complementary instrument that supports the implementation of appropriate policies in the sectors of land, fisheries, and forests, aiming to decrease hunger. They are addressed to states, implementing agencies, judicial authorities, local governments, organisations of farmers and small-scale producers, fishermen, foresters, pastoralists, indigenous peoples and other communities, civil society, the private sector, academia, and all persons concerned with assessing tenure governance and identifying and applying improvements. Consequently, this instrument covers a range of tools that might improve systems of governance designed to achieve food security. It might contribute to the improvement and development of policy, legal and organisational frameworks that regulate the range of tenure rights dealing with natural resources, enhance transparency, improve the functioning of tenure systems, and improve institutional infrastructures, judicial authorities, local governments, and organisations. Further, it may incorporate other stakeholders to promote cooperation.

The first part of the guidelines consists of a preamble outlining aims and goals. The second part describes the guiding principles of responsible tenure governance.[69] The principles require states to recognise, legitimise, and promote access to land and judicial systems as a way to prevent tenure disputes between stakeholders. The principles require all non-state actors involved in land businesses to protect HRs. The guidelines contain a set of mechanisms that enterprises could implement to prevent and address adverse impacts on HRs and legitimate tenure rights.[70] Such mechanisms also address human dignity, non-discrimination, equity and justice, gender equality, holistic and sustainable approaches, consultation and participation, rule of law, transparency, accountability, and continuous improvement.[71] The third part focuses on the obligations of states to recognise and allocate property rights. It makes special reference to minority groups, indigenous people, and other communities with traditional tenure systems.[72] The fourth part discusses

[68]Voluntary Guidelines on the Responsible Governance of Tenure of Land, Fisheries and Forests in the Context of National Food Security [2013] CL 144/9 C 2013/20.

[69]Ibid.

[70]Ibid.

[71]Ibid.

[72]Ibid.

issues regarding the transfer of and other changes to tenure rights and duties. In this part, the guidelines highlight the need to create free market structures that allow stakeholders to engage in transactions. The fifth part of the guidelines deals with the governance of the administration of land tenure, fisheries, and forests with regard to the registration of tenure rights, valuation, taxation, regulated spatial planning, resolution of disputes over tenure, and transboundary matters.[73] The sixth part addresses the connection between governance and climate change, as well as emergency situations resulting from natural disasters and potential conflicts affecting the tenure of land, fisheries, and forests.[74] The last part details the promotion, implementation, monitoring, and evaluation of the guidelines.[75]

Just like the European Union's Land Policy and the World Bank's Principles, the guidelines suggested by the Committee on World Food Security emphasise the role of transparency. The guidelines require states to uphold a minimum standard of legality in harmony with existing IL obligations. The guidelines also include a mechanism of interpretation that might be 'consistent with existing obligations under national and IL, and with regard to voluntary commitments under applicable regional and international instruments.'[76] Furthermore, they include the implementation of the legal recognition and allocation of tenure rights and duties. One relevant element of the guidelines is their level of detail and precision regarding the protection of rights, as well as the consideration of principles, e.g., human dignity, transparency, non-discrimination, gender, climate and environment, equity, and justice.

This instrument is not solely addressed to developing countries and LDCs. Instead, they were drafted in order to create a mechanism of protection for all vulnerable and marginalised people whose food security is threatened by restriction of land tenure and natural resources. The realisation of this instrument requires the participation of governments, who must implement the governance mechanisms. The guidelines' framework states that local governments and stakeholders are required to actively take part in the implementation process.

The guidelines require the creation of monitoring mechanisms to evaluate the impact of policies, specifically on LSLI contracts. The monitoring process should be inclusive, participatory, gender sensitive, implementable, cost effective, and sustainable.[77] The guidelines call for IOs to act as monitoring mechanisms to promote technical cooperation, financial assistance, institutional capacity, knowledge sharing, exchange of experiences, assistance in developing national tenure policies, and transfer of technology.[78] The guidelines also delegate the monitoring obligation to an Advisory Group. This group should report to the CWFS on the

[73]Ibid.

[74]Ibid.

[75]Ibid.

[76]Ibid.

[77]Ibid.

[78]Ibid.

progress of the implementation of the guidelines, as well as evaluate their impact and contribution to the improvement of the tenure governance.[79]

The guidelines do not include any sanction mechanisms in cases of non-fulfilment. One of the most critical problems of the guidelines is their failure to develop a strategic model promoting governance of natural resources. Instead, they include a set of principles and legal policies that might be further developed and adapted at the national level. Many nations, however, lack the institutional capacity to do so. While the guidelines include a commitment to gender equality and may contribute to the protection of disadvantaged social groups like minorities and indigenous peoples, they fail to include these groups in the implementation process and ignore other social groups that are even more affected in countries where LSLIs are introduced.

3.4.2.4 Framework and Guidelines on Land Policy in Africa

The framework and guidelines influencing land policy in Africa are instruments developed by regional institutions, governments, and African land experts from every corner of the continent.[80] The project, called the Land Policy Initiative, was designed and implemented by the African Union with the technical support of the UN Economic Commission for Africa and the African Development Bank. These guidelines provide a clear overview of the historical, political, economic, and social background of the land issue in Africa, and detail the role of land as a valuable natural resource endowment to achieve economic development and poverty reduction.

The purpose of the guidelines is to provide an instrument that helps African countries design land policies. They include a mechanism of implementation based on sustainable human development seeking to assure social stability, maintain economic growth, alleviate poverty, and protect natural resources from degradation and pollution. The guidelines also highlight the need for consensus and popular participation when introducing new land policies, suggest standards for best practices, create proactive mechanisms to address emerging issues, and promote cooperation. Further, they support the development of joint projects between states and stakeholders designed to ensure sustainable management and utilisation of land and associated resources shared by member states in various parts of Africa.

The framework and guidelines are presented in seven chapters. The first chapter explains why the framework and guidelines are needed. Chapters 2 and 3 contextualise and define the nature and characteristics of the land question in Africa and explain how this has impacted development policies. Chapter 4 is perhaps the most important chapter of the guidelines as it sets out the key operational processes that African countries need to follow in order to develop comprehensive land sector

[79]Ibid.

[80]Framework and Guidelines on Land Policy in Africa.

policies. Chapter 5 outlines the obstacles and limitations countries face when attempting to achieve the goals of the guidelines. Chapter 6 analyses and discusses policies that African countries may wish to put in place to track the progress of development and implementation of those policies. Chapter 7 offers a summary and concluding remarks.

The guidelines do not describe concrete measures that might be taken by member states in order to achieve the proposed goals. Instead, the document describes in general terms the social and economic problems faced by African countries due to persistent land conflicts. The guidelines primarily offer a historical perspective on land and development problems in the region and broadly describe the challenges African countries encounter when attempting to implement appropriate policies and achieve development goals. While the guidelines refer to the protection of HRs, mechanisms to achieve the level of protection required by the guidelines are absent. The discussion of HRs in the guidelines focuses only on indigenous rights and the non-discrimination of women. In both cases states are required to blend tradition and modernity in land rights regimes,[81] thus guaranteeing land resources access to women (who are, in many cases, discriminated against). Land policies must contain equal rights for women to inherit and bequeath land, guarantee co-ownership of registered land by spouses, and promote women's participation in land administration structures.[82] Even though the guidelines do not explicitly include additional HRs protections, the standards of transparency, participation, democracy, and non-discrimination require the fulfilment of international HRs standards. In addition, the mechanisms incorporated in the guidelines are designed not only to achieve sustainable stewardship and utilisation of Africa's primary development resource but to also deepen and consolidate peace, security, and democracy.[83]

The importance of transparency in achieving the proposed goals is stated throughout the guidelines. They demand that local institutions implement mechanisms guaranteeing transparency of governance and accountability if they hope to achieve the proposed objectives. One nuance of the guidelines is that while states are viewed as the coordinators of sustainable policy performance, the people are considered the essential drivers of land policies. In this regard the instrument focuses not only on agricultural activity, but also on the environment, gender issues, and the tourism industry.[84] The guidelines also demand that local laws and investment policies become more closely aligned. Further, the guidelines address the need for the provision of affordable and legally secure land and housing rights.[85] The elements of participation referred to by the guidelines include the extensive consultation of experts, ministers, and civil society in all African regions. The

[81] Ibid.

[82] Ibid.

[83] Ibid.

[84] Ibid.

[85] Ibid.

guidelines might be implemented by using tracking principles and standards of best practices as a benchmark.

Tracking principles are an effective mechanism for observing the development and implementation of land policy. The first principle is designed to assess the extent to which the actual processes of policy development and implementation conform to initial designs. The purpose of the second principle is to match land policy objectives with the expectations of beneficiaries and the requirement of sustainable development. The third principle assesses whether or not the objectives of the land policy were achieved. The fourth principle measures the effectiveness of resource utilisation. The fifth principle addresses the issue of sustainability. The sixth principle evaluates direct and indirect effects of land policy on beneficiaries and natural resources. The last principle considers the overall coherence and consistency of land policy including internal consistency, cross-sector consistency, and regional consistency.[86] The aforementioned principles are considered a sufficiently comprehensive evaluation mechanism for monitoring the effects of land policies. Complementing this monitoring mechanism, the guidelines include a feedback duty to the states that makes it possible to address institutional bottlenecks and, if necessary, readjust entire land policy systems.[87] Once again, however, the guidelines do not provide any enforcement mechanisms in case of non-compliance.

Following this broad overview of relevant soft law instruments, we will dedicate Sect. 3.5 to the IL regime that protects the HRs to food and property of local populations in sub-Saharan Africa. Section 3.6 examines how IL protects foreign investments. We will compare the different levels and mechanisms of protection offered to locals and investors in HRL and IIL in Sect. 3.7.

3.5 International Human Rights Protection for Local Populations in Sub-Saharan Africa

In this section we will analyse the substantive protection offered by HRL to third parties affected by certain aspects of LSLIs. We will focus on the rights to property and to food. By evaluating the treaties that protect these rights at a global and regional level, we are able to establish a link between the content of the treaties and the violation of the HRs to property and food. We will conclude that in some circumstances the violation of the right to food is a result of the violation of the right to property. Next, we will introduce the standards of treatment of HRL to explain the procedural alternatives available to individuals to enforce their rights, as well as the remedies they can expect.

---

[86] Ibid.

[87] Ibid.

3.5.1 The Right to Property

The right to property is considered a key institution in both HRL and IIL. This fundamental right, as well as the rules of the specific property regime in question, make it possible to allocate the use of land, the rights to land, and the fruits of the land to individuals. As a real right it protects against other individuals and the state. The interpretation of the right to property has been at the forefront of philosophical and legal debates for centuries. Since a shared interpretation of the right to property is crucial to the realisation of national policies, economic development, and the HRs agenda,[88] varying interpretations of this right have led to international conflicts. The right to property is internationally recognised in HRL. While the accumulation of property is often linked to the accumulation of political power,[89] it is also considered to be a human right of both nationals and foreigners.[90] Protecting the right to property also contributes to economic progress and to the further realisation of other HRs, for instance the right to food.[91]

At a regional level one finds some differences in the treatment of property rights due to historical and cultural particularities. For example, while language in Inter-American treaties strongly emphasises the protection of private property rights, the African region prioritises communal property rights.[92] The right to property does not emanate from the condition of being a human being, but rather from the fact that an individual owns something.[93] The protection of the right to property implies a relationship of exclusion vis-à-vis other legal persons that grants the owner certain legally regulated privileges to the property.[94] The right to property can also be seen as a vehicle to generate exchanges between legal persons. Having a recognisable title to land and being certain that the rights arising from this title will be protected, legal persons are able to operate and make use of their own property. Hegel considered property to be an expression of personality, independence, and self-government vis-à-vis third parties.[95] No less imperative is the fact that under some circumstances the right to property can serve as a mechanism to solve conflicts.[96] In the words of Monteagudo, 'it is a social mechanism that *naturally* links individuals that can be used to create competence and stimulate markets as proposed by the liberals, or as a common or collective good as proposed by the Marxists.'[97] Modern constitutions

[88]For a historical approach of the right to property in HRL see: Kriebaum (2008), p. 23.

[89]Theo van Banning (2002), p. 5.

[90]Contrary to other legal regimes, human rights law does not discriminate aliens. See *infra* at: 3.6.2.

[91]See *infra* at: footnote 225.

[92]See this book at Sect. 3.5.

[93]Monteagudo (2013). See also: Ledesma (2004), p. 70 ff.

[94]Cohen (1927), p. 8 13.

[95]Hegel (1821) paras 41–53 (Das Eigentum), special to be read are following annexs to paras 41, 46, 49.

[96]Monteagudo (2013).

[97]Ibid.

allow the state to impose some restrictions on public interest when confronted with the co-existence of communal and private property. In that case HRs treaties function to guarantee that the state does not interfere with the rights held by other legal subjects.[98]

3.5.1.1 UN Treaty-based Mechanisms

The extant compendium of UN treaties contains tools to implement and protect HRs. The content of the treaties provides authoritative guidance on HRs standards, advises on the correct application of treaties, and informs states how to fulfil their HRs obligations.

Article 17 of the Universal Declaration of Human Rights (UDHR) addresses the right to property. This article guarantees that everyone has the right to own property, by themselves or in association with others. In addition, it restricts the arbitrary deprivation of property.[99] Although the declaration itself is not a legally binding instrument, the very existence of the Declaration demonstrates the willingness of states to commit to and further implement the principles enshrined therein. The inclusion of the right to property in the UDHR represents great progress for HRL. Even though the details of the Declaration's promulgation exceed what is strictly necessary for our purposes, it is still significant to refer to the debates that influenced its formulation and determined the political positions of states in the development of the UN treaty-based system for years to come.[100] For instance, Article 17 has been subject to frequent criticism, with observers pointing out its overly broad and vague character.[101] Some critics claim that the meaning of 'arbitrarily' is not sufficiently clear. Although the article proscribes arbitrary seizures it does not define the meaning of 'arbitrarily'. Currently this criticism carries less weight because most of the literature agrees that arbitrariness does indeed occur in cases of discriminatory measures and when the public purpose cannot be substantiated.[102] Article 17 was formulated as a response to the political situation the international community found itself in after the Second World War. The article lacks more specific forms of protection because political tensions between signatory states precluded consensus on such specificity.[103] The historical debate's focus on whether to establish separate

---

[98]Ibid.

[99]General Assembly (UN) Universal Declaration of Human Rights [1948] UNGA Res 217A (III), UN Doc A/810 para 17.

[100]For example by discussing article 6 the *travaux prèparatories* show the political discussions based on the consideration of the inclusion of the right to property. In this case, the discussion was specifically on the protection of the right of minorities. Sub-Commission on Prevention of Discrimination and Protection of Minorities, *Record of Sixth Meeting* (Discussion of Article 6 (Continued) E/CN4/Sub2/SR6, 1947). For a complete compilation of most of the *travaux prèparatories* of the Declaration see: Schabas (2013).

[101]van Banning (2002), p. 42.

[102]See footnote: 100 as well as Krause (1999), p. 151.

[103]For an broad explanation about the ideological differences dominating the discussion of HRs see: Steiner and Alston (2000) at Part B.

protection mechanisms for private and common property rights shows the ideological influence of Soviet delegates on the discussion and illustrates the political positions, legal traditions, social convictions, and circumstances of the time.[104]

The right to property is included neither in the International Covenant on Civil and Political Rights (ICCPR) nor in the International Covenant on Economic, Social and Cultural Rights (ICESCR).[105] The inclusion of the right to property in the HRs bill was impeded by the failure of member states to find consensus. Australian delegates were the first to propose the inclusion of the right to property in the HRs bill. The *travaux préparatoires* provide a glimpse of the competing ideological stances dividing the discussion geopolitically between western and eastern countries, as well as between northern and southern countries.[106] Ultimately the proposal was rejected by the Drafting Committee because it represented a sensitive issue and required special consideration.[107]

The UN treaty-based system does not directly protect the right to property. However, some conventions consider the protection of the right to property a principle of non-discrimination. All of these more specific conventions, which are detailed in the following paragraphs, can be interpreted in the context of the Committee on the Elimination of Racial Discrimination (CERD). The Committee requires signatory states to prohibit and eliminate racial discrimination in all its forms and to guarantee *inter alia* the right to property.[108] Furthermore, parties to the Convention on the Elimination of all Forms of Discrimination against Women (CEDAW) are required to grant equal rights to women when concluding contracts and administering property.[109] The same Convention gives equal rights to both women and men when determining how marriage influences the control of property. Article 15 of the International Convention on the Protection of the Rights of All Migrant Workers and Members of Their Families (ICRMW) prohibits the arbitrary deprivation of individually or commonly held property. In a case of expropriation the victim must receive fair and adequate compensation.[110] Article

---

[104] Krause (1999), p. 364. See also: van Banning (2002), p. 39.

[105] Krennerich (2013), p. 33.

[106] Riedel (1986), p. 39. See also: Schabas (2013).

[107] Commission on Human Rights, *Summary Record of the Twenty-eight Meeting* (E/CN4/AC1/SR29, 1948).

[108] General Assembly (UN) International Convention on the Elimination of All Forms of Racial Discrimination [1965] 660 UNTS 195 art 5 (v).

[109] United Nations Convention on the Elimination of All Forms of Discrimination Against Women [1981] 1249 UNTS 14 art 15.

[110] International Convention on the Protection of the Rights of All Migrant Workers and Members of their Families [2003] 2220 UNTS 3. The 1989 International Labour Organisation Convention No. 169 in article 4 links the right to property with the right to work. It specially recognise s and requires the states to guarantee the right to property of Indigenous and Tribal People; which is a requirement to realise their right to work. However this Convention has been rarely ratified in Africa. The only African country that has ratified the convention is the Central Africa Republic on 30th August 2010. International Labour Organization (1996).

12.5 of the Convention on the Rights of Persons with Disabilities (CRPD) requires that signatory states take appropriate measures to guarantee the right to property of persons with disabilities.[111]

3.5.1.2 Regional Protection in Africa

HRL is geographically fragmented into three jurisdictions: European, American, and African. All of these jurisdictions contain regulations specific to the right to property. However, each jurisdiction offers different degrees of protection, as well as different forms. The African system—the only one considered here—places greater emphasis on collective property rights than the other two systems.[112] Two institutions, a Commission and a Court, supervise the compliance of member states. In this section we will only consider the general aspects of the African system, and will provide greater detail on structure and outcomes in later sections.

The African Charter on Human and Peoples' Rights (Banjul Charter) was adopted by the Assembly of Heads of State and Government of the Organisation of African Unity (OAU) in 1981.[113] It encompasses provisions protecting civil and political rights in Articles 3-14, and economic, social, and cultural rights in Articles 15–18. Furthermore, it includes provisions protecting collective rights and duties in Articles 19–25 and 25–29, respectively.[114]

The Banjul Charter is the cornerstone of the African HRs system. The Charter and its protocols protect the right to property in Article 14: 'The right to property shall be guaranteed. It may only be encroached upon in the interest of public need or in the general interest of the community and in accordance with the provisions of appropriate laws.'[115] Furthermore, the Banjul Charter in Article 13(3) grants equal access to public property and services to every individual, which is particularly relevant in the African context. In Article 21 the Banjul Charter recognises the right of all peoples to freely dispose of their natural resources. It obliges signatory states to eliminate all forms of foreign economic exploitation. The Banjul Charter Protocol on the Rights of Women places a special emphasis on the right to property and the equality of conditions between men and women in Articles 6(j) and 7(d).[116] Moreover, in Article 19(c) it emphasises the relevance of protecting the right to property in the pursuit of sustainable development. All African countries, with the

---

[111] General Assembly (UN) Optional Protocol to the Convention on the Rights of Persons with Disabilities [2006] A/RES/61/106 Annex II para 12.5.

[112] For a similar approach see: Cotula (2012), p. 49.

[113] African Charter on Human and Peoples' Rights (Banjul Charter) [1986] OAU Doc. CAB/LEG/67/3 rev. 5, 21 I.L.M. 58.

[114] Ibid.

[115] Ibid.; Protocol to the African Charter on Human and People's Rights on the Establishment of an African Court on Human and People's Rights [1998] OAU OAU/LEG/EXP/AFCHPR/PROT (III).

[116] Protocol to the African Charter on Human and Peoples' Rights on the Rights of Women in Africa [2000] CAB/LEG/66.6.

exception of Morocco, have ratified the Banjul Charter. The Protocol was ratified by only about half of all African countries.

Article 3(1) of the protocol to the Banjul Charter extends the Court's jurisdiction to all cases and disputes concerning the interpretation and application of the Charter. By considering other HRs treaties as sources of law it empowers the Court to apply not only the Banjul Charter, but also other HRs treaties.[117] It makes it possible for tribunals to use both systems complementarily so that legal gaps can be filled.

3.5.1.3 Relevant Soft Law Instruments in the Context of the Right to Property

A number of soft law instruments addressed the right to property. The concerns of soft law include food security, land tenure policies, fisheries, the protection of minorities, and the special protection of women. Generally, these instruments seek to promote discipline in LSLIs. Following the rapid increase in land deals, a number of NGOs contributed to the creation and proliferation of soft law instruments.[118] IOs and their sub-organs also began to elaborate soft law. In some cases projects initiated by NGOs were developed and completed by IOs. One example of this is the Code of Conduct developed by the International Food Policy Research Institute. This instrument was developed further by the World Bank, FAO, and UNCTAD.[119] As an interagency group they began a discussion about the development of principles to promote responsible agricultural investments. The first principle stated in this instrument is respect for existing rights to land including the right to property.[120] Authorities promoting land investments are required by this interagency group to identify the rights holders and to recognise their rights to land. Authorities are also required to include landholders in the negotiation process in a proactive way, and finally to provide fair and prompt payment for all lands acquired as a result of the negotiations.

The FAO Voluntary Guidelines are an additional relevant soft law instrument. The guidelines concern land tenure, fisheries, and forests with a particular focus on marginalised social groups. The guidelines expressly address the need to recognise

[117]Ibid.

[118]For instance the Tirana Convention; which is a Soft Law instrument aiming at securing land access for the poor in times of intensified natural resource competition. It was signed by over 150 representatives of civil society organisations, social movements, grassroots organisations, international agencies, and governments. Source: Tirana Declaration. Endorsed by the ILC Assembly of Members on 27 May 2011 Available http://www.landcoalition.org/sites/default/files/aom11/Tirana_Declaration_ILC_2011_ENG.pdf accessed 24 November 2013.

[119]Principles for Responsible Agricultural Investment that Respects Rights, Livehoods and Resources [2010] available http://siteresources.worldbank.org/INTARD/214574-1111138388661/22453321/Principles_Extended.pdf accessed 25 December 2013.

[120]Ibid.

and respect all legitimate tenure holders and their rights, to protect legitimate tenure rights against threats or infringements, and to promote and facilitate the enjoyment of legitimate tenure rights. This soft law instrument takes into account previously existing instruments such as the FAO Responsible Agriculture Investment Principles,[121] the Minimum Human Rights Principles elaborated by De Schutter as UN Rapporteur on the Right to Food,[122] and the Voluntary Guidelines on the Right to Food and the Principles of the International Conference on Agrarian Reform and Rural Development of the FAO. [123]

The Guidelines on Land Policy are a particularly relevant regional soft law instrument because its promoters are members of the African Union. The African Union itself has formed a joint initiative with the African Development Bank and the UN Economic Commission for Africa. These guidelines highlight the relevance of clearly defined property rights for the success of land policies. They address equal gender relations[124] and the need to clarify rights in agriculture.[125]

3.5.2 The Right to Food

The right to food is intrinsic to the human condition. The main goal of creating protection mechanisms of the right to food is to ensure that every person enjoys adequate access to nourishment. Nowadays, this is not only a moral obligation for states but it is a legally binding human right for at least 160 states who are signatories to the ICESCR.[126] In addition, this right was included in many humanitarian law instruments. These regulations provide legal security in the case of arrest and for prisoners of war,[127] protection of civilian persons,[128] and victims[129] of

---

[121]Committee on World Food Security (2011).

[122]The minimum standards were specially drafted in the context oft he proliferation of LSLIs. De Schutter (2009b).

[123]FAOVoluntary Guidelines to Support the Progressive Realization of the Right to Adequate Food in the Context of National Food Security [2004] available at http://www.fao.org/docrep/009/y7937e/y7937e00.htm accessed 13 July 2015.

[124]Framework and Guidelines on Land Policy in Africa 8.

[125]Ibid.

[126]The number of signatories is reported by the UN and can be consulted at: United Nations, 'Treaty Collection' (*UN*, 2015) https://treaties.un.org/pages/viewdetails.aspxchapter=4&lang=en&mtdsg_no=iv-3&src=treaty accessed 25 July 2015.

[127]Geneva Convention (III) Relative to the Treatment of Prisoners of War [1950] 75 UNTS 135 arts 20 and 26.

[128]Geneva Convention (IV) relative to the Protection of Civilian Persons in Time of War [1949] 75 UNTS 287 arts 23, 36, 49, 55 and 89.

[129]International Committee of the Red Cross (ICRC) Protocol Additional to the Geneva Conventions of 12 August 1949, and relating to the Protection of Victims of Non-International Armed Conflicts [1977] 1125 UNTS 609 art 14 and the ibid.

armed conflict and war. In Africa the right to food is not part of the Banjul Charter, but the ACHPR has considered it in its decisions. In the next section the diverse legal instruments regulating the right to food will be considered.

3.5.2.1 UN Treaty-based Mechanisms

Campaigns developed by the UN and the FAO promoting the right to food, as well as worldwide concerns over undernourishment and malnourishment in LDCs, have led to increased awareness and a general promotion of the right to food worldwide in recent years.

Article 25 of the UDHR guarantees to all people the right to a standard of living adequate for their health and well-being and that of their family. It offers a non-exhaustive list of the rights that constitute an adequate 'standard of living' including food, clothing, housing, medical care, social services, and the right to security for individuals in special situations such as unemployment, sickness, disability, widowhood, old age, or other circumstances beyond their own control.

Article 11.1 of the ICESCR recognises that the right to food is an essential right for every human being. It also recognises that the right to food is crucial for achieving an adequate standard of living. As a result the ICESCR creates the obligation for every state to ensure that all individuals who fall under its jurisdiction have access to a minimum amount of food deemed adequate, nutritious, and safe.[130] Similar regulations are found in other instruments including CEDAW in Article 12 and the Convention on the Rights of the Child in Article 24 paragraph 2 (c) and (e), and Article 27 paragraph 3.

3.5.2.2 The Regional Level

Although the Banjul Charter does not include a specific regulation concerning the right to food, the ACHR states that the right to food must be considered implicit in other rights included in the Charter as it is inextricably linked to the dignity of human beings.[131] The ACHR considers that for a state to fulfil its HRs obligations it must provide its residents with either food or the resources necessary for the production of food.[132] In *Social and Economic Rights Action Centre and Centre for Economic and Social Rights v Nigeria* decided in 2001, the ACHR stressed that the right to food is implicit in the Banjul Charter's provisions regulating the rights to life, health, and economic, social, and cultural development.[133] The ACHR found that the state, having

[130]General Assembly (UN) International Covenant on Economic, Social and Cultural Rights [1976] United Nations Treaty Series 993 available at http://www.refworld.org/docid/3ae6b36c0.html accessed 15 July 2015.

[131]*Social and Economic Rights Action Centre and Centre for Economic and Social Rights v Nigeria* [2001] Commission communication 155/96 (ACHPR) at para 64.

[132]Ibid at paras 47 and 67.

[133]Ibid at para 64.

failed in their three minimum duties concerning the right to food—those of respect, protection, and fulfilment—was in breach of the right to food regulated at the international and regional levels. As a result the ACHR required Nigeria to improve existing food sources and hence to ensure adequate food for the local population.[134] This case constitutes an important precedent because the ACHR explicitly mentions the duty of states to monitor multinational corporations operating in their territory.[135]

Article 15 of the Protocol on the Rights of Women in Africa places special emphasis on the obligation of states to uphold women's rights to nutrition and adequate food. In this concrete case the signatory states have a duty to provide access to clean drinking water, land, and the means to produce nutritious food. The obligation of states as considered in Article 15 of the Protocol is to establish adequate systems of supply and storage to ensure food security.

3.5.2.3 Relevant Soft Law Instruments in the Context of the Right to Food

Soft law contributes to guaranteeing the right to food through recommendations, guidelines, resolutions, or declarations for the implementation of the right to food. In these instruments actors express their commitment to fulfilling pre-existing obligations and developing national policies to progressively improve the standards regarding the right to food. Examples include the Declaration on Nutrition adopted at the International Conference on Nutrition of 1992,[136] the International Conference on Population and Development of 1994,[137] the Copenhagen Declaration on Social Development of 1995,[138] and the Rome Declaration on World Food Security.[139] These instruments provide policy-oriented mechanisms to improve domestic food systems. The FAO and WHO provided tools to help states not only improve their access to food, but also to improve its quality.

The Voluntary Guidelines adopted by the FAO council in 2004 aim to reinforce existing HRs standards and provide guidance to states on how to implement existing obligations.[140] They cover a wide range of actions governments can

---

[134]Ibid at para 65.

[135]For a broad analysis of the decision we recommend: Shelton (2002), p. 937.

[136]FAO and WH World Declaration and Plan of Action for Nutrition [1992] available at http://www.fao.org/docrep/003/w3613e/w3613e00.HTM accessed 14 July 2015.

[137]*Report of the International Conference on Population and Development United Nations Population Fund* (A/CONF171/13/Rev1 1994).

[138]World Summit for Social Development (UN) Copenhagen Declaration on Social Development [1995] A/CONF.166/9.

[139]FAO World Food Summit: Five Years Later. International Alliance Against Hunger [2002] WFS:fyl2002/3.

[140]FAOVoluntary Guidelines to Support the Progressive Realization of the Right to Adequate Food in the Context of National Food Security [2004] available at http://www.fao.org/docrep/009/y7937e/y7937e00.htm accessed 13 July 2015.

consider at the national level to promote the establishment of an environment that allows people to feed themselves with dignity and provides appropriate safety nets for those who are unable to do so. The guidelines also contain measures to hold governments accountable to rights holders.[141]

The General Comment on the Right to Adequate Food (General Comment 12)[142] interprets the substantive aspects of the human right to food. This interpretation includes the recognition of the human right to food as an indivisible right linked to the inherent dignity of the human person, and that is indispensable for the fulfilment of other HRs enshrined in the International Bill of HRs.[143] In addition the right to food is considered an essential requirement for social justice, eradication of poverty, and fulfilment of other HRs for all.[144]

The right to food is realised when every man, woman, and child, alone or in community with others, has physical and economic access at all times to adequate food or means for its procurement. States are obliged to introduce policies and implement appropriate measures to ensure the right to food and secure the protection of the right to food.[145] The provision of *respect* for the human right to food means that states are not allowed to take measures that may imperil or put at risk the conditions ensuring the right to food. States are required to maximise the use of their resources and allocate resources properly in order to progressively guarantee and *protect* the right to food.[146] Comment 12 highlights the obligation of states to facilitate and engage in activities that allow the population to have access to food. States must create the necessary mechanisms to make the right to food realisable at any time and in all circumstances.[147]

Among these mechanisms are non-binding norms suggesting implementation measures states may develop in order to comply with treaties. There are also legal policy recommendations made by the Committee on Economic, Social and Cultural Rights. These recommendations recognise the necessity for states to implement

[141] Office of the High Commissioner for Human Rights, *The Right to Adequate Food* (Fact Sheet No 34 2010) 9.

[142] CESCR, *Substantive Issues Arising in the Implementation of the International Covenant on Economic, Social and Cultural Rights. General Comment 12. The Right to Adequate Food.* (E/C12/1999/5, 1999b). For an academic interpretation of Comment 12 see: Söllner (2007).

[143] CESCR, Substantive Issues Arising in the Implementation of the International Covenant on Economic, Social and Cultural Rights. General Comment 12. The Right to Adequate Food. (E/C12/1999/5, 1999b) at para. 4.

[144] The Right to Food Guidelines. Information Papers and Case Studies at para 80.

[145] CESCR, Substantive Issues Arising in the Implementation of the International Covenant on Economic, Social and Cultural Rights. General Comment 12. The Right to Adequate Food. (E/C12/1999/5, 1999b) at para 6.

[146] Ibid.

[147] Krennerich develops broadly the scope of the right to food and the obligations of states regarding the right to food as well as the international political dimensions of obligations arising from the right to property. Krennerich (2013), pp. 252–267. Se also Economic and Social Council, *The Right to Food* (Report of the Special Rapporteur on the Right to Food, Jean Ziegler E/CN4/2006/44, 2006) and with special emphasis on LSLIs: De Schutter (2009c).

specific policies to reduce the vulnerability of certain groups. ICESCR requires states to create programmes that build on their commitments to guarantee the human right to food. These programmes should enable the affected populations to have better access to technology and education and become integrated in distribution processes and value chains through the incorporation of solid and sustainable mechanisms and production structures that avoid discrimination and make appropriate use of resources.[148]

3.5.3 Relationship Between the Violation of the Right to Property and the Right to Food

The Vienna Declaration and Programme of Action of the World Conference on Human Rights stresses the universality, indivisibility, and interdependence of all HRs.[149] Ergo, the realisation of one human right leads to the realisation of other HRs and *vice versa,* as they are mutually reinforcing. Some rights are more interconnected than others, e.g., the right to food and the right to life are more connected than the right to freedom of belief and the right to social security. The indivisibility of HRs can be seen in the fact that the violation of one specific right leads to the violation of a different right. In the context of the right to food, states are not only required to deal with issues that determine overall food security, but are also required to ensure progress in the exercise of other HRs. In other words, while the fulfilment of certain rights, such as the right to life, make it possible to realise the right to food, the fulfilment of the right to food also leads to the possibility of the fulfilment of other rights.[150] The Committee on Economic, Social and Cultural Rights (CESCR) in General Comment 12 affirms that:

> The right to adequate food is indivisibly linked to the inherent dignity of the human person and is indispensable for the fulfilment of other human rights enshrined in the International Bill of Human Rights. It is also inseparable from social justice, requiring the adoption of appropriate economic, environmental and social policies, at both the national and international levels, oriented to the eradication of poverty and the fulfilment of all human rights for all.[151]

The interrelation between the right to property and the right to food varies from case to case. In LSLIs the violation of the right to food is considered to be a

[148]See in this study at Sect. 3.4.

[149]The World Conference on Human Rights on Human Rights; Vienna Declaration and Programme of Action [1993] available at http://www.ohchr.org/en/professionalinterest/pages/vienna.aspx accessed 11 November 2014. In the case of the right to food see we recommend the following contribution: Vidar (2005), p. 141 ff.

[150]CESCR, Substantive Issues Arising in the Implementation of the International Covenant on Economic, Social and Cultural Rights. General Comment 12. The Right to Adequate Food. (E/C12/1999/5, 1999) paras 12–16.

[151]Ibid.

consequence of limited or denied access to land. The introduction of new agrarian policies in the form of LSLIs suggests a reformulation of property rights that in most cases leads to evictions. Reports of the weakened food security of subsistence farmers following deprivation of access to land have increased in weak states.[152] The international recognition of the relationship between denying access to natural resources and the deprivation of the right to food for subsistence farmers is well publicised.[153] In the *Ogoni* case, which concerned the violation of communal property rights in Nigeria, the ACHR formally highlighted the intrinsic relationship between the right to property and the right to food. The ACHR found that the Nigerian government brought about the destruction of local food sources through the authorisation of investment projects, leading to the infringement of others HRs including the right to food.[154] The ACHR applied an approach considering the minimum core duties of states. Minimum core refers to the minimum level of enjoyment of a right that should be guaranteed under all circumstances. These obligations include the duty not to destroy or contaminate food resources, not to allow private parties to destroy or contaminate food resources, and not to impede peoples' efforts to feed themselves.[155] The ACHR also stated that:

> The right to food is inseparably linked to the dignity of human beings and is therefore essential for the enjoyment and fulfilment of such other rights as health, education, work and political participation. The African Charter (*Banjul Charter*) and international law require and bind Nigeria to protect and improve existing food sources and to ensure access to adequate food for all citizens. Without touching on the duty to improve food production and to guarantee access, the minimum core of the right to food requires that the Nigerian Government should not destroy or contaminate food sources. It should not allow private parties to destroy or contaminate food sources, and prevent peoples' efforts to feed themselves.[156]

The written decision of the ACHR goes on to outline the relationship between the right to adequate housing and the right to protection against forced evictions. It addresses the effects of forced evictions on one's physical, psychological, and emotional wellbeing, leading to infringement of the right to health.[157] In 2009 the Special

[152]See in this book at Sect. 1.2.2 as well as footnotes: 8 in Chap. 1 and 192 in Chap. 2.

[153]See i.e.: Food and Agriculture Organization of the United Nations (2009), p. 74 that refers on the special protection needed by special vulnerable groups; The Right to Food Guidelines. Information Papers and Case Studies 12; Weatherspoon et al. (2001), p. 722; Food and Agriculture Organization of the United Nations, 'Fighting Poverty and Hunger' accessed 2010; Organización de las Naciones Unidas para la Agricultura y la Alimentación, '22 Países Sufren Crisis Prolongadas: Necesario Reorientar la Ayuda a los Países que Sufren Impactos Múltiples' (*FAO*, 2011) http://www.fao.org/news/story/es/item/46114/icode/ accessed 24 March 2015; De Schutter (2011), p. 249; Buxbaum and Caron (2010), p. 1. For the specific case of Ogoni communities see: Coomans (2003).

[154]*Social and Economic Rights Action Centre and Centre for Economic and Social Rights v Nigeria [*2001*] Commission communication 155/96 (ACHPR) paras 47 and ff.*

[155]Ibid.

[156]Ibid.

[157]Ibid.

Rapporteur on the Right to Food explained that: 'States would be acting in violation of the human right to food if, by leasing or selling land to investors (whether domestic or foreign), they were depriving the local populations from access to productive resources indispensable to their livelihoods.'[158] Like in the *Ogoni* case, violations occur where minimum core duties of the state are not fulfilled. These obligations include the duty not to destroy or contaminate food resources, not to allow private parties to destroy or contaminate food resources, and not to prevent peoples' efforts to feed themselves.[159] The ACHR established that Nigeria had condoned the destruction of natural resources by private investors that were used by the Ogoni community to produce food, and as a result found that Nigeria had violated the right to food.[160]

The Special Rapporteur on the right to food considers the right to food to be violated if states, through the implementation of investment policies, produce detrimental changes to the *status quo* regarding the access to food of the population.[161] This means that in regions where the right to food is already unfulfilled, new policies leading to even greater detriment constitute an infringement of the right to food. Thus an infringement occurs when there is a failure to create alternative and complementary mechanisms to ensure that new projects do not affect the food security of local people. Consequently, the human right to food is violated when states support and stimulate the introduction of investment projects that cause distortions in local structures affecting food supply, while disregarding the need to create new systems that protect the basic necessities of local people. Investors not only violate the human right to food when they coerce locals to abandon their lands, but also when the drastic changes brought about by investment projects spoil the land or water.[162]

The CESCR states that a violation of the right to food potentially occurs when minorities are denied access to the following:

- credit
- land ownership and other forms of property ownership
- natural resources and appropriate technology
- measures to respect and protect self-employment and work which provides a remuneration ensuring a decent living standard[163]

Furthermore, the FAO Guidelines establish a link between the potential violation of the human right to property and the human right to food.[164] This occurs when people are forced to leave their land without appropriate compensation. States violate the right to food when they expropriate land without providing appropriate

[158]De Schutter (2009b), p. 2.

[159]*Social and Economic Rights Action Centre and Centre for Economic and Social Rights v Nigeria [*2001*] Commission communication 155/96 (ACHPR) para 64.*

[160]Ibid.

[161]De Schutter (2009b) at para 4.

[162]Ibid.

[163]CESCR (1999b) paras 12 ff.

[164]The Right to Food Guidelines. Information Papers and Case Studies 8 guideline at 17 and 18.

compensation, as the land occupied or used by the local people is the only resource available to them to access the market and obtain other commodities.

States are also required to introduce measures that provide recourse to its citizens if their HRs are violated by third parties. In the *Ogoni* case, the ACHR established the responsibility of Nigeria because it allowed private oil companies to destroy resources previously held by the local people and to use terror operations to deny Ogoni communities to feed themselves.[165] The Nigerian state was deemed responsible for having failed to protect minimum standards of rights for the Ogoni communities. This clarifies that regional HRs institutions may sanction activities that harm third parties in cases that come before them. If we consider our first approach to the enforcement of third party rights explained in the introductory part, one can see that the legal linkage in the *Ogoni* case differs from the linkage proposed by Willimston.[166] In this case individuals do not claim the nullity of the contract between the state and the private actor but argue that the state failed to protect the right to food of locals. Consequently, remedies are *prima facie* oriented towards creating ways to tackle future violations rather than recommending the cessation of the economic activity that gave rise to the infringement.[167] These remedies are state oriented, while in the previous approach the success of legal action exercised by third parties would lead to the involvement of both contractual parties by calculating damages.

Some approaches consider trans-generational aspects associated with the protection of the human right to food, such as the conservation of soil, water, and ecosystems.[168] These practices are associated with the need to guarantee sustainable agricultural practices that contribute to the international agenda of sustainable development.[169] Due to the strong link between agriculture and environmental protection, the inclusion of acceptable farming techniques might be seen as an additional element of the protection of the human right to food. Even if this line of argumentation enriches the dogmatic body of IL and the international community generally accepts it, we consider the inclusion of such arguments in legal procedures to make the issue more complex.[170] For our purposes at least it is sufficient to consider the violation of HRs without trans-generational considerations. We will

---

[165]*Social and Economic Rights Action Centre and Centre for Economic and Social Rights v Nigeria [*2001*] Commission communication 155/96 (ACHPR) para 64.*

[166]See Chap. 1 of this study.

[167]The Commission appealed to introduce measures to avoid attacks against the Ogoni communities, to ensure adequate compensation tot he victims, to conduct an investigation into the human rights violations, ensuring appropriate environmental an social assessments are prepared in the future and providing information on health and environmental risks associated to the oil industry. *Social and Economic Rights Action Centre and Centre for Economic and Social Rights v Nigeria [*2001*] Commission communication 155/96 (ACHPR) para 69.*

[168]De Schutter (2009b) at para 21.

[169]See i.e.: The Right to Food Guidelines. Information Papers and Case Studies Section V.

[170]As well as the following approaches: De Schutter (2009a), Franco Suarez (2008), Mechlem (2004), p. 631; Eide et al. (1991), p. 415.

focus solely on the fact that the human right to food of a specific individual or group of individuals is violated and that this infringement is directly related to LSLIs.

3.5.4 Standards of Treatment

Standards of treatment refer to the substantive obligations contained in HRL. They are based on two types of obligations. The first category is contained in the duty to respect, protect, and fulfil HRs.[171] The second category concerns the availability, accessibility, acceptability, and adaptability of HRs.[172] Rather than constituting binding duties, these classifications should be seen as analytical tools that help to elucidate the content of the HRs obligations contained in treaties and help to create adequate policies to further advance domestic implementation. These schemas create a kind of guideline demonstrating how to bring about the necessary conditions for the fulfilment of a state's HRs obligations, distinguishing between 'absolute' and 'restricted' rights.[173] The difference between the two categories of rights concerns their flexibility and whether they must be observed at all times. While absolute rights must be respected at all times and are not derogable even for compelling reasons, other rights can be subject to some limitations in normal circumstances and increased restriction in situations of emergency or necessity.

Treaties and in some cases CIL grant states the option to limit HRs. HRs restrictions must fulfil the requirements of legality, legitimacy, and proportionality.[174] In the context of HRL, legality refers to the domestic legislation that applies to the restriction in a given set of circumstances. The Inter-American Court of Human Rights (IACHR) ruled that the element of legality is perhaps the most important in determining the scope of the right but also in offering guarantees to ensure that the inviolable attributes of the individual are not impaired.[175] Accordingly, the UN Sub-Commission on the Prevention of Discrimination and the Protection of Minorities states that the limitation on the exercise of HRs shall be provided by domestic law of general application and

[171]Eide et al. (1991), pp. 415, 452.

[172]This category was developed in the context of the right to education in General Comment No. 13. See: CESCR, *Implementation of the International Covenant on Economic, Social and Cultural Rights* (General Comment No 13 21st session E/C12/1999/10, 1999a).

[173]An example of such absolute obligation is the prohibition of torture article 7 ICCPR. See: De Schutter (2010), p. 257.

[174]United Nations Economic and Social Council, Siracusa Principles on the Limitation and Derogation Provisions in the International Covenant on Civil and Political Rights [1985] E/CN.4/1985/4 Annex A.10.

[175]In this regarding, the Advisory Opinion OC-06/86 establishes for the Inter American Jurisdiction the criteria of article 30. This gives the competence to the Court to attend issues regarding all kind of rights enunciated in the convention. It gives the competence to the Court itself with respect to each one of the protected rights. Inter American Court of Human Rights, *The Word "Laws" in Article 30 of the American Convention on human Rights* (Advisory Opinion OC-6/86, 1986).

must be consistent with the ICCPR at the time that the limitation is applied.[176] The restriction shall not be arbitrary or unreasonable. Rights shall be clear and accessible to everyone. In addition, the UN Sub-Commission on the Prevention of Discrimination and the Protection of Minorities requires states to provide effective local remedies against the illegal or abusive limitations imposed on or applied to HRs.[177] The legitimacy of a measure, which might rely on both national and international law, is determined by its upholding of public health, public morals, public safety, public order, national security, or the rights and freedoms of others.[178] The condition of legitimacy should provide for scrutiny of the motives behind the measure so that it can be considered whether the restriction of the right is in proportion to its restrictive effects in the context in which it was introduced.[179] Furthermore, the principle of proportionality, which is similar to the legitimacy requirement, provides that the interference with a protected right must be appropriate to the fulfilment of the legitimate aim pursued and must not exceed what is strictly necessary to achieve that aim.[180]

3.5.4.1 Non-Discrimination

Discrimination in *lato sensu* is at the core of standards of treatment in HRL. It is a guiding principle that has contributed to the further development of most specific standards in other legal areas, such as the standard of FET, equality of protection, access to justice, and mechanisms of compensation. While there is a well-established notion of discrimination in IL, it is still at an early stage of development in the African context due to a lack of jurisprudence. One might consider the substantive obligations contained in all binding HRs treaties but their operationalisation by African HRs institutions is limited. Article 3 of the Banjul Charter is phrased in a manner comparable to other regional HRs instruments. The Charter states that every individual is entitled to all rights, duties, and freedoms guaranteed by it without distinction of race, ethnic group, colour, sex, language, religion, political or any other opinion, national and social origin, fortune, birth, or other status. Respective protocols in the regional African system also include prohibitions against the discrimination of women and children.[181] The ACHR

[176] United Nations Economic and Social Council, Siracusa Principles on the Limitation and Derogation Provisions in the International Covenant on Civil and Political Rights [1985] E/CN.4/1985/4 Annex at A.8 and B.

[177] Ibid.

[178] In the framework of ICCPT the characters of public health, morals, security, safety rights and freedom of others and the restriction on public trials, have been also considered. Ibid.

[179] Ibid.

[180] Ibid; and also De Schutter (2010), p. 312.

[181] African Charter on Human and Peoples' Rights (Banjul Charter) [1986] OAU Doc. CAB/LEG/67/3 rev. 5, 21 I.L.M. 58 art. 18. In addition, the protocol defines what discrimination against women means in Art. 1.f. It reads: 'Discrimination against women' means any distinction, exclusion or restriction or any differential treatment based on sex and whose objectives or effects

heard the case of *CEMIRIDE and Minority Rights Group International v Kenya*. The ACHR found the Kenyan government guilty of violating the rights of the country's indigenous Endorois community by evicting them from their lands to make way for a wildlife reserve. The ACHR reaffirmed that state policies must be equitable, non-discriminatory, participatory, accountable, and transparent. The implication of this decision is that the ACHR considers indigenous peoples to be active stakeholders in society rather than passive beneficiaries of unenforceable rights. The ACHR adopted the same approach as the ECHR and recognised that the Banjul Charter's prescription does not consider differentiations made between individuals to always constitute a discriminatory measure.[182] This means that when national jurisdictions limit the right to property to nationals only, the measure alone does not represent a discriminatory measure against foreigners, including foreign investors.

A non-discrimination standard is also included in UDHR Article 10, ICCPR Articles 2(3) and 14(1), as well as in Article 3 of the Banjul Charter. In the ICCPR the norm refers to the equality of legal subjects before judicial institutions, not to their formal treatment (i.e. that all individuals must be treated identically). Article 3 of the Banjul Charter states that every individual shall be considered equal before the law and must be entitled to equal protection of the law. In the absence of jurisprudence *Legal Resources Foundation v Zambia* heard by the ACHR may be considered a kind of quasi-jurisprudence. In this case the solicitor claimed that Article 3 of the Banjul Charter had been violated when an amendment to constitutional provisions made it impossible for 35 per cent of the population to become a presidential candidate. The constitutional amendment provided *inter alia* that anyone seeking to run for the office of president must prove that both parents are or were Zambians by birth or descent.[183] The ACHR highlighted the relevance of the right to equality, which gives rise to the expectation among individuals to be treated fairly and justly within the legal system. It also underscored the relevance of this right in guaranteeing peace and economic stability. In this case the ACHR, rather than making a clear differentiation between equal treatment and discrimination, considered discrimination as a consequence of inequitable treatment. This leads us to expect that in future cases the ACHR will continue to take a broad approach to this standard of treatment.

---

compromise or destroy the recognition, enjoyment or the exercise by women, regardless of their marital status, of human rights and fundamental freedoms in all spheres of life' Protocol to the African Charter on Human and Peoples' Rights on the Rights of Women in Africa [2000] CAB/LEG/66.6 art. 1.f.

[182] *Centre for Minority Rights Development and Minority Rights Group International and Centre on Housing Rights and Evictions (intervening) (on behalf of Endorois Welfare Council) v Kenya* [2009] Merits communication no 276/2003 (ACHPR) para 237. In this case the ACHPR based part of its decision on the jurisprudence of the ECHR as can be read in *James and others v The United Kingdom* [2007] Judgement app no 8793/79 (ECtHR).

[183] *Resources Foundation v Zambia* [1998] 211/98 Legal Resources Foundation/Zambia (ACHPR) at 3.

3.5.4.2 Expropriation

Currently there is no well-established regional jurisprudence regarding the standard of treatment in cases of expropriation. The Banjul Charter allows states to restrict or interfere with the right to property in cases of public need or in the interest of the community.[184] It safeguards the requirements of legality, legitimacy, and proportionality concerning the limitation of HRs. The ACHR has highlighted the relevance of public order and legitimacy in cases involving indigenous peoples' rights.[185] However, the text of the Banjul Charter is silent on certain details concerning the scope of their treatment. Article 14 lacks an autonomous compensation provision in any form, let alone one that provides standards of compensation under differing sets of circumstances. It requires compliance with the relevant law. However, there still is no official stance on compensation. One reason for the continued absence of an official approach is that the ACHR has yet to implement institutional arrangements allowing for the establishment of monitoring mechanisms.

Article 14 of the Banjul Charter does not specify what group or groups of people are addressed by its provisions. As such, it is not clear whether it covers both natural and legal persons, and what types of property it addresses. While the question of legal persons remains unanswered, the ACHR has stated that every individual under the Charter's jurisdiction has the right to property. In addition, the ACHR's rulings regarding the protection of property rights indicate that both private property rights and common property rights are protected. In *John K. Modise v Botswana* the ACHR gave a ruling concerning the confiscation of private land,[186] and in *Minority Rights Group International v Kenya*[187] recognised common property rights. The ACHR has ruled to the benefit of victims by considering the interdependency of HRs. In this regard the Court developed arguments based on Article 14 to decide on the right to housing,[188] enforced displacement,[189] and confiscation.[190]

---

[184] African Charter on Human and Peoples' Rights (Banjul Charter) [1986] OAU Doc. CAB/LEG/67/3 rev. 5, 21 I.L.M. 58 art 14.

[185] *Centre for Minority Rights Development and Minority Rights Group International and Centre on Housing Rights and Evictions (intervening) (on behalf of Endorois Welfare Council) v Kenya [*2009*] Merits communication no 276/2003 (ACHPR) paras 211 ff.*

[186] *Modise v Botswana* [2000] Decision on Merits No 97/93 (ACHPR).

[187] *Centre for Minority Rights Development and Minority Rights Group International and Centre on Housing Rights and Evictions (intervening) (on behalf of Endorois Welfare Council) v Kenya [*2009*] Merits communication no 276/2003 (ACHPR).*

[188] As a manner of example we refer to the case: *Social and Economic Rights Action Centre and Centre for Economic and Social Rights v Nigeria [*2001*] Commission communication 155/96 (ACHPR).*

[189] See as example the case: *Centre for Minority Rights Development and Minority Rights Group International and Centre on Housing Rights and Evictions (intervening) (on behalf of Endorois Welfare Council) v Kenya [*2009*] Merits communication no 276/2003 (ACHPR).*

[190] *Institute for Human Rights and Development in Africa (on behalf of Esmaila Connateh & 13 others) v Angola* [2008] Merits communication no 292/2004 (ACHPR) see at para 17 and 22.

This standard of treatment also applies when owners lack a title to their property. In the *CEMIRIDE* case a pastoralist group—the Endorois— claimed and won restitution and compensation for ancestral land expropriated by the Kenyan government.[191] This dispossession was motivated by a development-related project granting concessions for the extraction of rubies.[192] In addition to the dispossession, areas of land were sold to third parties. Although the Kenyan government compensated some affected individuals, the test employed to determine the degree of compensation indicated that less than 40 per cent of the victims received any remuneration.[193] The ACHR applied a non-binding proportionality test in this case to determine whether the damage resulting from the application of the measure by the Kenyan government was in accordance with the level of compensation provided.[194] The ACHR expressly recognised the existence of collective land tenure and affirmed that collective property rights are protected HRs. It confirmed that the Endorois community was not only the possessor of the land but also its owner.

The ACHR highlighted the illegitimacy of any measure lacking control mechanisms or consultancy with the local population.[195] Moreover, the decision calls for the recognition of collective property rights,[196] traditional land tenure systems, and the restitution of disposed land.[197]

3.5.5 *Legal Capacity in Proceedings Before International Courts of Human Rights*

3.5.5.1 States, Individuals, Groups, and NGOs

States have the capacity to initiate inter-state complaints. However, these mechanisms have never been used. The UN treaty system and the African regional system allow individuals, groups, and NGOs to initiate complaints. Each person has the

---

[191] *Centre for Minority Rights Development and Minority Rights Group International and Centre on Housing Rights and Evictions (intervening) (on behalf of Endorois Welfare Council) v Kenya [2009] Merits communication no 276/2003 (ACHPR).*

[192] Ibid.

[193] The claimant alleged that only 170 of 400 families were compensated. See: ibid.

[194] The approach took in this decision was based on the notions implemented by the European Court of Human Rights. I.e. at para 237 the Commission stated that: 'These recommendations, which have been considered and applied by the European Court of Human Rights, set out the following principles for compensation on loss of land...' ibid.

[195] Ibid. In this case the Commission considered the common aspects as referred above regarding the similitudes between indigenous people and minorities. See the discussion relating the terms indigenous people and minorities *infra* at: 3.5.5.

[196] Ibid.

[197] Ibid.

right to access the system. The scope of claims extends to all other identical cases. Moreover, individuals may join a previously initiated complaint and file a joint complaint. The access of individuals and the recognition of their rights at the international level represent one of the most relevant successes in the international protection of HRs.[198]

Currently it is still unclear whether juridical entities under the jurisdiction of the Banjul Charter would be recognised as legal subjects in the same way as they are recognised in the European system. Some interpretations contend that due to Africa's colonial history, the tendency is for such a possibility to be ruled out, as it is in the inter-American system.[199] However, such interpretations were merely developed in the literature and are without legal precedent in the region. At the time of writing it is not possible to state with certainty which elements would be considered by an African court when transnational corporations claim HRL protection.

Due to the nature of protected rights the capacity of legal subjects to hold a specific right and to initiate a complaint (individually or collectively) differs among subjects. A distinction between legal and procedural capacities (*ius standi*) may be necessary. One must have procedural and legal capacity to have the legal right to initiate a claim. If an individual does not have the procedural capacity to bring a claim, a representative of the victim is given this capacity by law. This may be a person or persons (natural or legal) who initiate the claim on behalf of the victim.[200] In claims in the name of the public interest, the victim does not necessarily have to be identified. In cases where a group of legal subjects have identical legal interests, they can initiate a group complaint. In order to do so more than one legal subject must be the victim of HRs infringements. The right held by a group can be enforced either by one person as a member of the group, a representative of the group, or by some or all members of the group in their own name. These claimants may seek recourse in the case of an infringement of the communal right to property of minorities or indigenous peoples.

Under the African system NGOs lacking a direct legal interest can initiate complaints on behalf of an individual or a group of individuals. NGOs can initiate another kind of action where the victim(s) remain anonymous.[201] They can further initiate a

---

[198]For an analysis about the individual and NGOs complaints mechanisms before African human rights institutions see: Mohamed (1999), p. 202.

[199]Trindade (1998), pp. 1, 17.

[200]For a deep examination about the concept of 'victim' in the framework of Human Rights Law see: Trindade (1987), pp. 9, 262.

[201]It has been stated by the African Commission that the fact that NGOs can initiate procedures in name of non-determined victims it represents an advantage. The most relevant case of this kind is *Centre for Minority Rights and others v. Kenya*. In this case: 'The Commission thanks the two human rights NGOs who brought the matter under its purview: the Social and Economic Rights Action Center (Nigeria) and the Center for Economic and Social Rights (USA). Such is a demonstration of the usefulness to the Commission and individuals of actio popularis, which is wisely allowed under the African Charter.' *Centre for Minority Rights Development and Minority Rights Group International and Centre on Housing Rights and Evictions (intervening) (on behalf of Endorois Welfare Council) v Kenya [2009] Merits communication no 276/2003 (ACHPR) at para 49.*

complaint in the capacity of a substantive rightsholder and as the representative of the victims. In order to legally act in these different ways, NGOs must be registered. They can be called upon in an already initiated case in their capacity as experts. In such a situation NGOs provide specialised information or opinions on a matter for the court as *amicus curiae*. Participation as *amici curiae* is advantageous for NGOs as it allows them to impact upon a case without expending undue time and resources. In such cases, rather than having to demonstrate an interest in the case, the NGO is called upon by the tribunal as an expert. They are not required to prove a specific interest in the issue.[202] However, their capacity as *amici curiae* translates to a lack of control over the direction of the case. Their function is limited to answering the questions put before them by the tribunal.[203] The participation of NGO as *amici curiae* constitutes an improvement of the African regional system. While the intervention of *amici curiae* has been accepted in some cases presented before the inter-American and European systems, they were not initially admitted in the African system.[204]

The development of HRs treaties leads to the creation of special protections for specific vulnerable groups. While in some cases there are clear requirements to define what constitutes a member of a group (for example, in cases concerning gender issues or the protection of children), there are other areas in which HRL seems to lack specificity. When initiating a complaint there are real consequences from the determination whether specific individuals can be considered members of a group or not. In this sense the conceptualisation of minorities and indigenous peoples gains increased importance.

3.5.5.2 Minorities and Indigenous Peoples in International Human Rights Law

Discussions about the protection of minorities in IL are not new.[205] The League of Nations sought to create a special and effective regime for minorities but the political situation made this impossible. The system of protection for minority rights was first introduced after the First World War in some states but only became widespread much later through a new approach developed under the UN system.[206]

---

[202] van Aaken (2005) at fn 51.

[203] Shelton (1994), p. 611.

[204] Ibid.

[205] A short overview by: Kugelmann. For more complete approaches see: Ermacora (1983). For a wonderful study about the protection of indigenous people including on the one side the evolution of the protection of indigenous people, on the other side an analyses about human rights and their applicability with special emphasis on individual and collective claims we recommend: Ludescher (2004).

[206] A brief analysis of the mechanisms developed by the League of Nations can be read in a note of the Secretary General at: Economic and Social Council, *Note by the Secretary General, The International Protection of Minorities under the League of Nations, U.N. Sub-Commission on the Prevention of Discrimination and the Protection of Minorities* (UN Doc E/CN4/Sub2/6, 1947).

This system aims to foster peace and security and to protect HRs.[207] The discussion about minority groups and the design of international legal policies is closely related to the issue of indigenous peoples. However, minority groups and indigenous peoples cannot be treated identically due to legal implications at the international level.[208] Both groups may be seen as different legal subjects with some common aspects but also with relevant differences.[209] The historical dimension of these differences can be understood by comparing legislation concerning indigenous peoples and minority groups. Additionally, it might be recognised that the different mechanisms used to protect either indigenous peoples or minorities arise from variations across geographical regions. While discussions focused on the protection of minorities are somewhat eurocentric, debate over the protection of indigenous peoples' rights was influenced by realities specific to the Americas and Pacific regions.[210] The challenge for IL with regard to the African region is to provide legal security to individuals who can be considered either part of a minority group or part of an indigenous group using parameters accepted across different cultures. Additionally, it can be confusing that in some cases indigenous peoples may be (but are not necessarily) minorities, and *vice versa*.

The primary international legal source regulating the rights of minorities is Article 27 of the ICCPR. Article 27 states that where ethnic, religious, or linguistic minorities exist, the persons belonging to such minority groups shall not be discriminated against.[211] Article 2.1 of the UN Declaration on the Rights of Persons Belonging to National or Ethnic, Religious and Linguistic Minorities includes language that is very similar to Article 27 of the ICCPR. In addition, the Convention on the Rights of the Child incorporates the text of Article 27 of the ICCPR in its statement concerning the rights of children.[212] If IL confers rights or special treatment to minorities and indigenous peoples, it is necessary to delimit the application of these rights. There is no legal definition of minorities. The definition elaborated by the Special Rapporteur of the UN Francesco Capotorti is broadly accepted today, although it is not legally binding. For our purposes we may use it as a starting point in this discussion. It states that a minority is:

> A group numerically inferior to the rest of the population of a State, in a non-dominant position, whose members – being nationals of the State – possess ethnic, religious or

[207] Ludescher (2004), p. 21.

[208] Eide (2000) at para 43.

[209] Ermacora (1983), p. 250.

[210] Eide (2000) at para 25.

[211] Art 27 General Assembly (UN) International Covenant on Civil and Political Rights [2001] CCPR/C/66/GUI/Rev.2 reads: 'In those States in which ethnic, religious or linguistic minorities exist, persons belonging to such minorities shall not be denied the right, in community with the other members of their group, to enjoy their own culture, to profess and practise their own religion, or to use their own language'.

[212] General Assembly (UN) Declaration on the Rights of Persons Belonging to National or Ethnic, Religious and Linguistic Minorities [1992] A/RES/47/135. General Assembly (UN) Convention on the Rights of the Child [1990] 1577 UNTS 3.

linguistic characteristics differing from those of the rest of the population and show if only implicitly a sense of solidarity, directed towards preserving their culture, traditions, religion or language.[213]

The term 'indigenous peoples' is also not defined by IL. [214] Neither the Indigenous and Tribal Peoples Convention[215] nor the United Nations Declaration on the Rights of Indigenous Peoples[216] contain a definition of the term. Some legal scholars, as well as the Office of the United Nations High Commissioner for Human Rights (OHCHR), have elaborated approaches that suggest ways of determining whether or not an individual can be considered indigenous.[217]

Gupta's definition (2005) states that 'they are peoples who inhabited a land before it was conquered by other peoples or societies during colonisation by force or by treaty and they consider themselves distinct from the society currently governing those territories.'[218] The Commission on Human Rights in its preliminary Report on the Study of the Problem of Discrimination Against Indigenous Populations considers indigenous peoples as 'the descendants of the peoples who inhabited the present territory of a country wholly or partially at the time when persons from a different culture or ethnic origin arrived there from other parts of the world.'[219]

What these definitions bear in common is the mention of geographical, historical, and cultural traditions belonging to a collective. The notion of inhabiting specific territory is intrinsically related to cultural autonomy and plays an important role in traditions and religious practices.[220] Intergenerational continuity makes it possible to link current practices to ancient traditions that were performed before persons of a different origin arrived. The collective character of rights means that they can only be claimed by groups of people. Daes (2000) elaborates distinctions

[213] Francesco Capotorti and United Nations (1979) para 568.

[214] A brief overview of the discussion regarding the inclusion of a definition of indigenous see: van Genugten (2010), p. 29 and also United Nations (2010).

[215] International Labour Organization (ILO) Indigenous and Tribal Peoples Convention [1989] C169 is considered even though it has been rarely ratified by African States. See: International Labour Organization (1996), Gupta (2005).

[216] United Nations Declaration on the Rights of Indigenous Peoples Resolution [2007] A/61/L.67 and Add.1 61/295.

[217] With regard to the UN see: United Nations, Minority Rights: International Standards and Guidance for Implementation (HR/PUB/10/3, 2010).

[218] Kugelmann, 'The Protection of Minorities and Indigenous Peoples Respecting Cultural Diversity' Max Planck Encyclopedia of Public International Law, 258 http://www.mpil.de/files/pdf1/mpunyb_06_kugelmann_11.pdf accessed 14 Arpil 2011.

[219] Economic and Social Council (1983).

[220] It was confirmed by the African Commission in the case *Centre for Minority Rights Development and Minority Rights Group International and Centre on Housing Rights and Evictions (intervening) (on behalf of Endorois Welfare Council) v Kenya [2009] Merits communication no 276/2003 (ACHPR) para 290* in which the Commission agreed that the complaints had a legitimate expectation that even after their initial eviction, they would be allowed access to their land for religious ceremonies and medical purposes.

between indigenous peoples and minorities based on the faculty of indigenous peoples for self-determination. This faculty is associated with their autonomy of development and their sovereignty over land and natural resources.[221]

These differentiations do not negate the possibility of indigenous peoples also belonging to a minority group. Tribunals have clearly identifined approaches to hearing cases involving rights infrigements of different groups based on the determination of which group the victims belong to. Tribunals have had to separate affected individuals according to their belonging to either a group of indigenous peoples or a minority group.[222] Although the literature provides some guidelines on how a person's indigenous status might be ascertained, case law is still at an early phase. The first step is to determine whether legislation at the national level provides a definition of indigenous peoples. In such cases international tribunals will apply the national definition. In contrary cases the tribunal will apply a test on a case-by-case basis to determine whether a specific group should be considered a minority group or indigenous.

If a definition is absent from domestic law, a narrow interpretation of definitions found in the literature would lead to the conclusion that indigenous peoples feel themselves to be indigenous and fulfil the abstract requirements of sharing a religion, language, and longevity of customs. The lack of a legal definition at both the international and national levels could explain the underuse of binding and soft laws by victims. Although many legal scholars agree that it cannot be the role of IL to provide a definition of what constitutes indigenous peoples, it nonetheless increases the levels of legal insecurity as it is not possible *ex ante* to know

[221]Eide (2000) at para 43.

[222]There are some examples in which the rights that are given to a group, as the case of indigenous people, have been applied to single subjects. The Canadian case of *Lovelace v Canada* is one of the most relevant cases in which a case of discrimination could be argued in case that the claimant wouldn't be an indigenous, in this case the tribunal did not considered the fact that Sandra Lovelace lost the right to habit in the reserve with the community as discrimination given the fact that the Indian Act states that in cases that a woman marries a non-Indian man she loses the right to live in the reserve. However in case that a man marries a non-Indian woman, he wouldn't lose such right. *Lovelace v Canada* [1981] Commission Communication 24/1977, CCPR/C/13/D/ 24/1977 (UNHRC).

Another case, *Lubicon Lake Bankd v Canada*, concerned the indigenous rights' to self-determination and sovereignty over natural resources. In this case the question to be decided was not about the distortions produced by the incorporation of new development project, it was about the infringement of the right of indigenous people to self-determination. As the commentator states: 'The facts of this case were extremely complex, and hampered by fundamental disagreement between the parties over the interpretation of facts. Ultimately, the Band won its claim that historical and recent developments had undermined its traditional way of life, contrary to Article 27. However, the Human Rights Council then found that Canada's proposed solution, which was to transfer land and other benefits to the Lubicon Lake Band, was sufficient, despite arguments to the contrary by the Band. Therefore, the victory for the indigenous group was somewhat pyrrhic.' The case is available at: *Ominayak (on behalf of Lubicon Lake Band) v Canada* [1990] Commission Communication 167/1984, CCPR/C/38/D/167/1984 (UNHRC).

whether a person may be considered indigenous. This uncertainty is greater in states with weaker institutional capacities and where indigenous peoples are minorities.

In some cases legal subjects that could be members of either group might choose to make use of the advantages given to minorities. This may occur in regions where indigenous peoples are also members of a minority group. In certain circumstances individuals might also decide to use the legal instruments available to non-minorities or non-indigenous peoples. They are permitted to make use of these legal instruments because they belong to both the indigenous and the non-indigenous population. These individuals are equal to all other peoples, with the right to be different, to consider themselves different, and to be respected as such. If domestic jurisdiction does not define indigenous peoples, IL does not provide binding guidelines that would make it possible for victims to use the special protective mechanisms provided to indigenous peoples.

The relevance of the differentiation between the two groups is illustrated by the fact that the applicable law is subject to change in some cases. This means that indigenous peoples can sometimes use the advantages given to minorities by law to attain a higher level of protection. For IL the high level of discretion available to tribunals in such a case-by-case system could represent a problem. Some of the main interpretative issues that might arise in the future include the question of whether migration may lead to the preclusion of the protection of minority or indigenous rights. Even though this question goes beyond our current research purpose, it might play an important role in cases where communities are dispersed following the introduction of agrarian policies.

3.5.6 Enforcement Mechanisms

Now we turn to analyse the legal provisions contained in HRs treaties that make it possible to enforce the right to property and the right to food. Rather than discussing whether the system is effective or not, at this point we will concentrate on the mechanisms available to subjects with the legal capacity and legal interests to enforce their HRs. The mechanisms offered by HRL differ in their context; they were designed in diverse socio-economic contexts. Hence, all treaties do not work identically.

3.5.6.1 The UN Treaty-Based System

The UN treaty-based system is considered to be the link between universal standards and individuals. These treaties were designed to empower and protect individuals worldwide. Since they constitute binding norms, member states have to commit to the obligations imposed by these treaties.[223] Each member state has the

[223] Ki-moon (2012).

obligation to respect, protect, fulfil, and implement the rights contained in these treaties. The obligation to respect means that states must refrain from interfering with or curtailing the enjoyment of HRs. The obligation to protect requires states to protect individuals and groups against HRs abuses. The obligation to fulfil treaty obligations means that states must take positive action to facilitate the enjoyment of basic HRs.[224] The rights contained in this system are considered to be universal, indivisible, and interdependent. Their belonging to each human person is affirmed in Article 5 of the United Nations Vienna Declaration and Programme of Action, which was adopted in 1993.[225]

The UN treaty-based system is built around nine treaties. Seven of the treaties protect either the human right to food, the human right to property, or both.[226] None of them specifically mention the general principle in IL that local remedies must be exhausted before a complaint can be brought before an IL tribunal.[227] The committees that act as administrators of justice are institutions stemming from each treaty. Even though the views of committees may contribute to decisions in cases, they are not binding on states. Committees are made up of independent experts who undertake to hear or to make: (1) general comments, (2) states' reports, (3) inter-state complaints, (4) inquiries or visits, or (5) individual complaints. Of all of these mechanisms Individual Complaints are potentially the most effective.

General comments can be seen as prophylactic mechanisms in the sense that they are used to explain the meaning of specific treaty dispositions to states who may be committing HRs violations. Even though committees could prove that violations of property and food rights are in fact taking place, it is not expected that general comments will improve the situation as they lack a binding character and enforceability.

All treaties provide that states parties must submit reports to show the measures being taken to implement their obligations.[228] The first report submitted is used to set a baseline for evaluating improvements in later reports.[229] After receiving the report, the committee elaborates non-enforceable observations and recommendations. There are several drawbacks related to the states' reports mechanism. First, the committee lacks the authority to verify the information contained in reports. Second, the activity of the committees is deemed too slow, as it takes between

[224]An expansive explanation about the states obligations is developed by De Schutter (2010), p. 242 ff.

[225]See footnote: 10.

[226]We refer the following sections of this study: Sects. 3.5.1 and 3.5.2.

[227]On the principle of exhaustion of local remedies see: Amerasinghe (2004).

[228]ICERD article 9; ICCPR article 40; ICESCR article 16 (ECOSOC); CEDAW article 18; CAT article 19; CRC arts. 44–45; CMW arts. 73–74; CFD article 29; CRPD arts. 35–36.

[229]See part D of the initial report of the Consolidated Guidelines for State Reports Under the International Covenant on Civil and Political Rights [2001] CCPR/C/66/GUI/Rev.2. See the Guidelines on an Expanded Core Document and Treaty-Specific Targeted Reports and Harmonized Guidelines on Reporting Under the International Human Rights Treaties (Hamonized Guidelines) [2005] HRI/MC/2005/3 para. 9.

15 and 22 months to produce results. This situation may be changing, however, as some committees have installed permanent offices in certain countries.[230] That said, it is difficult to imagine concrete infringements being remedied in a timely manner through reports.

The mechanism of inter-state complaints allows states to report HRs violations carried out by other states. As a matter of procedure, the two states are then required to accept the competence of specific committees to take the role of mediators for the issue of concern. Certain political and diplomatic realities may make it less likely that a state will initiate this kind of complaint, even when private actors are involved.[231]

Inquires or visits allow committees to make direct observations, although their authority is limited.[232] The committee must have well-founded concerns about the deterioration of HRs in a state before conducting a visit. During missions, experts

[230]De Schutter (2010), p. 801. For a brief comment about the reluctance of states by submitting reports see: Pillay (2012), pp. 20–22.

[231]Legal source to initiate this inter-state mechanisms are: Art. 21 CAT, article 74 CMW, article 32 CED, article 10 of the Optional Protocol to ICESCR, and article 12 of the Optional Protocol (on a communications procedure) to the Convention on the Rights of the Child (not yet in force) set out a procedure for the relevant Committee itself to consider complaints from one sate party. It considers that another state party is not giving effect to the provisions of the Convention. This procedure applies only to States parties who have made a declaration accepting the competence of the Committee in this regard. CERD and CCPR: Arts 11–13 ICERD and arts. 41–43 ICCPR set out a more elaborate procedure for the resolution of disputes between states parties over a state's fulfilment of its obligations under the relevant Conventions through the establishment of an *ad hoc* Conciliation Commission. The procedure applies to all states parties to ICERD, but only to States parties to the ICCPR; which have made a declaration accepting the competence of the Committee in this regard. CERD, CEDAW, CAT, CMW and CED: Art. 22 ICERD, art. 29 CEDAW, art. 30 CAT, art. 92 CMW and art. 42 CED provides for disputes between States parties concerning interpretation or application of the Convention to be resolved in the first instance by negotiation or, failing that, by arbitration. One of the States involved may refer the dispute to the International Court of Justice if the parties fail to agree arbitration terms within 6 months. States parties may exclude themselves from this procedure by making a declaration at the time of ratification or accession, in which case, in accordance with the principle of reciprocity, they are barred from bringing cases against other States parties. Source: Commission on Human Rights (UN) Effective Functioning of Bodies Established Pursuant to United Nations Human Rights Instruments. Final Report on Enhancing the Long-Term Effectiveness of the United Nations Human Rights Treaty System [1997] E/CN.4/1997/74.

[232]The Committee Against Tortures as stated in General Assembly (UN) Convention Against Torture and Other Cruel, Inhuman or Degrading Treatment or Punishment [1984] 1465 UNTS 85 art 20; the Committee on the Elimination of Discrimination against Women General Assembly (UN) Optional Protocol to the Convention on the Elimination of All Forms of Discrimination Against Women [1981] 1249 UNTS 14 art 8; the Committee on the Rights of Persons with Disabilities General Assembly (UN) Optional Protocol to the Convention on the Rights of Persons with Disabilities [2006] A/RES/61/106 Annex II art 6; the Committee on Enforced Disappearances General Assembly (UN) International Convention for the Protection of All Persons from Enforced Disappearance [2006] Adopted by Resolution 61/177 art 33; the Committee on Economic, Social and Cultural Rights General Assembly (UN) Optional Protocol to the International Covenant on Economic, Social and Cultural Rights [1976] 999 UNTS 302 art 11.

evaluate the HRs situation in the state as well as the institutional, legal, judicial, administrative, and *de facto* situation under their mandates. However, whatever the outcome of a visit, the recommendations will lack enforceability.

Individual complaints allow victims to initiate complaints after fulfilling certain requirements. These procedures are contemplated by the CERD, CMW, CEDAW, CESCR and CRPD.[233] Under this procedure all individuals can submit a complaint. The conditions of admissibility are limited by the *ratione temporis* rule, which means that the treaty does not have a retroactive effect.[234] The complaint must be initiated either by the affected individual directly, through a representative, or through a third person acting on behalf of the victim.[235] The *actio popularis* is not permitted in any of the procedures. Although the admissions procedure forbids anonymity, a request can be made to the committee to maintain secret the identity of the solicitors involved. Furthermore, victims are required to have exhausted all domestic remedies.[236] This requirement aims to shine a spotlight on the failures of domestic institutions in adjudicating HRs issues. It is a control mechanism intended to improve domestic institutions so that the frequency of failure decreases.[237] A case brought before the committee may not be brought before another international tribunal. The case cannot be initiated on an abstract basis. In other words, the individual alleging the violation must demonstrate that they have *locus standi,* i.e. they must prove that they were personally affected by the state's activity.

After a case is admitted, there is an examination of the facts and arguments. If necessary, evaluation and working groups may be formed. Although the procedure is discussed in closed sessions and parties are usually required to provide written submissions, parties might still be called before the Committee. The outcome of the procedure is a published decision by the Committee that either recognises or denies the alleged violation. The claim can also be considered to be ill-founded. In some situations, a Special Rapporteur may be solicited to formally follow up a case.

Although the activities of these committees appear to be broad in theory, they are quite limited in reality. The procedures outlined above are rarely initiated, particularly in the developing world, and it is still a challenge to provide remedies to the

[233] A general article on the individual complaints: Trindade (1998), p. 1. On individual complaints under the African system see: Mohamed (1999).

[234] In this regarding the jurisprudence has had some difficulties to apply this requirement. One may differentiate between violations that occur once and violations that occur continuously. In the first case the *ratione temporis* rule will apply if the infringement occurred before the treaty entered in power. *J.L. v Australia* [1992] Communication No 491/1992, UN Doc CCPR/C/45/D/491/1992 (Human Rights Committee) at para 4.2. If the violation has been continued the complaint will be admissible from the day it entered in power. It was stated in: *Könye v Hungary* [1994] Communication No 520/1992, UN Doc CCPR/C/50/D/520/1992 (Human Rights Committee).

[235] On the concept of 'victim' see footnote: 200.

[236] The exception of this condition is given by Art. 5 para 2(b) of the Optional Protocol to the ICCPR that states: 'This shall not be the rule where the application of the remedies is unreasonably prolonged'.

[237] van Aaken (2005), p. 13.

victims. One reason for this may be a lack of legal infrastructure. Another point worth mentioning is the fact that in most cases it is developed countries who are the parties, in spite of the fact that HRs abuses arise much more frequently in developing countries and LDCs.[238]

3.5.6.2 UN Charter-Based System

Another set of HRs mechanisms emanate from the UN Charter. The system was profoundly reformed in 2006–2007. Even though the new system presented some achievements, it was criticised because undue political influence had diluted its credibility.[239] The main organ in the post-reform UN system is the HRC, established in 2006.[240] The HRC examines HRs violations that are catalogued as grave and persistent. The Council undertakes a Universal Periodic Review[241] that evaluates the HRs situation in all member states. Even though NGOs can play a relevant role by participating in evaluation procedures, their function is frequently overshadowed by state representatives or other state-financed NGOs. States may accept or deny the recommendations of the Council.[242] Consequently, the effects of this Periodic Review on violations of the right to property and food are very limited. In addition to the Periodic Review, the UN Charter-based system has the 1503 Revised Procedure and Special Procedures.

The 1503 Revised Procedure was established to address consistent patterns of gross and reliably attested violations of all HRs and all fundamental freedoms occurring in any part of the world and under any circumstances.[243] Its scope for action is very broad and cannot be derogated from by any member state. However, because it only applies to cases in which fundamental freedoms have been infringed, its scope is too limited for our purposes.

Special procedures evaluate the fulfilment of HRs obligations in specific situations.[244] They can be initiated as a collaboration mechanism with the state, as a

---

[238]De Schutter (2010), p. 242 ff.

[239]For a discussion about the UN Charter system we refer to: Pillay (2012). Specific criticisms of the UN Charter system can be read at: Joseph and McBeth (2010). See also: High Commissioner for Human Rights (2013).

[240]The Council was created by the United Nations General Assembly on 15 March 2006 by resolution 60/251. Its first session took place from June 19–30, 2006. One year later, the Council adopted its 'Institution-building package' to guide its work and set up its procedures and mechanisms. See: Joseph and Kyriakakis (2010), p. 10 ff.

[241]This review has its legal sources in the UN Charter and in the UDHR in combination with the international instruments that have been ratified by the specific country.

[242]Office of the High Commissioner of Human Rights (1996).

[243]For details of the complain mechanism see the detailed guide provided in the following website: Office of the United Nations High Commissioner for Human Rights (2013).

[244]In 2012 the OHCHR initiated special procedures in 80 different countries and visited 55 member states. In addition 603 communications to 127 member states were sent. The UN report shows that

warning mechanism, or as advocacy on behalf of the victims of HRs violations. Special procedures are comprised of individual complaints, communications to states (urgent appeals or letters), international public opinion alerts (press releases), and advice to states. This occurs through the publication of reports and by undertaking visits to member states. Individuals, groups of individuals, and NGOs can be solicited to undertake such procedures. The member states themselves can also invite the Special Rapporteur, *motu propio*.[245] The outcome of this procedure is a series of recommendations. The ideal scenario is that states take the recommendations seriously and endeavour to implement them to improve their domestic HRs situation. Given the importance of the right to food, a special set of procedures was put in place. In recent years the Rapporteur has focused on determining how LSLIs impact the right to food. The report on agribusiness and the right to food, published in 2009, focuses on the problem of asymmetric bargaining power of small producers and workers.[246] The Rapporteur makes recommendations whose implementation would contribute to guaranteeing small producers' market access, bargaining power, and the protection of their workers. The report recommends the introduction of legal policies to achieve such goals and the ratification of ILO conventions.[247] An additional Rapporteur concentrates specifically on LSLIs.[248] The purpose of these procedures remains to publicise the implications arising from the introduction of new agrarian policies. These reports may perhaps be consulted as a secondary source in the drafting of future judgments but in the short term, they do not provide remedies to affected locals. None of the mechanisms contained in the UN Charter system can be seen as potential mechanisms to remedy HRs violations in the short term.

74.3 per cent are joint communications issued by two or more mandates. Communications covered at least 1512 individuals and numerous groups of individuals. 295 communications concerned women. As of 31 December, States had responded to 40.1 per cent of communications sent between 1 January and 31 December 2011. Mandates followed up on 31.01 per cent of their communications, were submitted 129 reports to the Human Rights Council, including 60 on country visits, and 32 to the General Assembly, were issued 334 public statements; including 53 statements jointly with other special procedures and/ or mandate-holders from other mechanisms. 10 new Special Procedures mandate-holders into the system with the support of OHCHR and the respective committee. 92 States had extended a standing invitation to Special Procedures as of 31 December 2012. During 2012 Chad and Seychelles joined the growing number of States that have issued a standing invitation to the Special Procedures of the Human Rights Council. Source: Human Rights Council A/HRC/RES/5/1 General Assembly Institution-Building of the United Nations Human Rights Council The Human Rights Council [2007].

[245]In the last years some special state-based procedures have been completed. I.e: in 2013: Canada, Cameroon. 2012: China, Mexico, South Africa, and Madagascar. 2011: Syria, China. Source and details in: United Nations (2012), p. 37.

[246]De Schutter (2009c), p. 5.

[247]Ibid.

[248]Ibid.

3.5.6.3 Regional Mechanisms and Human Rights in Africa

The Organisation of African Unity—known as the African Union today—adopted the Banjul Charter in 1981.[249] This Charter is the cornerstone of the African system of HRs and includes a number of social and economic rights (Articles 15–18) and civil and political rights (Articles 3–14). One of the most emblematic characteristics of the Banjul Charter is the recognition of the collective rights of people and the rights of individuals (Articles 19–24).[250] The Banjul Charter considers states to be primarily responsible for HRs violations in their territories.[251] It is not clear to what extent the Banjul Charter can be applied to private actors.[252] Although the ACHR has suggested that private persons can violate rights enshrined in the Banjul Charter, there is no consensus on means to hold private persons accountable.[253]

In addition to the mechanism provided by the Banjul Charter through the ACHR, the Protocol of the Banjul Charter created the African Court on Human and Peoples' Rights, which is the principal judicial organ of the Charter.[254] Furthermore, the Charter on the Rights and Welfare of the Child (CRWC)[255] and five regional tribunals complement this regional HRs system.[256] The CRWC is not considered here as it does not provide mechanisms that individuals affected by LSLIs have recourse to.

3.5.6.3.1 The African Commission on Human and Peoples' Rights

The African Commission is charged with ensuring the promotion and protection of HRs in Africa. The Commission is the interpretative authority of the Banjul Charter.[257] It meets twice a year to adopt resolutions and to examine states' reports and communications on HRs violations submitted for its attention.[258] Individuals, groups of

---

249 African Charter on Human and Peoples' Rights (Banjul Charter) [1986] OAU Doc. CAB/LEG/67/3 rev. 5, 21 I.L.M. 58.

250 The importance of this recognition is not the recognition itself. It is given by the fact that the Banjul Charter breaches the generational classification of human rights, which broadly propagated in other regional systems. In the case of Africa, they are treated in the same tenor that other rights.

251 De Schutter (2010), p. 29.

252 South African Institute For Advanced Constitutional Public Human Rights and International Law (2010), p. 13.

253 In *Social and Economic Rights Action Centre and Centre for Economic and Social Rights v Nigeria [2001] Commission communication 155/96 (ACHPR)* the ACHR approached that non-state actors can infringe rights encompassed in the *Banjul Charter*. See paras 9, 55, 58 and 61.

254 Protocol to the African Charter on Human and People's Rights on the Establishment of an African Court on Human and People's Rights [1998] OAU OAU/LEG/EXP/AFCHPR/PROT (III).

255 Organization of African Unity African Charter on the Rights and Welfare of the Child [1999] OAU Doc. CAB/LEG/24.9/49.

256 For some details see Sect. 3.5.6 of this study.

257 See footnote: 113.

258 African Charter on Human and Peoples' Rights (Banjul Charter) [1986] OAU Doc. CAB/LEG/67/3 rev. 5, 21 I.L.M. 58 art 47.

individuals, NGOs, and state representatives can initiate complaints before the Commission.[259] Individuals may complain in their own name or on behalf of others.[260] Apart from the requirement of having exhausted all domestic remedies, the matter must be recent and cannot have already been adjudicated upon by an international HRs body. If a matter comes before the Commission in the form of a delayed action, the Commission determines whether or not it is admissible on a case-by-case basis.[261] When cases are denied judicial review at the national level, the ACHR as well as the African Court on HRs dispense with the exhaustion of local remedies.

The complaint must be compatible with the Banjul Charter and must indicate the complainant's name even if anonymity is requested. Furthermore, it must be written in an official language of the court.[262] When a case is deemed inadmissible it will be closed. Parties can make observations on the decision of admissibility. Thereafter, the Commission decides and informs the parties. The decision of admissibility is final but subject to review. If the Commission finds a violation it makes recommendations to the state party concerned. The Commission lacks the authority to either follow up such recommendations or enforce them. During the hearing of the case and before the last decision is published, the Commission may permit putting in place provisional measures for the protection of the individual(s) whose rights have potentially been violated.[263] Even though this procedure provides relatively uncomplicated access to the HRs system, and can be used to initiate a case before the African Court, its effectiveness is questionable due to the limited enforcement capabilities of the Commission. The main effect of the procedure is the potential reputational damage for states.

3.5.6.3.2 The African Court on Human and Peoples' Rights

After the Organisation of African Unity was replaced by the African Union, the African Court on HRs was replaced by a Court and the Commission.[264] The Court

---

[259]Ibid.

[260]For some considerations regarding the admissibility of *actio popularis* see: African Commission on Human and Peoples' Rights Resolution On Economic, Social And Cultural Rights In Africa [2004] ACHPR /Res.73(XXXVI)04. Some example of class actions are the following: *Zimbabwe Lawyers for Human Rights, Human Rights Trust for Southern Africa v The Government of Zimbabwe* [2005] Communication 314/05 (ACHPR); *Article 19 v State of Eritrea* [2003] Communication 275/03 (ACHPR); *Interights & Ditschwanelo v Botswana* [2006] Decision 319/06 (ACHPR).

[261]African Charter on Human and Peoples' Rights (Banjul Charter) [1986] OAU Doc. CAB/LEG/67/3 rev. 5, 21 I.L.M. 58 art 56(7).

[262]Ibid.

[263]Rules of Procedure of the African Commission on Human and Peoples' Rights [2010] available at http://www.achpr.org/files/instruments/rules-of-procedure-2010/rules_of_procedure_2010_en.pdf accessed 12 November 2013.

[264]Ibid., As to July 2013, 26 African States had accepted the Court's Jurisdiction.

decided its first case in 2009. The jurisdiction of the Court extends to the interpretation of the Banjul Charter, the Protocol, and other relevant HRs instruments ratified by the signatory states.[265] Its decisions are binding on signatory states.[266] Access to the Court is granted to the Commission, signatory states, and African intergovernmental organisations. NGOs are granted observer status before the Commission, although it may be presumed that under its rules of evidence the Court is free to admit NGOs as *amici curiae*.[267] Individuals of states that have accepted the jurisdiction of the Court also have access.[268]

The main procedures of the Court are in written form.[269] Diverse outcomes are possible before the Court since it can settle litigation, give advisory opinions as requested by the parties, and attempt amicable settlement.[270] In addition to these outcomes, the Court can also make use of provisional measures in cases of great gravity and urgency, including cases where imminent and irreparable harm to persons is likely.[271]

The most relevant characteristic of these measures is that they are binding. This is also the main difference between decisions taken by the Court and decisions taken by other organs. Member states are obliged to implement the Court's decisions. Even though the Court has no coercive mechanisms available to enforce its decisions, states usually comply to avoid the reputational costs of not implementing a decision. The Court's reports are submitted to the regular session of the Assembly. The Council of Ministers of the African Union also considers the Court's reports on behalf of the Assembly in order to monitor the execution of the decisions.[272]

---

[265]Mukundi (2008).

[266]Protocol to the African Charter on Human and Peoples' Rights [2004] OAU Doc. OAU/LEG/MIN/AFCHPR/PROT arts 3 and 4.

[267]This in concordance of arts 5 and 26 (2) Protocol Banjul Charter.

[268]African Charter on Human and Peoples' Rights (Banjul Charter) [1986] OAU Doc. CAB/LEG/67/3 rev. 5, 21 I.L.M. 58 art 56(6).

To July 2013 only seven States signed the Declaration allowing individuals direct access to the Court. Scholars see in this art. one of the most relevant limitations of the Protocol. The most tolerant view is that Art. 34 (6) is a filter to control floodgates. For others it constitutes a violation of the right to have access to justice constituting a contravention of the purpose of the Court. Mohamed (1999), p. 204.

[269]Rules of Procedure of the African Commission on Human and Peoples' Rights [2010] available at http://www.achpr.org/files/instruments/rules-of-procedure-2010/rules_of_procedure_2010_en.pdf accessed 12 November 2013. See i.e. rules 7, 20 and 65.2.

[270]Mgimba and Waters (2012), p. 9 ff.

[271]Protocol to the African Charter on Human and People's Rights on the Establishment of an African Court on Human and People's Rights [1998] OAU OAU/LEG/EXP/AFCHPR/PROT (III) arts 3, 5 and 27.2.

[272]Ibid.

3.5.6.3.3 The Courts of Justice of the African Economic Communities

Africa consists of eight different economic regions. These regions are: the Economic Community of West African States (ECOWAS), the Common Market for Eastern and Southern Africa (COMESA), the Economic Community of Central African States (ECCAS),tThe Southern African Development Community (SADC),tThe Intergovernmental Authority for Development (IGAD), the Arab Maghreb Union (AMU), the Community of Sahel-Saharan States (CEN-SAD), and the East African Community (EAC). Some of these regions created courts of justice to settle disputes. These courts also have explicit or implicit jurisdiction to hear HRs complaints. Nonetheless, the only regional court that openly accepts complaints from individuals is the Economic Community of West African States (ECOWAS) Court of Justice. While other courts, such as the East African Court of Justice[273] (EACJ), have heard pronouncements of HRs violations, private actors were not party to these cases.[274] These tribunals are complementary jurisdictional courts that work in unison with the African Court on Human and Peoples' Rights.

In 2005 the Economic Community of West African States (ECOWAS) Court of Justice was created.[275] The court has two jurisdictions:

1. advisory jurisdiction: the Court gives legal advisory opinions on any matter requiring interpretation.
2. contentious jurisdiction: zhe Court examines cases of failure by member states to honour their obligations under Community law.[276] The Court has jurisdiction to determine cases involving HRs violations occuring in any member State. It also adjudicates and makes declarations on the legality of regulations, directives, decisions, and other subsidiary legal instruments adopted by ECOWAS.[277]

[273]Ibid.

[274]The East African Court of Justice Rules of Procedure, 2010. Registered as a Newspaper at the G.P.O. available at: http://www.eacj.org/docs/EAC%20Gazette%205-5-10.pdf accessed 11 November 2013.

[275]For an analysis on the development of ECOWAS Court and the relevance it has gained with regard to HR decisions see: Alter et al. (2013), p. 737. ECOWAS organisational framework, functioning mechanism, powers, and procedure applicable before it are set out in: Ruhangisa (2011); Supplementary Protocol A/SP.2/06/06 of 14 June 2006, Regulation of 3 June 2002, and Supplementary Regulation C/REG.2/06/06 of 13 June 2006; Protocol on the Economic Community of West African States Court of Justice [1991] A/P.I/7/91; Economic Community of West African States Supplementary Amending the Preamble and Articles 1, 2, 9 and 30 of the Protocol A/P.1/7/91 Relating to the Community Court of Justice and Article 4 Paragraph 1 of the English Version of the Said Protocol [2005] A/SP.1/01/05.

[276]Rules of the Community (ECOWAS) Court of Justice [2002] available at http://www.courtecowas.org/site2012/pdf_files/rules_of_procedure.pdf accessed 11 November 2013.

[277]Protocol on the Economic Community of West African States Court of Justice [1991] A/P.I/7/91 art 96 ff.

The Court has no requirement to exhaust all domestic remedies; this allows victims of HRs violations to bypass national courts and access this court directly.[278]

Complaints cannot be submitted anonymously and must be made in written form.[279] The ECOWAS Court may apply all HRs treaties in force on the territory of the state where the complaint originates. Its decisions are not subject to appeal, however, they can be revised and subject to objection by interested third parties. Its decisions are binding on all member states, and the ECOWAS Court must specify the national authority that is competent to enforce the decision. Since its creation in 2005, the ECOWAS Court has decided 68 cases.[280] However, the ECOWAS Court has been underutilised by complainants for the purpose of defending HRs.[281] The Court's current workload is relatively low. This is surprising, considering the ease of access to the procedure and the fact that domestic remedies do not need to be exhausted to bring a complaint. The Court's workload in comparison with the ECtHR, which requires the exhaustion of local remedies but still receives in excess of 50,000 complaints per year, is particularly striking.[282]

3.5.6.4 Soft Law Mechanisms

In the specific case of LSLIs our analysis includes soft law mechanisms through which complaints can be initiated. We will also discuss unilateral and voluntary

[278]The direct access to the ECOWAS Court is one of the most relevant characteristics. Art. 4 of the ECOWAS Supplementary Protocol authorises the ECOWAS Court to attend complaints from 'individuals on application for relief for violation of their human rights'. Economic Community of West African States Supplementary Amending the Preamble and Articles 1, 2, 9 and 30 of the Protocol A/P.1/7/91 Relating to the Community Court of Justice and Article 4 Paragraph 1 of the English Version of the Said Protocol [2005] A/SP.1/01/05. For an analysis on the structure and special characteristics of ECOWAS Court we recommend: Alter et al. (2013), pp. 737, 753 ff.

[279]Economic Community of West African States Supplementary Amending the Preamble and Articles 1, 2, 9 and 30 of the Protocol A/P.1/7/91 Relating to the Community Court of Justice and Article 4 Paragraph 1 of the English Version of the Said Protocol [2005] A/SP.1/01/05 art. 10.

[280]Rules of the Community (ECOWAS) Court of Justice [2002] available at http://www.courtecowas.org/site2012/pdf_files/rules_of_procedure.pdf accessed 11 November 2013 art 40.2.

[281]In 2004 Niger has been founded responsible for failing to protect 24-year-old Hadijatou Mani from slavery. *Hadijatou Mani Koraou v The Republic of Niger* [2008] Decision ECW/CCJ/JUD/06/08 (ECOWAS). A second case was between *Ebrimah Manehh vs. The Gambia*, the court considered as illegal the arrest and disappearance of Mr. Manehh. In both cases the states were founded guilty. The remedies were payment of compensations; which were determined by applying domestic law. *Ebrimah Manehh v The Gambia* [2007] Decision ECW/CCJ/APP/11/07 (ECOWAS). Cases decided by ECOWAS Court of Justice are publicly available. Economic Community of West African States, 'List of Decided Cases From 2004 till Date' (*ECOWAS*, 2013) http://www.courtecowas.org/site2012/index.phpoption=com_content&view=article&id=157&Itemid=27 accessed 12 November 2013.

[282]Source: European Court of Human Rights (2014).

mechanisms including labelling and codes of conduct. There are mediation mechanisms created by states and IOs, as well as mechanisms created by private institutions, e.g. private banks. These mechanisms are briefly explained in the next paragraphs.

3.5.6.4.1 Mediation Mechanisms

There are three main mechanisms for the mediation of HRs claims in Africa. These include: ombudsmen, National Human Rights Institutions (NHRI), and the OECD Guidelines for Multinational Enterprises.

The institution of ombudsmen is an independent organ investigating complaints filed by individuals against governments and private organisations. Depending on the particular African nation, there are many national branches of this institution. Ombudsmen use set procedures to control and evaluate the impact of new public policies or private economic activities on HRs. Problems associated with dependency and impartiality have dominated the trajectory of this institution, not exclusively but particularly in developing countries. Problems associated with ombudsmen originate in the fact that they are appointed by governments but their main function is to investigate irregularities in state institutions. Often they work directly with parliamentary commissions, banks, ministries, NGOs, and civil groups. In some countries they are also incorporated into formal governmental structures.[283] Twenty-six African countries have created an Ombudsman Association that works to support and protect the independence and development of African ombudsman institutions by promoting information exchanges and best practices for the advancement of good governance and HRs in Africa. Even though this organisation tries to standardise the functioning of ombudsmen across the continent, its activity is limited. The last publicly accessible Ombudsman Association report was released in 2007.

Ombudsmen were also incorporated into finance corporations and IOs. Since 2013 the World Bank has engaged a Compliance Advisor Ombudsman with three complementary roles. The first role involves the resolution of disputes, the second ensuring compliance and being an advisor, and the third hearing complaints regarding projects financed by the International Financial Corporation (IFC)[284] and by the Multilateral Investment Guarantee Agency (MIGA).[285] While dispute resolution aims to solve

[283]African Ombudsman Association (2013).

[284]The IFC is the largest global development institution working with private investors in developing countries. It is owned by 184 members. Its goal is minimise risk abroad and make possible that investors realise their economic activity and impulse local development through the creation of jobs, generating tax revenues, improving corporate governance and environmental performance. See: International Finance Corporation (2015). For a discussion about the relevance of finance institutions and its relationship with other soft law mechanisms see: Wright (2009).

[285]The Convention Establishing the Multilateral Investment Guarantee Agency defines the objective of the agency to incentivise the flow of investment for productive purposes among member countries, and in particular to developing member countries, thus supplementing the activities of

pre-existing problems, compliance investigates and evaluates the performance of a project. The advisory role is based on insights gathered from the other two roles and focuses on policy design. Individuals and communities can initiate complaints but may not do so anonymously. Processing a complaint includes facilitation, information and fact sharing, dialogue, negotiation, mediation, and conciliation. The aim of this procedure is for parties to reach a mutually acceptable agreement which is followed up on by the Compliance Advisor Ombudsman.[286]

In 1993 the United Nations Paris Principles established NHRIs. NHRIs are independent public bodies that monitor and advise home governments.[287] By February 2013 one hundred and five States had created NHRIs. Seventy are accredited as compliant with the Paris Principles, 25 are not in full compliance, and the remaining ten are not compliant in any way. There is no formal or consistent structure to access NHRIs. In some countries such as Ghana, NHRIs can be accessed online. While their remedies are not binding, they do have a certain authority from giving an 'authoritative interpretation' that can be further enforced by national judicial bodies.[288]

The OECD Guidelines for Multinational Enterprises are part of the OECD Declaration on International Investment and Multinational Enterprises drafted in 1976. The Guidelines are a code of conduct for enterprises from the thirty-four OECD countries that invest abroad. In addition to the OECD members, eight non-OECD members and the European Commission (EC) have signed the guidelines.[289] One of the most important aspects of the 2011 revision of the Guidelines is that signatory states recognise that private actors can be violators of HRs. This key revision allows for the consideration of hard law sanctions for private actors.

The inclusion of a HRs chapter in the OECD guidelines is a considerable innovation. The chapter is consistent with the Guiding Principles on Business and Human Rights elaborated by Professor John Ruggie as Special Representative of the Secretary-General on the issue of HRs, transnational corporations, and other business enterprises.[290] The inclusion of such a chapter in the guidelines is of great

the International Bank for Reconstruction and Development, the International Finance Corporation and other international development finance institutions. Convention Establishing the Multilateral Investment Guarantee Agency [1988] available https://www.miga.org/documents/miga_convention_november_2010.pdf accessed 15 July 2015.

[286]The World Bank Group Office of the Compliance Advisor Ombudsman Guidelines [1999] available at http://www.cao-ombudsman.org/howwework/documents/CAOOperationalGuidelines2013_ENGLISH.pdf accessed on 15 July 2015 art 2.1.4.

[287]The Paris Principles, a set of international standards that frame and guide the work of National Human Rights Institutions (NHRIs). Drafted at an international NHRIs workshop in Paris in 1991, they were adopted by the United Nations General Assembly in 1993. Source: ibid.

[288]One example is Kenya where the decisions of the Kenya National Commission on Human Rights can be executed by tribunals. See: Office of the High Commissioner for Human Rights (2013).

[289]Argentina, Brazil, Egypt, Israel, Latvia, Lithuania, Peru, Romania.

[290]United Nations High Commissioner for Human Rights, 'Business and Human Rights: A Survey of NHRI Practices' (*UNHCR*, 2008) http://webcache.googleusercontent.com/search?q=cache:

relevance because of the broad protection it provides, the number of signatories, and the comprehensive forms of HRs protection it contains. This chapter creates a synchronicity between the UN system and the economic activities promoted by the OECD. It includes minimum standards and hard law under which violations of the framework guidelines can be considered.[291] Moreover, the guidelines include a comprehensive approach to due diligence and responsible supply chain management. They facilitate the tackling of bribery, extortion, environmental protection, consumer interests, disclosure, and taxation, which represents significant progress compared to earlier approaches.[292]

The National Contact Points (NCPs) are responsible for the promotion and implementation of the Guidelines at a national level.[293] Their functions include consultancy, mediation, conciliation, and interpretation.[294] NCPs are seen as an institutional development that may promote compliance with HRs abroad. NCPs furnish additional guidelines, such as obligations for states to create mechanisms to avoid HRs violations.[295] They establish links between the home and host states, as well as with civil society.[296] All NCPs are required to have Investment Committees. Investment Committees provide assistance in a variety of activities and areas and also offer interpretative advice when necessary. For example, if doubt arises over the interpretation of the Guidelines in a particular set of circumstances, the Investment Committee could be asked to interpret the Guidelines for the NCPs.[297]

---

oKxNkj0KlnsJ:www.reports-and-materials.org/OHCHR-National-Human-Rights-Institutions-practices-Apr-2008.doc+&cd=1&hl=en&ct=clnk&gl=ch&client=safari accessed 12 July 2015.

[291]In this regarding the guidelines reads:

> In all cases and irrespective of the country or specific context of enterprises' operations, reference should be made at a minimum to the internationally recognised human rights expressed in the International Bill of Human Rights, consisting of the UDHR and the main instruments through which it has been codified: the International Covenant on Civil and Political Rights and the International Covenant on Economic, Social and Cultural Rights, and to the principles concerning fundamental rights set out in the 1998 International Labour Organisation Declaration on Fundamental Principles and Rights at Work.

New OECD Guidelines for Multinational Enterprises to Protect Human Rights and Social Development para 38.

[292]Ibid.

[293]Ibid.

[294]Ibid.

[295]Ibid.

[296]Notwithstanding, the role and the quality of NCPs' contribution will vary of the institutional design at domestic level. One could speculate about potential problems of independence of NCPs due to protectionist policies. This topic is however beside of this study, it will be in a later contribution analysed.

[297]New OECD Guidelines for Multinational Enterprises to Protect Human Rights and Social Development at 2.C.

In most cases the complaints (which can be confidential) are made through NGOs. The NCPs determine whether the issues raised merit further examination.[298] When denying the merits of a particular matter the NCPs will issue a public statement substantiating the issues raised and the reasons for the decision taken. When accepting the merits of a particular matter the NCPs bring the parties together for a meeting to mediate the dispute. If a solution is not reached or a party is unwilling to participate in the mediation process, the NCPs will issue a statement including non-binding recommendations in accordance with OECD Guidelines. Where appropriate, the statement may also include the reasons why an agreement could not be reached. It is estimated that an average case is resolved within 1 year, however, some cases have taken twice that amount of time.[299] Among the numours criticisms that have been raised about the Guidelines the most serious is that they do not oblige member states to produce HRs assessments.[300]

3.5.6.4.2 Financial Institutions

The significant role played by financial institutions in investment projects and LSLIs is beyond dispute nowadays.[301] Globalisation is contributing to increased cooperation between diverse economic sectors. Some scholars have already written about the 'financialisation' of agricultural markets.[302] The potential contribution of these institutions in the agricultural economic sector is of increasing relevance. Social pressures, and in some cases governmental policies, have contributed to an increased level of accountability required of financial institutions. Different mechanisms can be initiated by victims (or by third parties on their behalf) to address HRs violations, even though these mechanisms are underused. The most well-known mechanisms are the ones developed by the World Bank, regional banks, and export credit agencies.

In addition to the compliance mechanisms of the World Bank previously mentioned, ombudsmen and inspection panels[303] hear complaints about projects financed by the International Bank for Reconstruction and Development (IBRD) and the International Development Association (IDA) of the World Bank Group.[304] If the IBRD and IDA are

[298]Ibid.

[299]For details in the procedure see: ibid.

[300]Accountability Counsel (2012). The UN-Rapporteur for the human right to food insists on creating consultation and participation mechanisms at a local level at the start of the process to decide whether a project can be realisable without affecting human rights.

[301]For the participation of finance institutions in LSLIs see Sect. 2.2.2 of this study. For the role of finance institutions in LSLIs and their potential contribution for sustainable development see: De Schutter (2009c) at 33.

[302]We recommend the contribution written by: Girardi (2012).

[303]The Panel was created in 1993, is composed of three members who are appointed by the Board of Executive Directors for a 5-year non-renewable term. Delphi International Ltd, *The Role of Financial Institutions in Achieving Sustainable Development* (1997).

[304]The mandate of the World Bank is poverty alleviation. The Group is made up of 184 member countries. These are only two of the institutions conforming the World Bank Group. The other are:

involved there is a HRs compliance procedure that can lead to a review or reconsideration of the performance of investment projects.[305] The procedure can be initiated by a group of individuals, a representative acting on behalf of the affected people, a foreign representative in exceptional cases, and an executive director of the Bank in special cases alleging serious violations. The remedies of this process are recommendations that are submitted to the board of executive directors of the IBRD and IDA, with the bank's management also receiving a copy. After the evaluation the bank management decides whether to approve the recommendations or not.[306]

When reviewing projects for approval, regional development banks consider some HRs issues by requiring the inclusion of environmental regulations, labour standards, and the observance of the 'local rights' of communities. However, such requirements are framed in very general terms and often remain unfulfilled. Mechanisms to enforce HRs are greatly underused.[307] Among all regional financial institutions the European Investment Bank has the most developed procedures for dealing with HRs violation claims.[308] However, because its investments in Africa represent only a small portion of its portfolio its relevance for our purposes is limited. Instead we concentrate on the African Development Bank (ADB), which is the most important regional financial institution for investments in Africa.

Created in 1964, the ADB operates out of Ivory Coast and has 53 African member states and 24 non-African member states. Its mandate is to 'combat poverty and improve the lives of the people on the African continent.'[309] The mission of the ADB is to promote economic and social development through loans, equity investments, and technical assistance. Many projects are co-financed by other international institutions, including the World Bank. Investments in agriculture represent the third most important investment sector of the ADB. This sector increased from 8.1 per cent in 2011 to 10.2 per cent in 2012.[310] This trend is directly linked to the effort to avoid food shortages by increasing support for agricultural infrastructure and management of

---

The International Bank for Reconstruction and Development (IBRD), The International Development Association (IDA), The International Finance Corporation (IFC), The Multinational Investment Guarantee (MIGA) and The International Centre for Settlement of Investment Disputes (ICSID).

[305] How to File a Request for Inspection to the World Bank Inspection Panel. General Guidelines The World Bank Group Office of the Compliance Advisor Ombudsman Guidelines [1993] available at http://ewebapps.worldbank.org/apps/ip/Documents/Guidelines_How%20to%20File_for_web.pdf accessed on 15 July 2015.

[306] The procedural principles are contented in: The World Bank (2013a) and the specificities about the procedure in: International Bank For Reconstruction and Development. International Development Association Resolution No. IBDR 93-10, Resolution No. IDA 93/6. The World Bank Inspection Panel available at: http://siteresources.worldbank.org/EXTINSPECTIONPANEL/Resources/ResolutionMarch2005.pdf accessed 14 November 2013.

[307] It is very hard to find cases in which human rights violations have been considered. Most of such procedures are run under secrecy. In few cases in which NGOs have been the window to filter some information, positive effects were missed.

[308] The World Bank (2013b).

[309] European Investment Bank Group (2012) at 16.

[310] African Development Bank Group (2013).

renewable natural resources.[311] In addition, the ADB addresses topics such as poverty reduction, the financial crisis, regional integration, quality assurance, and results.[312]

The complaint mechanism can be initiated by any group of two or more people in any country where an ADB-financed project is located.[313] The procedure only applies to cases in which liability can be determined in a direct and material way. NGOs can initiate the procedure, as well as a duly appointed local representative acting on explicit instructions as the agent of adversely affected people. Foreign representatives or the board of directors of a banking group may act as agents in cases where no adequate or appropriate representation is available in the country or countries where the project is located. The procedure is completed in writing and can be confidential if required.[314] There is an Independent Review Mechanism for the purpose of mediation, conciliation, and dialogue operated by the Compliance Review and Mediation Unit. The procedures apply to projects financed by the ADB. If allegations of HRs violations are substantiated, the panel elaborates suggestions for remedies and determines the steps to be taken to monitor their implementation.[315] The Compliance Review Report may not recommend the awarding of compensation or any other benefits to the requestors or any other person, entity, or government beyond that which may be expressly contemplated in a relevant bank group policy.[316]

Export Credit Agencies (ECAs) provide complaint mechanisms. ECAs are national public or semi-public institutions that offer private companies three different kinds of support: direct credit, credit insurance, and guarantees. They allow enterprises to reduce the financial risks associated with signing contracts in investment areas that are classed as high risk, which is often the case in developing

---

[311]Ibid.

[312]African Development Bank (2012), p. 9.

[313]The Independent Review Mechanism African Development Bank Operating Rules and Procedures (2010) available https://www.afdb.org/en/about-us/organisational-structure/independent-review-mechanism-irm accessed on 24 September 2014 at para 4.a.

[314]Ibid.

[315]Ibid at para I refer to the two different forms the procedure can take: (1) mediation or (2) compliance review. They are not independent therefore it can happen that they both are used for the same request. The mediation mechanism aims to bring parties together and dialogue to resolve the conflict. The exercise shall be a meeting or an exchange of views between the Bank's management representatives, the requester, and other interested persons. The director of the procedure has two make a report and specify the effects of the process. In the case that the process is unsuccessful (for the initiator) the director has to elaborate recommendations in steps to take deal with the issue. In the case that the process is successful the director shall prepare a report within 30 days after the conclusion of the exercise. The Compliance Review and Mediation unit will monitor the implementation of the solution agreed. The compliance review mechanism is used when there are well-founded evidences that the requesters are being harmed by the project. It can also be initiated after having finished the mediation procedure. However it is not considered as an appellation procedure. The results of these procedures consist in recommendations that are made by the director and experts. The panel conducts a review in the required time fame and may in particular solicit additional information form the interested parties or undertake on-site visits. The review will be submitted to the President or to the Board of the Bank.

[316]Ibid-60.

countries. More than 50 countries have created ECAs, their scope now covering almost all investment areas.[317] Today these agencies are considered highly influential actors in international trade and investment,[318] including the energy and carbon markets.[319] ECAs were forced to consider the protection of HRs and environmental rights in their activities following criticisms made by NGOs and civil society. These criticisms usually hinge on ECA's dependence on public funds. Therefore, as public or semi-public entities, the HRs obligations of the state should be extended to them.

Today ECAs include in their agendas an elaboration of their social responsibility policy[320] and complaint mechanisms. Some ECAs have adopted the Equator Principles and recommendations made by the OECD Council that include social environmental regulations and social impact assessments. Based on the due diligence process, some agencies have introduced HRs aspects to their agenda. Two examples of this are Export Development Canada[321] and the Overseas Private

[317]One of the most relevant aspects highlighted by the literature regarding the Export credit Agencies is the relevance they have at international level. This is given by the volume of investments they promote and the attractive guarantees they offer. As stated by Wright they contribute in LDCLDCs as: 'First, ECAs help expand energy supply in developing countries by providing risk cover to private companies involved in large, complex energy projects. They also mitigate energy poverty in cases where projects provide poor communities with access to new energy sources. Second, ECAs stimulate international trade in energy-related goods and services and facilitate the entry of multinational energy companies into countries associated with high political risk. They may also impact the relative international competitive- ness of energy companies by providing export companies in their own national jurisdictions with privileged access to export financing. Third, ECAs may influence the extent to which energy development in developing countries follows a carbon-intensive or low-carbon path.' ibid. A list of all Credit invest agencies can be seen at: ibid.

[318]Organisation for Economic Co-operation and Development (2015).

[319]Wright (2011), p. 133.

[320]On May 13th 2004 'Eksport Kredit Fonden' was created by private sector banks (see Part III on the Equator Principles) and then followed by the Canadian export credit agency. In 2003, the Coface (France) adopted environmental guidelines; however, these were the subject of severe criticism owing to the fact that they do not apply to all of the project categories.4 Some agencies have established complaints mechanisms. See for example: ibid 134.

[321]The Export Development Canada is owned by the Canadian Government. Its aim is to develop the Canadian export market and to profit from the possibilities and opportunities offered by international marketplace. Since 2004 this agency adopted a framework in which the agency affirms its respect for human rights and recognise s the need to be coherent with Canada's international obligations, including the UDHR and the necessity for financial institutions to evaluate potential negative impacts of their activities on human rights. This complains mechanism is accessible to any individual, group, community, entity or other party affected or likely to be affected by activities financed by the agency. Groups in behalf of thirds can also make claims. The outcome of the procedure is nonetheless quite limited, it only recommends to the board of Directors and be charged with the follow up. The possibility of stop financing a project in the case that irregularities are demonstrated is not considered. This mechanism has no judicial standing. Source: ibid.

Investment Corporation.[322] However, the remedies offered by these ECAs are limited to recommendations, and their mechanisms do not have judicial standing.

The Equator Principles are also considered to be a response to environmental and HRs violations in which private banks were directly or indirectly involved.[323] In this case private banks developed a self-regulation mechanism to increase their accountability by producing specific reputational effects in cases of HRs violations. The Equator Principles were implemented as voluntary environmental and social standards for private banks in project financing. Today 78 organisations, seventy-six banks, and two associated institutions are signatories. These organisations cover over seventy per cent of international project finance debt in emerging markets. The Equator Principles were conceived for large-scale projects financed by member banks in areas such as mining, the construction of dams, and telecommunications.[324] However, the principles do not contain an independent monitoring mechanism that is mandated to verify whether projects were prepared in line with the relevant provisions. The Equator Principles oblige signatory institutions to create a grievance mechanism. They compel borrowers to establish a mechanism to facilitate the resolution of concerns over the project's social and environmental impact raised by individuals or groups from project-affected communities.[325] Under the Equator Principles, financial institutions may not provide loans to projects where the borrower will not or is unable to comply with the respective social and environmental policies and procedures.[326] Such policies include sustainable

[322]The Overseas Private Investment Corporation. It is a US government agency that works in over 150 countries. It has established an independent office of accountability; which has two main functions: problem-solving and compliance review. For the problem-solving mechanism, the Office of Accountability will seek to create conditions that are conducive for affected communities and the OPIC client to resolve the conflict in a mutually acceptable manner. The OA does not take a position on any allegations that may be associated with the dispute. For the compliance-review process, the Office of Accountability will investigate and report on Overseas Private Investment Corporation implementation of relevant policies. The report may include recommendations for how the Corporation could strengthen its application of policies to the project in question or to future projects. This agency includes the topic of human rights as protected areas. The access to this complains mechanism is open to member of the local community affected by adverse environmental, social, worker rights or human rights impacts of a project supported by the agency. The President of the agency and also the directors can claim. *Corporate Social Responsibility Report 2012* (2012). See also: Complaint Mechanisms of Export Development Canada [2009] available at http://www.edc.ca/EN/About-Us/Management-and-Governance/Compliance-Officer/Documents/compliance-officer-steps-to-resolution.pdf accessed on 26 December 2013.

[323]Equator Principles available at http://www.equator-principles.com/documents/Equator_Principles.pdf, accessed 26 December 2013.

[324]At the beginning the principles applied for projects over 50 million dollars. After the first revision in 2006 and the second revision in 2012 they apply for projects exceeding 10 million dollars.

[325]Principles for Responsible Agricultural Investment that Respects Rights, Livehoods and Resources [2010] available http://siteresources.worldbank.org/INTARD/214574-1111138388661/22453321/Principles_Extended.pdf accessed 25 December 2013.

[326]Equator Principles available at http://www.equator-principles.com/documents/Equator_Principles.pdf, accessed 26 December 2013.

development, the protection of health, the protection of cultural heritage and biological diversity, the prevention and control of pollution, and consideration of the impact of projects on indigenous populations and communities.

The last revision of the Principles began in 2012, and discussions concerned an extension of their scope to project-related corporate and bridge loans, an adaptation to reflect the recent update of the International Finance Corporation Performance Standards, and new requirements regarding the management of social and environmental impacts. These revisions include consultation processes, independent reviews and monitoring mechanisms, and reporting obligations. They emphasise HRs considerations, due diligence, and a strengthening of reporting and transparency requirements.[327] Further, they acknowledge the UN 'Protect, Respect, and Remedy' Framework for Business and Human Rights and the Guiding Principles on Business and Human Rights.[328] As the principles lack an independent review or resource mechanism, any bank may adopt and apply them in a voluntary fashion. Moreover, the Equator Principles do not have a complaint mechanism for affected individuals, although affected people can alert the Equator Principles' Board of Violations. The fact that the principles apply only to projects worth more than USD 10 million reduces their scope. Beyond these criticisms the principles can be seen as a constructive effort to increase awareness of social and environmental issues in projects.

So far we have discussed the most relevant mechanisms in IL to protect the right to property and the right to food. We described not only hard law mechanisms but also soft law mechanisms at international and regional levels. Due to the nature of this project, special attention was paid to the African system. We covered enforcement mechanisms available in IL. In the next section we will turn to analysing protection mechanisms in IIL. These two approaches are the foundation of a comparative analysis that focuses on five main aspects, namely: (1) common aspects of both regimes, (2) standards of protection, (3) *standi*, (4) enforcement mechanisms, and (5) remedies. We will undertake this comparative analysis in an effort to establish whether the existent mechanisms in IL can contribute to blocking opportunistic behaviour in LSLIs.

[327] Silvina González, 'Equator Principles' Max Planck Encyclopedia of Public International Law, at para 44 http://opil.ouplaw.com/view/10.1093/law:epil/9780199231690/law-9780199231690-e1038?rskey=vuep8N&result=1&prd=OPIL# accessed 21 December. 2013.

[328] Equator Principles available at http://www.equator-principles.com/documents/Equator_Principles.pdf, accessed 26 December 2013 principle 6.

3.6 International Investment Law and the Protection of Investors in Sub-Saharan Africa

Over the past 40 years the structure of IIL has contributed to increasing the protection of foreign investments. Today it can be catalogued as an area of public IL that successfully limits political risk by including specific provisions.[329] It allows for a review of the legality of states' decisions in a neutral judicial forum. Put succinctly, IIL provides the necessary structures for states to voluntarily restrict their sovereign power with the goal of attracting foreign investment into their country. The promise of increased investment is traded off against reduced regulatory space for states, while investors gain increased predictability as well as guarantees to be treated at least in the same way as a domestic investor. IIL often grants international tribunals broad discretionary powers in settling disputes between the host state and the investor. This regime provides high levels of effectiveness in enforcing the tribunals' decisions. IIL allows countries to attract foreign investment and to profit from the know-how, infrastructure, and technological skills associated with FDI.[330]

In recent years the empirical literature has shown that even though such goals can be achieved, success depends on diverse variables within the host state.[331] It was widely recognised that the positive effects expected from FDI remained unfulfilled due to omnipresent institutional weaknesses of host countries.[332] The challenge of IIL has been to create a framework where the particularities of each economic sector become manageable for all actors involved. For example, long-term contracts contain large amounts of risk due to weak institutions in the host country. These risks concern political stability, regulatory activity (including drastic changes in tax policies), technological advances, and political ideology. In these areas IIL might provide guarantees for the completion of certain economic activities.[333]

Today highly developed and specialised IIAs have far surpassed their initial structure.[334] While bilateral relationships were successful, attempts at multilateral regulation failed due to divergent interests between developed and developing

[329]As subscribed by Steward, credible enforcement is essential for legal systems. Steward (2012). See also: Ruggie (2011).

[330]This is the classical assumption behind foreign direct investments. For a brief commentary of the evolution of IIL see: Wright (2009), p. 61 http://www.loc.gov/catdir/toc/ecip0825/2008032291.html.

[331]Relevant contributions in this regard are: van Aaken (2014), p. 1; Moran (2006).

[332]See for example: Moran (2011), Franck (2005), pp. 1521, 1524; Guzman (1998), p. 639; Hallward-Driemeier (2003), Yackee (2007).

[333]For an analysis about the political risks and guarantees in IIL see footnote: 238 in Chap. 2.

[334]The learning process of investment actors has been used to explained the increment on the complexity that investment treaties have had since the emanation of the first treaty until today, see: Montt (2007), p. 150. For a broad analysis of the history of such treaties see: Nadakavukaren (2013), p. 209.

countries, and also between developed countries themselves.[335] Bilateral Investment Treaties (BITs) are the most widespread form of treaty in IIL. UNCTAD reported that by the end of 2014, the overall number of IIAs stood at 3236 agreements including 2902 BITs and 334 'other IIAs'. This number principally refers to free trade agreements with investment provisions, economic partnerships, and regional agreements.[336]

All these instruments are designed to ensure that investments are protected. They achieve this by creating incentives for investors to invest abroad. In this sense the objective of IIL is to protect investments by focusing on the potential effects on investors' property rights when regulatory measures are introduced by host states. Although there are no tribunal cases directly related to LSLIs, the jurisprudence has dealt with cases involving the expropriation of land. Similar cases can be expected when states subject to LSLI on their territory introduce new land policies leading to land redistribution, restitution, or privatisation, as well cases in which states react to social pressures following invasions or occupations.

In the following section we will analyse the mechanisms of protection in IIL available to foreign investors. We will consider three mechanisms of protection: investments made without an investment contract, investments made with an investment contract, and investments made under the protection of IIAs. When states sign IIAs, they reduce the cost of negotiating investment contracts. However, they potentially increase the cost of introducing regulatory measures in the future. Without IIAs, the negotiation cost of an investment contract will increase considerably because investors will make many demands of their host state before making an investment in LDCs.[337] We will then proceed to introduce the standards of protection offered by IIL, adjudication mechanisms, and their enforcement.

---

[335]For documentation about the negotiation process and some causes for the failure see: Álvarez (2010), for a fresh discussion about a new negotiation of MIA see: Salacuse (2010), p. 78; International Economic Law and Policy Blog, 'A Multilateral Investment Agreement' available at http://worldtradelaw.typepad.com/ielpblog/2013/01/a-multilateral-investment-agreement.html accessed 11 November 2013 and also Nicolle Graugnard, 'Toward a Multilateral Framework for Investment' Columbia FDI Perspectives Perspectives on topical foreign direct investment issues by the Vale Columbia Center on Sustainable International Investment No 103 accessed 11 November 2013.

[336]Katia Tieleman, 'The Failure of the Multinational Agreement on Investment (MAI) and the Absence of a Global Public Policy Network' available at http://www.gppinet/fileadmin/gppi/Tieleman_MAI_GPP_Network.pdf [accessed 11 November 2013].

[337]The classification of mechanisms of protection we offer is developed by Franck as mechanisms to shift investment costs. See: United Nations Conference on Trade and Development, World Investment Report 2014 (World Investment Report 2014, 2015) 115.

3.6.1 Mechanisms of Protection

The term 'property' is rarely used in IIL. Instead, IIL refers to 'investments'. The relationship between investors and their investments vis-à-vis other legal subjects is characterised by the right to property.[338] Considering the concept of property, one may focus on the principle of excludability. This principle, as understood by Barnes (2009), *excludes* others from one's property. It protects against interference by other parties with the investor's property, allowing the holder of the property right to achieve and maintain pre-established economic expectations should such interference arise.[339] This definition intrinsically considers the fruits of the property to be a part of it. Foreign direct investments may be defined as the transfer of tangible or intangible assets from one country to another for the purpose of their use in that country to generate wealth under the total or partial control of the owner of the asset.[340] IL protects investments and the right to property in at least three different forms: investments made without an investment contract, investments made with an investment contract, and investments made under the protection of IIAs.

3.6.1.1 Investments Made Without an Investment Contract

When there exists no contract between the state and the investor, IL mechanisms to protect the rights of aliens apply. These mechanisms constitute the minimum standards of protection and are considered to be customary IL.[341] It is disputed whether additional standards of treatment, such as National Treatment and FET, could be considered minimum standards. Regarding National Treatment it was affirmed that states may establish differences between foreign and national investors as long as measures do not contravene pre-defined IL obligations.[342] Regarding FET the literature and jurisprudence agree that it is part of customary IL.[343]

In the case of direct and indirect expropriation, which is not forbidden under IL, HRL protects investors.[344] An expropriation is legal under some circumstances, for

[338]Franck (2011), p. 769.

[339]Kriebaum and Schreuer (2007), p. 2. For different approaches of Property see: Barnes (2009), p. 28.

[340]Cohen (1927), p. 8 12.

[341]Butler (2013), pp. 847 853 ff.

[342]In the absence of a contrary rule of international law binding on the States parties, whether of conventional or customary origin, a State may differentiate in its treatment of nationals and aliens. Salacuse (2010) 18 as well as 160 and 169.

[343]See i.e.: Hollin Dickerson, 'Minimum Standards' Max Planck Encyclopedia of Public International Law http://opil.ouplaw.com/view/10.1093/law:epil/9780199231690/law-9780199231690-e689?rskey=muCNrC&result=1&prd=EPIL accessed 21 December. 2013. The literature also refers to: *Methanex Corporation v United States* [2005] Final Award (Ad hoc UNICTRAL) Part IV, Chapter C, 25; Dolzer (2005), p. 87; Dolzer and von Walter (2007).

[344]Mishra and Mishra (2012), p. 107.

instance if it is deemed to be in the public interest, non-discriminatory, and compensated.[345] It has become a common standard that compensation should fulfil the requirements of the Hull Formula, which states that compensation must be prompt, effective, and adequate.[346] The violation of these norms constitutes a wrongful international act for which the state will be deemed responsible under IL.

The protection of investors without investment contracts is limited, as IIL can only mitigate some political risks. For example, it does not guarantee the right to transfer capital abroad or to repatriate it. Discriminatory measures can be introduced easily, and states can enact policies that progressively benefit national investors.

It is one thing to be the holder of a right, and quite another to have the legal capacity to enforce that right. This legal capacity is known as *ius standi*. Legal subjects with this capacity can access the judicial system and initiate a claim. In IL it is only in exceptional cases that legal subjects have this capacity. In the absence of this capacity the domestic law of host countries governs investments. The general rule of IL as included in the Brussels Convention of 1968 regarding the exclusivity of jurisdiction might apply here. It states that in cases involving immovable property or the tenancy of immovable property, the local courts have exclusive jurisdiction.[347] After having exhausted domestic remedies, aliens can make use of HRs protection—if possible—and diplomatic protection. Diplomatic protection is an inter-state measure through which the home state can make a claim against the host state if the latter has violated IL and adversely affected investors from the home state.[348] Naturally investors cannot directly partake in this mechanism of protection, and they automatically delegate bargaining power to politicians. Thus, it can be said that the protection IL offers to investors contains real limitations because the *locus standi* of investors is limited, their legal personality is not broadly recognised (even in HRL at the regional level), and diplomatic protection is more akin to a political mechanism than a legal one. Under this system aliens depend more on political decisions than judicial ones.

3.6.1.2 Investments Made with an Investment Contract

Investment contracts are one instrument available to foreign investors to mitigate the risks of an investment. Investment contracts can balance the shortcomings of IL by providing adequate investment protection for investors in the host country. They usually contain certain clauses that increase legal certainty for the investor. Some of

[345]Schreuer (2005), p. 115; Herzt (1941), p. 253 and also Reisman and Sloane (2004) Paper 1002 YLSLSR 115.

[346]Gazzini (2010), p. 36.

[347]Griebel (2008), p. 18.

[348]A brief explanation about Diplomatic Protection is developed by: Brussels Convention on Jurisdiction and the Enforcement of Judgments in Civil and Commercial Matters [1968] OJ C 027 at 1-27 art 16.1. A more complete approach: Stephan Wittich, 'Diplomatic Protection' Oxford Bibliographies http://www.oxfordbibliographies.com/view/document/obo-9780199796953/obo-9780199796953-0020.xml accessed 21 December 2013.

the main issues that can be addressed in an investment contract include the law applicable to an investment, conflict resolution mechanisms, and renegotiation. In light of this, the level of protection that the contract can provide will depend on the investors' bargaining power when negotiating a contract. Contracts have to be designed in a way that balances the regulatory power of the state with the property rights of the investors. This balance can be achieved in a variety of ways, for instance by applying international standards and mechanisms to solve conflicts. Bilateral contracts between states and investors can mitigate political risks, but investors must be able to internalise high negotiation costs.

3.6.1.3 Investments Made Under the Protection of IIAs

IIAs are broad instruments that aim to mitigate political risk for investors. These agreements are negotiated at an inter-state level and establish the terms and conditions for private investment by nationals and companies of one state to another state. One of the advantages they offer is that they automatically decrease negotiation costs for future investments by establishing a negotiation baseline that offers guarantees otherwise not available to investors. IIAs create alternative legal avenues for investors who would otherwise be restricted to making a claim for breach of contractual obligations in the domestic legal system. Investors may be reluctant to take cases involving sensitive matters such as expropriation before a national court for fear of host country bias, particularly in states with less developed judicial systems and an equivocal separation of powers. However, IIAs have developed a standardised contractual structure in which protection mechanisms are included. These mechanisms were designed to offer an increased level of protection to investors.

Regarding investment protection under IIAs, the definition of investment is contained in the relevant treaty and constitutes a jurisdictional requirement in the framework of the International Centre for Settlement of Investment Disputes (ICSID) Convention as stated in Article 25 (1). Hence, the jurisdiction of IIL is framed *ratione materiae* by defining 'investment'. Contracting parties have the authority to define investments, delegate the interpretation of contracts to an external entity, and provide the applicable rules for the resolution of conflicts. This means that contracting parties define investments in the treaty and give the tribunal the authority to apply this definition.

In the past, investment treaties contained a relatively broad definition of investment that often centred on 'property, rights and interest'.[349] Modern treaties focus more on the process or transaction constituting the investment, on the asset acquired as a result of the process, or on transaction.[350] The tendency is that IIAs broaden the

---

[349]The evolution of IIL and also referring to the definition of investment see: Sornarajah (2010), p. 8. About the diplomatic protection we recommend the book by: Amerasinghe (2008).

[350]For a broad explanation about the coverage of investments in IIAs see: Dolzer and Schreuer (2008), pp. 17–24.

scope of an investment's definition, thereby amplifying the protection of the treaty. Due to the proliferation of economic activity associated with FDI, parties are able to delegate more competence to investment law adjudicators by broadening the definition of investment.[351] In most cases IIAs contain clauses defining investment. Even though these definitions are not always identical, modern IIAs combine broad terms with a list of the specific economic activities considered to constitute an investment. Most of the treaties include landholdings in the definition of investment. Definitions of investment tend to be rich in words and aspire to be broad in scope.[352] If an economic activity is the cause of a dispute, the definition of

[351]Ibid.

[352]For instance Art 1139 NAFTA is a clear example in which the parties defined what is and what is not an investment. It states that Salacuse (2010) 18, pp. 160–169 investment means: (a) an enterprise; (b) an equity security of an enterprise; (c) a debt security of an enterprise (I) where the enterprise is an affiliate of the investor, or (ii) where the original maturity of the debt security is at least three years, but does not include a debt security, regardless of original maturity, of a state enterprise; (d) a loan to an enterprise (i) where the enterprise is an affiliate of the investor, or (ii) where the original maturity of the loan is at least three years, but does not include a loan, regardless of original maturity, to a state enterprise; (e) an interest in an enterprise that entitles the owner to share in income or profits of the enterprise; (f) an interest in an enterprise that entitles the owner to share in the assets of that enterprise on dissolution, other than a debt security or a loan excluded from subparagraph (c) or (d); (g) real estate or other property, tangible or intangible, acquired in the expectation or used for the purpose of economic benefit or other business purposes; and (h) interests arising from the commitment of capital or other resources in the territory of a Party to economic activity in such territory, such as under (i) contracts involving the presence of an investor's property in the territory of the Party, including turnkey or construction contracts, or concessions, or (ii) contracts where remuneration depends substantially on the production, revenues or profits of an enterprise. It also includes what is not meant by investment. It includes: (i) claims to money that arise solely from (i) commercial contracts for the sale of goods or services by a national or enterprise in the territory of a Party to an enterprise in the territory of another Party, or (ii) the extension of credit in connection with a commercial transaction, such as trade financing, other than a loan covered by subparagraph (d); or (j) any other claims to money, that do not involve the kinds of interests set out in subparagraphs (a) through (h).

The Energy Charter structures in a different way the concept of investments. It encompasses a list of activities that are considered as investments without a further specification about what is not considered as investment. The Art. 1.6 reads as following: 'Investment' means every kind of asset, owned or controlled directly or indirectly by an Investor and includes: (a) tangible and intangible, and movable and immovable, property, and any property rights such as leases, mortgages, liens, and pledges; (b) a company or business enterprise, or shares, stock, or other forms of equity participation in a company or business enterprise, and bonds and other debt of a company or business enterprise; (c) claims to money and claims to performance pursuant to contract having an economic value and associated with an Investment; (d) Intellectual Property; (e) Returns; (f) any right conferred by law or contract or by virtue of any licences and permits granted pursuant to law to undertake any Economic Activity in the Energy Sector. A change in the form in which assets are invested does not affect their character as investments and the term 'Investment' includes all investments, whether existing at or made after the later of the date of entry into force of this Treaty for the Contracting Party of the Investor making the investment and that for the Contracting Party in the Area of which the investment is made (hereinafter referred to as the 'Effective Date') provided that the Treaty shall only apply to matters affecting such investments after the Effective Date. 'Investment' refers to any investment associated with an Economic Activity in the Energy Sector and to investments or classes of investments designated by a Contracting Party in its Area as 'Charter efficiency projects' and so notified to the Secretariat.

'investment' in the IIA must actually describe the activity in question in order for this activity to be considered an investment. Some IIAs contain exhaustive lists and specify whether any given activity is an investment under the agreement. Other IIAs include lists of characteristics that economic activities must fulfil in order to be considered investments, as well as illustrative lists.[353] In other cases still, a list illustrates some of the characteristics or activities that constitute an investment.[354] For example, some IIAs include the concept of property interest in land and natural resources concessions, while others refer to 'concessions to search for, cultivate, extract or exploit natural resources.'[355] Some IIAs actually exclude land from their scope of protection.[356] Here, a differentiation can be made if the IIA has retroactive effect. Other factors may include the scope of IIAs and the domestic authorities' approval in the host country.[357] In addition to the definition of investments, IIAs include a set of standards of protection that are much more specific than the minimum standard of protection regularly offered. Since IIAs constitute the most important source of law in IIL, in the next segment we will briefly analyse the standards of protection they offer to incentivise FDI.

[353]Such a model is included in BIT between Ghana and Benin for instance. As in the case of the BIT Ghana-Benin. Agreement Between Canada and the Republic of Peru for the Promotion and Protection of Investment (Canada-Peru) [2006] available at: http://investmentpolicyhub.unctad.org/Download/TreatyFile/626 accessed 20 September 2015.

[354]See the art. 1 of the BIT between India and Ghana. Agreement Between the Government of the Republic of Ghana and the Government the Republic of Benin for the Promotion and Protection of Investments (Ghana-Benin) [2001] available at: http://investmentpolicyhub.unctad.org/IIA/country/79/treaty/567 accessed 17 September 2015.

[355]Ethiopia-UK BIT 2009, Article 1(a)(v), emphasis added. Other UK treaties use similar formulations (e.g. Article 1(a)(v) of Laos-UK BIT 1995 and Tanzania- UK BIT 1999, and Article 2(a)(v) of Colombia-UK BIT 2010), as do some treaties concluded by Malaysia (e.g. Chile-Malaysia BIT 1992, Article 1(a)(v)).

[356]E.g. ASEAN Comprehensive Investment Agreement of 2009, Article 14, footnote 10 in Chap. 1.

[357]In a conflict originated under the protection of the Sweden-Malaysia BIT the stated alleged the lacking of approbation by competent authorities leads out of the scope of the BIT the investment of the company Gruslin regarding an investment made in securities listed on the Malaysian Stock Exchange. The tribunal highlighted that since the approval of an investment was a regulatory measure considered as a requirement of an investment, missing such a requirement it is not possible to consider a project as an investment. The substantive law considered by the tribunal was the Art. 1 e (i) BIT Sweden-Malaysia. Agreement Between the Government of the Government of the Republic of India and the Government of the Republic of Ghana for the Reciprocal Promotion and Protection of Investments (India-Ghana) [2000] available at http://investmentpolicyhub.unctad.org/IIA/country/79/treaty/1785 accessed 16 September 2015. Source of the decision: Agreement Between the Government of Sweden and the Government of Malaysia Concerning the Mutual Protection of Investments (Sweden-Malaysia) [1979] SÖ 1979:17 available at: http://investmentpolicyhub.unctad.org/IIA/country/202/treaty/2484 accessed 17 September 2015.

3.6.2 Standards of Treatment

3.6.2.1 Expropriation

The development of rules protecting against the expropriation of alien property has a long tradition in IL, as this is the most severe form of interference with property.[358] In addition to the norms considered to be part of customary IL, all contemporary IIAs include specific provisions for expropriations. IIAs often outline the legal fallout of an expropriation for states. In IIL, only investments that are legal objects can be subject to expropriation, and the term investment itself is defined in IIA. Consequently, for an action to be considered an expropriation, it must apply to an investment that was previously defined as such in an IIA.

Since there is no prohibition on expropriation, one of the most relevant issues—after determining whether or not an act constitutes expropriation in the first place—is to test whether it can be considered a legal or a wrongful act. This will have meaningful effects on calculating compensation. Where the expropriation is legal, compensation will not exceed the value of the investment. In *Bernardus Henricus Funnekotter v Zimbabwe*, a case dealing with land expropriation in Zimbabwe, the tribunal clarified that a genuine value has to be calculated in order for compensation to be made. In this context 'genuine value' is used as a synonym for market value.[359] To define the terms under which an expropriation can be legal, most modern investment treaties incorporate the following conditions: the measure must serve a public purpose, the measure must not be arbitrary and discriminatory, and the principles of due process and prompt, adequate, and effective compensation must be satisfied.[360] In practice, the notion of public purpose was used broadly by states to justify expropriations because it allowed them to give a face of legality to otherwise illegal acts. The case *ADC Affiliate Limited and ADC & ADMC Management Limited v Republic of Hungary* placed limits on the notion of public purpose.[361] The tribunal hearing this case stated that

> a treaty requirement for 'public interest' requires some genuine interest of the public. If mere reference to 'public interest' can magically put such interest into existence and therefore satisfy this requirement, then this requirement would be rendered meaningless since the tribunal can imagine no situation where this requirement would not have been met.[362]

The requirement of non-discrimination is considered to be a basic and fundamental part of IL.[363] The requirement of due process originates in the minimum

---

[358] Dolzer and Schreuer (2008), p. 89.

[359] *Bernardus Henricus Funnekotter and Others v Zimbabwe* [2009] Award ARB/05/6 (ICSID) 127 and ff.

[360] United Nations Conference on Trade and Development (2007), p. 47.

[361] *ADC Affiliate Limited and ADC & ADMC Management Limited v Hungary* [2006] Award on Jurisdiction, Merits, and Damages ARB/03/16 (ICSID).

[362] Ibid para 432.

[363] The Tribunal in case *Libyan American Oil Company (LIAMCO) v Libya* stated that it is a well-established rule that a purely discriminatory nationalisation is illegal and wrongful. *Libyan American Oil Company v Libya* [1977] Award 53 ILR 422 (Ad Hoc Tribunal) at 194.

standards of treatment protected under CIL. For Dolzer and Schreuer the association of due process with CIL and FET makes it unclear whether it can even be considered an independent requirement.[364] The requirement of prompt, adequate, and effective compensation originates in the Hull Formula. There the term 'prompt' means compensation without undue delay. The term 'adequate' means that which is equivalent to the market value, and the term 'effective' indicates that payment should be made in readily transferable currency. In the event of an unlawful expropriation, tribunals not only require that payment is effectuated in the fashion agreed upon in the contract but also that measures resulting from the illegal act be reversed and the investor be restored to the position preceding injury.

Previously, the concept of expropriation applied only to cases of direct expropriation, which are relatively easy to determine. Direct expropriation means that the state physically takes the investment. Today, indirect expropriation is the most common form of expropriation. This type of expropriation occurs via the slow erosion of the alien's ownership rights through regulatory measures.[365] Identifying indirect expropriation is difficult for observers because the lines between the licence of states to introduce regulatory policies and expropriation are not always clear.[366] One may reference the wealth of jurisprudence in this area to determine whether an indirect expropriation has taken place. Actions constituting indirect expropriation might include, for instance, disproportionate tax increases,[367] interference with contractual rights,[368] unjustified interference with the management of the investment,[369] and revocation or denial of government permit or licence.[370] Tribunals deliberating whether an indirect expropriation has in fact taken place considered the degree of intensity of interference with the investor's property rights

---

[364]Dolzer and Schreuer (2008), p. 91.

[365]As stated by tribunal *Feldmann v Mexico*: 'Recognising direct expropriation is relatively easy: governmental authorities take over a mine or factory, depriving the investor of all meaningful benefits of ownership an control' *Feldman v Mexico* [2002] Award ARB(AF)/99/1 (ICSID) para 100.

[366]For a broad treatment of indirect expropriation see: United Nations Conference on Trade and Development, World Investment Report 2012 (World Investment Report 2012, 2013) XX.

[367]In the case *Occidental Exploration and Production Company v Republic of Ecuador*, the claimant considers that the disproportioned increment of taxes led to an indirect expropriation. However the tribunal dismissed the expropriation on the ground that the measure did not substantially affect the investment. *Occidental Exploration and Production Company v Ecuador* LCIA Case UN 3467 at para 89. A negative interpretation of the decision led to the affirmation that the tribunal consider that in case that a tax increase substantially affect an investment, it might be considered as indirect expropriation.

[368]*CME Czech Republic B.V. v The Czech Republic* [2003] Award (UNCITRAL) paras 591 ff.

[369]Reisman and Sloane (2004).

[370]In the case between *Goetz and Others v Republic of Burundi*, the ICSID was occupied with a la withdrawal of the certificate of free zone that the company was granted in 1993. This certification gave the investors privileges in tax and customs exemptions. In this case the tribunal considered that the measure constituted a tantamount to expropriation. This was decided with reference to the BIT between Belgium-Luxembourg Economic Union and Burundi. *Antoine Goetz and others v Republic of Burundi* [1995] Award ARB/95/3 (ICSID).

(i.e. the severity of the economic impact and the duration of the measure) and the frustration of the investor's legitimate expectations. Further, these tribunals considered lack of proportionality, transparency, arbitrariness, discrimination, and the purpose of the measure. As these examples make apparent, tribunals focussed on the consequences of the measures rather than the causes leading to them. It appears to be less relevant whether it was the intention of the state to expropriate.[371] The issue of expropriation could increase in relevance in cases where LDCs implement new land redistribution programmes. In certain cases governmental measures have indeed led to expropriation. For example, in Venezuela landholdings were expropriated through a new land distribution programme.[372] A second example is Zimbabwe, where claims arose following a fast-track land reform programme implemented by the government.[373]

3.6.2.2 Prohibition of Arbitrariness and Discrimination

The protection of investors from arbitrary or discriminatory measures is common in IIAs.[374] Language in some treaties may lead to the assumption that the two terms—arbitrariness and discrimination—are used interchangeably, while in other treaties they are not.[375] The prohibition of arbitrariness and discrimination is a standard in IIL. Given the discretion of arbitrators in judging states' activities, these prohibitions are highly significant.

With regard to arbitrariness, tribunals have stated that measures that were not decided upon through a rational decision-making process may be deemed arbitrary.[376] The differences between tribunals in deciding what is considered arbitrary tend to regard how restrictively they interpret the standard and how they construct comparative approaches. Many tribunals have applied the framework used by the International Court of Justice (ICJ) in the famous ELSI case, in which the Court defined arbitrariness as a violation of the rule of law.[377] One example is the case *Genin v*

---

[371] Dolzer and Schreuer (2008), p. 96.

[372] *Vestey Group Ltd v Bolivarian Republic of Venezuela* [2016] Award ARB/06/4 (ICSID).

[373] *Bernardus Henricus Funnekotter and Others v Zimbabwe [2009] Award ARB/05/6 (ICSID).*

[374] Heiskanen (2009), p. 87.

[375] Tribunals have also considered the terms separately. In the case *Azurix v Argentina*, the tribunal stated that: 'The Tribunal agrees with the interpretation of the Claimant that a measure needs only to be arbitrary to constitute a breach of the BIT.' [. . .] 'The Tribunal is required to consider the ordinary meaning of the terms used in the BIT under Article 31 of the Vienna Convention.' *Azurix Corporation v Argentina* [2006] Award ARB/01/12 (ICSID) para 391.

[376] *LG&E Energy Corporation and others v Argentina* [2006] Decision on Liability ARB/02/1 (ICSID) para 158.

[377] In this case the ICJ stated that arbitrariness is not so much something opposed to a rule of law, as something opposed to the rule of law. . . .It is a wilful disregard of due process of law, an act which shocks, or at least surprises, a sense of judicial propriety. *Elettronica Sicula SpA (ELSI), United States v Italy* [1989] Judgment GL No 76 (ICJ) 15.

Estonia,[378] where the tribunal had to decide whether the withdrawal of a banking licence could be considered arbitrary. The tribunal decided that since it was not made in bad faith, did not violate due process, and did not constitute an extreme insufficiency of action, the measure could not be considered arbitrary. In the case *Azurix v Argentina*, the tribunal took the approach of integrating diverse definitions of expropriation and comparing these with the facts in question.[379] This led the tribunal to the conclusion that domestic authorities in Argentina took arbitrary actions that damaged the operations of Azurix.[380] In other cases where states argued that the measure taken had a basis in domestic law, tribunals used comparative methods to test whether the state's measure would have been justified under comparable circumstances in other countries. A comparison vis-à-vis other national jurisdictions led the tribunal to rule in favour of Romania when it was sued by Noble Ventures.[381] In other cases tribunals used more creative approaches. For instance, in *LG&E v Argentina,* the tribunal referred to 'apparent' measures mentioned in the bilateral investment treaty (BIT) to define what it considered arbitrary.[382]

Discrimination can occur based on nationality, race, religion, political affiliation, and minority status. By testing a discriminatory measure through the lens of this principle, judges do not have to consider elements of domestic law, as they do in determining the existence of an investment. An act considered discriminatory under IIL can be perfectly legitimate under domestic law.[383] In most cases discrimination occurs based on nationality—which is included under National Treatment and Most Favoured Nation provisions—and the violation of international standards as in the case *Lauder v The Czech Republic*.[384] In deciding whether discrimination based on nationality has occurred, tribunals applied comparative methods focussing on the nationality of investors and on the economic sector in question.[385] After a tribunal has deemed a measure to be discriminatory, there is an

---

[378] *Genin and others v Estonia* [2001] Award ARB/99/2 (ICSID) para 371.

[379] *Azurix Corporation v Argentina [2006] Award ARB/01/12 (ICSID) para 392.*

[380] Ibid.

[381] *Noble Ventures Incorporated v Romania* [2005] Award ARB/01/11 (ICSID).

[382] In *LG&E Energy Corporation and others v Argentina [2006] Decision on Liability ARB/02/1 (ICSID) at para 158* the tribunal described the measures constitutive of a discriminatory measure.

[383] Nadakavukaren (2013), p. 272.

[384] One of the most prominent cases dealing with violation of international standards: *Ronald Lauder v The Czech Republic* [2001] Final Award 9 UNCITRAL Rep 66 (UNCITRAL) Ver en el parrafo 20 y 9 ICSID Reports 66.

[385] The tribunals have applied comparative approaches with different levels of specification or deepness. In the case *Saluka Investments v The Czech Republic* the tribunal did not need a deep analysis to decide on the issue of discrimination. In the cases *Occidental v Ecuador* and *Enron v Argentina* the tribunals compares the treatment of other investors in the same economic sector and whether there had been ‚any capricious, irrational of absurd differentiation' respectively. *Saluka Investments BV v Czech Republic* [2006] Partial Award 210 (PCA) at paras 313 f. *Occidental Exploration and Production Company v Ecuador* [2004] Final Award UN3467 (LCIA) para 12 CREO and *Enron Corporation and Ponderosa Assets, L.P v The Argentine Republic* [2005] Decision on Jurisdiction ARB/01/3 (ICSID) at para 282.

additional issue that has to be dealt with. This regards the effects of the measure and the intention of the measure. While the intention of the measure appeared to be of secondary consideration in *Siemens v Argentina*,[386] in *GL&E v Argentina* the tribunal treated both elements—intention and effects—in the same way.[387]

We have shown that tribunals applied diverse methods to establish whether a violation of this standard of protection has occurred. Such diverse and unexpected approaches bring a degree of legal uncertainty for investors.[388]

3.6.2.3 Fair and Equitable Treatment

FET is one of the most extensive standards included in IIAs. This standard protects investors against serious instances of arbitrary, discriminatory, or abusive conduct by host states.[389] FET is an absolute standard of treatment, the meaning of which must be considered in the terms of the agreement it is contained within. FET has a dual function because prior to the investment, FET sets the legal basis that makes investment possible but also limits the subsequent protection in case of future disputes.[390] Nevertheless, the standard of FET was included in the framework of IIAs in order to fill the gaps that more specific standards could not cover. This means that its specific operationalisation varies depending on the gap it fills in any given case. FET is used extensively, and while in some cases it has contributed to investment protection, it has posed new risks in others. These risks arise from the specific wording of the clauses; in determining the appropriate threshold for liability, it is necessary to balance investment protection with competing state policies. Moreover, tribunals have not been consistent in determining when an infringement of FET occurs. By definition, this standard sets out the obligation for host states to treat foreign investors 'fairly' and 'justly'. The meaning of these concepts varies due to the nature of the standard of flexible interpretation. In most cases it will also vary depending on the context and the motives behind the introduction of the measure.[391]

The nature of FET as an absolute standard of treatment means that parties have to define the scope of its protection. This definition then provides a reference point if a dispute should arise. Due to the fact that FET provides a common touchstone of interpretation, the essence of the standard will not be subject to change in the future.

---

[386]The tribunal stated at para 321 that 'intent; is not essential to determine whether a measure is discriminatory. See: *Siemens AG v Argentina* [2007] Award and Separate Opinion ARB/02/8 (ICSID).

[387]*LG&E Energy Corporation and others v Argentina [2006] Decision on Liability ARB/02/1 (ICSID)at para 146* The tribunal stated that a measure is discriminatory if it is intended or if it has discriminatory effects.

[388]For similar see the conclusion of: Kriebaum (2013 forthcoming) 17 http://papers.ssrn.com/sol3/papers.cfm?abstract_id=2268927 accessed 13. 05. 2014.

[389]Nadakavukaren (2013), p. 272.

[390]Dolzer (2005), pp. 87, 103.

[391]Griebel (2008), p. 70.

The application of the standard protects investors from discrimination. However, the application of FET has been dominated by friction in IIL. While in some cases tribunals decided that the norms included in IIAs do not require more protection than the minimum standards of protection in IL,[392] others ruled that FET constitutes an autonomous standard of IIL,[393] while others still determined that an infringement of FET can be decided by analogy or by basing the reasoning on preliminary decisions. Describing measures that can be considered a violation of FET, tribunals have used phrases such as 'unjust or arbitrary',[394] 'wilful neglect of duty',[395] 'arbitrary, grossly, unfair, unjust or idiosyncratic, discriminatory and exposes the claimant to sectorial or racial prejudice, or involves a lack of due process leading to an outcome which offends judicial property.'[396] The literature has also made an attempt to clarify what exactly constitutes FET. A lack of FET may refer to a variety of governmental actions affecting investments for which more specific rules would be unsuitable. These actions, as stated in the literature, include failing to protect the investor's legitimate expectations, failing to act transparently, acting arbitrarily or discriminatorily, denying access to justice or procedural due process, or acting in bad faith.[397] Many tribunals have affirmed that FET should be considered in an international context, and not only in a framework of domestic law. This means that an international investment receiving the same treatment as national investment may also be considered a violation of FET.[398]

The fact that FET is a broad standard of protection leads one to expect that it will continue to change and take new forms in conjunction with changes to investment activities and state measures. An interesting aspect of the development of FET is that through its expansive interpretation and the legal uncertainty surrounding it, the standard has become even more indeterminate. Further, the potential to strike an adequate balance between private and public interests has become even more difficult.[399] As a result, IIL must deliver stability and predictability in decisions and indirectly promote more investment while also contributing to a desirable climate of cross-border investment.

---

[392]*Occidental Exploration and Production Co. v Republic of Ecuador* LCIA Case No. UN3467. *Siemens AG v Agentine Republic* CSID Case No. ARB/02/8, *Tecmed v Mexico* ARB(AF)/00/2; *Genin and others v Estonia [*2001*] Award ARB/99/2 (ICSID) at para 367.*

[393]*Técnicas Medioambientales Tecmed SA v Mexico* [2003] Award ARB(AF)/00/2 (ICSID) at para 360.

[394]*S.D. Myers, Inc. (Claimant) v Government of Canada (Respondent)* [2000] First Partial Award 40 ILM 1408 at para 263 that refers to art. 1105 of the IIAs which content the protection of FET.

[395]*Genin and others v Estonia [*2001*] Award ARB/99/2 (ICSID) para 367* refers to art. II(3)(a) oft he BIT that refers tot he „fair and equitable' treatment the state shall guarantee.

[396]*Salini Costruttori S.p.A. v Jordan* [2007] Decision on Jurisdiction ARB/02/13 (ICSID) para 198.

[397]For an examination of all these elements see: United Nations Conference on Trade and Development, *Fair and Equitable Treatment* (United Nations 2012) 1; Salacuse (2010), pp. 205 until 243.

[398]*Genin and others v Estonia [*2001*] Award ARB/99/2 (ICSID) para 17*; *CME Czech Republic B.V. v The Czech Republic [*2003*] Award (UNCITRAL) para 9.*

[399]Salacuse (2010), p. 222.

3.6.2.4 Full Protection and Security

Full protection and security is a standard of protection in IIAs and also in CIL. This was recognised in many awards affirming that states are liable for failing to protect foreigners.[400] It is an absolute standard of protection that is almost always included in IIAs. It protects the foreign investor against third party interference, including by states and individuals. The state guarantees to protect the investor from industrial action by employees or civil disturbances, and pledges to refrain from threatening behaviour towards the investor.[401] This standard protects investors against the invasion of the premises of their investment, as well as against infringements of their rights through laws and regulations of the host states. States are not allowed to use their armed forces to harm foreign investors, and the state shall protect the property of the investor from violence if this could be anticipated. Physical security includes an obligation of the state to prevent external forces affecting the investment's physical integrity.[402] Where the investor is a natural person, guarantees might be provided against injury, harassment, or threat. This also includes a guarantee that investments won't be damaged, which extends to protection against physical violence and harassment. One classic example is the case *Wena Hotels v Egypt,* in which Egypt was deemed liable because state employees seized the hotel while police authorities, who were aware of the seizure, did not act to protect the investor before or after the invasive action.[403] In another case, *AAPL v Sri Lanka,* it was claimed that security forces had destroyed the infrastructure of a counter-insurgency operation. The tribunal stated that the actions of the security forces had been excessive and infringed the standard of protection against physical violence and harassment.[404]

Even though the name of the standard indicates 'full' protection, there is consensus among legal scholars that it does not provide absolute protection.[405] The ICJ and numerous arbitration tribunals decided that if the state uses all possible resources to avoid damages for the investor and they nevertheless occur, the state may not be

[400] Schreuer (2010), p. 1; Reinisch (2009), p. 131.

[401] See footnote: 238 in Chap. 2.

[402] Nadakavukaren (2013), p. 311.

[403] *Wena Hotels Limited v Arab Republic of Egypt* [2002] Decision on Annulment ARB/98/4 (ICSID) For a comment of the case see: Ursula Kriebaum, 'Wena v Egypt Case' Max Planck Encyclopedia of Public International Law http://opil.ouplaw.com/view/10.1093/law:epil/9780199231690/law-9780199231690-e1784?rskey=JSZ16c&result=3&prd=EPIL accessed 14 April 2011.

[404] *Asian Agricultural Products Limited v Sri Lanka* [1990] Award ARB/87/3 (ICSID) para 45 ff.

[405] Dolzer and Stevens (1995), p. 61; *Elettronica Sicula SpA (ELSI), United States v Italy [1989] Judgment GL No 76 (ICJ) at para 108*; *Técnicas Medioambientales Tecmed SA v Mexico [2003] Award ARB(AF)/00/2 (ICSID) at para 177*. See also the case *Elettronica Sicula SpA (ELSI), United States v Italy [1989] Judgment GL No 76 (ICJ)* at para 111 where the tribunal explains the scope of the full protection and security.

considered liable.[406] The *ELSI* case before the ICJ is of note here.[407] In this claim against Italy, workers occupied a factory building for a long period of time. The tribunal agreed that the building was occupied for what constituted a long period of time, and that this could result in negative effects for the investor. However, the tribunal did not find the state liable for this.[408] The existence of legal protection in addition to physical protection was also considered in an ICSID case, *Azurix v Argentina*. The tribunal affirmed that the infringement of legal protection also constituted an infringement of the standard of full protection and security.[409] A further extension of the notion of full protection and security could be problematic.

3.6.2.5 Umbrella Clauses

Umbrella clauses are provisions that guarantee the observance of obligations assumed by the host state vis-à-vis the foreign investor in the framework of IIAs.[410] Their aim is to determine which acts constitute a violation of IIAs.[411] Umbrella clauses were developed to make diplomatic protection broadly available even if CIL had not been infringed.[412] It is not the aim of umbrella clauses to transform the contractual relationship between investor and state; instead, they seek to link the investment contract to the IIA. In this sense the source of the obligation is in the contract and granted by the umbrella clause through the protection mechanisms encompassed in IIAs.[413] The crucial aspect is to determine whether, if the state breaches the investment contract, it also breaches the IIA.

---

[406] *Asian Agricultural Products Limited v Sri Lanka [*1990*] Award ARB/87/3 (ICSID) at para 51.* In the ELSI case A Chamber of the ICJ estated that 'The reference in Article V of the provision of 'constant protection an security' cannot be constructed as the giving of a warranty that property shall never in any circumstances be occupied or disturbe.' *Elettronica Sicula SpA (ELSI), United States v Italy [*1989*] Judgment GL No 76 (ICJ) at para 108.*

[407] *Elettronica Sicula SpA (ELSI), United States v Italy [*1989*] Judgment GL No 76 (ICJ).*

[408] Ibid.

[409] *Azurix Corporation v Argentina [*2006*] Award ARB/01/12 (ICSID) at para 336.*

[410] Ibid. See also: Dolzer and von Walter (2007), p. 99.

[411] As manner of example the Article II(2)(c) United States-Argentina BIT reads: 'Each party shall observe any obligation it may have entered into with regard to investments'. See also: Dolzer and Schreuer (2008), p. 153. The 2008 German BIT Model also estates in Art. 7(2): 'Each contracting State shall fulfil any other obligation it may have entered into with regard to investments in its territory by investors of the other Contracting State'. Treaty with Argentina concerning the reciprocal encouragement and protection of investment (USA-Argentina) [1991] available at http://2001-2009.state.gov/documents/organization/43475.pdf accessed 9 July 2016.

[412] We recommend the following contributions that lead with the invention en evolution of umbrella clauses. German Model Treaty -2008 [2008] available at http://www.italaw.com/sites/default/files/archive/ita1025.pdf accessed 9 July 2016; Sinclar (2004), pp. 411, 416.

[413] Katia (2008) stated: 'the effect of the umbrella clause is not to transform the obligation which is relied upon into something else; the content of the obligation is unaffected, as is its proper law'.

While the scope of application of umbrella clauses does not appear limited from a substantive point of view, it does in practice. Tribunals have been far from unanimous and consistent in their decisions in this regard. In some cases tribunals have opted for a restrictive interpretation of umbrella clauses, while others have opted for an expansive interpretation. These divergent decisions, their meaning, and impact on understanding of umbrella clauses will be explained in the next paragraphs.

Restrictive interpretation means that tribunals build arguments that weaken the import of umbrella clauses in order to avoid interference with traditional expectation under IL.[414] In these cases tribunals acknowledge similarities between breach of international contracts and breach of IIAs.[415] The decision in *SGS v Pakistan*[416] changed the traditional view which held that IL only applies in cases arising from contracts that were signed by states in their capacity as IL subjects.[417] In the aforementioned case the tribunal had to decide whether the breach of the investment contract between a Swiss company and Pakistan translated to a breach of the Swiss-Pakistani BIT.[418] The tribunal concluded that an umbrella clause does not elevate all contractual claims to treaty claims.[419] Moreover, the tribunal was of the view that the umbrella clause in the Swiss-Pakistani BIT failed to explicitly specify that breaches of the investment contract should be considered a breach of IL.[420] The tribunal in *Joy Mining v Egypt* also followed a restrictive approach.[421] Here the tribunal had to settle a dispute over bank guarantees for equipment at a desert mining site. The tribunal was of the view that bank guarantees were 'somewhat

[414] *CMS Gas Transmission Company v Argentina* [2007] Decision on Application for Annulment ARB/01/8 (ICSID) at para 95 (c).

[415] Potts (2011), pp. 1005, 1012.

[416] Ibid.

[417] I.e. the decision of the Serbian Loan case the ICJ stated: 'any contract which is not a contract between States in their capacity as subjects of international law is based on the municipal law of some country'.

[418] Specifically, the Swiss-Pakistan BIT's umbrella clause read: 'Either Contracting Party shall constantly guarantee the observance of commitments it has entered into with respect to the investments of the investors of the other Contracting Party'.

[419] The decision of the tribunal read as following:

'A treaty interpreter must of course seek to give effect to the object and purpose projected by that Article and by the BIT as a whole. That object and purpose must be ascertained, in the first instance, from the text itself of Article 11 and the rest of the BIT.174 Applying these familiar norms of customary international law on treaty interpretation, we do not find a convincing basis for accepting the Claimant's contention that Article 11 of the BIT has had the effect of entitling a Contracting Party's investor, like SGS, in the face of a valid forum selection contract clause, to 'elevate' its claims grounded solely in a contract with another Contracting Party, like the PSI Agreement, to claims grounded on the BIT, and accordingly to bring such contract claims to this Tribunal for resolution and decision.' *SGS Société Générale de Surveillance SA v Pakistan* [2003] Decision on Objections of Jurisdiction ARB/01/13 (ICSID) at para 165.

[420] Ibid.

[421] Ibid.

simpler' (with regard to previous cases) since they are inherently commercial activities (and not subject to expropriation). Ergo, there were no grounds to consider it as an investment-related issue. Even though the bank guarantees were associated with the investment in dispute, the tribunal did not consider the matter to be an investment-related dispute.[422]

El Paso v Argentina concerned the removal of fundamental rights and safeguards from investors in the Argentine energy sector.[423] The tribunal took an even narrower approach by stating that one must differentiate between the state as a sovereign and a merchant entity.[424] The case *Hamester v Ghana* is also notable for its approach to umbrella clauses.[425] In this case, involving a German company that had entered into a joint venture with a public Ghanaian corporation, the tribunal had to determine the scope of the umbrella clause. The tribunal saw no reasons under IL to apply the umbrella clause because the issue only concerned the breach of an investment contract.[426] The tribunal also extended its opinion, arguing that the umbrella clause was too weak to 'transform' the breach into IL.[427]

Contrary to the aforementioned approach, other tribunals have interpreted umbrella clauses to have an extensive scope. In these cases contractual breach may actually lead to treaty breach. *SGS v Philippines*'s tribunal concluded that the umbrella clause transforms all claims arising from the relationship between foreign investor and the host state.[428] In *CMS v Argentina* the foreign investor claimed not only contractual but also treaty breach.[429] Here the tribunal ruled that not all breaches of contract result in a treaty breach.[430] It also determined that only breaches of enumerated treaty rights and obligations or violations of specifically protected contract rights would trigger the BIT's protections.[431] In *Noble v Romania* the tribunal left open the possibility that

---

[422] *Joy Mining Machinery Limited v Arab Republic of Egypt* [2004] Award on Jurisdiction ARB/03/11 (ICSID).

[423] Ibid.

[424] *El Paso Energy International Company v Argentina* [2006] Decision on Jurisdiction ARB/03/15 (ICSID), 'it is necessary to distinguish the State as merchant from the State as sovereign'. Tribunal that also have followed this approach is: ibid: 'The Tribunal fully shares the view that ordinary commercial breaches of a contract are not the same as Treaty breaches'.

[425] *Sempra Energy International v Argentine Republic* [2007] Award ARB/02/16 (ICSID) at para 310.

[426] *Gustav F W Hamester GmbH & Co KG v Ghana* [2010] Award ARB/07/24 (ICSID).

[427] Ibid: 'In these circumstances, the contractual commitments of Cocobod, being a separate entity from the State, cannot be considered as elevated – and transformed in nature – by Article 9(2) of the BIT, into treaty commitments of the State itself. It follows that a violation by Cocobod – if such a violation had been found – could not have constituted a violation of the BIT.

[428] Ibid. The tribunal stated that: '[Umbrella clause] makes it a breach of the BIT for the host State to fail to observe binding commitments, including contractual commitments, which it has assumed with regard to specific investments'.

[429] *SGS Société Générale de Surveillance SA v Philippines* [2004] Decision on Objections to Jurisdiction and Separate Declaration ARB/02/6 (ICSID) ara para 128.

[430] *CMS Gas Transmission Company v Argentina* [2005] Award ARB/01/8 (ICSID).

[431] Ibid.

umbrella clauses might elevate breaches of contract to breaches of BITs.[432] In *BIVAC v Paraguay* the tribunal had to decide whether the umbrella clause encompassed in the BIT or the forum selection clause included in the investment contract applies.[433] On the one hand it was apparent to the tribunal that allocating jurisdiction to national courts (as stated in the forum selection clause) would create some advantages for the host state. On the other hand the umbrella clause imposed a requirement that the host state alone was required to honour its contractual obligation. To resolve this issue, the tribunal suggested that the host country must ensure that the domestic courts are equipped and willing to resolve any disputes arising from the contract.[434]

3.6.2.6 Access to Justice, Fair Procedure, and the Denial of Justice

One reason why parties enter into IIAs is to bypass the domestic court system of the host country. This is not the case with regard to the standards of access to justice, fair procedure, and denial of justice. These three standards of protection are mainly designed for instances requiring action from the domestic legal system or for exceptional cases where these standards need to be applied in international arbitration procedures. They guarantee the rights of parties to bring a claim before a domestic court, to be treated fairly throughout the case, and to obtain a judicial decision at the end of the case. Depending on the wording of the IIA, these standards can also be applied during the arbitration process.[435]

These standards indicate the guarantees given by the host state to administer justice at the domestic level so that foreign investors may exercise their substantive rights, which must comply with the minimum international standards.[436] They protect the investor against procedural irregularities.[437] If procedural irregularities do occur, the state is deemed responsible and the investor can initiate a claim at arbitration. This procedure does not review the domestic decision because the object and subject of the cases, as well as the applicable law, differ. Rather than conducting a review of the domestic decision, the tribunal will decide whether the state's action could be considered a wrongful act. The case law shows that a denial of justice is carried out when states use their power in an unjust way, refuse to entertain a case, delay the procedure, or misuse the law.[438] There are two distinct

[432]ibid.

[433]*Noble Ventures Incorporated v Romania [2005] Award ARB/01/11 (ICSID) 61 ff.*

[434]*Bureau Veritas, Inspection, Valuation, Assessment and Control BIVAC B.V. v The Republic of Paraguay* [2009] Award ARB/07/9 (ICSID).

[435]Ibid, regarding the denial of justice in paras 128 ff. See also: *Waste Management, Inc. v United Mexican States* [2004] Award ARB(AF)/00/3 (ICSID) paras 118 et seqq.

[436]As it was considered in *Loewen v USA* and Dolzer and Schreuer (2008), p. 163.

[437]*Loewen Group Incorporated and Loewen (Raymond L.) v United States* [2004] Decision on Respondent's Request for a Supplementary Decision ARB(AF)/98/3 (ICSID) para 121.

[438]Ibid.

possible scenarios: the tribunal might commit an error that brings about a wrongful and unjust decision, or the tribunal might act in a wrongful way.[439] A judgment that is grossly and inordinately unjust is the most important situation in which this standard applies. In these cases an international tribunal might consider denial of justice to arise from the partiality of the national judge and the decision may be annulled. International tribunals are relevant to proving whether the national tribunal has acted in bad faith.[440] The main limitation of the protection offered by this standard is that the protection of public officers, for instance, might prevent the initiation of lawsuits against the state.[441]

3.6.2.7 The Preservation of Rights

The preservation of rights standard refers to the guarantee given by the host state to foreign investors that the investment environment shall prevail in the host country. In giving a guarantee of this kind, the host country has a duty not to diminish the rights and privileges the investor enjoyed when the investment was initially undertaken.

3.6.2.8 National Treatment

The national treatment (NT) principle prevents a host state from differentiating between foreign and national investors when enacting and applying its rules and regulations. NT thus brings about a situation in which foreign investors can expect at least the same level of treatment as nationals. This standard has two implications. The first is that investors are usually permitted to operate in the host country under better conditions than nationals. The second implication is that after the investor has entered into the host country, foreign investors are conferred the same advantages and privileges enjoyed by nationals. This standard commonly applies with some exceptions that allow the host state to discriminate between foreign investors, e.g. in activities in which the economic conditions between foreign and national investors are not the same.[442] The national treatment standard does not prohibit the host state from introducing policy measures that affect investors—it only stipulates that foreign investors must be treated in the same way as national investors. For this

---

[439]The procedural irregularities played an important role in *Loewen v USA*. The tribunal considered that domestic institutions were disgraceful and that domestic judge failed at protecting the interests of the investor. Sornarajah (2010), p. 354.

[440]*Loewen Group Incorporated and Loewen (Raymond L.) v United States [2004] Decision on Respondent's Request for a Supplementary Decision ARB(AF)/98/3 (ICSID) para 53.*

[441]For an analysis on the state immunity in the cases of access to justice, denial of justice in IIL see: ILC (2001).

[442]Franceso Francioni (2010).

reason, treaties also include other standards of protection that shield the investor from harsh measures.

The application of this standard in case law leads to a comparative approach. It requires the claimant to prove differential treatment from national investors. To do this, the first step is to test whether both investors are comparable with regards to their economic activity. Tribunals, however, have applied different tests to establish to what extent economic activities are identical. For example, in the case *Marvin Feldman v Mexico* the tribunal interpreted 'in like circumstances' to refer to the same business in a narrow sense. The tribunal limited the application of the approach to firms that 'resell/export cigarettes' but not to firms that manufacture them.[443] In another case in which Ecuador was sued, the tribunal referred to local producers in a much more general way.[444]

To verify a violation of the NT principle tribunals test whether differential treatment has occurred and whether the circumstances for such treatment were justifiable or not. If differential treatment has in fact taken place, further questions arise over whether the treatment was *de jure* or *de facto*. In this sense the tribunal is required to determine whether the measure is discriminatory from a purely legal viewpoint or whether its effects can be considered discriminatory in practice.[445] Some tribunals have stated that the production of some effects is not sufficient for treatment to be considered differential. The tribunal in the case *GAMI v Mexico* asserted that an incidental differentiation resulting from misguided policy decisions is not sufficient to demonstrate differential treatment.[446]

The next question concerns the justification for this treatment. To do this, states are required to substantially justify the introduction of new measures. Hearing cases like these, tribunals have demonstrated that the comparative test based on 'like circumstances' or 'similar situations' is not sufficient to demonstrate the breach of this standard.[447] Policies that are conceived in pursuit of public interest and rationally implemented can be successful before a tribunal if they can be considered lawful under IL.[448]

---

[443] *MTD Equity Sdn Bhd and MTD Chile SA v Chile* [2004] Award ARB/01/7 (ICSID) paras 119 ff.

[444] *Feldman v Mexico [2002] Award ARB(AF)/99/1 (ICSID) para 23.*

[445] *Occidental Exploration and Production Company v Ecuador [2004] Final Award UN3467 (LCIA) para 173.*

[446] *Feldman v Mexico [2002] Award ARB(AF)/99/1 (ICSID) at para 171.*

[447] *Occidental Exploration and Production Company v Ecuador [2004] Final Award UN3467 (LCIA) at para 73.*

[448] *ADF Group Incorporated v United States* [2003] Award ARB(AF)/00/1 (ICSID) paras 61 ff.

3.6.3 Who Can Violate the Investors' Property Rights?

Primarily, IIL protects investments from hostile actions of the state. States have the capacity to directly or indirectly infringe on investors' property rights due to their power to affect investors' economic activity. States directly infringe on the right to property when investments are negatively affected through the exercise of their power. This can come about through unfair and inequitable treatment, by denying access to justice, or through arbitrary or discriminatory measures. Furthermore, states are held responsible for not acting when other legal subjects violate an investors' right to property. The section on full protection and security already outlined when a state can be held liable. Although standards of protection will be explored further in a subsequent section, the obligation of full protection and security merits examination here.

3.6.4 Legal Capacity in Proceedings Before International Investment Tribunals

The capacity of aliens to access the judicial system of the host country has historically been a topic of discussion in IL.[449] Access to justice as understood in customary IL presupposes that the legal subject that has suffered damages must be given the opportunity to obtain a reparation of damages before a tribunal or a judicial agency. If this is not allowed, a 'denial of justice' takes place leading to international responsibility. However, access to diplomatic protection is conditional on the exhaustion of domestic remedies. In the past it was common that after having exhausted domestic remedies without success, diplomatic protection could be used to protect the interests of investors. Access to justice as presupposed in customary IL is thus limited to the courts of the host state. It covers neither access to international justice nor to third states' courts.[450]

The benefit of IIL is that it offers natural and juridical legal subjects direct access to international tribunals without the need to exhaust domestic remedies.[451] In disputes between private persons and investors, the domestic jurisdiction of the host country applies. In most cases the ICSID Convention and IIAs frame the *ius standi* for accessing the IIL regime. This regime applies in disputes between a contracting state and a 'national of another contracting state' which are understood to be natural and juridical persons.[452] Due to the design of IIAs it is not possible for legal persons other than investors to initiate a claim. Thus in most cases states may only act as the respondent.

---

[449] See Sect. 3.6.

[450] *International Thunderbird Gaming Corporation v Mexico* [2006] Award 136 (UNCITRAL) at para 177.

[451] Griebel (2008), p. 6.

[452] Convention on the Settlement of Investment Disputes Between States and Nationals of Other States [1965] 17 UST 1270 TIAS 6090 575 UNTS 159 art 25.

3.6.5 Enforcing the Right to Property in Investment Law

IIL guarantees foreign investors access to international arbitral tribunals without the requirement of exhausting remedies at the domestic level. The ICJ has elucidated that since the delegation of jurisdiction is made through IIAs, the exhaustion of national remedies does not apply as long as the parties agree to it.[453] IIAs create a legal relationship between investors and host states, and in most cases investors are the only parties authorised to initiate arbitration proceedings. Adjudication in IIL is gaining more and more importance on the one hand due to the number of cases being brought and on the other hand because of the high amounts of these claims. It is difficult to estimate the number of cases in IIL because of the confidentiality governing some procedures. However, the data provided by UNCTAD gives us some idea. It appears that most procedures were initiated in 2012. Fifty-eight new cases were initiated, with more than 50 per cent involving developing or transition economies. Most of these cases were initiated by investors from developed countries.[454] In 2012 the number of known cases reached a total of 514, involving 95 states worldwide.[455] Considering these numbers, as well as the fact that claims have reached amounts exceeding 1.5 billion dollars,[456] the importance of adjudicating institutions in IIL becomes indisputable.

There are different dispute resolution forums in IIL. Examples include: the International Chamber of Commerce, the London Court of International Arbitration, the Stockholm Chamber of Commerce, the Permanent Court of Arbitration, the United Nations Commission on International Trade Law (UNCITRAL), and the International Centre for Settlement and Investment Disputes (ICSID). The International Court of Justice presides over some cases, although this occurs in exceptional circumstances only. A specific institution is given the jurisdiction to preside over investment cases by the parties involved through their consent, which is the cornerstone of these treaties (*rationae voluntatis*).[457] The most relevant forum, in terms of the number of cases decided, is the ICSID. From a total of 58 cases in 2012, thirty-eight were initiated before the ICSID,[458] followed by seven cases at UNCITRAL, five cases at the Stockholm Chamber of Commerce, and one case each at the International Chamber of Commerce and the Cairo Regional Centre for International Commercial Arbitration.[459]

---

[453]Ibid 52.

[454]Ibid.

[455]United Nations Conference on Trade and Development, *Recent Developments in Investor-State Dispute Settlement* (UNCTAD, N 1 May 2013, 2013) 1.

[456]Ibid 3.

[457]United Nations Conference on Trade and Development, World Investment Report 2014 (World Investment Report 2014, 2015) xiii.

[458]*Philip Morris Brands Sàrl, Philip Morris Products S.A. and Abal Hermanos S.A. v La República Oriental del Uruguay* [2013] Decision on Jurisdiction ARB/10/7 (ICSID) at fn 1.

[459]United Nations Conference on Trade and Development, Recent Developments in Investor-State Dispute Settlement (UNCTAD, N 1 May 2013, 2013b) 2.

The most important feature of all these institutions is that their decisions are binding and the remedies offered by the tribunals are effective.[460] Most of these arbitration forums are linked to, or are correctly subordinated to, the New York Convention.[461] The advantages offered by the New York Convention include the ease of enforcing awards and its high number of signatories. Since the Convention extends its jurisdiction to the territory of all signatory states, it is possible to enforce a decision abroad if it cannot be enforced in the territory of the state involved. The further implication of this is that awards of tribunals are subject to the limitations and reasons for non-enforcement of awards contained in Article V of the New York Convention. The exemptions contemplated in Article V are contained in an exhaustive list that includes substantial and formal procedural errors leading to the decision not being enforced.[462] In cases of non-compliance, the New York Convention makes it possible to execute sanctions against states, including the freezing of bank accounts or intervening in economic activities of the state so that its interests can be harmed.

ICSID is the leading international arbitration institution devoted to investor-state dispute settlement. The delegation of competence in investment disputes is made *inter partes* through IIAs. Its goal is to promote economic development through the creation of a favourable investment climate.[463] It provides facilities for the conciliation and arbitration of international investment disputes. From an institutional point of view, ICSID contributes to the structure of proceedings and to 'organisational' aspects. Even though the parties select their own arbitrators, ICSID assigns delegates who partake in the procedure as legal secretaries. ICSID manages all finances in the procedure. Its procedures are self-contained and cannot be intervened upon by any other legal body. Domestic courts cannot set aside ICSID decisions. Its jurisdiction is tested through the requirements of Article 25 of the ICSID Convention and specific requirements established by the parties in IIAs. These requirements focus on *ratione personae*, *ratione materiae*, *ratione voluntatis,* and *rationae temporis*.

---

[460]Some examples are: ibid; Convention on the Settlement of Investment Disputes Between States and Nationals of Other States [1965] 17 UST 1270 TIAS 6090 575 UNTS 159 para 53 ff. UNICTRAL Arbitration Rules Art. 32(2), United Nations General Assembly Resolution 65/22 UNCITRAL Arbitration Rules as Revised in 2010 [1976] A/RES/31/98 15 ILM 701 art 32(2); United Nations Commission on International Trade Law, *UNCITRAL Model Law on International Commercial Arbitration* (United Nations 1985) art 28(6).

[461]I.e. Art. 19 ICSID Convention states that arbitration procedure shall be held only in States that are parties to the 1958 UN Convention on the Recognition and Enforcement of Foreign Arbitral Awards. The London Court of International Arbitration. Arbitration Rules [1998] available at http://www.lcia.org/Dispute_Resolution_Services/LCIA_Arbitration_Rules.aspx accessed on 14 July 2015 art 26.9.

[462]Convention on the Settlement of Investment Disputes Between States and Nationals of Other States [1965] 17 UST 1270 TIAS 6090 575 UNTS 159.

[463]General Assembly (UN) Convention on the Recognition and Enforcement of Foreign Arbitral Awards [1968] 330 UNTS 38; 21 UST 2517; 7 ILM 1046 art V.

ICSID decisions are binding; they can only be reviewed in a limited set of circumstances.[464] The pecuniary obligations arising from ICSID decisions must be enforced in the same manner as the final decision of a local court.[465] The binding nature of ICSID awards originates in the concept of arbitration expressed in terms of *res judicata*.[466] The strength of awards is facilitated by an *inter partes* agreement that includes a commitment to permit the bypassing of national jurisdiction and a recognition of the power of tribunals to produce binding decisions. Article 53 (1) of the ICSID Convention reiterates the binding nature of ICSID awards. These awards are exhaustive and self-contained in their nature, and cannot be appealed. This aspect differentiates the ICSID Convention from the rules of the International Criminal Court (ICC) or UNCITRAL, which are potentially subject to domestic review.[467] Additionally, ICSID awards are exclusive, meaning that dissatisfied parties cannot take the same case to another forum.[468]

In most cases awards granting the reparation of damages to investors are supplemented by pecuniary compensation.[469] Restitution is not excluded as a remedy but is frequently left out due to the nature of the cases. Needless to say this does not mean that a tribunal may not apply a different form of reparation that exists in IL, such as restitution, compensation, or satisfaction. However, the strong enforcement obligation attached to ICSID decisions only extends to the pecuniary obligations imposed by the award. In the case of restitution or any other performance, the award is subject to recognition by the state.[470] The award must describe the findings of the tribunal as well as the reasons why certain measures are considered to infringe an agreement. Article 54 obliges signatory states to recognise the award, to enforce it, and to designate competent authorities to the Centre for these purposes. States shall inform the ICSID authorities of the modalities of execution at the domestic level.[471] Commentators have observed that ICSID provisions on sovereignty do not apply at the stage of recognition.[472] Recognition is a waiver of immunity in proceedings in order to have the award enforced. As stated by Schreuer and others, 'the award applies irrespective of any immunity from execution.'[473]

[464]Convention on the Settlement of Investment Disputes Between States and Nationals of Other States [1965] 17 UST 1270 TIAS 6090 575 UNTS 159 at preamble.

[465]Ibid.

[466]Ibid.

[467]See: Schreuer et al. (2009) art 53 at para 10.

[468]Parra (1997), p. 287.

[469]Schreuer et al. (2009) art 53.

[470]Convention on the Settlement of Investment Disputes Between States and Nationals of Other States [1965] 17 UST 1270 TIAS 6090 575 UNTS 159 art 54.

[471]Schreuer et al. (2009) art 54 at paras 46.

[472]Convention on the Settlement of Investment Disputes Between States and Nationals of Other States [1965] 17 UST 1270 TIAS 6090 575 UNTS 159 art 54(3).

[473]Ibid.

In addition to arbitration procedures, the ICSID Convention also contains rules on the interpretation, revision and annulment of awards.[474] The broad acceptance of both the ICSID and New York Conventions in Africa leads us to believe that the enforcement of arbitration awards would be guaranteed in most cases. This general assessment might be impacted by challenges to final judgements allowed under domestic laws and the invocation of state immunity from execution.[475] Additionally, the Cotonou Agreement,[476] which has been ratified by most African states, contains some specific clauses relevant to investment.[477]

3.7 Human Rights Protection Vis-à-Vis International Investment Law Protection

In the previous segment we analysed the mechanisms available in IL to protect the rights to property and food. HRL and IIL contribute to the whole of IL by not only achieving the specific goals of the legal subjects they protect, but also by achieving more general goals, e.g. international cooperation, development, and the maintenance and improvement of public order. HRL and IIL, as regimes of IL, are dynamic areas that constantly interact. Their relationship can be defined as symbiotic: in some of its features HRL benefits from IIL and *vice versa*. While this connection and cross-fertilisation is neglected by the literature to some extent, the fragmentation of both systems has been rationalised and is now taken for granted. This leads us to analyse similarities between the two jurisdictions as well as some of their differences in order to assess the extent to which affected third parties can enforce their rights. At the same time we will elucidate to what extent IL as a whole, and also the two regimes of IIL and HRL, are able to incentivise economic actors to achieve compliance.

3.7.1 Common Aspects of the Two Regimes

We have seen throughout the previous segments that both the HRL and IIL regimes are based on the power of individuals to act against the state and make it accountable for the violation of protected rights. These are, for our purposes, the right to

[474]For a comment of the annulement procedures see: Schreuer et al. (2009) Art 54 at para 48.

[475]The comparative analysis written by Baetens highlights some weaknesses of ICSID and New York Convention enforcement systems. See: Dolzer and Schreuer (2008), p. 271.

[476]Baetens (2013), p. 9.

[477]Partnership Agreement between the members of the African, Caribbean and Pacific Group of States of the one part, and the European Community and its Member States, of the other part [2000] OJ L 287.

food and the right to property, the latter being protected by IIL and HRL. In many cases they are essential rights that are also found in national legislation, for instance the right to access to justice, fair treatment, the right to food, the right to property, and the right to not be discriminated against. Both regimes commit to protecting these rights by limiting states' sovereignty. The state is seen as an entity that may exercise its power to interfere with the right to property and food of its legal subjects and aliens on its territory.[478] However, the point of view in HRL considering states to be the only potential violators of HRs is expanding to also consider private actors as potential HRs violators.[479]

At a very general level IIL and HRL offer identical protection through CIL. Such cases arise when foreign investments are protected by neither IIAs nor by investment contracts. At this level the interaction between the two regimes is more tangible due to the application of indistinguishable norms. At a more specific level the same principles apply, but due to jurisdictional specificities their scope will differ. For example, this could mean that what is considered discrimination might not be the same in the two regimes. This would also apply to other principles such as fair treatment and the access to justice.

There is the possibility of punishing the state in the two regimes, not only when it breaches contractual promises but also when third parties perturb the enjoyment of protected rights. In HRL the duty to protect extends to third parties. Article 2.1 of the CESCR states that the state party is obliged to take necessary steps to progressively achieve the full realisation of the rights recognised in the Covenant. The CESCR has also made this interpretation, stating in General Comment 12, paragraph 15 that 'the obligation to protect requires measures by states to ensure that enterprises or individuals do no deprive individuals of their access to adequate food.'[480] The ACHR reads article 14 of the Banjul Charter to oblige states to protect the right to property, which includes an obligation to protect against the interference of third parties. It states:

> Its [the state's] obligations to protect obliges it to prevent the violation of any individual's right to housing by any other individual or non-state actors like landlords, property developers, and land owners, and where such infringements occur, it should act to preclude further deprivations as well as guaranteeing access to legal remedies.[481]

With regard to the right to food, the ACHR in the *Ogoni* case declared that:

> The Government's treatment to the Ogonis has violated all three minimum duties of the right to food. The government has destroyed food sources through its security forces and State Oil Company; has allowed private oil companies to destroy food sources; and, through terror has created significant obstacles to Ogoni communities trying to feed themselves.[482]

---

[478] Schrijveri (1999), p. 65.

[479] Ibid.

[480] CESCR, *Right to Adequate Food* (General Comment No 12 (1999) E/C12/1999/5 1999).

[481] *Social and Economic Rights Action Centre and Centre for Economic and Social Rights v Nigeria [*2001*] Commission communication 155/96 (ACHPR) at para 61.*

[482] Ibid.

In IIL, states are obliged to offer full protection and security to investments, which in practical terms is no different from the obligation to 'protect' in HRL. In both regimes this absolute standard of protection is limited to the capacity of the state to guarantee protection.[483] It is possible in both regimes to hold actors accountable when their economic activities cause damage to third parties. In both regimes judicial action does not try to intervene in the state-investor relationship but holds the state accountable for the violation of an extra-contractual obligation.[484] Victims are not holders of a contractual right but do hold an extra-contractual right that has been infringed upon as a result of the performance of the contract. The active legitimation of the victim of a violation of the right to property and food does not arise from the contract producing damages (state-investor) but emanates from the failed obligation of a state to fulfil pre-established commitments. The technical reason why individuals cannot intervene in the investor-state contractual relationship is their lack of *locus standi*. Ergo, by invoking the nullity of the contract at the international level (as they could also do at the national level), they can invoke states' responsibility for their violation of HRs.[485] This affects the allocation of responsibility and, therefore, the potential remedies, as the state and the victims are the only parties in the procedure.

In addition to these similarities between the two regimes, IIL and HRL have demonstrated their capacity to interact. This might be seen as natural since both regimes are part of the whole of IL. As a result, cross-fertilisation can be observed in the jurisprudence where investment adjudicators share ideas and methods developed by HRs adjudicators. This inter-jurisdictional communication is mostly found in awards in the areas of expropriation, the exhaustion of local remedies, the allocation of costs, and the assessment of damages.[486] This communication goes back to the possibility given by invoking Article 31.3(c) of the VCLT, which permits the interpretation of legal norms in the context of any relevant rule of IL applicable in the relations between parties. Let us consider some examples. In the case of expropriation, HRL has provided IIL jurisprudential tools to develop concepts applicable in the area of treaty interpretation. In the famous case *Lauder v Czech Republic* the investment

[483]See for example the case between *Zaire v the United States* in which the tribunal held that: 'the obligation incumbent on the [host state] is an obligation of vigilance, in the sense that [the host state] shall take all measures necessary to ensure the full enjoyment of protection and security of its investments and should not be permitted to invoke its own legislation to detract from any such obligation.,,' American Manufacturing and Trading, Inc. v. Republic of Zaire [1997] Case ARB/93/I (ICSID) at 28. Another tribunal in the case between *AAPL v Sri Lanka* stated that: 'absolute obligation which guarantees that no damages will be suffered, in the sense that any violation thereof creates automatically a 'strict liability' on behalf of the host State' *Asian Agricultural Products Limited v Sri Lanka [*1990*] Award ARB/87/3 (ICSID) at 545.*

[484]It was the main difference we stated after having analysed in the first part the legal mechanisms for third-party enforcement national law vis-à-vis IL.

[485]See Sect. 1.5 of this research project.

[486]For an elaborated approach about all the approaches see: Human Rights Council, Business and Human Rights: Mapping International Standards of Responsibility and Accountability for Corporate Acts (Report of the Special Representative of the Secretary-General (SRSG) on the Issue of Human Rights and Transnational Corporations and Other Business Enterprises [2007] A/HRC/4/035, 2007).

tribunal adopted the method of the ECHR to frame the measures constituting formal and *de facto* expropriations.[487] *Tecmed v Mexico* was the first case in which the tribunal not only looked at decisions of the IACHR[488] but also of the ECtHR.[489] Having looked at the former, the tribunal determined that expropriation had taken place.[490] Then the latter's' jurisprudence was used twice. First it was used to rely on the standard of proportionality regarding the public interest in expropriation, and second to develop an applicable rule on regulatory expropriation.[491] In the case *Saipem S.p.A v Bangladesh* the tribunal again relied on the ECtHR to determine whether certain measures constituted expropriation.[492]

HRL and IIL have the ability to interact. Furthermore, there is a complementary relationship between the two regimes in which HRL provides IIL with substantive principles and norms to decide specific issues. Even though both jurisdictions are considered 'close', 'independent wholes', or 'self-contained' regimes, their interaction and interdependence, as demonstrated in the jurisprudence, shows that in fact they cannot be described as entirely independent legal bodies.[493] Completely closed or self-contained systems would lack the sort of mechanisms described above allowing engagement between the two regimes. Were they completely autonomous, cross-fertilisation that currently exists would not be possible. Needless to say we recognise their interconnectedness to be limited, otherwise one could not talk about the fragmentation of IL. Even though the two regimes interact, the links between them are not the result of HRs contributing protected rights to IIL. These rights were picked up by tribunals rather than brought into IIL in an integrative approach, isolated from the further development of investment jurisprudence. The benefits to HRL are marginal.

Both systems protect the right to property as a mechanism for promoting development.[494] As a result it would be difficult to find either HRs or investment

---

[487]In this case the UNCITRAL tribunal used the case *Mellacher v. Austria* to define 'formal' and 'de facto' expropriation of private property. *Mellacher et al. v Austria* [1989] Judgement app nos 10522/83, 11011/84 and 11070/84 (ECtHR).

[488]*Matos e Silva, LDA., and others v Portugal* [1996] Application 15777/89 (ECtHR) at paras 77 ff.

[489]Ibid.

[490]*Técnicas Medioambientales Tecmed SA v Mexico [*2003*] Award ARB(AF)/00/2 (ICSID) para 117.*

[491]Ibid.

[492]*Mellacher et al. v Austria [*1989*] Judgement app nos 10522/83, 11011/84 and 11070/84 (ECtHR) see at para 30.*

[493]See i.e. Dupuy (1999), p. 791 and see also Fry (2007–2008), p. 77, Part III.

[494]Most of the BTIs include the specific goal of promote economic development, i.e.: the US BITs Model states: "*Recognizing* that agreement on the treatment to be accorded such investment will stimulate the flow of private capital and the economic development of the Parties" The Hague Convention (I) for the Pacific Settlement of International of International Disputes [1908] 1 Bevans 577; 2 AJIL Supp. 43. Moreover the General Comment No. 14, the Committee emphasises that it is particularly incumbent on all those in a position to assist, to provide "international assistance and cooperation, especially economic and technical" to enable developing countries to fulfil their core obligations. U.S. Model Bilateral Investment Treaty [2004] Available at http://www.state.gov/documents/organization/117601.pdf accessed 17 November 2013.

treaties from which the idea of the promotion of development is absent. The protection of the right to property is probably reflected in all HRs instruments and constitutes an element of the definition of investment in IIL. Even though it has been interpreted broadly, one condition for classifying an economic activity as investment is its contribution to development in the host country.[495] Development has an indisputable economic component, which, if implemented jointly with appropriate redistributive polices, improves the host state's welfare. HRL and IIL both promote the increase of social welfare and the reduction of poverty. In this regard the shared economic components of both legal regimes have to be considered necessary elements in fulfilling the requirements of legal policies and, therefore, as an important contribution to the achievement of major IL goals.

As outlined in the UDHR, HRL considers poverty to be harmful to the well-being of human beings.[496] In order to combat poverty IOs have created different programs ranging from humanitarian aid to technological development in feeds and plantations. The goal of eliminating extreme poverty and hunger has become even more pressing in the last two decades. This goal is the first item on the UN's millennium agenda, and the one with the most severe time constraints. The UN's Millennium Development Goals aim to reduce poverty by promoting development.[497] This agenda might also interpreted as a response to the UN's legal obligation to reduce poverty and promote development. The most recent draft outcome document of the UN summit for the adoption of the post-2015 development agenda also highlights the determination to end poverty and hunger in all forms and dimensions, and to ensure that all human beings can fulfil their potential in dignity and equality and in a healthy environment.[498]

It is not possible to separate one human right from another when seeking to achieve HRL goals. This is known as the principle of indivisibility.[499] HRs are

---

[495]Schreuer and others refer that: "the only possible indication of an objective meaning that can be gleaned from the Convention is contained in the Preamble's first sentence, which speaks of 'the need for international co-operation for economic development and the role of private international investment therein'. This declared purpose of the Convention is confirmed by the Report of the Executive Directors which points out that the Convention was 'prompted by the desire to strengthen the partnership between countries in the cause of economic development.' Therefore it may be argued that the Convention's object and purpose indicate that there should be some positive impact on development". Schreuer et al. (2009), p. 125.

[496]The Preamble to the UDHR and the common Preamble to the ICCPR and the ICESCR emphasise the importance of "freedom from . . . want".

[497]In addition to the reduction of poverty, the reduction of HIV/AIDS and they provide universal primary education were topics also included in the agenda. General Assembly (UN) Universal Declaration of Human Rights [1948] UNGA Res 217A (III), UN Doc A/810. Seminal report: United Nations Millennium Project (2005).

[498]Human Rights Council A/69/L.85 General Assembly Draft outcome document of the United Nations summit for the adoption of the post-2015 development agenda [2015] 2.

[499]This based on the principle that human rights are interdependent and interrelated. Each one contributes to the realisation of a person's human dignity through the satisfaction of his or her developmental, physical, psychological and spiritual needs. The fulfilment of one right often

interconnected: guaranteeing compliance with the protection of one specific right requires and often brings about the support of other rights. As a result, upholding the rights to work, housing, a standard of living, food, and a peoples' right to dispose freely of their natural resources is considered necessary to bringing about a reduction in levels of poverty and underdevelopment. These rights can most likely be achieved in an environment where property rights are well defined and protected.[500] Considering this, FDI could contribute to this agenda by encouraging growth in the domestic economies of LDCs. Different IOs, especially the World Bank, also follow this model and try to promote development through market liberalisation and the promotion of FDI similar to that of developed nations.

We saw in a previous section that the structure developed by IIL creates a unique institutional environment in LDCs. This institutional environment seeks to boost the confidence of investors who would otherwise be reluctant to invest in LDCs due to the associated political risk. In this regard the impact of investments on HRL is visible in the fact that they reduce the costs for states to fulfil their HRs obligations. This means that states can provide a higher level of security to foreign investors and as a result can expect the creation of jobs, the transfer of know-how, the development of local infrastructure, and the facilitation of access to markets. The fact that FDI can contribute to the realisation of the HRs agenda shows the close relationship and interdependence of the two regimes. If both regimes work in unison, FDI and HRs in LDCs will improve. Most IIAs state in their preamble the necessity of signing such instruments due to their ability to promote and stimulate the prosperity of the contracting states.[501] Additionally, there is a broadly accepted view that FDI can play a positive role in promoting economic development, reducing poverty, and improving local standards.

Notwithstanding the commonalities of the two regimes, fundamental differences remain between them. On the one hand these regimes play a decisive role in protecting investors who perpetuate rights violations in the context of LSLIs, while on the other hand they fail to enforce the rights of affected third parties. We will compare the two regimes in the next part and focus on the following aspects: standards of treatment, systems of adjudication, standards of protection,

---

depends, wholly or in part, upon the fulfilment of others. For instance, fulfilment of the right to health may depend, in certain circumstances, on fulfilment of the right to development, to education or to information. See: Pillay (2012), p. 12.

[500]Ibid.

[501]See i.e. BIT between Germany and Benin states: Recognizing that encouragement and contractual protection of such investments are likely to stimulate private economic initiative and to increase the prosperity.; US Model 2004([...] Recognizing that agreement on the treatment to be accorded such investment will stimulate the flow of private capital and the economic development of the parties. Ruggie, 'Obstacles to Justice and Redress for Victims of Corporate Human Rights Abuse', 311 http://ohrh.law.ox.ac.uk/about/opbp/ accessed 17 July 2015. BIT Canada Model states: "Recognizing that the promotion and the protection of investments of investors of one Party in the territory of the other Party will be conducive to the stimulation of mutually beneficial business activity, to the development of economic cooperation between them and to the promotion of sustainable development." U.S. Model Bilateral Investment Treaty [2012] available at http://www.state.gov/r/pa/prs/ps/2012/04/188199.htm accessed on 12 July 2015.

awards, and remedies. Our goal remains to elucidate to what extent affected individuals can make use of IL to obtain remedies if they are affected by an investor-state relationship.

3.7.2 Standards of Treatment

Standards of treatment refer to substantive norms that create a basis for defining the level of protection guaranteed under each regime. We have seen that even though the two regimes offer similar standards, these standards have proliferated more in IIL than in HRL. Although some of these standards have the same background, their level of specification has limited their scope. HRs treaties are of a more general nature than those found in IIL. This could be related to the fact that IIL only protects one right, whereas HRL protects many rights that are governed by the same standards of treatment. It might also result from the negotiation costs of the treaties. As most HRs treaties are multilateral, it is assumed that their negotiation costs are higher than the costs of negotiating IIAs, which are usually bilateral. A clear illustration of this statement is the long history of disputes during the negotiation of HRs treaties where states attempted to set out aspects of the regulation of the right to property. While in the framework of HRL parties have been willing to internalise higher negotiation costs (which are probably balanced by *ex post* flexibility mechanisms), negotiation costs in IIL treaty negotiations increase more quickly, becoming prohibitive and leading to the frustration of multilateral treaties.

Even though the standards of treatment in the two regimes are mostly vague and allow some room for interpretation, the level of protection offered by standards of treatment in HRL allows signatory states to breach obligations more easily than in IIL. We have shown that the legal authority given to states to limit rights over time can be used to justify rights violations. Some HRs can be derogated from in certain circumstances, including for the maintenance of public order, public morality, public health, the promotion of democracy, and freedom.[502] On the one hand such parameters impose limits on regulatory power. On the other hand their level of precision is too low to accurately make an *ex ante* consideration. Let us consider the following examples. Article 6 of the Banjul Charter states that freedom should not be curtailed except for reasons and conditions previously laid down by law. Article 8 of the Banjul Charter contains provisions regarding the freedom of religion and conscience stating that no one may be submitted to measures restricting their exercise. Both clauses establish subjective standards that can be restricted by states through the enactment of domestic legislation. In well-functioning states upholding the rule of law it can be expected that parliamentary controls will prevent the misuse of such laws.

[502]Model BIT Canada available [2004] at http://www.italaw.com/documents/Canadian2004-FIPA-model-en.pdf accessed 14 September 2014.

The African domestic legal order, however, does not seem to be able to prevent the misuse of such international provisions. One improvement can be seen in the case *Media Rights Agenda and Others v Nigeria*, in which the African Commission stated that international HRs standards must prevail over contradictory national laws.[503] This statement creates a new limitation for states imposing restrictive policies. It is, however, less authoritative than the limitations established through stabilisation clauses in IIL. Such clauses provide that any alteration in the legal system affecting the activity of the investor can be sanctioned.[504] The use of such clause is widespreah across industries and regions of the world. It is not be the case of LSLI, nonetheless.[505] This ensures that the state will bear the excessive cost of implementing new policies, e.g. in environmental and social areas. Even though such clauses vary in their scope, they can include protection against fiscal and non-fiscal laws with respect to an investment for the duration of a project. This protection against the financial implications of changes in the law is ensured by requiring compensation or adjustments to the deal concluded between the investor and the state to compensate the investor where changes to the law occur.

States can differentiate in their treatment of nationals and aliens if they do not contravene obligations previously entered into.[506] The less favourable treatment that aliens tend to be confronted with is balanced by the standards of protection in IIL and HRL, which apply as customary international norms. Since different forms of treatment do not necessarily constitute a discriminatory measure, legal subjects are only discriminated against when they have been treated less favourably than other legal subjects operating under the same conditions. In IIL this protection is also guaranteed through the most favoured nation standard, which balances the rights of all foreign investors, and through the standard of national treatment, which guarantees foreign investors at least the same treatment as national investors. The

---

[503]Dumberry and Dumas-Aubin (2012), p. 349.

[504]A complete research project on Stabilization Clauses and Human Rights has been developed by Andrea Shember as legal advisor to the United Nations Special Representative to the Secretary-General for Busniess and Human Rights. See: Andrea Shemberg, 'Stabilization Clauses and Human Rights' A research project conducted for IFC and the United Nations Special Representative of the Secretary-General on Business and Human Rights http://www.ifc.org/wps/wcm/connect/9feb5b00488555eab8c4fa6a6515bb18/Stabilization%2BPaper.pdf?MOD=AJPERES accessed 23. March 2017. Our investigation does not further develop the concept of stabilization clauses since they are not included in LSLI analysed in Sect. 2.2.3.

[505]See Sect. 2.2 of this paper that analyses LSLI.

[506]The Iran-US Claims Tribunal recognized in the case of *Amoco v. Iran*, that Iran owed compensation for expropriation measures, and also acknowledged the rule of non-discrimination. It stated that: "discrimination is widely held as prohibited by customary international law in the field of expropriation," although the Tribunal found no discrimination in this case (para. 140). Most prominently also *Methanex Corporation v. United States of America* para. 179: "But as a matter of general international law, a non-discriminatory regulation for a public purpose, which is enacted in accordance with due process and, which affects, inter alias, a foreign investor or investment is not deemed expropriatory and compensatory".

legal security in HRL is weaker than in IIL, even where protection could be drawn from the standard of discrimination.

We might also consider the protection offered by IIL through the standard of full protection and security.[507] Similar protection is found in HRL under the notion of non-interference of third parties, which is also part of the duty of protection.[508] States have the duty to guarantee that third parties do not interfere with the rights of other protected subjects. In this case the state might create incentives at the national level so that one individual does not infringe the right to property or food of another individual. In IIL this standard also obliges states to ensure that third parties do not negatively impact an investor's assets. As we already explained, this does not mean that the state will always be responsible for damages to an investment caused by third parties. It means that the state has to use all existing mechanisms to prevent third parties from damaging the investment. In this case investors once again enjoy a higher level of protection than in HRL. This is because states guarantee investors full protection and security so that third parties cannot violate their rights, but if investors violate the rights of third parties, affected individuals or groups of individuals cannot make use of IIL to enforce their rights. Consequently, this does not incentivise investors to avoid violating the HRs of third parties. Additionally, as investors also have access to the HRL adjudication system, they are doubly protected.

The standard of treatment in cases of expropriation is a sensitive issue in the two regimes. The reasons for this are the importance of the right to property for economic activity, as well as the contribution of the right to property to human dignity. Following this point of view, the African Commission has pursued a broad approach that considers HRs to be interdependent. In its approach it has pointed out the impossibility of enjoying the best state of mental and physical health as a result of the violation of the right to property.[509]

Neither HRL nor IIL prohibit expropriation. The relevant issue is rather to determine whether the restriction of the right to property fulfils the requirements of legality, the remedies, and the possibility to enforce judicial decisions. Determining the legality of an expropriation affects the calculation of compensation. In this sense the following two elements are relevant: (1) whether it serves a public purpose and (2) whether the measure is arbitrary or discriminatory.[510] In practice these two requirements rarely provide grounds for declaring an expropriation unlawful. It has been affirmed by some tribunals that states have 'extensive discretion' in determining what public purpose means.[511] Other tribunals have, to the contrary, ruled that 'some genuine interest of the

---

[507] See Sect. 3.5.4 of this study.

[508] See: *Media Rights Agenda v Nigeria* [2000] Communication 224/98 (ACHPR) para 36.

[509] Human Rights Council, *Report of the Special Representative of the Secretary-General on the issue of human rights and transnational corporations and other business enterprises, John Ruggie* Business and human rights: mapping international standards of responsibility and accountability for corporate acts* (A/HRC/4/35, 2011) para 10.

[510] De Schutter (2010), p. 379 ff.

[511] *Social and Economic Rights Action Centre and Centre for Economic and Social Rights v Nigeria [2001] Commission communication 155/96 (ACHPR) at para. 60.*

public' is necessary to consider a measure to fall within the framework of public purpose.[512] Two additional elements also require consideration: (3) whether the procedure of expropriation satisfies the principles of due process,[513] and (4) whether the expropriation is accompanied by prompt, adequate, and effective compensation.

In the case of HRL it is also necessary to demonstrate that the measure fulfils the requirement of proportionality. This might include consideration of compensation, which in the case of HRL must be 'reasonable'. In IIL it must fulfil requirement number 4. Compensation in HRL has a different purpose than in IIL. In HRL the adjudicator must consider whether the compensation is reasonable at the domestic level, taking into account the public purpose. Under the regime of IIL the full value of the expropriated property must be paid on the basis of the market price of the investment in order for compensation of land expropriation to be legitimate.[514] If an expropriation is deemed unlawful, tribunals not only require the payment to be made in the way the parties agreed to in the contract, but also that the principle of restitution in *integrum* is observed. This principle means that as a consequence of the illegal act, measures must be taken to re-establish the situation prior to the occurrence of the unlawful act.

In addition to norms protecting against direct expropriation, IIAs include norms protecting against indirect expropriation, or the slow erosion of an alien's ownership rights through regulatory measures. Indirect expropriation is of great importance due to the effects that regulatory measures can have on investments. It is not a new issue but its importance has grown in recent years. Tribunals take more cases as states realise they cannot simply expropriate directly. The problem with indirect expropriation is that its scope can be very broad. The jurisprudence, however, has helped to address this problem by developing a 'catalogue' of specific measures that are recognised as indirect expropriation. The fact that there is no established mechanism to differentiate between non-compensable and compensable indirect expropriation creates some uncertainty about the procedures used in determining what constitutes indirect expropriation.[515] Some guarantees against indirect

---

[512]In *ADC Affiliate Limited and ADC & ADMC Management Limited v Hungary [*2006*] Award on Jurisdiction, Merits, and Damages ARB/03/16 (ICSID) at paras 429* and also in the case *British Petroleum Exploration Company (Lybia) v Lybia*. In these cases the tribunal encountered that the governmental measure was made for purely extraneous political reasons" and therefore it was declared unlawful.

[513]*Amoco International Finance Corporation v Islamic Republic of Iran* Partial Award Treaty of Amity and Customary International Law Requirements for Compensation for Expropriation; Calculation of Compensation International Legal Materials American Society of International Law, International Materials 27 1314–1405 (Iran-United States Claims Tribunal) in which the tribunal stated that: "The legal procedure must be of a nature to grant an affected investor a reasonable chance within a reasonable time to claim its legitimate rights an have its claims heard".

[514]*ADC Affiliate Limited and ADC & ADMC Management Limited v Hungary [*2006*] Award on Jurisdiction, Merits, and Damages ARB/03/16 (ICSID)*.

[515]In the case between *Compañía del Desarrollo de Santa Elena S.A v Costa Rica* the tribunals for example stated that environmental purpose had no bearing on issue of compensation. The tribunal considered the case a direct expropriation and not as indirect taking. In this case the tribunal made clear that although an expropriation can be justified with environmental issues, it does not affect

expropriation are offered by stabilisation clauses, which are complemented by umbrella clauses. Although there are some critical aspects of expropriation, IIL has shown its ability to solve cases and offer relatively guaranteed legal remedies when investments are affected by states' activities.

Apart from these standards, there are no comparable standards of protection or treatment at a more specific level shared by HRL and investment law in the African system. In this sense the level of specificity of standards offered in IIL through IIAs is considered much higher than the level of specificity in HRs treaties. This higher level of specificity in IIL translates to more legal security for investors. IIL has progressively developed and complemented standards of treatment that apply in HRL. This is the case with fair and equitable treatment, which is regularly interpreted and applied in IIL.[516]

When HRs complaints are initiated, HRL must interpret contracts to clarify their scope. The reasons for the level of specificity in HRs treaties are the broad catalogue of rights that are protected under HRL, as well as the negotiation costs associated with discussing highly specific matters in multilateral treaties. This contrasts with the narrower scope of investment law, which only covers the protection of investments, generally speaking. The fact that HRs treaties provide less specific information about the standards of protection necessitates the use of additional resources for parties to know *ex ante* to what extent and under what conditions their rights may or may not be protected. This work is contained in the comments and reports published by different committees, and also in the decisions of tribunals.

3.7.3 Standi

IL does not admit, *prima facie*, natural persons as legal subjects. However, HRL opens this door and makes it possible for the victims of abuses carried out principally by states to enforce the rights contained in HRs treaties. IIL also grants *locus standi* to natural persons. For instance, Article 25 of the ICSID Convention regulates the conditions under which its jurisdiction applies. Its jurisdiction extends to any legal dispute arising between a contracting state and a national of a different contracting state. It is understood that on the date that the parties submit a dispute, the claimant is a natural person of another contracting state other than the state standing as the defendant. The difference between the two regimes is that in IIL the nationality of the individuals who are claimants must be from another contracting

the measure of the compensation. By doing so, the tribunal omitted all explanations regarding the obligations of Costa Rica to preserve the unique Santa Elena ecological site. *Mike Campbell (Pvt) ltd. & 78 Others v Zimbabwe* [2008] Judgement T02/07_JUD (SADC).

[516]Some examples in the case law are: *Compañía del Desarrollo de Santa Elena SA v Costa Rica* [2000] Award ARB/96/1 (ICSID), *Técnicas Medioambientales Tecmed SA v Mexico [2003] Award ARB(AF)/00/2 (ICSID).*

state. Nationality is not a condition for claiming the protection of HRs as they are recognised for all human beings. HRs are part of the framework of humanism rather than the framework of nationalism, as is the case in IIL.

The requirement of exhausting domestic remedies, which is a prerequisite for accessing adjudication in HRL, constitutes a further difference between the two systems. While in HRL all avenues of domestic jurisdiction must be exhausted (with the exception of *ius cogens* issues), in IIL access to IL does not require the existence of a previous domestic judicial decision. In this regard the two systems show their differences and crucial principles. While IIL focuses on the protection of investments, HRL is of broader application and is more directly concerned with fundamental rights and the rule of law. HRL requires the state to create appropriate mechanisms to fulfil its HRs obligations. The exhaustion of local remedies should lead to a situation where states demonstrate the effectiveness of their judicial system by fulfilling the obligations they have undertaken in HRs treaties. In IIL national jurisdictions are excluded. The requirement for victims to exhaust domestic remedies in order to access international HRL dramatically increases the costs of bringing a case. These costs are not limited to the time-consuming nature of bringing multiple cases and appeals, but also extend to potential personal retaliations against those bringing cases. In most cases these costs cannot be internalised. This perhaps answers the question why IIL internationalised so rapidly in Africa, and clarifies why this has not occurred in HRL. Direct access to international courts constitutes a considerable advantage in situations where there are institutional weaknesses at a domestic level affecting the independence of the judicial system. In African HRL the fact that claimants must have recourse to the ACHPR after having exhausted domestic remedies before accessing the Court becomes a disadvantage. The binding character of its decisions increases the relevance of the Court, nonetheless.

African HRL permits states, individuals, groups of individuals, and NGOs to access the administration of justice. This applies either to individuals, groups, or agents acting on behalf of third parties, depending on the nature of the right in question. The member state has to give its approval for nationals to exercise this right, nevertheless. As only five states allow their nationals to access the African Court, its scope is limited. The ECOWAS Court of Justice is an exception to this rule.[517] It permits the natural citizens of ECOWAS member states to access its system of justice. Article 9.4 of the supplementary protocol to the ECOWAS Court of Justice states that the Court can rule on alleged HRs violations that occur in its jurisdiction. The Court has been a pioneer in decisions concerning the human right to education and the prohibition of slavery. As Nigeria was guilty of tolerating the practice of slavery in the past, it was an important decision for the ECOWAS Court of Justice to condemn this practice.[518]

[517]*Loewen Group Incorporated and Loewen (Raymond L.) v United States [*2004*] Decision on Respondent's Request for a Supplementary Decision ARB(AF)/98/3 (ICSID).*

[518]The ECOWAS Court of Justice has already made a number of rulings on human rights issues. In 2008, the Court took a pioneering decision concerning slavery: The State of the Niger was

Access to IIL is narrower than to HRL. Under many IIAs this right is reserved for foreign investors alone. NGOs and nationals of the host state do not have *locus standi* in IIL. The most relevant implication of this is that individuals cannot initiate a legal action against investors under the dispute settlement mechanism of an IIA when the activities of investors produce damages.[519] As analysed in the introductory section, this is one of the fundamental reasons why the structure of contracts in IIL fails to offer relief to third parties. However, the fact that third parties cannot access IIL as a complainant does not mean that these legal subjects cannot take part in arbitration. In some circumstances, IIL does allow third parties to take part in the process (*amici curiae*). As already mentioned, states cannot initiate IIL claims. Under the vast majority of IIAs, arbitral tribunals only have jurisdiction to adjudicate claims brought by investors and not those submitted by states. In addition to this, counterclaims are often not considered. One important exception is India's model BIT allowing the state to counterclaim.[520]

In the specific case of LSLIs the most important and transcendental implication is for cases where investors do not fulfil the commitments they made to the state, and this affects the local population by infringing HRs. Individuals cannot enforce the contract under the IIL regime even though they are directly affected by the breach of the IIA. In this situation, two main difficulties arise. The first is that states cannot initiate investment law cases, and the second is that in LDCs it is possible for the interests of governmental decision makers to be implicated in the investment, leading these decision makers to ignore potential violations of HRs. This complicity between the investor and the political elites creates barriers to the administration of justice and to the ability of NGOs to work freely because of the peril of personal retaliation.

Therefore, even though investors, and often states as their accomplices, infringe HRs, from the point of view of IIL the investment activity seems to be completely

---

convicted having violated the human rights of one of its citizens. While the Court found that Niger was not itself responsible for the discrimination—the plaintiff was subjected to by a non-State actor, namely her former master—the country was found in violation of its international obligations to protect Mrs Hadijatou Mani from slavery under international as well as national law because of its tolerance, passivity, inaction, and abstention with regard to the practice. Niger had to pay reparations in the amount of 10 million CFA francs (more than 20,000 US-Dollar). The judgment has been referred to as historic, because this is one of the first slavery cases ever to be won at the international level. Alter et al. (2013), p. 737. See also: *Hadijatou Mani Koraou v. The Republic of Niger* Merits, Suit No ECW/CCJ/APP/08/08, Judgment No ECW/CCJ/JUD/06/08, IHRL 3115 (ECOWAS 2008), 27th October (ECOWAS).

[519]We do not consider at this point the potential intervention by *amicus curiae* since it is not an intervention *per se* because, although they could have legal interest to participate in the process, their intervention will depend on the parties of the process.

[520]Deutsche UNESCO-Kommission e.V. and Commission française pour l'UNESCO, 'Guide to International Procedures Available in Cases of Human Rights Violations in Africa. The ECOWAS Court of Justice' (*A joint project of the National Commissions for UNESCO of France and Germany*, 2013) http://www.claiminghumanrights.org/ecowas.html accessed 29.07.2015.

legal. This is a problem arising from the conflict of norms between HRL and IIL that goes back to the fragmentation of the law and affects the unity of IL.

We now consider it pertinent to analyse how states can make use of IIL to justify domestic behaviour that aims to protect HRs. Since states usually cannot initiate cases in IIL, as respondents they have at least two possibilities. First, states can argue that the activity performed was necessary in order to fulfil pre-existing HRs obligations. This would be the case if an investor claimed contractual breach because of legislative changes.[521] These allegations might have their legal foundations in constitutional law as well as UN treaties that create the obligation to progressively protect, respect, and remedy HRs at the national level. This argument was supported by the ECHR when it stated that:

> . . .it is clear that, if a State contracts treaty obligations and subsequently concludes another international agreement which disables it from performing its obligations under the first treaty, it will be answerable for any resulting breach of its obligations under the earlier treaty.[522]

The second possibility is that the host state argues that the investor him- or herself committed HRs violations against locals in the context of the investment.[523] Some cases help us to elucidate to what extent such lines of argument could contribute to legalising a states' activities in IIL. The success of states when arguing HRs protection has been low. The Argentina cases are probably the most recent examples dealing with HRs issues. In this regard we consider the cases *CMS*, *Azurix,* and *Siemens*, all of which were against Argentina.[524] The case *Sempra v Argentina* is, up until now, the only case in which the tribunal recognised the complexity of the issues involving HRs protection and investments. However, in its final decision it did not make a finding that there had been HRs violations. A first tribunal did not consider the fact that expropriation had taken place under very unusual circumstances. After Sempra won the case, Argentina introduced an annulment petition that was granted. In this case the *ad hoc* tribunal declared the nullity of the previous decision, however, its decision was not based on the HRs argument made by Argentina but on fact that the original tribunal had exceeded the limitations of its power.[525]

Argentina had failed in all of the other cases when it argued its obligation to protect HRs as a justification for its legislative changes, which brought about a direct or indirect expropriation. However, it is relevant to note that none of the

[521] The most recent examples are the Argentina cases we have referred to throughout his research in which indirect expropriation was claimed due to the legislative measures taken during the economic crisis.

[522] Model Text of the Indian Bilateral Investment Treaty, available at: https://mygov.in/sites/default/files/master_image/Model%20Text%20for%20the%20Indian%20Bilateral%20Investment%20Treaty.pdf accessed 17 August 2015 at para 14.2.

[523] This notion is broadly developed by Subedi in: *Kahn v Germany* Commission Decision 235/56/EEC [1958] Yearbook 2, p 256 para 256 and Dumberry and Dumas-Aubin (2012), pp. 349, 361.

[524] Subedi (2008); *CMS Gas Transmission Company v Argentina [2005] Award ARB/01/8 (ICSID)*; *Azurix Corporation v Argentina [2006] Award ARB/01/12 (ICSID)*.

[525] *Siemens AG v Argentina [2007] Award and Separate Opinion ARB/02/8 (ICSID)*.

tribunals mentioned their lack of competence to deal with issues of HRs violations in investment cases.

In the case *CMS v Argentina* the line of argumentation employed by the host country was that decisions affecting the investment were taken because of a moment of national crisis and therefore Argentina did not consider it possible that investment treaties could take precedence over recognised constitutional rights: 'no investment treaty could prevail as it would be in violation of such constitutionally recognized rights.'[526, 527] In this case the tribunal did not see the correlation between the measure taken by Argentina and the protection of fundamental rights.[528]

In the case *Azurix v Argentina* the argumentation for the expropriation was the protection of local consumers. The host country considered the compatibility between BITs and its HRs obligations. Argentina was of the view that where a conflict arises between BITs and HRs, the decision should be in favour of the state's HRs obligations because the public interest must prevail over the private interest of a company.[529]

In *Siemens v Argentina*, Argentina tried to justify its actions by arguing that it was protecting HRs.[530] The tribunal found that there was no relationship between the measures taken during the crisis and the protection of HRs. These cases show that tribunals tend to be reluctant to consider arguments brought by states with regard to the protection of HRs. Only in one case did the tribunal consider the complexity of the HRs issues (*Sempra v Argentina*), although this was without success, as the tribunal did not agree with the argumentation of the host state that the Argentine crisis led to the collapse of the state.[531] These cases confirm the difficulties—in the framework of IIL—for a state to introduce domestic policies to fulfil obligations arising from non-investment related activities.

It needs to be clarified whether the investor can make use of HRs arguments in investment cases. The legal status of the investor rarely facilitates the invoking of HRs protection, which is only allowed under the European HRs system. Furthermore, since the level of protection offered by IIL is higher than that of HRL, it would be counterproductive for investors to take a case under HRL. One attempt to do so was made in *Biloune v Ghana*,[532] but in this case the UNCITRAL tribunal did not recognise its jurisdiction to preside over cases of HRs violations. This does not mean that it is not possible for investors to appeal on HRs grounds. The legal foundation of such an appeal might be seen in the principle of non-discrimination.

---

[526] *Sempra Energy International v Argentine Republic [*2007*] Award ARB/02/16 (ICSID) at para 332.*

[527] *CMS Gas Transmission Company v Argentina [*2005*] Award ARB/01/8 (ICSID) at para 114.*

[528] The Tribunal stated: "In this case, the Tribunal does not find any such collision. First because the Constitution carefully protects the right to property, just as the treaties on human rights do, and secondly because there is no question of affecting fundamental human rights when considering the issues disputed by the parties." Ibid at paras 114–121. See also: Reinisch (2006), p. 13.

[529] *Azurix Corporation v Argentina [*2006*] Award ARB/01/12 (ICSID) para 254.*

[530] *Siemens AG v Argentina [*2007*] Award and Separate Opinion ARB/02/8 (ICSID).*

[531] *Sempra Energy International v Argentine Republic [*2007*] Award ARB/02/16 (ICSID) para 332.*

[532] *Biloune and Marine Drive Complex Limited v Ghana Investments Centre and Ghana* [1994] Award on Jurisdiction and Liability 95 (UNCITRAL).

In very limited cases third parties can take a case under IIL (*amici curiae*).[533] It should be noted that the intervention of third parties is not free of risk to the case, given the fact that they could lack political or economic independence. However, their participation in cases has been seen as a possibility to provide vital information to the tribunal.[534] Such interventions give the tribunal precise information about the social impact of investments, as well as the legitimacy of both the project and the governmental measure.

Since the revision of ICSID rules, there is no doubt that tribunals accept *amicus curiae*.[535] Before the reform tribunals were reluctant to accept the intervention of third parties in cases. These difficulties were classified in the literature under the substantive and procedural aspects of cases.[536] In the case *Aguas del Tunari v Bolivia*[537] the tribunal considered the acceptance of third party participants to be impossible because the parties did not mutually agree upon the submission, nor did the treaty make any stipulation in this regard. In the view of the tribunal the admittance of a submission from a third party by the tribunal would constitute an excess of its authority. In the cases *Aguas Proviciales de Santa Fe v Argentina*[538] and *Biwater Guaff v Tanzania*[539] the tribunals accepted *amicus curiae* briefs because of the public interest issues in the case. However, even when reference to HRs abuses was consistently made in the second case, the tribunal centred its analysis on arguing that the inclusion of *amicus curiae* briefs occurred for transparency reasons. It stated that the tribunal responds primarily to public interest rather than to HRs considerations.[540]

In cases taken under UNCITRAL, tribunals have accepted the participation of *amicus curiae* as a third party interested in the case based on their substantive elements, namely the right to have access to justice and a fair trial. However, in *Methanex v United States*[541] the participation of *amicus curiae* was also accepted based on public interest. Additionally, the tribunal justified the participation of *amicus*

---

[533]For the cases in which NGOs can intervene as *amici curiae* see above at page 119.

[534]See: Reiner and Schreuer (2009), p. 88, and more concrete about the role of NGOs in international law *Biloune and Marine Drive Complex Limited v Ghana Investments Centre and Ghana [*1994*] Award on Jurisdiction and Liability 95 (UNCITRAL)*. See also: Astrid Epiney, *Die völkerrechtliche Verantwortlichkeit von Staaten für rechtswidriges Verhalten im Zusammenhang mit Aktionen Privater* (1. Aufl. edn, Nomos Verl.-Ges. 1992).

[535]Simmons (2009), p. 31 ff. Dupuy and Vierucci (2008).

[536]Simmons (2009), p. 31 ff.

[537]Convention on the Settlement of Investment Disputes Between States and Nationals of Other States [1965] 17 UST 1270 TIAS 6090 575 UNTS 159 art 37 (2).

[538]*Aguas del Tunari v Bolivia* [2005] Decision on Respondent's Objections to Jurisdiction ARB/02/3 (ICSID).

[539]*Aguas Provinciales de Santa Fe SA and others v Argentina* [2006] Order in Response to a Petition for Participation as Amicus Curiae ARB/03/17 (ICSID).

[540]See: *Biwater Gauff (Tanzania) Ltd v Tanzania* [2008] Award and Concurring and Dissenting Opinion ARB/05/22 (ICSID).

[541]*Biwater Gauff (Tanzania) Ltd v Tanzania* [2006] Procedural Order No 3 ARB/05/22 (ICSID) para 70.

Table 3.1 Access to justice in HRL and IIL in Africa

	Human rights	Int. investment law
Owners (Social delegates or chiefs)	√	X
Foreign investors	√	√
States	√	√ (in some cases)
Third parties	√	X

Source: Prepared by the author

curiae by pointing out that it increased procedural transparency. Since the American Free Trade Commission clarified the application of the principle of non-disputing party participation, a new spectrum of discretionary power for tribunals has been opened. This clarification increases the possibility of affected individuals to access IIL.

Table 3.1 depicts access to justice in HRL and in IIL. It is distributed specifically and applied to the cases relevant for this research.

3.7.4 Enforcement Mechanisms

Enforcement is a key element of every legal system because it leads to the sanctioning of parties that breach an agreement. Enforcement involves monitoring the performance of parties and punishing those who violate the obligations of the contract or agreement.[542] Many different types of enforcement mechanism exist in IL. They differ from regime to regime and also from protected right to protected right. The mechanisms of enforcement are dynamic and need to adapt to specific circumstances at specific moments in time. These two elements were taken into consideration by Born in his attempts to classify the mechanisms of enforcement that are offered in IL and that have proliferated over the last decades.[543] This goes back to the effects that enforcement mechanisms have on the achievement of the goals proposed by each regime. Born (2012) classifies adjudication mechanisms in IL chronologically in terms of first and second generations. The chronology does not represent a hierarchy but corresponds to the time the mechanisms were created. The first generation's scope is broad and covers the classic areas of dispute in IL. This kind of adjudication was established as a result of multilateral negotiations whose role was to promote cooperation between signatory states.[544] The institutions belonging to the first generation were not empowered to hand down effective and enforceable decisions. This means that even though the adjudicator can decide whether a state has breached a previously

[542] *Methanex Corporation v United States* [2001] Decision on *Amici Curiae*, IIC 165 (Ad hoc UNICTRAL).

[543] Cooter and Ulen (2012), p. 92.

[544] To the first generation belongs the group of treaties that emerged at the outset of the twentieth century with the creation of Permanent Court of Arbitration, Permanent Court International Justice and International Court of Justice.

made promise, the enforcement of its decision relies on the state doing so voluntarily. These tribunals have only been used reluctantly by their legal subjects, and their effects have been very limited.[545]

HRs treaties belong to this first generation, which includes the African Commission on HRs. The upholding of HRs depends on the capacity of the state to enforce them, and the progressive realisation of HRs requires states to create national institutions to do so, including judicial institutions. In this regard the question of the enforceability of HRs becomes political, as the creation of the appropriate infrastructure for a state to fulfil its HRs obligations depends on its power and willingness.[546] Consequently, in states with acute problems of corruption and poor governance, HRs agreements entered into by the state are insufficiently enforced. Most of the judicial decisions belonging to this kind of enforcement mechanism are merely reputational. Decisions affirming the violation of a human right by a state could, in theory, lead to some diversion of trade away from that state. Investors that make use of HRL to enforce their rights will also be subjected to this form of enforcement.

Needless to say the improved legal security of IIAs goes far beyond what is offered by first-generation treaties. The second generation arose from a need to adopt a more precise and pragmatic adjudication system that also aimed to increase transparency, impartiality, efficiency, and effectiveness in resolving disputes, with special emphasis on specific areas of trade and investment.[547] The second generation emerged, in most cases, from bilateral relationships; these treaties have compulsory jurisdiction and the power to enforce decisions.[548] It is no surprise that this generation was used much more frequently than the first. This generation does not restrict the application of the first generation of treaties, since the first generation pertains mostly to disputes between states. Instead, it applies *prima facie* in cases where specific issues cannot be answered by the first generation. The first generation complements the second.[549] The ICSID, NAFTA, WTO, and national courts adjudicating claims against foreign states[550] all belong to the second generation. This adjudication mechanism facilitates the resolution of conflicts by applying legal norms instad of utilising diplomatic forums.[551] It creates adequate enforcement mechanisms in cases where not only states but also private legal subjects are involved. In addition, this mechanism frames efficient norms that, if

---

[545] Born (2012), p. 775.

[546] Guzman (2008), p. 51.

[547] Born (2012), pp. 775, 794.

[548] Krennerich (2013), p. 346 ff.

[549] In this form an interaction between national, international and private adjudicators is created. The creation of private adjudicators in forms of tribunals or arbitration institutions leads to a delegation of authority by governments to private actors, or from new private initiatives that are approved by governments and that regulate the behaviour of involved actors. See: Born (2012), pp. 775, 792.

[550] Ibid.

[551] Eyal and Downs (2012).

Table 3.2 Allocation of HRL and IIL enforcement mechanisms in Africa

	Jurisdiction	
	Human rights law	Investment law
First generation	√	
Second generation		√

Source: Prepared by the author

followed, will lead to increased compliance. The ICSID Convention and the UNCITRAL Rules are the most relevant legal instruments in investment disputes between contracting states and investors pursuant to IIAs. The ICSID Convention not only offers a system for settling disputes, it also includes norms for conducting the case and guaranteeing the enforcement of decisions.[552] The mechanisms to enforce ICSID are not only applicable on the basis of voluntary compliance, they also apply in cases where only one party initiates the procedure.[553] ICSID tribunals' decisions are not subject to appeal and are binding for the parties.[554] One of the most important provisions of the ICSID Convention is the obligation for states to recognise the awards of tribunals. The obligations stemming from awards are pecuniary and are enforced and treated as if the award were the final judgment of a court of the state. The obligation to recognise the outcome of the procedure applies to all states that are party to the ICSID Convention.[555]

Table 3.2 shows the allocation of IIL and HRL in the categorisation of enforcement mechanisms based on the approach developed by Born (2012).

3.7.5 *Remedies*

Remedies guarantee the enjoyment of protected rights. The guarantee to a remedy is also considered to be a human right at the international and regional levels.[556] It encompasses, on the one hand, the obligation of states to create adequate facilities for the administration of justice and, on the other hand, it refers to the obligation of states to guarantee the effectiveness of remedies. The Banjul Charter gives every individual the right to appeal to competent national organs against acts violating their fundamental rights guaranteed by conventions, laws, regulations, and customs that are in force.[557] In Article 21 the Banjul Charter refers to 'adequate compensation' if spoliation of the resources of a people has occurred. Article 26 obliges the

[552]Born (2012), pp. 775, 819.

[553]Ibid.

[554]Schreuer et al. (2009) at 6 ff..

[555]Convention on the Settlement of Investment Disputes Between States and Nationals of Other States [1965] 17 UST 1270 TIAS 6090 575 UNTS 159 art 45 (2).

[556]In Art 2.3 ICCPR, Art 9.5 ICCPR Art. 14.6 ICCPR.

[557]Art 2.1 Convention on the Settlement of Investment Disputes Between States and Nationals of Other States [1965] 17 UST 1270 TIAS 6090 575 UNTS 159 Art 53 (1).

state to create 'independent institutions' to guarantee freedom. Neither are there limitations on the kinds of remedies that states can provide, nor on the remedies available in HRs claims. Therefore, an infringement of the right to property—under the two regimes—and the right to food can be remedied through compensation or *restitutio in integrum,* or payment in compensation. Limitations on remedies might arise through arrangements contained in HRs treaties or IIAs.

If an aliens' rights have been violated in the absence of an IIA, CIL and diplomatic protection provide remedies. IL primarily provides remedies where investment rights protected by investment contracts are breached. While payment, as a form of compensation, is by far the most widespread remedy, *restitutio in integrum* was catalogued as taking primacy in Articles 34 and 35 of the Draft Articles on Responsibility of States for International Wrongful Acts (ARSIWA). Regarding cases where expropriation is illegal, the ICJ stated in the *Chorzów* case that:

> The essential principle contained in the actual notion of an illegal act ... is that reparation must, as far as possible, wipe out all the consequences of the illegal act and re-establish the situation, which would in all probability, have existed if that act had not been committed. [558]

This means that in cases where an expropriation has been determined to have taken place, the due compensation can extend to gains that the investor did not receive as a result of the state's measure. In HRL the payment of money is of secondary importance. What is most relevant is the requirement for states, considering states are the greatest potential violators of HRs, to take concrete action to remedy the victim's grievance, but also to eliminate the cause of the violations of HRs. In cases where a *quantum* needs to be defined, Article 14 of the Banjul Charter does not establish an autonomous compensation mechanism. Positive actions, such as special treatment, economic measures, and benefits can also be considered remedies. In the case of IIL it can be affirmed that, in practically all cases,[559] the payment of compensation is the remedy used.

Problems could technically arise between the two regimes regarding their remedies. In HRL, remedies commonly focus on *restitutio in integrum.* Restitution consists of returning objects and returning to the *status quo ante.*[560] In cases of expropriation it consists of transferring ownership back to the previous owner so that the individual or group of individuals can make use of the legal object. In cases where a violation of the right to food has occurred, it is not completely clear whether restitution can compensate for the damage produced, or whether compensation should also be given. In these cases restitution would mean that the state must improve the *status quo* at least to the

[558] African Charter on Human and Peoples' Rights (Banjul Charter) [1986] OAU Doc. CAB/LEG/67/3 rev. 5, 21 I.L.M. 58.

[559] One of the very seldom examples was *Texaco overseas petroleum company and California Asiatic oil company v Libya*. However In this case the restitution could not be performed leading to a payment of compensation. *Factory At Chorzów, Germany v Poland* [1928] Judgment 13 (PCIJ) at para 124.

[560] See i.e.: *Texaco Overseas Petroleum Company & California Asiatic Oil Company v Government of the Libyan Arab Republic* (Award of 19 January 1977) (1978) 17 ILM 1.

level previous to the state introducing the measure. Even though this type of remedy is not forbidden in IIL, given the characteristics of this regime, it may be less appropriate because the investor probably does not have any particular economic interest in the host country. However, if restitution applies and the African Court obliges the state to return the land to the affected local population, yet the land has already been transferred to a third party (investor), it would result in further legal conflicts. Since HRs decisions are not binding in the investment regime, and enforceability in the investment regime is more guaranteed than in HRL, it is expected that the decision taken by the investment tribunal may be contrary to the decision taken by HRs tribunals.

Notwithstanding, both systems have mechanisms that lead to binding decisions; they differ, however, in their power of enforcement. As we have already seen, decisions of the African Court can hardly be enforced effectively. In IIL, arbitration cases lead to binding and enforceable decisions. In the ICSID, signatory states of the ICSID Convention are required to enforce decisions as if they were final decisions at the domestic level. Pecuniary remedies are enforced even without the recognition of the state. In cases where the ICSID Convention does not apply, the New York Convention, which has been ratified almost worldwide, guarantees the enforceability of decisions. The difference between these two forms of enforcement is that the New York Convention contains an exception providing immunity to state activities. Article 55 of the ICSID Convention cannot be construed as a derogation from the law of any contracting state or from applicable rules on state acts that are considered to grant immunity.

Our approach suggests that the binding and enforceable character of arbitration procedures guarantees a higher level of effectiveness to property rights protection in the legal regime of IIL than under the protection of HRL. Even though the recommendations made by HRs organs have authoritative character, they can only bring about a limited number of effective consequences. The same applies to decisions of the African Court, since the effects depend on the 'will' of the states concerned. Due to the fact that the Protocol of the African Charter on Human and Peoples' Rights on the Establishment of the African Court on Human and Peoples' Rights was signed and ratified by only 24 countries (24 countries have signed, but not yet ratified it and five countries have not yet signed or ratified it),[561] the scope of the African Court, as the only judicial institution that can produce binding decisions, is still limited.

The remedies offered in IIL and HRL constitute the most relevant differences between both regimes. The remedies offered in IIL can be seen as the most pertinent incentive for foreign investors to access the protection mechanisms of IIL rather than HRL. The special protection enjoyed by foreign investors, and the possibility of protecting their investment against state and third party interference, reduce both the costs and the political risks of investment incentives (Table 3.3).

[561] Source: CESCR, Substantive Issues Arising in the Implementation of the International Covenant on Economic, Social and Cultural Rights. General Comment 12. The Right to Adequate Food. (E/C12/1999/5, 1999) at para 32.

Table 3.3 Remedies in HRL and IIL enforcement mechanisms

Type of remedy	Regime	
	Human rights law	Investment law
Pecuniary	Not mandatory	Most widely used. A recognition of the tribunal decision is not required to enforce this remedy
Restitutio in integrum	Not mandatory	Can be considered by tribunal but rarely used
Recommendations and Guidelines to improve the situation	Most widely used remedies. However, their implementation is not mandatory	Can be used by tribunals, however, they have to be recognised by states.

Source: Prepared by the author

3.8 Intermediate Result: International Legal Context Leads to Opportunistic Behaviour

We started this chapter by considering IL in its entirety. We briefly analysed the issue of legal fragmentation, which, as stated by the ILC, is a phenomenon associated with globalisation, and has proliferated throughout international legal regimes. The primary causes of this fragmentation are the absence of a general legislative body and the manner in which the law governing the revision and interpretation of treaties has developed. We observed the potential conflict arising from the fact that regimes that belonging to the unity of IL become isolated. We assumed that the effects of LSLIs are consequences of the fragmentation in IL. We were interested in elucidating whether individuals, considered to be affected third parties, have legal remedies to enforce their right to property and their right to food. In order to do so we analysed how national jurisdictions solve similar problems, for instance when legal subjects harm third parties through the performance of a contract.

The cross-jurisdictional and comparative analysis of HRL vis-à-vis IIL contributed to illustrating the different mechanisms of protection of the rights to property and food at the international level. We showed that IL does have legal remedies for third parties who are victims of HRs violations when LSLIs are introduced, however, they are ineffective because the actors involved have asymmetric incentives to comply with the law. This does not mean that states are not willing to comply with HRs treaties in full or all of the time,[562] what it does mean is that states' priorities to comply with pre-established obligations are formed by legal incentives included in treaties. We demonstrated that, in fact, IIL offers a better level of protection of the right to property than HRL. We also showed that even though IIL offers a higher level of protection than HRL, affected individuals cannot

[562]In this same line of argumentation see: African Commission on Human and Peoples' Rights, 'Protocol to the African Charter on Human and Peoples' Rights on the Establishment of the African Court on Human and Peoples' Rights. Legal Instruments' (*ACHPR*, 2013) http://www.achpr.org/instruments/court-establishment/ accessed 29 July 2015; Simmons (2009), pp. 12, 122 ff.

make use of IIL because of jurisdictional restrictions regarding access to the judicial system. Additionally, IIL has a narrower scope than HRL. The sole right protected by IIL is the right to property of foreign investors, compared to the large number of rights HRL protects. This was made evident in the interpretation of the standard of protection in the two regimes. Standards of protection in HRL are more elastic than those in IIL, which make it possible for states to easily legitimate political decisions. The most relevant difference between the two regimes is the fact that IIL offers remedies that are enforceable, while HRL's remedies are, in most cases, prohibitively costly either for victims or for states.

National institutions hold a key role in fulfilling HRs obligations. In this sense HRL establishes duties that might be fulfilled through national policies. However, there is no higher designated authority to effectively ensure the fulfilment of these obligations by states. This is contrary to what happens in IIL, where IIAs effectively monitor and sanction state activities. In the case of investments protected by IIAs, domestic institutions play a less relevant role than in HRL because IIAs create a special institutional environment at the international level. Studies conducted in the field of agricultural investment have demonstrated that a weak domestic environment contributes to investors and governments decreasing the cost of projects because legal and legitimacy requirements do not play a relevant role. When deciding whether to permit an investment or not, national institutions might be seen as control organs that make it possible for the investment to be negotiated in a legal and legitimate way. In doing so negotiation costs increase but performance costs of the investment should compensate for this. If domestic institutions are weak, IL can be expected to have a complementary function to the domestic system so that goals can be achieved. This chapter also considered the weaknesses of domestic institutions through an analysis of the bargaining power of locals to enforce their rights to property and food. In these specific cases it seems that the mechanisms contained in HRL are not sufficient to produce desirable outcomes and to tackle opportunistic behaviour. This means that there may be cases where states can infringe HRs obligations, or where they are complicit in such infringements. When national institutions fail, HRL is neither effective nor enforceable because it depends on national institutions. In IIL, where locals lack *locus standi,* it is not wrong to affirm that it is possible within this framework for states to sign contracts with investors to the detriment of third parties and that victims' rights remain unenforced because of legal gaps. It is up to the competence of arbitrators to decide to what extent such economic activities can be considered investments. Some scholars have asked whether investors should be concerned about the domestic institutional environment of the host country and the legal consequences of infringements. This question has gained relevance in the HRs literature through scholars considering the possibility of making private actors accountable if HRs violations occur.[563] In the jurisdiction of IIL we saw that HRs violations by investors are unlikely to be considered as procedural arguments. The reluctance

[563]See for some examples at footnote: 890 in Chap. 4.

of arbitrators to consider claims of HRs violations originates in the narrowness of their jurisdiction. This narrowness seems to impede the consideration of states' measures to fulfil extra-contractual obligations (in this case HRs obligations) as they fall outside of the arbitrators' jurisdictional scope. This could be performed, depending on the case at issue, either by applying IL (which would be highly costly to enforce), or according to the law of the investors' domicile. In this case the extraterritorial application of HRs obligations is at issue. In recent years it has gained relevance mostly in some European jurisdictions[564] and the United States. Nevertheless, a recent decision of the United States Supreme Court opened a broad legal avenue for US tribunals to claim a lack of jurisdiction to hear such cases.[565]

The literature has expressed concerns about the fragmentation of IL. For better or worse, it is currently accepted that fragmentation represents a new challenge for IL. Most of the legal contributions dealing with the issue of fragmentation offer a set of solutions that are oriented towards giving recommendations to arbitrators about how to deal with this issue. The approaches have been in line with the ILC study on the application of interpretative techniques, applying *ad hoc* hierarchies on a case-by-case basis and solving normative conflicts in line with the VCLT.[566] Today, even though the problem of fragmentation has been researched and many questions have been answered, one can still observe the persistent reluctance of arbitrators to follow such recommendations.

It might be expected that due to the higher level of protection offered by IIL vis-à-vis HRL and the increase of LSLIs in recent years, IIL will be confronted with issues necessitating decisions on the HRs to land and food. The cases involving Argentina demonstrated that arbitrators are not formally required to consider the existing normative conflict between the two regimes when interpreting the law. Under the current conditions in IIL one cannot expect arbitrators who promote the defragmentation of IL as a way of guaranteeing HRs obligations to do the same in IIL. The cases involving Madagascar also gave rise to an issue that might concern

---

[564]In Germany for example the European Centre for Constitutional and Human Rights is probably the leading organization initiating procedures against German companies producing in LDCs. Some relevant cases include proceedings against supermarkets relating exploitation of workers in Bangladesh and Pakistan. Source: Chayes and Chayes (1993), p. 175.

[565]We understand in this context as extraterritorial jurisdiction the competence of a State to make, apply and enforce rules of conduct in respect of persons, property or events beyond its territory. Such competence may be exercised by way of prescription, adjudication or enforcement. For a comment and overview we suggest: European Center for Constitutional And Human Rights, 'Neueste Publikationen' (ECCHR 2015) http://www.ecchr.de accessed 05.04.2015. For the application of the principle but much more focused on European jurisdiction see: Menno Kamminga, 'Extraterritoriality' Max Planck Encyclopedia of Public International Law http://opil.ouplaw.com/view/10.1093/law:epil/9780199231690/law-9780199231690-e1040?rskey=6HTneo&result=1&q=extraterritoriality&prd=EPIL accessed 20 August 2013.

[566]Nicola Wenzel, 'Extraterritoriality. Human Rights, Treaties, Extraterritorial Application and Effects' Max Planck Encyclopedia of Public International Law http://opil.ouplaw.com/view/10.1093/law:epil/9780199231690/law-9780199231690-e819?rskey=FcIcM0&result=2&q=extraterritoriality&prd=EPIL&print> accessed 20 August 2013.

IIL.[567] This situation is becoming more and more dangerous for IIL, as it seems to directly or indirectly support violations of rights protected by HRL. Up to this point the negative aspects of fragmentation appear to arise from the way that investment arbitrators construct their decisions. It seems that if arbitrators were concerned about HRL obligations, their decisions would take a different face.

We have shown that the problem of infringements of the rights to property and food cannot be associated with a lack of substantive norms protecting these rights. Instead, these infringements are linked to the lack of enforcement mechanisms. Since the emergence of enforceable mechanisms in HRL cannot be expected in the short term, the fulfilment of obligations arising from HRs treaties should be approached in light of two facts: HRs treaties fail to enforce protected rights, and an improvement in the domestic institutional environment of LDCs contributing to an increase in the contractual governance of LSLIs contracts cannot be expected in the short run. These two elements make it necessary to formulate alternatives that are less dependent on the discretion of arbitrators and on domestic institutions in LDCs. If policymakers claim that LSLIs contribute to the reduction of poverty and the promotion of development, they must at least consider the reality that these goals are dependent on well-functioning local institutions. The fact that these conditions are not a given in LDCs constitutes a structural bias of the development agenda. In addition, since HRs obligations are highly dependent on national institutions, it cannot be expected that violations of HRs in the presence of LSLIs can be solved at the national level. It would also constitute a bias to consider IL to lack enforcement mechanisms to promote governance in LSLI activities. One only needs to look at the broad range of enforcement possibilities in IL apart from judicial mechanisms, and at the many instances of successful governance through the design of legal policies whose enforcement does not depend on judicial mechanisms. However, the price in these models is increased complexity because legal theory can only offer limited solutions. This is the reason why the application of social science theory and methodology is required for the design of appropriate enforcement mechanisms to tackle opportunism in LSLIs.

We elucidated two significant and relevant points. Although IL contains mechanisms to alleviate fragmentation, arbitrators seem to ignore these mechanisms in their decisions in the case of IIL. This behaviour leads to detrimental effects for HRL. If we correctly assume that the main problem is caused by arbitrators, the solution can take two different forms. One solution is to look for alternative enforcement mechanisms that do not involve arbitrators. Another possibility is to design and allocate legal incentives so that arbitrators' decisions conform to HRs obligations.

In the next chapter, we will consider two proposed methods that encompass both judicial and extra-judicial strategies. While the literature has broadly investigated judicial strategies, authors have ignored the question of the incentives that should be at the disposal of an adjudicator in deciding whether or not to consider HRL. The

[567]For a short documentation of the experience of Madagascar with regard LSLIs see: ILC (2006).

question is relevant for several reasons. First, international tribunals have a high degree of autonomy, especially international investment arbitrators. Second, there is a lack of control institutions that might balance failures, e.g. an appellate body. Finally, there is a danger that biased or misbalanced judicial decisions could contribute towards the toleration of HRs violations. That said, incentives need to be allocated in a way that leads adjudicators to apply methods that will contribute to the defragmentation of IL.

As a preliminary step to the development of the aforementioned strategies, we will introduce a theoretical approach that relies on economic theory. This will elucidate the origin of the failures leading to the existence of opportunism in LSLIs. The model will frame preferred strategy requirements so that the expected goals of land policies can be realised. In addition to this, the economic approach makes it possible to determine where incentives should be allocated so that strategies oriented towards defragmentation can come into being and produce effects upon the system. We firstly elaborate the economic approach and later concentrate on the design of strategies.

References

Abbott, K., & Snidal, D. (2003). Hard and soft law in international governance. *International Organization, 54*, 421.

Accountability Counsel. (2012). *Accountability resource guide* (Vol. 7.1). Natalie Bridgeman Fields, Esq.

ADC Affiliate Limited and ADC & ADMC Management Limited v Hungary [2006] Award on Jurisdiction, Merits, and Damages ARB/03/16 (ICSID).

ADF Group Incorporated v United States [2003] Award ARB(AF)/00/1 (ICSID).

African Charter on Human and Peoples' Rights (Banjul Charter) [1986] OAU Doc. CAB/LEG/67/3 rev. 5, 21 I.L.M. 58.

African Commission on Human and Peoples' Rights. (2013). *Protocol to the African Charter on human and peoples' rights on the establishment of the African Court on human and peoples' rights. Legal instruments.* ACHPR, http://www.achpr.org/instruments/court-establishment/. Accessed 29 July 2015.

African Commission on Human and Peoples' Rights Resolution On Economic, Social And Cultural Rights In Africa [2004] ACHPR/Res.73(XXXVI)04.

African Development Bank. (2012). *The 2012–2014 programme and budget.*

African Development Bank Group. (2013). *Bank Group mandate.* African Development Bank, http://www.afdb.org/en/topics-and-sectors/sectors/water-supply-sanitation/bank-group-mandate/. Accessed 13 November 2014.

African Ombudsman Association. (2013). *About the AOMA.* AOMA, http://www.aoma.org.za/content/view/3/2/. Accessed 13 November 2014.

Agreement Between the Government of Sweden and the Government of Malaysia Concerning the Mutual Protection of Investments (Sweden-Malaysia) [1979] SÖ 1979:17 available at: http://investmentpolicyhub.unctad.org/IIA/country/202/treaty/2484. Accessed 17 September 2015.

Aguas del Tunari v Bolivia [2005] Decision on Respondent's Objections to Jurisdiction ARB/02/3 (ICSID).

Aguas Provinciales de Santa Fe SA and others v Argentina [2006] Order in Response to a Petition for Participation as Amicus Curiae ARB/03/17 (ICSID).

Alter, K., Helfer, L., & McAllister, J. (2013). A new international human rights court for West Africa: The Ecowas Community Court of Justice. *American Journal of International Law, 107*, 737.

Álvarez, J. (2010). Comparison U.S. Model BIT (1984) and U.A. Model BIT (2004). *Transnational Dispute Management.*

Amerasinghe, C. F. (2004). *Local remedies in international law*. Cambridge.

Amerasinghe, C. F. (2008). *Diplomatic protection*. Oxford University Press.

Antoine Goetz and others v Republic of Burundi [1995] Award ARB/95/3 (ICSID).

Article 19 v State of Eritrea [2003] Communication 275/03 (ACHPR).

Asian Agricultural Products Limited v Sri Lanka [1990] Award ARB/87/3 (ICSID).

Azurix Corporation v Argentina [2006] Award ARB/01/12 (ICSID).

Baetens, F. (2013). Enforcement of arbitral awards. In T. Weiler & I. Laird (Eds.), *The Furute of ICSID, Juris Arbitration Series*. Martinus Nijhoff Publishers.

Barnes, R. (2009). *Property rights and natural resources*. Oregon: Oxford and Portland.

Benvenisti, E., & Downs, G. (2007). The empires new clothes: Political economy and the fragmentation of international law. *Stanford Law Review, 60*, 595.

Bernardus Henricus Funnekotter and Others v Zimbabwe [2009] Award ARB/05/6 (ICSID).

Biloune and Marine Drive Complex Limited v Ghana Investments Centre and Ghana [1994] Award on Jurisdiction and Liability 95 (UNCITRAL).

Biwater Gauff (Tanzania) Ltd v Tanzania [2006] Procedural Order No 3 ARB/05/22 (ICSID).

Biwater Gauff (Tanzania) Ltd v Tanzania [2008] Award and Concurring and Dissenting Opinion ARB/05/22 (ICSID).

Born, G. (2012). A new generation of international adjudication. *Duke Law Journal, 61*, 775.

Brownlie, I. (1988). The rights of peoples in modern international law. In J. Crawford (Ed.), *The rights of peoples*.

Brussels Convention on Jurisdiction and the Enforcement of Judgments in Civil and Commercial Matters [1968] OJ C 027 at 1-27.

Bureau Veritas, Inspection, Valuation, Assessment and Control BIVAC B.V. v The Republic of Paraguay [2009] Award ARB/07/9 (ICSID).

Butler, L. (2013). Resilience of property. *Arizona Law Review, 55*, 847.

Buxbaum, R., & Caron, D. (2010). The Alien Tort Statute: An overview of the current issues. *Berkeley Journal of International Law, 28*, 1.

Capotorti, F., & United Nations (1979). *Study on the rights of persons belonging to ethnic, religious, and linguistic minorities* (UN Doc E/CN4/Sub2/384/rev1).

Centre for Minority Rights Development and Minority Rights Group International and Centre on Housing Rights and Evictions (intervening) (on behalf of Endorois Welfare Council) v Kenya [2009] Merits communication no 276/2003 (ACHPR).

CESCR. (1999a). *Implementation of the international covenant on economic, social and cultural rights* (General Comment No. 13 21st session E/C12/1999/10).

CESCR. (1999b). *Substantive issues arising in the implementation of the international covenant on economic, social and cultural rights. General comment 12. The right to adequate food* (E/C12/1999/5).

Charter of the United Nations [1945] 1 UNTS XVI.

Chayes, A., & Chayes, A. (1993). On compliance. *International Organization, 47*, 175.

CME Czech Republic B.V. v The Czech Republic [2003] Award (UNCITRAL).

CMS Gas Transmission Company v Argentina [2005] Award ARB/01/8 (ICSID).

CMS Gas Transmission Company v Argentina [2007] Decision on Application for Annulment ARB/01/8 (ICSID).

Cohen, M. (1927). Property and sovereignty. *Cornell Law Quarterly, 13*, 8.

Commission on Human Rights (UN) Effective Functioning of Bodies Established Pursuant to United Nations Human Rights Instruments. Final Report on Enhancing the Long-Term Effectiveness of the United Nations Human Rights Treaty System [1997] E/CN.4/1997/74.

Committee on World Food Security. (2011). *Final Report of the Thirty-seventh Session* (CFS:2011).

Compañía del Desarrollo de Santa Elena SA v Costa Rica [2000] Award ARB/96/1 (ICSID).

Complaint Mechanisms of Export Development Canada [2009] available at http://www.edc.ca/EN/About-Us/Management-and-Governance/Compliance-Officer/Documents/compliance-officer-steps-to-resolution.pdf. Accessed 26 December 2013.

Convention Establishing the Multilateral Investment Guarantee Agency [1988] available http://www.miga.org/documents/miga_convention_november_2010.pdf. Accessed 15 July 2015.

Convention on the Settlement of Investment Disputes Between States and Nationals of Other States [1965] 17 UST 1270 TIAS 6090 575 UNTS 159.

Coomans, F. (2003). The Ogoni case before the African Commission on human and peoples' rights. *International and Comparative Law Quarterly, 52*.

Cooter, R., & Ulen, T. (2012). In D. Battista (Ed.), *Law & economics* (6th ed.). Pearson Adison Wesley.

Cotula, L. (2012). *Human rights, natural resources, and investment law in a globalised world: Shades of grey in the shadow of the law*. Routledge Research in International Economic Law.

De Schutter, O. (2009a). Realising the right to food. *Pambazuka* (Kenya, 24.07.2009), http://pambazuka.org/en/category/comment/55794. Accessed 24 March 2011.

De Schutter, O. (2009b). *Report of the Special Rapporteur on the right to food* (A/HRC/13/33/add2).

De Schutter, O. (2009c). *Report of the Special Rapporteur on the right to food. Agribusiness and the right to food* (A/HRC/13/33).

De Schutter, O. (2010). *International human rights law*. Cambridge.

De Schutter, O. (2011). How not to think of land-grabbing: Three critiques of large-scale investments in farmland. *Journal of Peasant Studies, 37*, 249.

Deininger, K., & World Bank. (2003). *Land policy framework for growth and poverty reduction*. Oxford University Press.

Delphi International Ltd (1997). *The role of financial institutions in achieving sustainable development*.

Desta, M. G. (2012). Soft law in international law: An overview. In A. Bjorklung & A. Reinisch (Eds.), *International investment law and soft law*. Edwar Elgar.

Dickerson, H. *Minimum standards*. Max Planck Encyclopedia of Public International Law, http://opil.ouplaw.com/view/10.1093/law:epil/9780199231690/law-9780199231690-e689?rskey=muCNrC&result=1&prd=EPIL. Accessed 21 December 2013.

Dolzer, R. (2005). Fair and equitable treatment: A key standard in investment treaties. *International Lawyer, 39*, 87.

Dolzer, R., & Schreuer, C. (2008). *Principles of international investment law*. Oxford University Press.

Dolzer, R., & Stevens, M. (1995). *Bilateral investment treaties*. M. Nijhoff.

Dolzer, R., & von Walter, A. (2007). Fair and equitable treatment-lines of jurisprudence in customary law. In F. Ortino, et al. (Eds.), *Investment treaty law current issues II*.

Dörr, O. (2012). Section 3 interpretation of treaties. In O. Dörr & K. Schmalenbach (Eds.), *Vienna Convention on the law of treaties*. Springer.

Dörr, O., & Schmalenbach, K. (Eds.). (2012). *Vienna Convention on the law of treaties*. Springer.

Dumberry, P., & Dumas-Aubin, G. (2012). When and how allegations of human rights violations can be raised in investor-state arbitration. *Journal of World Investment and Trade, 13*, 349.

Dupuy, P.-M. (1999). The danger of fragmentation or unification of the international legal system and the international court of justice. *New York University Journal of International Law and Politics, 31*, 791.

Dupuy, P.-M., & Vierucci, L. (Eds.). (2008). *NGOs in international law. Efficiency in flexibility?* Edward Elgar.

Ebrimah Manehh v The Gambia [2007] Decision ECW/CCJ/APP/11/07 (ECOWAS).

Economic and Social Council. (1983). *Study of the problem of discrimination against indigenous populations. Final Report (last part) submitted by the Special Rapporteur, Mr. José Martínez Cobo* (E/CN4/Sub2/1983/21/Add4).

Economic Community of West African States. (2013). *List of decided cases from 2004 till date*. ECOWAS, http://www.courtecowas.org/site2012/index.phpoption=com_content&view=article&id=157&Itemid=27. Accessed 12 November 2013.

Economic Community of West African States Supplementary Amending the Preamble and Articles 1, 2, 9 and 30 of the Protocol A/P.1/7/91 Relating to the Community Court of Justice and Article 4 Paragraph 1 of the English Version of the Said Protocol [2005] A/SP.1/01/05.

Eide, A. (2000). *Working paper on the relationship and distinction between the rights of persons belonging to minorities and those of indigenous peoples* (E/CN4/Sub2/2000/10).

Eide, A., Oschaug, A., & Barth, E. W. (1991). Food security and the right to food in international law and development. *Transnational Law & Contemporary Problems, 1*, 415.

El Paso Energy International Company v Argentina [2006] Decision on Jurisdiction ARB/03/15 (ICSID).

Elettronica Sicula SpA (ELSI), United States v Italy [1989] Judgment GL No 76 (ICJ).

Enron Corporation and Ponderosa Assets, L.P v The Argentine Republic [2005] Decision on Jurisdiction ARB/01/3 (ICSID).

Epiney, A. (1992). *Die völkerrechtliche Verantwortlichkeit von Staaten für rechtswidriges Verhalten im Zusammenhang mit Aktionen Privater* (1. Aufl. ed.). Nomos Verl.-Ges.

Ermacora, F. (1983). *The protection of minorities before the United Nations* (Vol. 182). Martinus Nijhoff Online.

EU Guidelines to Support Land Policy Design and Reform Processes in Developing Countries. Annex to the Communication. Commission Staff Working Paper [2004] SEC(2004)1289.

European Center for Constitutional And Human Rights. (2015). *Neueste Publikationen*. ECCHR, http://www.ecchr.de. Accessed 05 April 2015.

European Court of Human Rights. (2014). *The ECHR in 50 questions*.

European Investment Bank Group. (2012). *Operational plan 2013–2015*.

Eyal, B., & Downs, G. (2012). National court and transnational private regulation. In F. Cafaggi (Ed.), *Enforcement of transnational regulation*. Edward Elgar.

Factory At Chorzów, Germany v Poland [1928] Judgment 13 (PCIJ).

FAO and WH World Declaration and Plan of Action for Nutrition [1992] available at http://www.fao.org/docrep/003/w3613e/w3613e00.HTM. Accessed 14 July 2015.

FAO World Food Summit: Five Years Later. International Alliance Against Hunger [2002] WFS: fyl2002/3.

FAOVoluntary Guidelines to Support the Progressive Realization of the Right to Adequate Food in the Context of National Food Security [2004] available at http://www.fao.org/docrep/009/y7937e/y7937e00.htm. Accessed 13 July 2015.

Feldman v Mexico [2002] Award ARB(AF)/99/1 (ICSID).

Food and Agriculture Organization of the United Nations. (2009). In FAO (Ed.), *Guide on legislating for the right to food*. FAO.

Food and Agriculture Organization of the United Nations. (2014). *Committee on World Food Security. Principles for responsible agricultural investment*. FAO, http://www.fao.org/cfs/cfs-home/resaginv/en/. Accessed 11 August 2014.

Francioni, F. (2010). Access to justice, denial of justice, and international investment law. In D. Pierre-Marie, F. Francioini, & E.-U. Petersmann (Eds.), *Human rights in international investment law and arbitration*. Oxford University Press.

Franck, S. (2005). The legitimacy crisis in investment treaty arbitration: Privatizing public international law through inconsistent decisions. *Fordham Law Review, 73*, 1521.

Franck, S. (2011). Rationalizing cost awards in investment treaty arbitration. *Washington University Law Review, 88*, 769.

Franco Suarez, A. M. (2008). *How to promote the justiciability of the human right to food*. FIAN International.

Fry, J. (2007–2008). International human rights law in investment arbitration: Evidence of international law's unity. *Duke Journal of Comparative & International Law, 18*, 77.

Gazzini, T. (2010). Drawing the line between non-compensable regulatory powers and indirect expropriation of foreign investment – An economic analysis of law perspective. *Manchester Journal of International Economic Law, 7*, 36.

General Assembly (UN) Convention Against Torture and Other Cruel, Inhuman or Degrading Treatment or Punishment [1984] 1465 UNTS 85.

General Assembly (UN) Convention on the Recognition and Enforcement of Foreign Arbitral Awards [1968] 330 UNTS 38; 21 UST 2517; 7 ILM 1046.

General Assembly (UN) Convention on the Rights of the Child [1990] 1577 UNTS 3.

General Assembly (UN) Declaration on the Rights of Persons Belonging to National or Ethnic, Religious and Linguistic Minorities [1992] A/RES/47/135.

General Assembly (UN) International Convention for the Protection of All Persons from Enforced Disappearance [2006] Adopted by Resolution 61/177.

General Assembly (UN) International Convention on the Elimination of All Forms of Racial Discrimination [1965] 660 UNTS 195.

General Assembly (UN) International Covenant on Civil and Political Rights [2001] CCPR/C/66/GUI/Rev.2.

General Assembly (UN) International Covenant on Economic, Social and Cultural Rights [1976] United Nations Treaty Series 993 available at http://www.refworld.org/docid/3ae6b36c0.html. Accessed 15 July 2015.

General Assembly (UN) Optional Protocol to the Convention on the Elimination of All Forms of Discrimination Against Women [1981] 1249 UNTS 14.

General Assembly (UN) Optional Protocol to the Convention on the Rights of Persons with Disabilities [2006] A/RES/61/106 Annex II.

General Assembly (UN) Optional Protocol to the International Covenant on Economic, Social and Cultural Rights [1976] 999 UNTS 302.

General Assembly (UN) Universal Declaration of Human Rights [1948] UNGA Res 217A (III), UN Doc A/810.

Geneva Convention (III) Relative to the Treatment of Prisoners of War [1950] 75 UNTS 135.

Geneva Convention (IV) relative to the Protection of Civilian Persons in Time of War [1949] 75 UNTS 287.

Genin and others v Estonia [2001] Award ARB/99/2 (ICSID).

Girardi, D. (2012). *A brief essay on the financialization of agricultural commodity markets*. University of Siena, Department of Economics and Statistics, Centro Studi CRESME.

González, S. *Equator principles*. Max Planck Encyclopedia of Public International Law, http://opil.ouplaw.com/view/10.1093/law:epil/9780199231690/law-9780199231690-e1038?rskey=vuep8N&result=1&prd=OPIL. Accessed 21 December 2013.

Graugnard, N. Toward a multilateral framework for investment. Columbia FDI Perspectives. Perspectives on topical foreign direct investment issues by the Vale Columbia Center on Sustainable International Investment No. 103. Accessed 11 November 2013.

Griebel, J. (2008). *Internationales Investitionsrecht: Lehrbuch für Studium und Praxis* (1st ed.). Beck.

Guidelines on an Expanded Core Document and Treaty-Specific Targeted Reports and Harmonized Guidelines on Reporting Under the International Human Rights Treaties (Hamonized Guidelines) [2005] HRI/MC/2005/3.

Gupta, A. (Ed.). (2005). *Human rights of indigenous peoples* (Vol. 1). Isha Books.

Gustav F W Hamester GmbH & Co KG v Ghana [2010] Award ARB/07/24 (ICSID).

Guzman, A. T. (1998). Why LDCs sign treaties that hurt them: Explaining the popularity of bilateral investment treaties. *Virginia Journal of International Law, 38*, 639.

Guzman, A. T. (2008). *How international law works: A rational choice theory*. Oxford University Press.

Hadijatou Mani Koraou v The Republic of Niger [2008] Decision ECW/CCJ/JUD/06/08 (ECOWAS).

Hadijatou Mani Koraou v. The Republic of Niger Merits, Suit No ECW/CCJ/APP/08/08, Judgment No ECW/CCJ/JUD/06/08, IHRL 3115 (ECOWAS 2008), 27th October (ECOWAS).
Hafner-Burton, E. (2009). *Forced to be good: Why trade agreements boost human rights*. Cornell University Press.
Hallward-Driemeier, M. (2003). Do bilateral investment treaties attract FDI? Only a bit and they could bite. World Bank Policy Research Working Paper No. WPS 312, http://wdsbeta.worldbank.org/external/default/WDSContentServer/IW3P/IB/2003/09/23/000094946_03091104060047/Rendered/PDF/multi0page.pdf. Accessed 14 April 2014.
Harten, G. V., & Scott, D. (2016). Investment treaties and the internal vetting of regulatory proposals: A case study from Canada. *Journal of International Dispute Settlement, 1*, 92.
Hegel, G. W. F. (1821). *Grundlinien der Philosophie des Rechts*.
Heiskanen, V. (2009). Arbitrary and unreasonable measures. In A. Reinisch (Ed.), *Standards of investment protection* (Repr. ed.). Oxford University Press.
Herzt, J. H. (1941). Expropriation of foreign property. *American Journal of International Law, 35*.
High Commissioner for Human Rights. (2013). *Human rights bodies - Complaints procedures*. UN, http://www.ohchr.org/EN/HRBodies/TBPetitions/Pages/HRTBPetitions.aspx-interstate. Accessed 12 November 2013.
How to File a Request for Inspection to the World Bank Inspection Panel. General Guidelines The World Bank Group Office of the Compliance Advisor Ombudsman Guidelines [1993] available at http://ewebapps.worldbank.org/apps/ip/Documents/Guidelines_HowtoFile_for_web.pdf. Accessed 15 July 2015.
Human Rights Council. (2011). *Report of the special representative of the Secretary-General on the issue of human rights and transnational corporations and other business enterprises, John Ruggie* Business and human rights: Mapping international standards of responsibility and accountability for corporate acts* (A/HRC/4/35).
Human Rights Council A/69/L.85 General Assembly Draft outcome document of the United Nations summit for the adoption of the post-2015 development agenda [2015].
Human Rights Council A/HRC/RES/5/1 General Assembly Institution-Building of the United Nations Human Rights Council The Human Rights Council [2007].
ILC. (2001). Draft articles on responsibility of states for internationally wrongful acts. In *Yearkbook of the International Law Commission* (Vol. II). United Nations.
ILC. (2006). *Fragmentation of international law: Difficulties arising from the diversification and expansion of international law* (A/CN4/L682).
Institute for Human Rights and Development in Africa (on behalf of Esmaila Connateh & 13 others) v Angola [2008] Merits communication no 292/2004 (ACHPR).
Inter American Court of Human Rights. (1986). *The word "Laws" in Article 30 of the American Convention on human rights* (Advisory Opinion OC-6/86).
Interights & Ditschwanelo v Botswana [2006] Decision 319/06 (ACHPR).
International Committee of the Red Cross (ICRC) Protocol Additional to the Geneva Conventions of 12 August 1949, and relating to the Protection of Victims of Non-International Armed Conflicts [1977] 1125 UNTS 609.
International Convention on the Protection of the Rights of All Migrant Workers and Members of their Families [2003] 2220 UNTS 3.
International Economic Law and Policy Blog. *A multilateral investment agreement*, available at http://worldtradelawtypepad.com/ielpblog/2013/01/a-multilateral-investment-agreementhtml. Accessed 11 November 2013.
International Finance Corporation. (2015). *Sustainability*. IFC, http://www.ifc.org/wps/wcm/connect/corp_ext_content/ifc_external_corporate_site/home. Accessed 12 July 2015.
International Labour Organization. (1996). *Ratifications of C169 - Indigenous and Tribal Peoples Convention, 1989 (No. 169)*. ILO, http://www.ilo.org/dyn/normlex/en/f?p=1000:11300:0::NO:11300:P11300_INSTRUMENT_ID:312314. Accessed 08 August 2015.
International Labour Organization (ILO) Indigenous and Tribal Peoples Convention [1989] C169.
International Thunderbird Gaming Corporation v Mexico [2006] Award 136 (UNCITRAL).

J.L. v Australia [1992] Communication No 491/1992, UN Doc CCPR/C/45/D/491/1992 (Human Rights Committee).

James and others v The United Kingdom [2007] Judgement app no 8793/79 (ECtHR).

Janeba, E. (2016). *Regulatory chill and the effect of investor state dispute settlements*. CESifo Working Paper Series No. 6188, https://papers.ssrn.com/sol3/papers2.cfm?abstract_id=2887952##. Accessed 16 February 2017.

Jenks, C. W. (1953). The conflict of law making treaties. *British Year Book of International Law, 30*, 401.

Joseph, S., & Kyriakakis, J. (2010). The United Nations and human rights. In S. Joseph & A. McBeth (Eds.), *Research handbook on international human rights law*. Edward Elgar.

Joseph, S., & McBeth, A. (Eds.). (2010). *Research handbook on international human rights law*. Edward Elgar.

Joy Mining Machinery Limited v Arab Republic of Egypt [2004] Award on Jurisdiction ARB/03/11 (ICSID).

Kahn v Germany Commission Decision 235/56/EEC [1958] Yearbook 2, p 256.

Kamminga, M. *Extraterritoriality*. Max Planck Encyclopedia of Public International Law, http://opil.ouplaw.com/view/10.1093/law:epil/9780199231690/law-9780199231690-e1040?rskey=6HTneo&result=1&q=extraterritoriality&prd=EPIL. Accessed 20 August 2013.

Katia, Y.-S. (2008). What about this "Umbrella Clause"? In Y.-S. Katia (Ed.), *Arbitration under international investment agreements: A guide to the key issues*. Oxford Universtiy Press.

Ki-moon, B. (2012). *Secretary-General's remarks at treaty body strengthening consultation for states parties*. New York, 2 April 2012, http://www.un.org/sg/statements/?nid=5967.

Kneer, D. (2013). *Investitionsschutz und Menschenrechte*. Nomos.

Koskenniemi, M., & Leino, P. (2002). Fragmentation of international law? Postmodern anxieties. *Leiden Journal of International Law, 15*, 553.

Krause, A. (1999). Article 17. In G. Alfreðsson & A. Eide (Eds.), *The universal declaration of human rights: A common standard of achievement*. Martinus Nijhoff Publishers.

Krennerich, M. (2013). *Soziale Menschenrechte*. Wochen Schau Verlag ed.

Kriebaum, U. (2008). *Eigentumsschutz im Völkerrecht: Eine Vergleichende Untersuchung zum Internationalen Investitionsrecht sowie zum Menschenrechtsschutz*. Duncker & Humblot.

Kriebaum, U. (2013 forthcoming). Arbitrary/unreasonable or discriminatory measures. In M. Bungenber & J. Griebel (Eds.), *International investment law*. Baden Baden: Nomos, http://papers.ssrn.com/sol3/papers.cfm?abstract_id=2268927. Accessed 13 May 2014.

Kriebaum, U., & Schreuer, C. (2007). The concept of property in human rights law and international investment law. In S. Breitenmoser, et al. (Eds.), *Human rights, democracy and the rule of law: Liber amicorum Luzius Wildhaber*. Nomos.

Kugelmann, D. *The protection of minorities and indigenous peoples respecting cultural diversity*. Max Planck Encyclopedia of Public International Law, http://www.mpil.de/files/pdf1/mpunyb_06_kugelmann_11.pdf. Accessed 14 Arpil 2011.

Ledesma, H. F. (2004). *El Sistema Interamericano de Protección de los Derechos Humanos. Aspectos institucionales y procesales*. IIDH.

LG&E Energy Corporation and others v Argentina [2006] Decision on Liability ARB/02/1 (ICSID).

Libyan American Oil Company v Libya [1977] Award 53 ILR 422 (Ad Hoc Tribunal).

Loewen Group Incorporated and Loewen (Raymond L.) v United States [2004] Decision on Respondent's Request for a Supplementary Decision ARB(AF)/98/3 (ICSID).

Lovelace v Canada [1981] Commission Communication 24/1977, CCPR/C/13/D/24/1977 (UNHRC).

Ludescher, M. (2004). *Menschenrechte und Indigene Völker*. Peter Lang.

Matos e Silva, LDA., and others v Portugal [1996] Application 15777/89 (ECtHR).

Mechlem, K. (2004). Food security and the right to food in the discourse of the United Nations. *European Law Journal, 10*, 631.

Media Rights Agenda v Nigeria [2000] Communication 224/98 (ACHPR).

Meinzen-Dick, R., & Markelova, H. (2009). Necessary nuance: Toward a code of conduct in foreign land deals. In M. Kugelman & S. L. Levenstein (Eds.), *Land grab? The race for the world's farmland*. Woodrow Wilson International Center for Scholars.

Mellacher et. al. v Austria [1989] Judgement app nos 10522/83, 11011/84 and 11070/84 (ECtHR).

Methanex Corporation v United States [2001] Decision on *Amici Curiae*, IIC 165 (Ad hoc UNICTRAL).

Methanex Corporation v United States [2005] Final Award (Ad hoc UNICTRAL).

Meyer, T. (2009). Soft law as delegation. *Fordham International Law Journal, 32*.

Mgimba, L. M., & Waters, S. J. (2012). *Jurisprudential analysis of the African Court on human and peoples' rights: From 2004 to 2010*. Martinus Nijhoff Publishers.

Mike Campbell (Pvt) ltd. & 78 Others v Zimbabwe [2008] Judgement T02/07_JUD (SADC).

Mishra, A., & Mishra, A. (2012). Fair and equitable treatment standard in international investment law: An analysis vis-a-vis public international law. *Korea University Law Review, 107*, 107.

Model BIT Canada available [2004] at http://www.italaw.com/documents/Canadian2004-FIPA-model-en.pdf. Accessed 14 September 2014.

Model Text of the Indian Bilateral Investment Treaty., available at: https://mygov.in/sites/default/files/master_image/Model%20Text%20for%20the%20Indian%20Bilateral%20Investment%20Treaty.pdf. Accessed 17 August 2015.

Modise v Botswana [2000] Decision on Merits No 97/93 (ACHPR).

Mohamed, A. (1999). Individual and NGO participation in human rights litigation before the African Court of human and peoples' rights: Lessons from the European and Inter-American Courts of human rights. *Journal of African Law, 43*.

Monteagudo, M. (2013). *The right to property in human rights and investment law: A Latin American perspective of an unavoidable connection*. SECO/WTI Academic Cooperation Project Working Paper Series 2013/06, http://ssrn.com/abstract=2613890. Accessed 28 August 2015.

Montt, S. (2007). The BIT generations emergence as a collective action problem: Prisoners dilemma or network effects? *Latin American Caribbean Journal of Legal Studies, 2*, 150.

Moran, T. (2006). *Harnessing foreign direct investment for development*. Center For Global Development.

Moran, T. (2011). *Foreign direct investment and development*. Peterson Institute for International Economics.

MTD Equity Sdn Bhd and MTD Chile SA v Chile [2004] Award ARB/01/7 (ICSID).

Mukundi, G. (2008). *African Court on human and peoples' rights: Ten years on and still no justice*. United Kingdom: MRG.

Nadakavukaren, K. (2013). *International investment law*. Edward Elgar.

Noble Ventures Incorporated v Romania [2005] Award ARB/01/11 (ICSID).

Occidental Exploration and Production Company v Ecuador [2004] Final Award UN3467 (LCIA).

Office of the High Commissioner for Human Rights. (2010). *The right to adequate food* (Fact Sheet No. 34).

Office of the High Commissioner for Human Rights. (2013). *Paris principles: 20 years guiding the work of National Human Rights Institutions*. UNHR, http://www.ohchr.org/EN/NewsEvents/Pages/ParisPrinciples20yearsguidingtheworkofNHRI.aspx. Accessed 12 July 2015.

Office of the High Commissioner of Human Rights. (1996). *Background information on the human rights council*. UN, http://www.ohchr.org/EN/HRBodies/HRC/Pages/AboutCouncil.aspx. Accessed 08 August 2013.

Office of the United Nations High Commissioner for Human Rights. (2013). *Human rights council complaint procedure*. OHCHR, http://www2.ohchr.org/english/bodies/chr/1503.htm. Accessed 26 July 2015.

Ominayak (on behalf of Lubicon Lake Band) v Canada [1990] Commission Communication 167/1984, CCPR/C/38/D/167/1984 (UNHRC).

Organisation for Economic Co-operation and Development. (2015). *Official export credits agencies*. OECD, http://www.oecd.org/tad/xcred/eca.htm. Accessed 12 July 2015.
Organization of African Unity African Charter on the Rights and Welfare of the Child [1999] OAU Doc. CAB/LEG/24.9/49.
Parra, A. (1997). Provisions on the settlement of investment disputes in modern investment laws, bilateral investment treaties and multilateral instruments on investment. *ICSID Review: Foreign Investment Law Journal, 12*, 287.
Partnership Agreement between the members of the African, Caribbean and Pacific Group of States of the one part, and the European Community and its Member States, of the other part [2000] OJ L 287.
Pauwelyn, J. *Fragmentation of international law*. Max Planck Encyclopedia of Public International Law, http://opil.ouplaw.com/view/10.1093/law:epil/9780199231690/law-9780199231690-e1406?rskey=0dMLs5&result=1&prd=EPIL. Accessed 18 August 2015.
Philip Morris Brands Sàrl, Philip Morris Products S.A. and Abal Hermanos S.A. v La República Oriental del Uruguay [2013] Decision on Jurisdiction ARB/10/7 (ICSID).
Pillay, N. (2012). *Strengthening the United Nations human rights treaty body system*. United Nations Human Rights Office of the Commissioner.
Potts, J. (2011). Stabilizing the role of umbrella clauses in bilateral investment treaties: Intent, reliance, and internationalization. *Virginia Journal of International Law, 51*, 1005.
Principles for Responsible Agricultural Investment that Respects Rights, Livehoods and Resources [2010] available http://siteresources.worldbank.org/INTARD/214574-1111138388661/22453321/Principles_Extended.pdf. Accessed 25 December 2013.
Prost, M. (2012). *The concept of unity in public international law*. Hart.
Protocol on the Economic Community of West African States Court of Justice [1991] A/P.I/7/91.
Protocol to the African Charter on Human and People's Rights on the Establishment of an African Court on Human and People's Rights [1998] OAU OAU/LEG/EXP/AFCHPR/PROT (III).
Protocol to the African Charter on Human and Peoples' Rights [2004] OAU Doc. OAU/LEG/MIN/AFCHPR/PROT.
Protocol to the African Charter on Human and Peoples' Rights on the Rights of Women in Africa [2000] CAB/LEG/66.6.
Reiner, C., & Schreuer, C. (2009). Human rights and international investment arbitration. In P.-M. Dupuy, F. Francioni, & E.-U. Petersmann (Eds.), *Human rights in international investment law and arbitration*. Oxford.
Reinisch, A. (2006). Necessity in international investment arbitration - An unnecessary split of opinions in recent ICSID cases? Comments on CMS v. Argentina and LG&E v. Argentina. *Transnational Dispute Management, 3*.
Reinisch, A. (2009). *Standards of investment protection* (Repr. ed.). Oxford University Press.
Reisman, W. M., & Sloane, R. D. (2004). *Indirect expropriation and its valuation in the BIT generation*. Boston University School of Law Working Paper 06-43, http://www.bu.edu/law/faculty/scholarship/workingpapers/2006.html. Accessed 14 April 2014.
Republic of Guinea v Democratic Republic of the Congo [2007] Preliminary Objections and Judgment, ICJ Report 2017, p 582 (ICJ).
Resources Foundation v Zambia [1998] 211/98 Legal Resources Foundation/Zambia (ACHPR).
Riedel, E. (1986). *Theorie der Menschenrechtsstandards: Funktion, Wirkungsweise und Begründung wirtschaftlicher und sozialer Menschenrechte mit exemplarischer Darstellung der Rechte auf Eigentum und Arbeit in verschiedenen Rechtsordnungen*. Duncker & Humblot.
Ronald Lauder v The Czech Republic [2001] Final Award 9 UNCITRAL Rep 66 (UNCITRAL).
Ruggie, J. (2011). *UN guiding principles for business & human rights*. United Nations Human Rights Office of the High Commissioner, New York, 2011 No. A/HRC/17/32.
Ruhangisa, J. E. (2011). The East African Court of Justice: Ten years of operation. In *Sensitisation Workshop on the Role of the EACJ in the EAC Integration*, Imperial Royale Hotel, Kampala, Uganda November.

Rules of Procedure of the African Commission on Human and Peoples' Rights [2010] available at http://www.achpr.org/files/instruments/rules-of-procedure-2010/rules_of_procedure_2010_en.pdf. Accessed 12 November 2013.

Rules of the Community (ECOWAS) Court of Justice [2002] available at http://www.courtecowas.org/site2012/pdf_files/rules_of_procedure.pdf. Accessed 11 November 2013.

S.D. Myers, Inc. (Claimant) v Government of Canada (Respondent) [2000] First Partial Award 40 ILM 1408.

Salacuse, J. (2010). *The law of investment treaties*. Oxford University Press.

Salini Costruttori S.p.A. v Jordan [2007] Decision on Jurisdiction ARB/02/13 (ICSID).

Saluka Investments BV v Czech Republic [2006] Partial Award 210 (PCA).

Schabas, W. (Ed.). (2013). *The universal declaration of human rights: The travaux préparatoires*. Cambridge University Press.

Schaffer, G., & Pollack, M. (2011). Hard versus soft law in international security. *Boston College Law Review, 52*, 1147.

Schreuer, C. (2005). The concept of expropriation under the ETC and other investment protection treaties. *Transnational Dispute Management, 5*.

Schreuer, C. (2010). Full protection and security. *Journal of International Dispute Settlement*, 1.

Schreuer, C., Malintoppi, L., Reinisch, A., & Sinclair, A. (2009). *The ICSID Convention. A commentary*. Cambridge University Press.

Schrijveri, N. (1999). The changing nature of state sovereignty. *British Yearbook of International Law, 70*, 65.

Sempra Energy International v Argentine Republic [2007] Award ARB/02/16 (ICSID).

SGS Société Générale de Surveillance SA v Pakistan [2003] Decision on Objections of Jurisdiction ARB/01/13 (ICSID).

SGS Société Générale de Surveillance SA v Philippines [2004] Decision on Objections to Jurisdiction and Separate Declaration ARB/02/6 (ICSID).

Shelton, D. (1994). The participation of nongovernmental organizations in international judicial proceedings. *American Journal of International Law, 88*, 611.

Shelton, D. (2002). Decision regarding communication 155/96 (Social and Economic Rights Action Center/Center for Economic and Social Rights v. Nigeria). Case No. ACHPR/COMM/A044/1. *American Society of International Law, 96*, 937.

Shelton, D. (2008). Soft law. In *Handbook of international law*. The George Washington University Law School, http://ssrn.com/abstract=1003387. Accessed 13 November 2013.

Siemens AG v Argentina [2007] Award and Separate Opinion ARB/02/8 (ICSID).

Simmons, B. A. (2009). *Mobilizing for human rights*. Cambridge.

Sinclar, A. (2004). The origins of the umbrella clause in the international law of investment protection. *Arbitration International, 20*, 411.

Social and Economic Rights Action Centre and Centre for Economic and Social Rights v Nigeria [2001] Commission communication 155/96 (ACHPR).

Söllner, S. (2007). The "Breakthrough" of the right to food: The meaning of general comment no. 12 and the voluntary guidelines for the interpretation of the human right to food. In A. von Bogdandy & R. Wolfrum (Eds.), *Max Planck yearbook of United Nations law* (Vol. 11). Martinus Nijhoff Publishers.

Sornarajah, M. (2010). *The international law on foreign investment* (3rd ed.). Cambridge University Press.

South African Institute For Advanced Constitutional Public Human Rights and International Law. (2010). *The state duty to protect, corporate obligations and extra-territorial application in the African regional human rights system*.

Steiner, H. J., & Alston, P. (2000). *International human rights in context: Law, politics, morals: Text and materials* (2nd ed.). Oxford University Press.

Steward, R. (2012). Enforcement of transnational public regulation. In F. Cafaggi (Ed.), *Enforcement of transnational regulation*. Edward Elgar.

Sub-Commission on Prevention of Discrimination and Protection of Minorities. (1947). *Record of Sixth Meeting* (Discussion of Article 6 (Continued) E/CN4/Sub2/SR6).

Subedi, S. (2008). *International investment law: Reconciling policy and principle*. Oxford and Portland.

Técnicas Medioambientales Tecmed SA v Mexico [2003] Award ARB(AF)/00/2 (ICSID).

The East African Court of Justice Rules of Procedure, 2010. Registered as a Newspaper at the G.P.O. available at: http://www.eacj.org/docs/EACGazette5-5-10.pdf. Accessed 11 November 2013.

The Hague Convention (I) for the Pacific Settlement of International of International Disputes [1908] 1 Bevans 577; 2 AJIL Supp. 43.

The Independent Review Mechanism African Development Bank Operating Rules and Procedures (2010) available http://www.afdb.org/en/about-us/organisational-structure/independent-review-mechanism-irm/. Accessed 24 September 2014.

The London Court of International Arbitration. Arbitration Rules [1998] available at http://www.lcia.org/Dispute_Resolution_Services/LCIA_Arbitration_Rules.aspx. Accessed 14 July 2015.

The World Bank. (2013a). *Panel mandate and bank policies*. The World Bank, http://ewebapps.worldbank.org/apps/ip/Pages/Panel-Mandate.aspx. Accessed 12 July 2015.

The World Bank. (2013b). *Processing a request*. The World Bank, http://ewebapps.worldbank.org/apps/ip/Pages/Processing-a-Request.aspx. Accessed 12 July 2015.

The World Bank Group Office of the Compliance Advisor Ombudsman Guidelines [1999] available at http://www.cao-ombudsman.org/howwework/documents/CAOOperationalGuidelines2013_ENGLISH.pdf. Accessed 15 July 2015.

The World Conference on Human Rights on Human Rights; Vienna Declaration and Programme of Action [1993] available at http://www.ohchr.org/en/professionalinterest/pages/vienna.aspx. Accessed 11 November 2014.

Thomas, C. A. (2014). The uses and abuses of legitimacy in international law. *Oxford Journal of Law and Economics*, 1.

Thürer, D. *Soft law*. Max Planck Encyclopedia of Public International Law, http://www.mpepil.com/subscriber_article?script=yes&id=/epil/entries/law-9780199231690-e1469&recno=1&searchType=Quick&query=soft+law. Accessed 05 March 2012.

Tieleman, K. *The failure of the multinational agreement on investment (MAI) and the absence of a global public policy network*, available at http://www.gppinet/fileadmin/gppi/Tieleman_MAI_GPP_Network.pdf. Accessed 11 November 2013.

Tirana Declaration. Endorsed by the ILC Assembly of Members on 27 May 2011 Available http://www.landcoalition.org/sites/default/files/aom11/Tirana_Declaration_ILC_2011_ENG.pdf. Accessed 24 November 2013.

Trachtman, J. (2011). *Fragmentation, synergy and institutional choice*.

Treaty with Argentina concerning the reciprocal encouragement and protection of investment (USA-Argentina) [1991] available at http://2001-2009.state.gov/documents/organization/43475.pdf. Accessed 9 July 2016.

Trindade, A. A. C. (1987). Co-existence and co-ordination of mechanisms of international protection of human rights. *Collected Courses of the Hague Academy of International Law, 202*, 9.

Trindade, A. A. C. (1998). The consolidation of the procedural capacity of individuals in the evolution of the international protection of human rights: Present state and perspectives at the turn of the century. *Columbia Human Rights Law Review, 30*, 1.

U.S. Model Bilateral Investment Treaty [2004] Available at http://www.state.gov/documents/organization/117601.pdf. Accessed 17 November 2013.

U.S. Model Bilateral Investment Treaty [2012] available at http://www.state.gov/r/pa/prs/ps/2012/04/188199.htm. Accessed 12 July 2015.

United Nations. (2010). *Minority rights: International standards and guidance for implementation* (HR/PUB/10/3).

United Nations. (2012). *United Nations special procedures. Facts and figures 2012*. Office of the United Nations High Commissioner for Human Rights Geneva, February 2013.

United Nations Commission on International Trade Law. (1985). *UNCITRAL model law on international commercial arbitration*. United Nations.
United Nations Conference on Trade. (2013a). *Investment facilitation compact*. UNCTAD, http://unctad.org/en/Pages/DIAE/InvestmentFacilitationCompact/Investment-Facilitation-Compact.aspx. Accessed 12 April 2015.
United Nations Conference on Trade. (2013b). *Recent developments in investor-state dispute settlement*. UNCTAD, N 1 May 2013.
United Nations Conference on Trade and Development. (2007). *Bilateral investment treaties in 1995–2006: Trends in investment rulemaking*.
United Nations Convention on the Elimination of All Forms of Discrimination Against Women [1981] 1249 UNTS 14.
United Nations Declaration on the Rights of Indigenous Peoples Resolution [2007] A/61/L.67 and Add.1 61/295.
United Nations Economic and Social Council, Siracusa Principles on the Limitation and Derogation Provisions in the International Covenant on Civil and Political Rights [1985] E/CN.4/1985/4 Annex.
United Nations High Commissioner for Human Rights. (2008). *Business and human rights: A survey of NHRI practices*. UNHCR, http://webcache.googleusercontent.com/search?q=cache:oKxNkj0KlnsJ:www.reports-and-materials.org/OHCHR-National-Human-Rights-Institutions-practices-Apr-2008.doc+&cd=1&hl=en&ct=clnk&gl=ch&client=safari. Accessed 12 July 2015.
United Nations Millennium Project. (2005). *Investing in development: A practical plan to achieve the millennium development goals*. New York.
van Aaken, A. (2005). *Making international human rights protection more effective: A rational-choice approach to the effectiveness of Ius Standi provisions*. Preprints of the Max Planck Institute for Research on Collective Goods 2005/16 1.
van Aaken, A. (2006). Fragmentation of international law: The case of international investment law. In J. Klabbers & K. Creutz (Eds.), *Finnish yearbook of international law* (Vol. 17). Martinus Nijhoff Publishers.
van Aaken, A. (2014). Delegating interpretative authority in investment treaties: The case of joint commissions. *Transnational Dispute Management, 1*.
van Banning, T. (2002). *The human right to property*. Intersentia.
van Genugten, W. (2010). The African move towards the adoption of the 2007 declaration on the rights of indigenous peoples: The substantive arguments behind the procedures. *American Journal of International Law, 104*, 29.
Vestey Group Ltd v Bolivarian Republic of Venezuela [2016] Award ARB/06/4 (ICSID).
Vidar, M. (2005). The interrelationships between the right to food and other human rights. In W. B. Eide & U. Kracht (Eds.), *Food and human rights in development: Legal and institutional dimensions and selected topics* (Vol. I). Intersentia.
Voluntary Guidelines on the Responsible Governance of Tenure of Land, Fisheries and Forests in the Context of National Food Security [2013] CL 144/9 C 2013/20.
von Braun, J., & Meinzen-Dick, R. (2009). "Land Grabbing" by foreign investors in developing countries: Risks and opportunities. *International Food Policy Research Institute Policy Brief, 13*, 1.
Waibel, M. (2011). International investment law and treaty interpretation. In R. Hofmann, et al. (Eds.), *From clinical isolation to systemic integration*. Nomos. Accessed 18 August 2015.
Waste Management, Inc. v United Mexican States [2004] Award ARB(AF)/00/3 (ICSID).
Weatherspoon, D., Cacho, J., & Christy, R. (2001). Linking globalization, economic growth and poverty: Impacts of agribusiness strategies on Sub-Saharan Africa. *American Journal of Agricultural Economics, 83*, 722.
Wena Hotels Limited v Arab Republic of Egypt [2002] Decision on Annulment ARB/98/4 (ICSID).
Wenzel, N. *Extraterritoriality. Human rights, treaties, extraterritorial application and effects*. Max Planck Encyclopedia of Public International Law, http://opil.ouplaw.com/view/10.1093/law:epil/9780199231690/law-9780199231690-e819?rskey=FcIcM0&result=2&q=extraterritoriality&prd=EPIL&print. Accessed 20 August 2013.

World Summit for Social Development (UN) Copenhagen Declaration on Social Development [1995] A/CONF.166/9.

Wright, C. (2009). Setting standards for responsible banking examining the role of the international finance corporation in the emergence of the equator principles. In F. Biermann, B. Siebenhüner, & A. Schreyögg (Eds.), *Routledge research in environmental politics.* Routledge, http://www.loc.gov/catdir/toc/ecip0825/2008032291.html.

Wright, C. (2011). Export credit agencies and global energy: Promoting national exports in a changing world. *Global Policy, 2*, 133.

Yackee, J. (2007). *Do BITs really work? Revisiting the empirical link between investment treaties and foreign direct investment.* Univ of Wisconsin Legal Studies Research Paper No. 1054, http://ssrn.com/abstract=1015083. Accessed 20 September 2014.

Zimbabwe Lawyers for Human Rights, Human Rights Trust for Southern Africa v The Government of Zimbabwe [2005] Communication 314/05 (ACHPR).

Chapter 4
Opportunism in LSLI Contracts: An Economic View

4.1 Overview

Following the analysis of legal mechanisms in IL to enforce the rights to food and property, and showing how IL fails to protect the rights of locals, this chapter will follow a social science approach to LSLIs. In order to do so, we will consider the effects of LSLIs as a result of opportunistic behaviour producing detrimental effects for third parties. We will apply NIE to analyse what gives rise to opportunism and how it can be tackled. After this brief overview we will introduce NIE and the concept of opportunism. We will suggest that opportunism has two sources, namely prohibitively high agency costs and incomplete contracts.

The justification for applying NIE is that it allows the observer to penetrate national and local structures to discover legal failures whose effects will materialise upon completion of new LSLIs. In order to achieve our goal we apply principal-agent theory (PAT) and contract theory (CT) from a political economic perspective. They allow us to offer a detailed description of LSLIs by breaking down the investment process and institutional setting from the household to the international level. We will attempt to find the sources of opportunism to then propose mechanisms to tackle it. Our hypothesis posits that opportunism is a result of principal-agent problems arising from exorbitant agency costs at the local level. This problematic is framed by the application of a property rights approach. After assessing the situation at a local level we can better understand further failures arising from LSLIs. Institutional weakness at the household level creates a unique scenario in which investors and state representatives can sign incomplete contracts (i.e. their performance produces the effects we described above). Explaining LSLIs through the lenses of PAT and CT allows us to further apply these theories and follow the solutions that social science theory offers to mitigate the effects of opportunism. Consequently, the next chapter will focus on control mechanisms that can be used in the framework of IL to mitigate negative effects.

L.T. Montilla Fernández, *Large-Scale Land Investments in Least Developed Countries*, International Law and Economics, DOI 10.1007/978-3-319-65280-1_4

4.2 New Institutional Economics

4.2.1 *Justification*

The use of economic theory to analyse and solve legal problems has increased continuously in recent decades, although its growth has been slower in Europe than in the United States.[1] IIL and HRL were not absent in this process but have not been subject to the broad use that L&E has enjoyed in private law.[2] In the framework of L&E the use of a theory based on institutions has contributed to providing answers to legal problems.[3] Applying both theoretical and empirical approaches, NIE contributes to determining and efficiently ameliorating shortcomings in the legal system that lead to failures with relevant negative welfare effects. In order to do so we will offer positive and normative analyses which empirically test the answers to two different variable-oriented questions.[4] The first uses the law as an *explanans* by answering the question about the effects of the law. The second is to use the law as *explanandum*; in this case the answer examines why the law exists as it does.[5]

Nowadays the NIE approach is widely used in the school of L&E.[6] Already in the late 1980s it was catalogued as the liveliest area in economics.[7] It employs normative and positive analyses to model legal structures in which the contractual and delegation problems of moral hazard, adverse selection, and opportunism need to be solved.[8] As NIE's object of study, institutions are considered to set 'the rules

---

[1]We recommend the empirical examination on the importance of L&E at European Law Schools written by: Andrianirina-Ratsialonana et al. (2011). We also recommend the following contribution that analyses the future of L&E: Gazal-Ayal (2007), p. 3.

[2]Some examples are: Calabresi (2016), Posner (1973), Trachtman (2008), Posner and Sykes, p. 72134; van Aaken (2005, 2006), van Aaken (2009a), p. 483; van Aaken (2010). Susan Frank has also collected some data making some empirics analysis of IIL. In the area of trade law the some contributions have also been written: Guzman (2008), Franck (2005), p. 1521; Schropp (2009), Cashore et al. (2004).

[3]See the explanation of Williamson about the progress of NIE as well as the fields it covers: Posner and Sykes, p. 72134. As well as Posner in: Posner (1973).

[4]See also: Williamson (2000), p. 595.

[5]For an approach see: Posner (1993a), p. 73.

[6]As stated by Posner (1993a) when comparing NIE and L&E, both movements are valuable and they overlap in many aspects making its application fruitful. Posner refers to Williamson to affirm that: '[...]law is one of the legs of the interdisciplinary tripod on which NIE rests the seems no to be referring to the economic analysis of law.' For basics on NIE: Guzman (2008). For specific application of NIE in agricultural issues see: van Aaken, 'Rational Choice Theory' available at http://www.oxfordbibliographies.com/view/document/obo-9780199796953/obo-9780199796953-0051xml?rskey=qyeNms&result=21&q= [accessed on 26 November 2013].

[7]This was stated by R. C. O. Matthews In his presidential address to the Royal Economic Society. Quoted by: Menrad and Shirley (2005).

[8]The theoretical framework of principal-agent relationships was also used in the legal literature to explain and solve efficiency problems. Some of the classical contributions in which contractual structures are explained as well as the problems of moral hazard, adverse selection and

of the game in a society' or, more formally, they are seen as 'the humanly devised constraints that shape human interaction.'[9] Following Ostrom's definition institutions refer to the rules, norms, and strategies used by humans in repetitive situations.[10] Ostrom's approach considers rules to be prescriptions that are understood and enforced in particular situations by agents that are responsible for monitoring and imposing sanctions. Norms are known and accepted prescriptions involving costs and benefits rather than material sanctions or inducements. Strategies represent the steps taken by economic actors to make use of the incentives produced by rules and norms. As defined by North, institutions provide for more certainty in human interaction, influence human behaviour, and impact outcomes such as economic performance, efficiency, economic growth, and development.[11]

NIE has a Coaseian background.[12] In contrast to other economic traditions such as the neoclassical approach, which takes institutions as a given and focuses on their efficiency, NIE centres on the development of institutions at different levels and examines their efficiency and welfare. NIE as approached by Williamson (2000) considers institutions on two levels; these levels are part of a total of four levels examined in a social institutional analysis.[13] They include embeddedness, the institutional environment, governance, and resource allocation.[14] The first level is the most static. It contains norms that change over long periods of time, e.g. customs, religion, and traditions.[15] Classical economists consider this level to be a given. The second level is composed of 'formal rules' such as constitutions, laws, and property rights. The norms included here are a product of the norms at the first level. The second level encompasses the institutional environment that forms the framework in which economic subjects interact. North states that this interaction is possible because 'the major role of institutions in a society is for Institutions to reduce uncertainty by providing a structure to everyday life.'[16] This level includes the norms that formalise state power and state functions. The property rights approach is included at this level.[17] Williamson includes the contributions of positive political theory (PPT)[18] because NIE is a part of it, and because it provides

opportunism are offered by: Kherallah and Kirsten (2002), p. 110; Williamson (2000), p. 595; Williamson (1979), p. 233. More specific and applied to the field of L&E see: Braverman and Stiglitz (1982), p. 695; Milgrom and Roberts (1992), Mahoney (1999), Shavell (2004), van Aaken (2014b), Hermalin et al. (2007), Schropp (2009).

[9]van Aaken (2009b), p. 507.

[10]North (1990), p. 3; Ostrom (1998, 2005b).

[11]Ostrom (2005a).

[12]Seminal works: North (1990), p. 3; Coase (1937), p. 386. A review of Coase's work: Coase (1988).

[13]Williamson (1989), p. 223.

[14]Williamson (2000), pp. 595, 597.

[15]As stated by Williamson, 'this level is undertaken by historians and other social scientists'. Ibid.

[16]Ibid.

[17]North (1990), p. 3.

[18]For complete application of Political Theory see: Williamson (2000), pp. 595, 598.

a positive analysis that contributes to NIE.[19] The third level focuses on governance mechanisms in which the role of contracts, their anatomy, and their function take a central position.[20] Williamson defines governance as 'an effort to *craft order*, thereby to mitigate *conflict* and realise *mutual gains*.'[21] Therefore, this section focuses on *ex ante* incentives to increase governance in unavoidably incomplete contracts. PAT and CT were developed at this level. The *ex post* stage of contracts is the focus of transaction cost economics.[22] Neoclassical analysis comes in at the fourth level. This level includes the firm described as a production function where optimisation plays a relevant role. The approach developed by NIE relates to the second and third levels. Williamson described these two levels as representing the macro and micro levels.

The rapid development of this field may be attributed to its eclecticism and flexibility in proposing models. NIE compiles variables from old economic theories, increases their flexibility, reuses them, and proposes solutions. It relaxes the variable of full rationality[23] and recognises the existence of transaction costs,[24] thus arguing at a macro level that the institutional arrangement of a country (i.e. its legal, political, and social frameworks) will influence economic performance in a determinant way.[25] Applying these approaches, NIE analyses legal, social, economic, and political institutions that govern everyday life and focuses on explaining how economic actors achieve their goals through the creation of incentives. Hence, it follows a model of strict methodological individualism.[26]

In the next section we will analyse the application of NIE in agricultural economics where the rise of opportunism takes a prominent role.

---

[19]Mueller (2008).

[20]Some of the most relevant contributions in this strand are: Williamson (2000), pp. 595, 598; Williamson (1996), Fudenberg and Tirole (1990).

[21]Milgrom and Roberts (1992).

[22]As stated by North: 'The costliness of information is the key to the costs of transiting, which consist of the costs of measuring the valuable attributes of what is being exchanged and the costs of protecting rights and policing and enforcing agreements. These measurements and enforcement costs are the source of social, political en economic institutions'. Williamson (2000), pp. 595, 599.

[23]Posner (1993b) offers a brief description of the differences between the 'old' school and the 'new' school. His distinction focuses on the rejection of the classical economic theory (the theory of Adam Smith) by old institutional economics. He also focuses on the economic formal aspects as seen by both schools and the NIE theory, as expounded for example by Paul Samuelson.

[24]North (1990), p. 26.

[25]See for example some works made by: Menrad and Shirley (2005), p. 41; Feld and Voigt (2003), p. 497.

[26]See Sect. 1.5 of this study.

4.2.2 Assumptions

NIE offers an approach that is closer to reality than the conditions assumed under the perfect competition model. The latter posits a large number of actors in the market, profit and utility maximisation, perfect information, homogenous products, easy entry and exit to the market, no economies of scale or production externalities, and a complete set of markets. The perfect conditions created by this model produce equilibrium. For new institutional economists, this model lacks realism. NIE considers the classical model but relaxes its assumptions.[27] While the classical model assumes individuals to be completely rational, NIE proposes that even individuals trying to be completely rational are limited by cognitive restrictions. Economic actors cannot perceive the state of the world with complete accuracy. This means that even when individuals try to be completely rational, their lack of complete information[28] about the world leads them to overlook some of the risks associated with the transaction they are engaging in. Individuals *intend* to be rational but are *limited* in their rationality, thus operating with so-called 'bounded rationality'.[29] These two elements, namely bounded rationality and limited cognitive capacity, determine transaction costs. These costs arise because information is valuable and held asymmetrically by the parties. Ergo, parties have to make decisions under conditions of uncertainty.[30] This means that economic actors are neither able to know the probability of a determined outcome, define a comprehensive set of outcomes, nor make a decision based on the probability of their favoured outcome.[31] Under the described circumstances, rational actors will maximise their expected gains. Some authors prefer to describe this process not as the profit-maximisation approach but as the satisfaction of one's own necessities.[32] This means that individuals operating under the above-mentioned restrictions will act when they are sure that transacting satisfies their needs. In this sense NIE constructs a *homo economicus* whose anatomy differs from the profit maximisers found in classic economic theories. After considering the assumptions of NIE it should now be mentioned that the contribution of NIE is seen to be its acknowledgement of informational asymmetries and its assertion that institutions do matter.

---

[27]Voigt and Hazo (2007), p. 269.

[28]For a comprehensive illustration of the different types of distribution of asymmetrical information applied to principal-agent problems that can also be considered in other NIE approaches see: Furubotn and Richter (2008), p. 2.

[29]Volker (1995), pp. 821, 824.

[30]Furubotn and Richter call it as 'Imperfect Individual Rationality' Milgrom and Roberts (1992) at chapter 5; Voigt (2009), p. 30. For uncertainty applied to international relations see:; Furubotn and Richter (2008).

[31]Komoremos (2005), p. 49.

[32]Williamson (1985), p. 49 and Chayes and Chayes (1993), pp. 175, 197. Both quoted in footnote 39 in Chap. 1 by: Simon (1957).

NIE allows us to apply its assumptions and approaches to our problem through the lens of political economy. The framework of political economy focuses on non-market decision-making.[33] Assuming politicians are rational, we shift the picture to benevolence by analysing the contribution of politicians' behaviour to social welfare.[34] Ergo, we consider politicians to be profit maximisers who satisfy their own preferences as well as those of specific social groups by undertaking measures in exchange for support so that they can remain in power.

4.2.3 *Implications*

Since individuals have cognitive limitations and asymmetric access to information, conflicts of interest may arise. The actor with more information has a competitive advantage over others individuals. Institutions are created as an environment in which both parties can interact. Parties will interact when their expected gains are at least greater than zero. Parties need information in order to make this calculation, the disclosure of which will depend on the relevant institutions. The problem of unbalanced information may give rise to opportunism. If institutions understand that individuals have limited resources to make a decision, they might create incentives to provide these resources—such as information—so that uncertainty decreases and individuals can transact. Without institutions the cost of transacting becomes higher and affects the willingness of actors to interact. The limitations of NIE are clear from the fact that it is still not possible to predict how individuals will act in future situations. It presupposes an unresolved behavioural aspect regarding individual preferences and models for individuals to make decisions. Therefore, at least for now, it seeks to offer institutional models that completely guarantee that individuals will not behave opportunistically.[35]

NIE has developed diverse tools and theories that contribute to analysing many types of contractual relationships between economic actors. These theories make it possible to understand behaviours in specific circumstances while allowing for predictable outcomes and avoiding opportunism. Applying these tools to the political scenario, politicians can make use of coercive mechanisms to achieve specific goals. The alignment of interests between politicians and their supporters makes these goals achievable. NIE concerns moral hazard and rent-seeking behaviour while also framing solutions for public policies to achieve expected social welfare goals. PAT and CT are applied to the problem discussed in this research. Opportunism plays a central role in both theories. However, the difference between them

[33]van Aaken (2013), p. 227.

[34]Mueller (2008), p. 1.

[35]Indirectly this statement can be perceived in the contribution by Schropp (2009). He graphically shows the limitations of CT, such limitations have the common characteristic resulting in the impossibility of model aspects related to the sources of the preferences. See: ibid.

is that PAT presupposes a delegation of activity, while CT does not. In the next section we will introduce the notion of opportunism and proceed to apply PAT and CT.

4.3 Opportunism

4.3.1 General Overview

Williamson defines opportunism as the strongest expression of self-interest.[36] He incorporates the conditions 'simple self-interest seeking'[37] and 'obedience'[38] into opportunism as forms of self-interested behaviour. Even though the opportunism literature has made significant progress in recent decades it still remains a controversial subject.[39] Research has focused on understanding risk and its implications in trade scenarios. The classical notion developed by Williamson considers opportunism to be a violation of an explicit contract.[40] He affirms that opportunism is 'self-interest seeking with guile.' Expressed in legal terms, Williamson associates opportunism with bad faith.[41] It is a troublesome source of behavioural uncertainty in economic transactions, and is motivated by a self-interest-seeking assumption that relies on neoclassical economics. It is curious in so far as it includes the element of guile. The analogy between bad faith and opportunism was also suggested by Williamson when he defined guile as 'lying, stealing, cheating, and calculated efforts to mislead, distort, disguise, obfuscate, or otherwise confuse.'[42]

Opportunism has important practical and negative implications for negotiation processes.[43] This is because it represents a risk for contracting parties of failing to

---

[36]Schropp (2009).

[37]It is explained by Williamson (1985), p. 49 as follows: 'although neoclassical man confronts self-interested others across markets, this presumes that bargains are struck on terms that reflect original position. But initial positions will be fully and candidly disclosed upon inquiry, state of the world declarations will be accurate, and execution is oath- or rule-bound in the manner described above. Accordingly, whereas parties realise all advantages that their wealth, resources, patents, know-how, and so forth lawfully entitle them, those are all evident from the outset. Inasmuch as there are no surprises thereafter, a condition of simple self-interest seeking may be said to obtain. Issues of economic organisation thus turn on technological features (e.g. scale economies), there being no problematic behaviour attributable to rule deviance among human actors'.

[38]Williamson uses the definition of obedience introduced by Georgescu-Roegen in which a collective follows the instructions imposed by functionaries who establish macro goals. The economic problem is reduced to a problem of 'technical manipulation. See: Williamson (1985), p. 47.

[39]By way of example see: ibid; Georgescu-Rogen quoted at 49 ibid.

[40]Wathne and Heide (2000), p. 36.

[41]In the context of this research the two terms are used synonymously.

[42]Davis et al. (1997), p. 20.

[43]Williamson (1985), p. 49.

realise their goals. When the risk produced by opportunism is sufficiently high in a particular relationship, considerable effort must be spent on controlling and monitoring resources. Opportunism affects transaction and opportunity costs[44] in the form of high-value deals going unperformed. The reasons go back—from a methodological point of view—to the general assumptions of NIE.

Williamson classifies opportunism as having two different forms. The first arises from a deliberate misrepresentation during the negotiation stage, while the second emerges after the negotiation stage when the contract is being performed. These forms are commonly known as *ex ante* and *ex post* opportunism, respectively. The difference between the two lies in the moment they arise, namely before or after the signing of a contract.[45] In order to prevent *ex post* opportunism from arising, Williamson states that two conditions must be observed: (1) parties promise at the outset to disclose all relevant information candidly and to behave in a cooperative way during contract execution and renewal intervals, and (2) the promises are self-enforcing, meaning that parties adhere to the agreement as long as each gains more from continuing with the agreement than from abrogating it.[46] In addition, Williamson presents a category through which opportunism may be defined. He uses the term 'lawful opportunism' to describe infringements that are outside the scope of formal contracts but still produce the effects of opportunism.[47] This means that there are certain kinds of behaviour that are not included in the contractual relationship, and their performance cannot be sanctioned.

In the area of 'self-enforcing' promises and opportunism, different types of contracts, including 'social contracts' and 'synallagmatic contracts', are considered. These contracts are based on relational activities governing a particular aspect of complex social relationships. In these cases, due to the absence of a specific contract, the determination of the constitutional elements of opportunism can be more difficult. Therefore, it is necessary to fix a baseline to differentiate 'guile' from acceptable behaviour, and then use it as a reference to determine the existence of opportunism. For the purpose of this research it shall be taken into consideration that an actor taking advantage of another actor within a contractual relationship cannot be seen as opportunistic. Should the actor take such an advantage, and by doing so violate an existing norm or legally protected value (at the national or international level), this actor might be considered an opportunist and therefore could be held accountable.[48] The form taken by accountability is defined by law, which in our case encompasses the

---

[44]Transaction costs are the object of study of transaction economics. This discipline is a part of the NIE research tradition. Arrow understands transaction costs as the costs of running the economic system. They are different from production costs, which is the cost category which neoclassical analysis researches.

[45]Transaction economics understands contracts not only in a narrow legal way. The idea of the social contract is also part of the understanding of contract.

[46]Williamson (1985), p. 64.

[47]Williamson (1993), p. 97.

[48]We concentrate however only on cases in which the human rights to food and property are infringed.

enforcement mechanisms described in Chap. 2. This means that in our case the baseline that needs to be crossed for an actor to be considered opportunistic is defined by law. It should be highlighted that in our case the violated norm does not necessarily have to be the one stipulated by the contractual parties—e.g. relational contracts. More general norms included in governance systems may be considered. We also consider other norms such as those regulating different economic activity that might produce the infringement of norms upon completion.

4.3.2 Opportunism in LSLIs

Having approached the general aspects of NIE and opportunism, we will now proceed to elaborate our theoretical framework by defining opportunism in LSLIs. In this manner we suggest that self-interest-seeking behaviour with guile that carries out HRs transgressions sets the baseline for opportunism. This behaviour produces detrimental effects either for a contractual party or for third parties. We nevertheless separate negative externalities from opportunism based on chronological reasons. Opportunism is the behaviour that produces negative externalities. In many cases parties will determine the existence of opportunistic behaviour when negative externalities are nevertheless appreciable. Now we will consider different sources of opportunism in LSLIs. We suggest that opportunism arises from two different sources:

(1) Opportunism results from a delegation activity, which itself derives from a principal-agent relationship that produces principal-agent problems because the agency costs are high. In this case opportunism arises from contracts in a broad sense, such as social contracts, for example the contract between voters and politicians or between indigenous authorities and their subordinates. This situation occurs at the ground level. We define it as *ex ante* opportunism because it is already present before the LSLI contract is signed. In fact the LSLI contract *per se* does not accentuate the existence of opportunism in the principal-agent relationships we are considering. Investment contracts, as they are signed, are the effect of principal-agent problems. This means that if principal-agent problems wouldn't exist, transaction costs of signing these investment contracts would probably be higher because they would require better standards of governance and information. In the political arena LSLI contracts can be seen as the payment from politicians to investors in order for them to remain in power.

In this structure we identify what Williamson defined as lawful opportunism. It takes place because the institutional framework in which negotiations take place—specifically property rights to land—fails in scenarios dominated by principal-agent problems. Due to the existence of moral hazard and adverse selection, agency costs are excessively high.[49] Thus there might be an institutional gap the closure of which

[49]For a broad explanation of the models including both moral hazard and adverse selection see: Williamson (1993), pp. 97, 98.

would efficiently limit the opportunistic behaviour of economic actors. A poor allocation of incentives exists in so far that economic actors are not properly incentivised to act on behalf of their principals, and decision makers are not sanctioned when they follow their own interests. This produces detrimental effects for less politically relevant actors. The problem we now face is determining where the problem is located.

(2) Opportunism also results from synallagmatic contractual relationships. In this case LSLI contracts are properly considered. Opportunism arising from these contracts is considered *ex post* opportunism because it comes about after having signed the contract. This means that opportunism occurs when the negotiation process is over and the parties are performing the contract. It arises from incomplete contracts. From the implications we explained, incompleteness can be traced back to, *inter alia*, strategic motives from the parties and cognitive limitations of the parties. Incomplete contracts are those contracts that fail to regulate events that might be regulated, and where the negative externalities are linked to institutional failures and the contractual governance designed by the parties during the negotiation process.[50] The fact that decision makers and investors behave opportunistically after closing negotiations is caused by the *ex ante* misallocation of incentives, when parties make their own law through the contract. In addition to the contractual conundrum that makes up the institutional agreement, the institutional environment also fails to create incentives to discourage opportunistic behaviour. Such incentives might relate to the regulatory framework of the state where the negotiations take place, access to justice, and the credibility of the judicial system, *inter alia*. In the IIL regime the domestic institutional environment would be less relevant, as in most cases the presence of an IIA means that the requirement of having to exhaust domestic remedies may be bypassed. This leads us to highlight that if opportunism arises at the international level, this is due to the asymmetric level of protection offered by IL and the absence of incentives to not behave opportunistically.

Having highlighted the different types of opportunism in LSLIs, their specific source and moment of occurrence need to be determined. The two different types of opportunism are found at five negotiation levels. Again, we consider the moment in which the investment contract is signed to be the determinant for *ex ante* and *ex post* considerations. The negotiation levels include the most relevant economic actors that interact in the negotiation process. The first three levels refer to the three scenarios which take place before the contract is signed (*ex ante*). These three scenarios include the negotiation process between:

1. local authorities and government representatives,
2. local authorities and local owners,
3. and government representatives and local owners.

Investors are not considered at these three levels, and 'lawful opportunism' takes place at each of them. These levels of negotiation are situated at a national level

[50] A detailed approach, *infra* at: Sect. 4.5.

Table 4.1 Types of opportunism at different negotiation levels in LSLI contracts

Level of neg.	Economic actors	Type of relationship	Type of opport.
1	Owners—Social delegate(s)	Principal—Agent	Ex ante
2	Social delegate(s)—Governmental Agency	Principal—Agent	Ex ante
3	Owners—Governmental Agency	Principal—Agent	Ex ante
4	Owners (including social delegate(s)—Investors	Contracting parties	Ex post
5	Investors—State	Contracting parties	Ex post

Source: Prepared by the author

between domestic authorities and owners or tenants. A transmission of property rights takes place (through purchase, lease, or expropriation) so that the state has the land at its disposal and can introduce investment projects. It is as part of this process that moral hazard problems can arise. They will only be palpable, however, when the land investment is performed.

At levels four and five, which take place after the contract has been signed (*ex post*), opportunism arises if *ex ante* parties did not design incentives to promote co-operation or did not design enforceable promises. Table 4.1 displays who the actors are, what kind of contractual relationship governs them, and the type of opportunism that we suggest might arise.

When contractual parties know all the elements that can affect the profit, as well as all the costs associated with each of their transactions, and they regulate each one of them, the possibility of behaving opportunistically is zero. However, as we explained earlier, applying the assumptions of NIE it is almost impossible to imagine that such a Panglossian world might exist. Economic actors differ in the amount of information and knowledge they hold, and the greater the asymmetry of information, the higher the probability that behaviour of an opportunistic nature will occur.

The contracting process requires a balance between transaction costs and incentives to contract. If transaction costs become too high, economic actors will not contract. Williamson posits that if parties knew that transactions were subject to potential *ex post* opportunism, *ex ante* measures might help them to avoid these detrimental effects. These measures might occur in the framework of an 'institutional environment' and 'governance.'[51] While the institutional environment contributes towards balancing the bargaining power of the parties, governance structures contribute towards incentivising compliance. Disclosing information incentivises cooperation between actors.[52] Governance structures are relevant for avoiding *ex post* opportunism. Such incentives will vary depending on the form of government, the possibility of access to judicial mechanisms, the recognition of

[51] Williamson (1993), pp. 97, 98 ff.

[52] Williamson (1985), p. 49.

potentially violable rights, the establishment of clear rules on rights restrictions and expropriation, and the monetary cost of having access to competent institutions. We will now proceed to analyse the forms that opportunism can take in LSLI contracts.

4.3.3 Expressions of Opportunism

Case studies analysing the effects of LSLIs mostly focus on unfulfilled political promises leading to two different issues, which in legal terms constitute the violation of the human right to property and to food.[53] As we have previously deliberated upon, such violations are considered to be a consequence of opportunistic behaviour. While we do not deny the existence of other effects associated with opportunism, we will primarily concentrate on these two effects as they are most frequently mentioned. However, our approach can be extended to other rights.

Thus, we consider the infringement of the right to property and food to be a consequence of the opportunistic behaviour of economic actors. In Chap. 2 we analysed the mechanisms in IL to prevent infringements of property rights and the right to food and to make a claim following the violation of these rights. In this section it is our goal to explore the factors that make it possible for agents to behave opportunistically. It is our claim that if we can determine the source of opportunistic behaviour, it is possible to design legal policies incentivising economic actors to behave in a more desirable way. Therefore, we need to focus on potential sources of opportunism to show who behaves opportunistically and how this behaviour can be tackled. The role of the law may be to create a balance so that market failures are minimised and opportunistic behaviour can thus be tackled.

In order to do this, as previously stated, we will apply two of the tools available in NIE. These tools are PAT and CT. Even though the fundamentals of these two theories go back to the existence of a contractual relationship and their assumptions are linked, they each have a different notion of contracts, and the delegation of economic activity to a second individual is only found in PAT. This delegation of activity implies a hierarchical relationship between the economic actors, which is absent in contractual relationships. In these relationships actors are contractual parties and not delegators of a specific activity that might be realised on behalf of another individual. In the next section we will explain how the two theories work and then proceed to apply them in order to comprehensively understand how the actors involved negotiate. Knowing how actors negotiate will help us to figure out how policies might be formulated to create and allocate incentives correctly so that opportunism can be tackled. Of course, the aim of this is to achieve the original goal of the associated policies, namely to increase social welfare.

[53]See *supra* Sect. 2.3.

4.4 Opportunism in Principal-Agent Relationships

4.4.1 Introduction

The research of PAT confronts us with the principal-agent problem. The development of PAT began with the contributions of Wilson and Arrow in 1968 and 1971, respectively.[54] Their scholarship framed part of the exploratory phase of this early development. Thereafter, this theory was applied to a huge spectrum of problems from the micro to the macro level. It is one of the oldest and most commonly used codified models of social interaction.[55] It seeks to describe the risks faced by contractual parties seeking to cooperate when they contend with uncertainty and different interests. It has made a great contribution to expanding the literature on risk sharing[56] as well as to understanding the social, political, and cultural structures influencing economic outcomes.[57] Different approaches and research areas have applied the research agenda proposed by PAT, and some of the most important contributions have been in the areas of insurance,[58] labour relationships,[59] common property rights,[60] and institutions in the agricultural sector.[61] In the field of L&E it has been frequently used to analyse corporation structures,[62] international relations, arbitrators, courts, and the problems arising from delegating competences to specialised bodies.[63]

PAT attempts to solve the problems emanating from agency relationships. These problems arise from asymmetric information, which affects the desires or goals of the principal. Agency relationships are defined as a contract under which one or more persons (the principal) engage another person (the agent) to perform some service on their behalf.[64] Following the assumptions of NIE, problems might arise if the goals of the parties diverge at the time of contracting. Individuals, including politicians, are assumed to be utility maximisers who do not have complete

---

[54]Williamson (1985), p. 49; Wilson (1968).

[55]Arrow (1971). Williston in 1902 already told about the principal-agents problems applied to legal issues. On this regarding see footnote 43 in Chap. 1.

[56]Ross (1973), p. 134.

[57]Here we refer to the contributions of Williamson and Ostrom.

[58]Eisenhardt (1989), p. 57.

[59]Miller (2008), p. 351.

[60]Jensen and Meckling (1976), p. 305, 5.

[61]Ostrom and Hess, 'Private and Common Property Rights' http://ssrn.com/abstract=1304699 accessed 26 August 201 Schlanger and Ostrom (1992), p. 249; For an overview about the classical applications of PAT see: Bardhan (1987, 1989).

[62]One of the most famous examples of applying PAT in Corporate Law was written by: Volker (1995), pp. 821, 822.

[63]Some examples of these contributions include:; Reinier et al. (2009) as well as van Aaken (2014b).

[64]Paul and Stephan (2002).

information about other party's preferences.[65] Agency costs increase linearly as a function of the size of the divergence of interests between the parties. The greater the divergence, the more agency costs increase, as does the conflict of interest between principal and agent.[66] PAT studies the design of *ex-ante* incentive mechanisms to reduce agency costs in the face of adverse selection and potential moral hazard for agents. The contractual relationship between principal and agents cannot be viewed narrowly. It does not necessarily refer to what legal theory defines as synallagmatic contracts. It includes contractual relationships along a broad spectrum, e.g. the relationship between voters and politicians.[67]

It is difficult for the principal to verify what the agent is doing and whether the actions of the agent are made on behalf of the principal or on his own behalf. Therefore, PAT proposes an approach that allows for the lowering of transaction risks. On one side of the equation the problem is that the principal is not able to corroborate that the activity carried out by the agent is to the benefit of the principal, and not to the benefit of himself (the agent). On the other side of the equation it constitutes a problem that the agent and the principal, being rational economic actors, are unwilling to share risks to an equal extent.[68] Consequently, the agent might make decisions following his own preferences and not the principal's. This may cause serious damage to the principal in some cases. This leads to the question of why the principal delegates activities if it is well known that the agent is a rational actor and will therefore follow his own interests. The PAT literature answers this question primarily by arguing that the agent plays a complementary role in the economic activity of the principal because he—the agent—has experience and information that are not easily accessible to the principal. Therefore, the principal creates incentives for the agent to provide this information. In our case a principal-agent relationship exists between government representatives (a general term for all of the politicians or decision makers including indigenous chiefs) and the local population. The existence of the principal-agent relationship is not rare at all. National regulations are designed so that principal-agent problems can be minimised. If national legislation fails, the question arises whether IL can be used as a control mechanism to avoid further detrimental effects produced by principal-agent problems or whether IL can be used as a monitoring mechanism to avoid an increase in agency costs. In the next section we will review the applicability of PAT to agricultural economics and the potential benefits that its application may bring about at the international level.

[65]Jensen and Meckling (1976), p. 305.

[66]Ross (1973), pp. 134, 5.

[67]This refers to the cases in which a more abstract notion of what constitutes a contract exists. In the political economic field, the relationships between voters and politicians is also seen as a principal-agent relationship in which a contract exist. See: Volker (1995), pp. 821, 823.

[68]Furubotn and Richter (2008), p. 476.

4.4.2 PAT and Agricultural Law & Economics

L&E analysis of agrarian law is still in the initial stages of development.[69] PAT has, however, made a contribution to agricultural economics by explaining the emergence of specific institutions[70] as an effect of the existence of asymmetric information, huge transaction costs, transaction risks, and delegation problems in which moral hazard and adverse selection play a role.[71] In political economy PAT has been extensively used to analyse rent-seeking behaviours as well as regulatory processes.[72] These contributions mostly focus on sharecropping, vertical integration, the regulation of labour markets, the interlinking of contracts in credit and land leases, labour hiring, output sales, and institutions for risk hedging, interlocking credit, input and produce transactions, cooperative institutions in production, and credit. It has also contributed to understanding the existence of some contractual arrangements, particularly in cases of sharecropping. Other academic contributions have concentrated on the creation, improvement, or performance of agrarian institutions' contribution to development at a local and national level.[73]

Elinor Ostrom offers different approaches to applying PAT by addressing the problem of the commons and the decision-making processes of groups. In *Governing the Commons* she analyses possible solutions to *ex ante* agency problems by focusing on production in the presence of common property rights. She models different situations in order to define how to design policies to govern common property rights and increase their productivity. Today, Ostrom's contribution is probably the first and most important reference in research dealing with common property rights.[74] Ostrom constructs different scenarios, which are described as 'games'. In her example, herders working in the same meadow year after year are the players of these games.[75] Therefore, the individuals know the productivity and carrying capacity of the land, and there exists a situation in which there is a homogeneous level of information among the herders. This fact will allow the individuals to act when they perceive that other contracting parties are breaching the contract of the commons. The different scenarios she uses to analyse diverse possibilities are based on contractual arrangements. In general terms, she presents two models in which a central agency is allowed to sanction the wrongful behaviour of individuals. In one game the central agency has complete information, and in the second it does not. By analysing the two scenarios Ostrom concludes that

[69]Even though there are some economic approaches in the field of NIE that consider legal systems as variables, a well-developed application of theory of L&E on agrarian law as it exists in contract, civil, criminal, trade, international law, is still missing. The field is open for research.

[70]For an approach on agrarian institutions see: Volker (1995), pp. 821, 823 ff.

[71]See i.e. Bardhan (1989).

[72]For an overview of the application of PAT in political economy see: Harriss et al. (1997).

[73]For example Mueller (2008), p. 340 ff. Braverman and Stiglitz (1982), p. 695.

[74]Binswanger and Rosenzweig (1986), p. 503.

[75]Ostrom (2005b).

a central agency can solve problems between herders, but only if it has complete information.[76] The fact that the agency needs complete information in order to sanction correctly means that participation costs will increase. If individuals correctly assume that the agency does not have complete information, an incorrect sanction might result. This means that the preferences of the participants would change because the agency would introduce and misallocate new incentives.

Next, Ostrom analyses cases where participants have similar information and proposes a game in which the herders delegate the competence to sanction wrongful behaviour to a third body, called arbitrators. She states that in this case:

> Arbitrators may not need to hire monitors to observe the activities of the contracting parties. The self-interest of those who negotiated the contract will lead them to monitor each other and to report observed infractions so that the contract is enforced. A regulatory agency, on the other hand, always needs to hire its own monitors. The regulatory agency then faces the principal-agent problem of how to ensure that its monitors do their own job.[77]

Such arrangements have to be self-enforcing. Her empirical studies conclude that it was not possible to design a general solution in the specific structures she analysed; her institutional arrangements cannot be seen as a panacea. She therefore suggests a case-by-case approach. The arrangements presented in the various cases have many weaknesses associated with asymmetric information.[78] It is economically evident that the agent and the principal introduce specific arrangements that make it possible to tackle opportunism in complex ownership structures.

4.4.3 PAT Contribution

The contribution of PAT is to have found an efficient way to regulate principal-agent problems. Principal-agent relationships become problematic when agency costs are high.[79] Agency costs are defined by Jensen and Meckling as the sum of (1) the monitoring expenditures of the principal, (2) the bonding expenditures of the agent, and (3) the residual loss.[80] Residual loss is the decrease in welfare experienced by the principal due to his divergent preferences from the agent.[81] In other words it represents the potential gains from trade not realised because principals cannot provide perfect incentives for agents to perform some tasks, but only have imperfect indications of the agent's performance. PAT addresses the problem of the general assumptions of NIE. Additionally, it assumes that there are some conflicts between participants in every organisational process due to discrepancies in their

---

[76] Ibid.

[77] Ibid.

[78] Ibid.

[79] Ibid.

[80] Ross (1973), pp. 134, 114.

[81] Jensen and Meckling (1976), pp. 305, 6.

personal goals. PAT considers efficiency a criterion of effectiveness, and it also assumes that not all participants have the same information either *ex ante* or *ex post*. Thus, PAT proposes the implementation of monitoring and control mechanisms to ensure that the *ex ante* promises will not remain without substance and that the expected gains of the principal can be achieved.[82] PAT solves the motivational problem of one party—the agent—so that they will act on behalf of the principal. In interpersonal relationships the arrangements necessary to achieve a certain level of governance are contained in contracts.[83] At the state level, the law might call for institutions to incentivise economic actors while at the international level, this function is within the scope of IL. The synergy that ideally exists between national law and IL should contribute to correctly creating and allocating incentives if this does not occur at the national level.

4.4.4 Identifying Sources of Opportunism: Principal-Agent Problems

We have identified three different agency problems related to delegation activities that occur when the agrarian policies introduced by states include LSLIs. The three agency problems are between communal owners and their local social delegates, investment agencies and the local chiefs, and between owners and investment agencies. In the next paragraphs we will justify the assumption of the existence of principal-agent problems.

The first agency problem arises from the relationship between the communal owners and their local social delegates (see Table 4.1). A social delegate is a person who has political power in the community in which the future investment will take place. This person was usually the chief in the geographical area of interest to our study. The chief is vested with the characteristics of the agent. He is the representative of the local community and he is traditionally responsible for ensuring its welfare. His position vis-à-vis the community is comparable to the *bonus pater familias* in ancient Roman law. A person becomes chief for cultural or political reasons, and often but not always because of his lineage.[84] The ancestors of the community agreed to accept this person, or a member of the chief's family, as chief. The chief makes most of the decisions regarding the community's resources. This means that the communal owners transfer some attributions of their property rights to the chief so that he can exercise his authority. In this case, the decision of whether his people will enter into an investment contract or not—either with a local public agency, a national investor, or a foreign investor—and whether some property

[82] Ibid.

[83] Volker (1995), p. 821, 114.

[84] A very well elaborated contribution that explains the role of Chiefs by resolving local conflicts see: Jensen and Meckling (1976), p. 305, 7.

rights are transferred either definitively or temporarily is made either by the chief alone or by a very small group of individuals with homogenous preferences.

On the other side of this agency relationship are the members of the community: the principals. They are considered to be the owners of the commons who delegate authority to the person fulfilling the role of chief. They recognise the authority of the chief. Their membership of the community has a strong economic component, in addition to cultural and historical elements, as the village or community provides jobs (often in subsistence agriculture), education, medical services, housing, and in some cases personal security. In the hierarchical relationship between the chief and community members it is not possible for the owners to directly influence the decisions of the chief. There is no voting mechanism for dissatisfied members of the community, but principals are free to leave the village since there are no fixed rules for entering and exiting the community. Since the members of the community pay royalties to the chief, the chief has an incentive for the population to continually increase. The decision maker, who is either the chief or a very small and homogenous group of individuals, has sufficient power not to be controlled by the principals. The principals' mechanisms for improving governance in most of the communities are co-extensive with their autonomy as actors in that they are free—or almost free—to enter and exit the community. This means that because agents have an interest in obtaining the fruits of their principals who are the economic motor of the community, it is also in their interest to ensure that their decisions are supported by the principals at least to some extent.

The second agency problem arises between investment agencies and chiefs. In this relationship the chief is the principal and the investment agency takes the role of agent. Investment agencies in this context are formal state institutions—investment agencies, ministries of agriculture, or ministries for development—that in turn are represented either by one individual or by a small homogenous elite who make decisions; they are part of the governmental structure of the state. Their goals are the promotion of FDI and development. In this agency relationship the principal transfers a bundle of property rights to the investment agency so that it can use them to create incentives for foreign investors to use the land. In the negotiation process between the investment agency and the chief, promises regarding the positive effects of investments on local education, health, and work places are made. However, it is not possible for the chief to keep all the promises he had previously made to members of his community through negotiation with foreign investors. The chief can also not be certain whether the representative of the investment agency is negotiating on their own behalf alone. The institutional environment and the governance mechanisms created by the contracts are insufficient to put in place an appropriate level of incentives to mitigate opportunistic behaviour.

The third type of agency problem arises between owners and investment agencies. This problem occurs in communal land tenure systems when there is no specific person who is vested with the authority to govern the community (such as the chief in our example). This means that there is no well-established hierarchical relationship between individuals. An example of this can be found in certain nomad communities. It also applies when the owners of the land do not have an ownership title, which means they are private or communal owners without title. We include here traditional farmers with small pieces of land (subsistence farmers) without clear delimitations. In these cases the individuals are considered to be principals and the investment agency is considered to be the agent. Here, principal-agent problems arise for reasons similar to those explained in the previous case. While investment agencies seek to acquire the land for development-oriented purposes in which the owners are direct beneficiaries, it is not possible for the principal to follow whether the agent's behaviour is the most conducive to them achieving the aims previously agreed upon. This means that principals cannot know whether the agent is acting in their own best interest or in the best interest of the principal. Asymmetries of information and bargaining power dominate the relationship between principal and agent, resulting in potentially unequal grounds for negotiation. The result of this is that due to the institutional framework, which includes the positive law governing the relationship, the owners may not be able to get their land back. Even though in most cases agencies do not buy the land but lease it, the effects are more or less the same since the lease contracts are drawn up to 99 years (see Chap. 2).

When decisions are taken in groups, the requirements of the institutional environment might increase the cost of transacting due to the higher costs of coordination that are implicit in the decision-making process. Elinor Ostrom demonstrates that the size of the groups influences the efficiency of decision-makers.[85] If the coordination costs are too high, it will be difficult for the parties to engage in collective action, which in turn will influence their bargaining power. In well-functioning systems the delegation of functions to a specialised group or commission can contribute to balancing the position in negotiations and to decreasing the exorbitant agency cost.[86] However, it also creates another challenge due to the new principal-agent relationship created between the commission and the principal. This structure is not covered in our analysis at this stage.

After having explored various types of opportunism, the moment when opportunism arises, and the actors involved in the negotiation process, it is now our goal to explain why it is possible for agency costs to be as high as they are and why it is unlikely that the affected actors will behave in a correct or non-opportunistic manner in many cases. The assumptions of NIE are now applied to the property rights approach. Individuals lacking information about their legal property rights will have to make deals in a context of high levels of uncertainty and risk. In these situations their bargaining power is low. Without bargaining power, meaning that a party agrees to a contract only because it does not have all the relevant information at its disposal, property rights alone lose their importance. In order to substantiate our argument we will apply an approach to property rights developed by Schlanger and Ostrom (1992). This approach describes how communal property rights are

[85]Brobbey (2008).

[86]This is so because in the presence of high coordination costs, collective decision-making processes will also be more expensive than in small and homogenous groups.

structured and how decisions concerning their redefinition are taken.[87] The redefinition of property rights occurs via the introduction of a new policy, which in our research refers to the implementation of LSLIs. By redefinition we mean a transformation of the original property right that alters the existing *de jure* or *de facto* situation; this can be done by transmitting all or some bundles of property rights. Our analysis breaks down the system of property rights and examines its structure so that the function and role of each actor involved can be observed individually.

4.4.5 Property Rights Approach: Motivation

As already noted in previous sections, the idea of increasing agricultural production on idle or underused land in order to produce food and other derivatives is highly welcome. The increase in market prices generates profits that stimulate FDI in LDCs. LSLIs are seen as an instrument for the definition of property rights through market transactions between involved economic actors (contractual parties). The fact that a clear definition of property rights exists and that these rights are enforceable provides the essential incentive for investment. To reiterate: without clearly defined property rights, economic actors would not cultivate the land in the first place. Having rights that are defined leads investors to provide the capital necessary for economic growth.[88] Problems associated with the formal distribution of land have dominated the modern history of the sub-Saharan region and they have featured heavily in some economist's explanations of the why certain agrarian policies fail continuously.[89] In colonial times the situation was very simple because local governments or authorities did not play an important role in decision-making processes. Land was not considered a *res commercium* per se.[90] However, a new market was formalised when land was made transmissible. The purpose of the institutional environment created through constitutional and IL is to make rights enforceable.

The existence of opportunism means that there is a lack of legal incentives to protect or enforce the rights of either an individual (private property rights) or a group of individuals (common property rights). The origin of the problem lies in the structure of the common property rights system that allows one owner to transmit property rights irregularly due to a principal-agent problem. This happens because highly asymmetric information makes it possible for decision makers to behave opportunistically, while for the rest of the owners it is almost impossible to take action to enforce their rights and hold the decision maker accountable.

[87] Ostrom and Hess, 'Private and Common Property Rights', 338 http://ssrn.com/abstract=1304699 accessed 26 August 2015.

[88] More detailed at Sect. 2.2.

[89] See: Schlanger and Ostrom (1992), p. 249; Mannathukkaren (2011), p. 379.

[90] See Sect. 2.2.1.2.

To understand how this occurs, a descriptive fragmented analysis of common property rights is needed. Knowledge of the structure of the property rights system allows us to understand why principal-agent problems, and therefore opportunism, arise. Furthermore, it allows us to understand the impact on the protection of the right to food. The property rights approach justifies the existence of a principal-agent relationship. After having shown why principal-agent problems arise and how they facilitate opportunistic behaviour, the application of PAT will elucidate how opportunistic behaviour might be tackled in the context of LSLIs.

4.4.5.1 Fragmented Property Rights Approach

Elinor Ostrom offers one of the most relevant contributions to modern common property rights research. Ostrom was able to explain why some common property rights systems fail while others have been successful. We will consider a piece of her research to further construct our approach. Together with Edella Schlanger, Ostrom authored a text on property rights focussing on natural resource regimes. Schlanger and Ostrom's approach explains how the productivity in common property rights systems may be increased.[91] Contrary to other schools of economic thought that qualify and rationalise common property rights as inefficient, these authors conducted in-depth analysis and studied their structures. Some economic schools of thought consider such systems to create insufficient incentives for owners to increase productivity, mainly because they do not realise that their own work matters.

The model proposed by Schlanger and Ostrom proceeds as follows: they classify the different boundaries that define the common property rights system. They place individuals within a pyramidal structure, depending on their personal qualities. The closer to the peak a person is, the more rights—and subsequently the more power—the person has. The individual or small homogenous group at the peak is the only entity with the power to decide on the access, withdrawal, management, and exclusion of other persons from the community. This person or small homogenous group can also alienate the land without any kind of previous consultation. All of these actions illustrate the boundary-free nature of property rights.

The contribution of this model to the present research question lies in its demonstration of how the existing property rights system in LDCs leads to opportunistic behaviour at different levels. Additionally, it highlights the presence of coordination problems and their effects on the bargaining power of potential actors, as well as the ramifcations of entering into negotiations. Therefore, with the help of the conceptual approach of Schlager and Ostrom, we will aim to clarify and analyse whether and how it is possible to avoid the undesirable but apparent opportunistic effects arising from agency problems in the LSLI contracting process. This approach is limited to the technical solutions the theory can offer; however, it has

[91]Deininger et al. (2008), p. 1786.

some implications for policy design. The question about the role of IL in avoiding or tackling such effects will be addressed separately.

4.4.5.2 Definition of Common Property Rights

Property rights are basically a bundle of rights that enable the holder to freely dispose of an asset and to exclude others from its use or enjoyment. Common property rights afford the authority to undertake particular actions related to a specific domain. This contribution describes a bundle of common property rights as authorising specific individual(s) to take decisions regarding shared property titles. It also includes in its definition individuals without a formal ownership title, since for customary and constitutional reasons they are considered owners as well,[92] and partake in communal ownership. In our case this group of persons is comprised of the individuals represented by chiefs in local communities. The chief is an authority figure who represents the community. The community does not elect him but he consults with the members of the communities (or some of them) when making decisions. If there are no chiefs the model may still be applied. This is because a local politician, local authority, or unilateral decision maker will replace the chief in the model.[93]

4.4.5.3 Rules, Rights, and Property Regimes

Different rules and rights might play a role in distinct categories and at different levels of action in the property rights system. These are (1) operational-choice and (2) collective-choice rules. Rules are generally agreed upon and enforced prescriptions that require, forbid, or permit specific actions for more than a single individual. The rules come from collective choice; this allocates the competence of the participants and necessary consensus. Rights are considered particular actions related to a specific domain that is authorised.

4.4.5.4 Operational Levels

The distribution of capacities to use one or more bundles of property rights occurs at certain operational levels. These levels consist of the different possibilities of access that an individual has in the bundle of property rights. To coordinate the

---

[92]See Sect. 2.2.1.4 of this study.

[93]There are other systems such as that of Ethiopia where the institution of the Chief does not exist. In this particular case, since the land is completely owned by the state, the local authority takes decisions. Nevertheless given the fact that Chiefs do not exist in the theoretical model, the place of the Chief belongs to the state-authority.

operation of property rights, the owners have different degrees of participation in using the rights. Some individuals will have access—the right to enter a defined physical property—and withdrawal—the right to obtain the 'products' of a resource, e.g. planting and harvesting—from the property rights. Other individuals have the right to manage the property, which includes regulating internal use patterns and transforming the resource by making improvements, or the right to exclude, which includes determining who will have access to certain rights and how they may be transferred. Others have the right to alienate, which includes transmitting part or all of the property rights from one party to another. The operational levels of actors are determined by their level in the pyramidal structure, and are defined below.[94]

Individuals are assigned a certain operational level. The more rights an individual has, the more power he or she has to administrate and enforce *de facto* property rights. When it comes to communal rights, all individuals belonging to the community are owners (even when they do not have a title), given national and international legal recognition from constitutional law and international treaties.[95] Through a 'social contract', rights are transferred to an authority that administers them on behalf of the community. Having explained this, the following graph shows the implicit hierarchy of the system. The largest area is allocated to the operational level of those with only the right to access and withdrawal. This level represents the area in which the highest number of individuals are operating. The right to manage the resources is reserved for a smaller group of individuals who also have the right to access and withdrawal. Individuals at the base of the trapeze accumulate all rights, including the right to alienate (Fig. 4.1).

Some modern states with communal systems have constitutional rules that delimit the competence of the two extremes (Access, Withdrawal and Alienation), which implies that the bargaining power of group members decreases, at least *de jure*. Control mechanisms to alienate the land include the register of the transaction that in some cases requires the approbation of the community and their expertise.[96] In the following section we will describe the economic actors and their roles in the property rights system.

4.4.5.4.1 Actors

Three different types of actors can be found in the system of property rights: (1) the chief or social delegate, (2) owners, and (3) foreigners or investors. The only person

---

[94]Schlanger and Ostrom (1992), p. 249.

[95]This statement is given by the fact that most of the African countries have ratified the 538; additionally domestic law in most African countries, protects the right to property of indigenous people at a constitutional level Last but not least, the African Commission on Human and People Rights ratified the guarantees concerning common property rights. See: ibid.

[96]In the case of Ghana for example where the Land Registry offices are catalysts for the Chiefs' political power. Shelton (2002), p. 937.

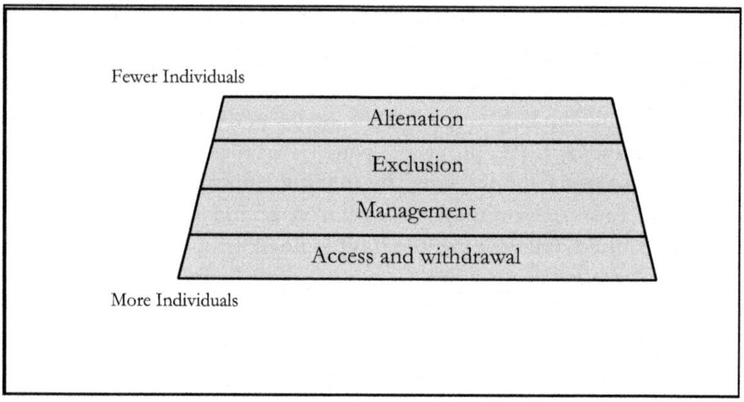

Fig. 4.1 Bundles of property rights. Source: Prepared by the author

who can use all the attributes of the system is the chief (at least with some limitations, as expressed above). Again, if there is no chief, the person exercising the power of the chief will be considered the decision maker. The owners are the members of the community. They have the option of Access and Withdrawal, despite the limitation of having to pay royalties to the chief, and they can also manage the land. Frequently, the royalties they pay are directly proportional to their production output. This could explain why in some cases owners are not incentivised to increase their production. The foreigners or investors are completely external to the community and have limited rights of access and withdrawal to the land. Their bundle of rights is achieved only through the positive result of a negotiation, and is formalised through purchase or lease contracts.

The lease contract creates a new sub-level of property rights that are not considered in the graph above. These rights are distributed between access, withdrawal, and management. This is a different configuration of management because investors have a fixed quota to pay, given the contractual specification of the lease contract. In these cases it does not matter whether the investors produce anything or not, which distinguishes the treatment of investors from local people. Local people must pay royalties depending on their production, while investors make a monetary payment. Investors fulfil the contract by paying rent. This payment is made either once every year or once every contract period, also in contracts whose duration is for 25 years or more.[97]

[97]Due to the nature of the agricultural activity this has implicit high investment costs. Investment contracts are necessarily long-time contracts and firms must be big in order to be able to internalise risks and production costs.

4.4.5.4.2 *De Facto* and *de Jure* Property Rights

Property rights remain *de facto* as long as the government authorities do not formally recognise them. Recognition can be given through administrative or judicial acts, e.g. through constitutional protection. These acts grant authority to the government to enforce and to accord such rights to the users of land.

In defining property rights one finds that law functions in two different ways depending on the relationship between occupiers and resources. In *de facto* property rights the function of the law will be a declarative one. Hence an act of law that recognises such rights will not result in a new status for the individual; it will simply affirm or legalise a previously existing relationship. However, is there is no *de facto* property right the function of the law will be a constitutive one.

De facto property rights are relevant for four reasons: (1) they influence the form of the incentives being created; (2) self-control and collective-choice arrangements can produce operational rules closely matched by the physical and economic conditions of a particular site; (3) they introduce 'sweeping reforms'; and (4) since the regulation of these *de facto* ownership regimes is undertaken by locals who benefit from them, the costs of regulation are largely borne by these same beneficiaries. Institutional arrangements that internalise the cost of monitoring and exclusion among beneficiaries reduce inefficiencies.

Taking into account the different structural analyses up to this point, one can affirm that the problem with communal property rights—at least from the legal point of view, but with important economic consequences—is that given the nature of such rights, it is almost impossible to enforce individual rights. This is the case because the enforcement costs associated with minimum coordination between communal owners is very high. Individuals are owners without a title, except in some cases for the chief. This may be the result of hierarchical local structures, weak policies, or individual strategies. It is also problematic that even when such rights are recognised at the constitutional level, formal mechanisms to enforce them are missing.

The most frequently practiced form of enforcement is still the traditional one, which is also exercised by the chiefs. The aspect that needs to be highlighted here is that the chief is *de jure chief* and *de facto owner* of all the land the community he represents owns. This means that this person has at his disposal both the traditional power to control the land and the cooperation of weak national institutions to make his own position much more powerful. Consequently, it is possible and completely legal for the chief to act as the *de facto owner* and exercise all the rights of a legal owner even when he is not the legal owner of all the land. This weakness increases the likelihood of chiefs behaving opportunistically.

4.4.5.5 Incentives and Outcomes of Property Rights

The most important difference between property rights in different systems noted by Schlanger and Ostrom (1992) is the relationship between individuals, the property right (*de jure* or *de facto*) as such, and the relationship between individuals and bundles of property rights. The authors affirm that the most important and crucial bundle is the right to alienate. It is the ultimate expression of power. Therefore, it is an economic incentive that increases efficiency. The right to alienate can also facilitate finding equilibrium between incentives coming from owners and incentives coming from investors. If communal owners overvalue their land, investors will lose interest in investing; otherwise, over-exploitation or misuse of natural resources could result.

Exclusion also increases the incentives to cooperate and to create favourable conditions for investors, and by doing so the owners can capture benefits related to withdrawal rights. The crucial element is the minimal coordination that is needed between owners allocated across the different levels of the trapeze and their relationship with the chiefs to capture and distribute the benefits. If coordination costs are high, bargaining power decreases. In consequence, due to high coordination costs, the agent can act opportunistically. Given that agents do not cooperate (i.e. monitor the investors) because the principal does not encourage them to do so, as a result it is not possible to get the expected returns on investments. This means that one way of increasing the expected gains is to incentivise agents to act on behalf of the principals, meaning that agency costs might decrease.

Furthermore this situation will overlap on a second level. This happens when a national entity (investment agency or ministry) gets involved in the negotiation. These institutions are competent to deal with the local authority (chiefs or local decision makers) who provide the land where the investment will take place. Investment agencies, as national legal authorities, will take the land provided by the local authority and allocate the property rights to investors. The local representatives will also be confronted with asymmetric bargaining power resulting from high coordination costs if they are the owners *de jure* and *de facto*. If the state is the *de jure* owner of the land, bargaining asymmetries will be even more palpable.

Some countries have implemented policies oriented towards the redistribution of property rights through entitlements. However, even when these policies received support from IOs, for instance in the region of sub-Saharan Africa, they have failed.[98] The reasons for these outcomes have not been fully understood in academia; however, it seems that political power at the domestic level resisting calls to register land is a causal factor. Local political leaders such as chiefs would lose control of their land if they were to register it, as it would lead to the formalisation of the rights of the other members of the community. Even though this power is also lost when new agrarian policies are introduced, calls for land registration leads to conflict between communities and government but not between the members of the communities themselves.

Up until now we have learned that certain failures create incentives for opportunistic behaviour. These failures are not necessarily associated with LSLIs—they are factual elements pre-dating the arrival of investors. However, the fact that

[98]One recent study on land register: Goldstein and Udry (2008), p. 981.

investments take place potentially magnifies such failures and creates negative externalities, the cost of which can usually not be internalised.

By applying the approach described, a key failure is the extreme difficulty principals have in incentivising agents to act on their behalf at the local level, with repercussions at the international level due to the framework that protects investors. The cost of taking decisions is very high for principals as their level of coordination is low. This makes it possible that the agents, rather than taking decisions for the benefit of society as a whole, maximise their own utility function by remaining in power or obtaining direct benefits from supporters. We have shown that this occurs as a result of missing governance mechanisms, as well as from the absence of an appropriate institutional environment that creates efficient monitoring and control mechanisms at the local level. Ergo, there are clear incentives for local decision makers to act opportunistically and maximise their own gains. These facts produce negative spill-overs and create incentives to transfer property rights to investors, the legitimacy of which is broadly questionable. The goal of this segment has been to analyse the structures of property rights in order to find the primary source of principal-agent problems. Having done this we now examine the literature on principal-agent relationships to elucidate how opportunism can be tackled. IL instruments are used to assess whether IL has suitable tools to operationalise the solutions proposed.

4.4.6 Tackling Opportunism Through PAT

By applying NIE-based assumptions, PAT offers a strategy seeking to ensure that the agent behaves to the benefit of the principal through the analysis of their relationship (taking principal and agent as units of analysis). Expressed in PAT vocabulary, it offers a solution to tackling opportunistic behaviour in a contractual relationship in which delegation or coordination activities are present. It cannot be expected that PAT provides a general or standardised answer for all problems.[99] However, PAT may indeed elucidate concrete problems, and its implications should certainly be testable. PAT offers a multiple-solution system and in some cases it will state that there is not an optimal solution. Instead, it will indicate an alternative solution that is closest to the optimal one.[100]

The solution offered by PAT is the creation of monitoring mechanisms that decrease agency costs and allow the principal to have some control over the agent. These mechanisms might create incentives for individuals to behave in conformity with norms. They also contribute to defining the structure of property rights and thus make it possible to increase agricultural productivity independently of the type of

[99]As many studies have concluded. Some examples: Cotula (2015), Miller (2008).

[100]This approach would follow the acceptance of the second best solution; as considered by individuals given the fact that they cannot obtain the best solution due to their cognitive limitations. For a seminal work: Kirsten et al. (2009).

property rights. Therefore, the literature establishes that the principal can introduce measures that limit divergences with the agent through monitoring systems. In some cases the principal will create monetary incentives for the agent not to harm the principal or to ensure that the agent will compensate the principal if damages arise. The costs incurred by the parties are not necessarily pecuniary; they can also be gains or losses of welfare. Such mechanisms are understood to be efforts on the part of the principal to control the behaviour of the agent through budget restrictions, compensation policies, or operating rules. They are more than just measurements or observations of the agent's behaviour.[101] Instead, a mechanism might function by creating incentives to balance informational asymmetries and thereby tackle opportunism. Monitoring mechanisms generally seek to establish a context of equilibrium in information flows. The information thus provided can be used to incentivise agents to fulfil promises and to behave on behalf of the principal. They can also be used by the principal to demonstrate before a third institution—a judge or arbitrator—that there has been a contractual breach and thus demand compensation.

Based on the classical solutions proposed by the literature, Milgrom and Roberts developed four principles which prevent increases in agency costs if they are applied during the period of contractual activity. They might have effects if an institutional environment can be considered a given; in other cases the implementation of these principles could represent an exorbitant cost for contracting parties. The principles are (1) the information principle: any measure of performance that (on the margin) reveals information about the level of effort chosen by the agent should be included in the compensation contract; and (2) the incentive-intensity principle: an optimal intensity of effort is devoted to solving the principal-agent problem, so it will never be 'fully resolved'. As a result principal-agent issues are always subject to contest and further experimentation in the public and private sectors. The next principle is (3) the monitoring intensity principle: situations in which the optimal intensity of incentives corresponds highly to those in which the optimal level of monitoring is also high; and (4) the equal-compensation principle: activities equally valued by the employer should be equally valuable (in terms of compensation, including non-financial aspects such as pleasantness) to the employee.[102] This principle refers to the problem that employees may be engaged in several activities, and if some of these activities are not monitored or are monitored less frequently they will be neglected, as activities with higher marginal returns to the employee are favoured. Targeting certain measurable variables may cause others to suffer. For example, if agricultural workers are rewarded in relation to the volume of input packages sold to farmers or the number of loans granted to farmers, they may de-emphasise equally or more important aspects of their role which were not explicitly targeted in their performance contract.[103] In state activities these principles might be incorporated into the legal system at different levels.

[101] For this definition see Lipsey and Lancaster (1956).

[102] Jensen and Meckling (1976), p. 305, at footnote 9 in Chap. 1.

[103] Milgrom and Roberts (1992).

The principles proposed by Milgrom and Roberts lead to a solution that is identical to that proposed by Ostrom. They propose a specific design of the governance and institutional arrangements that are necessary for enforcement (including self-enforcement). Correct arrangements increase the governance of the contract by reducing performance and renegotiation costs.

In order to achieve monitoring goals, states have legal systems that are responsible for creating the institutional environment to enforce protected rights. At the most general level constitutional law has basic mechanisms that guarantee the realisation of social values, which are expressed in the form of principles.[104] They function as channels to enable the flow of information, incentivise economic actors to interact, and to create judicial or administrative monitoring mechanisms to enforce sanctions. Without the existence of principles at a constitutional level and procedural norms to enforce them, it is not possible to obtain a specific level of efficiency, which is required to maximise the net surplus of society.[105] Efficiency is not a benchmark but constitutional principles are used as a proxy for those principles agreed upon by society.[106] Society must recognise and accept the significance of a monitoring mechanism before it can be added to existing constitutional values and principles. Not only the inclusion and definition of property rights (which, depending on the state structures, might be common or private) belong to this level, but also the judicial guarantees to protect them and the reparation mechanisms in case of infringement. An institutional balance might exist that creates economic incentives for individuals to interact and to balance their bargaining power. These incentives are created not only by *de jure* protection but also by *de facto* protection of rights.

There is a need for more concrete mechanisms to implement protections guaranteed at a constitutional level. In order to do so further policies targeting legal and economic activities are required. These policies will create a more specific institutional framework for economic actors to interact, i.e. they set the standards for contracting, create guarantees by transmitting property rights, prohibit contracting in certain situations—including areas that are monopolised by the state—and in some cases regulate the exploitation of natural resources or the property rights to land. In agricultural markets, which are characterised by high levels of uncertainty and risk,[107] the institutional framework regulating the activity plays a decisive role. This is the case even more so in LDCs where the agricultural sector is the most important. At this level the legal institutional design makes it possible for parties to exchange important

[104]Such principles vary depending on national idiosyncrasies and the political orientation of the government.

[105]Milgrom and Roberts (1992), van Aaken (2003).

[106]van Aaken (2008), p. 659. The term 'Efficiency' coming from welfare economics searches for the welfare of society. Van Aaken states that welfare might be derived from individual utilities and preferences (according to the classical school as well as Kaplow/Shavell) or might be constituted by individual capabilities and rights through an objective justification (following Sen). The important element of this approach is that it seeks to maximise human well-being as L&E does.

[107]See for example the role of entitlement of land on decreasing uncertainty in LDCs with a special emphasis on Sub-Saharan Africa. Ibid.

information and thus to decrease transaction costs. Legal norms make it possible to create a potentially balanced relationship between contracting parties: a legal baseline. They might incentivise individuals to contract and thus ensure that their actions produce legal effects. In a system of property rights, internal institutional weaknesses create failures and negative externalities arise as a result. These are due to a lack of enforcement in the institutional environment.

Contractual arrangements are responsible for creating specific norms for the achievement of specific goals. The relevance of national institutions lies in their facilitating the alignment of development-oriented policies and coordinating the interests of different groups to achieve commonly proposed goals. However, in most LDCs these structures are weak or missing, the judicial system tends to be insufficiently independent, and there are high levels of corruption and a lack of independence in the judicial system, which all affect the institutional environment. This leads to increasing agency costs, which make it possible for individuals to behave opportunistically. IL comes into play to fill such institutional gaps. A complementary relationship between the two mechanisms makes it possible to control for the potential opportunism of agents and to adapt monitoring mechanisms for specific economic transactions. This might include the creation of an obligation to provide specific valuable information that is essential to the success of specific economic activities, or the obligation to demonstrate legal capacity to enter into a legal business. Since the general mechanisms are abstract it is necessary to specify the activity they are planning to undertake when principals and agents negotiate. This is the interaction between the institutional environment and governance arrangements that was previously referred to, and which might be applied and socially accepted at the domestic level to guarantee desired goals.

These failures become increasingly relevant when foreign investors are involved due to the asymmetric level of protection between groups of legal subjects entering into the same economic activity. We have already shown that the difference in treatment between nationals and foreigners creates a legal grey zone where it is possible for investors, who have a higher level of protection and a competitive advantage due to economic power, knowledge, and technology, to detrimentally affect the local and traditional systems of production. Local farmers are competing under different levels of protection than foreign investors. Hence, a state that introduces LSLIs as a policy to guarantee food security (which is relevant to fulfilling national and international HRs obligations) will have two different groups of actors involved in the production. Rather than one party complementing the other or promoting competence, the result is that the most powerful party dominates the market and negatively affects local food security, even though global food security seems to improve as a result of the investment. This is the case because locals are often shut out from the market created by foreign investors due to their lack of access to it as consumers.

Therefore, monitoring mechanisms are needed in order for IL to function correctly. Further, incentives are needed to counteract the possibility of agents maximising their own welfare and creating better conditions for their groups of supporters. Some mechanisms that were explained in Chap. 2 constitute the basis of the international institutional environment in which a framework based on judicial incentives with reputational effects governs. We have seen that these mechanisms often fail to help affected locals due to their unenforceability and the fact that their remedies offered in other cases lack sufficient incentives for actors to enforce their rights. They do not create sufficient incentives to balance the flow of information between the parties and therefore to allow principal-agent problems to become principal-agent relationships. This failure is evident from the fact that HRs obligations are often not observed. Judicial mechanisms protecting HRs often fail, and due to the fragmentation of IL it seems impossible to enforce HRs through IIL. We believe, and we will be able to demonstrate, that different kinds of mechanisms and legal strategies that have already been developed in the L&E and legal literature can contribute to alleviating the effects of domestic failures by implementing new agrarian policies. We also believe that once incentives to achieve specific goals are correctly allocated, agency costs will decrease. We are not blind to the fact that, looking through the lens of NIE, there are sufficient reasons to believe that the impracticality of including HRs issues in investment law is rooted in a principal-agent background (this aspect will be briefly treated in Chap. 5).[108] We will scrutinise legal strategies as instruments used by states to implement, regulate, and incentivise investment negotiations so that contractual goals are achievable. These strategies are not only judicial but also extra-judicial in nature. We reserve explanation and evaluation of such legal strategies for the next chapter, as well as the necessary mechanisms to incentivise political actors to behave in a way that allows social welfare to prevail over their own welfare. For now we turn to justifying our argument regarding the emergence of opportunism from synallagmatic contracts.

4.5 Opportunism in Synallagmatic Contractual Relationships: A Contract Theory Approach

4.5.1 Introduction

We now turn to analysing contractual activity *per se* as a source of opportunism in LSLI contracts and will apply CT and political economy. It has been suggested that applying CT to the analysis of international contracts can enrich the research agenda.[109] In addition to political economy models it has been frequently applied

[108]The considerations of Arbitrators as profit maximisers can be deduced from this seminal work by Atwood, p. 659. More focused on arbitrators see: Posner (1993b), p. 1. Focusing on courts: van Aaken (2014b), p. 5.

[109]Relevant contributions in CT are: Paul and Stephan (2002), Dunoff and Trachtman (1999), p. 1; Bhandari and Sykes (1998), Posner (1973), Scott (2006), p. 279; Williamson (1979), p. 233; Shavell (1980), Mahoney (1999), Brousseau and Glachant (2002). CT applied to IIL: Shavell (2004), van Aaken (2009b), p. 507.

in L&E to explain legal phenomena in HRs, tax law, criminal law, and IIL.[110] Its application is highly interesting for lawyers because, in contrast to the legal analysis of contracts, CT as applied in this investigation shifts the focus of analysis to an *ex ante* perspective. It makes it possible to frame outcomes and therefore to consider specific structures for improving governance. An *ex post* perspective as offered by legal theory allows us to interpret the contract rather than adapt it to a specific economic activity.[111] Through CT we can explain the preferences of contracting parties, their considerations and preferences when entering negotiations, as well as their aims and the approach they use to achieve their proposed goals. CT also constitutes a comprehensive approach to understanding why opportunism arises and what can be done to tackle it. Additionally, contract activity seen through the lens of political economy allows us to understand rent-seeking behaviour and how politicians behave like economic actors imbued with power that is used to maximise their own utility functions. By using CT we explain why parties contract and why they choose the contractual arrangements they do. Furthermore, it helps us to answer the question of optimal contracting and to design legal policies to achieve pre-established goals. This theoretical approach provides a foundation for defining different contractual structures based on ownership and control, which is highly relevant in agricultural markets.[112] It explains how different organisational structures assign property rights to resolve the issues that arise when contracts are considered incomplete. To apply CT we first refer to Table 4.1 showing the two levels at which opportunism arises due to the structure of synallagmatic contracts that are signed between locals and investors or between states and investors. While opportunism arises in both cases, we will focus on investor-state relationships. In the application of PAT we mostly focused on situations previous to the negotiation of LSLI contracts in which the delegation of an activity was the common characteristic. We will now deal with contractual commitments and their enforcement. In order to analyse contracts as a source of opportunism, we will first develop a theoretical approach to introduce the theory and thereafter apply it to LSLI contracts.

[110]See: Hrabrin Bachev, 'Framework for Analysis of Agrarian Contracts' Munich Personal RePEc Archive http://mpra.ub.uni-muenchen.de/20264/1/MPRA_paper_20264.pdf accessed 21 July 2015; See also van Aaken (2009b), p. 507 and Scott (2006), p. 279.

[111]Scott considers that the major conceptual advance proposed by CT is that it analyses the contract from an *ex ante* perspective which differs from how it is done in legal theory which focuses on the *ex post* perspective. The approach offered by CT makes it possible for parties to consider the inclusion of specific rules or standards in the contract that make contractual outcomes predictable in light of courts' decisions. See: Scott and Stephan (2006), Scott (2006), pp. 279, 281.

[112]It is of increasing relevance for agricultural activities as a result of potential governmental interventions in agricultural markets. See: Scott and Stephan (2006), p. 62.

4.5.2 *Contract Theory in LSLIs*

4.5.2.1 Contractual Actors

The starting point in our approach is to refresh our basic assumptions, which are founded on the cognitive limitations of economic actors that affect their perception of the real world and thus give rise to informational asymmetries, *inter alia.*[113] Bounded rationality and profit maximisation are characteristics of economic actors in CT and play a relevant role by defining their preferences.[114] Information differs from economic actor to economic actor, and since contracting parties have divergent interests, the exchange of information is costly. The implications of these assumptions in the framework of CT are clearly explained by Scott, who states that:

> Parties who enter into contracts typically face a conundrum. They want to write a contract that is optimal *ex ante*, that at the time of contracting is one that encourages each party to invest in the contractual relationship so as to maximise the anticipated joint benefits. In particular, parties wish to make credible (i.e., enforceable) promises to motivate their contracting partners to invest in jointly profitable activities. They also want to write a contract that is optimal ex post, that is, one that is still value maximizing after all future uncertainties have been resolved as of the time of performance.[115]

In this scenario the problem is that on the one hand parties are reluctant to give away their own information, but on the other hand they need as much information as possible about the other party's position. Their aim is to design the commitments contained in the contract as inflexibly as possible and to guarantee enforcement.[116] Additionally, due to their cognitive limitations parties are not able to foresee probable but uncertain events. This means that uncertainty is a barrier to drafting a complete contract. These constraints will create tensions, requiring *ex post* flexibility of commitments to adapt them to future uncertainties. Parties will sign a contract when they have solved the tensions surrounding commitment and flexibility.

In CT, contracts (*lato sensu*) are the unit of analysis. They are considered to be an exchange of promises for future performance. This means that contracts are intended to guarantee credible commitments in a future-oriented relationship. From the economic point of view, enforceability is a requirement for efficiency; it is the element that creates incentives for parties to fulfil their promises.[117] As stated by Calabresi and Melamed in 1972, contracting parties 'make their own law' by assigning themselves residual ownership rights or 'entitlements'.[118] In our specific

---

[113]See Sect. 1.5 of this study.

[114]This statement is derived from our main assumptions; which have been broadly treated in previous chapters. Even though this is the case, we refer to the specific consideration of these assumptions as applied in CT (Wu (2006), p. 490) as well as the basic literature of L&E: Scott and Stephan (2006).

[115]Cooter and Ulen (2012), p. 276 ff.

[116]Scott and Stephan (2006), p. 61.

[117]Dunoff and Trachtman (1999), pp. 1, 35.

[118]Cooter and Ulen (2012), p. 283.

case, CT contributes to understanding the contractual design of LSLIs, the reasons why it produces certain effects, and what should be done to create and allocate incentives to avoid opportunism through *ex ante* contractual commitments.

4.5.2.2 Contractual Motivation

One of the most challenging tasks of CT is to explain why economic actors contract. Following our own assumptions in addition to those developed in the specialised literature by Calabresi and Melamed, it can be stated in very general terms that the motivation of parties to contract is to make use of the regulatory function of the contract; these regulatory functions are able to guarantee that promises will be fulfilled.[119] Assuming that parties are rational actors, they enter into contracts because each of them values gains more than losses.[120] An exchange of promises produces a welfare surplus, meaning an expected win-win situation for contracting parties. Parties contract when an objective can be more effectively achieved by cooperating. Otherwise, rational economic actors would prefer to use informal institutions without incurring the costs associated with legally binding activities.[121] Considering motivation from an informational point of view, parties contract because they know that one party has information that the other party lacks but needs to make a profit; information asymmetry thus plays an essential role in contracting. While an individual's information regarding a better form of production is an essential element of motivation, information about risks and profit guarantees is also indispensible. Promises can take different faces; they may consist of an exchange of goods, unilateral promises, or services. Economic actors will contract when their commitments have a minimum value; this is expressed through a contract. Contracts are also considered coordination instruments that guarantee future exchanges and the timely completion of production. Furthermore, they provide rules indicating how to deal with future problems which often also outline a governance structure.[122] The relevance of contracts increases when parties have to fulfil their commitments at different points in time. It increases even more in complex relationships such as long-term investment contracts. Hence, contracts are used as a guarantee for the party who first fulfils its part of the promise that the other party will fulfil their part of the promise as well.[123] Scott considers the most plausible answer to be that the motivation to enter into contracts is that 'promises formalised through a contract produce welfare surplus.'[124] By cooperating, parties obtain mutual benefits leading to an expected win-win situation.

---

[119]Calabresi and Melamed (1972), p. 1089.

[120]Ibid.

[121]Ibid.

[122]Ibid.

[123]Hermalin et al. (2007), p. 8.

[124]Ibid.

In political economy, the approach we also rely on, remaining in power is analogous to profit maximisation. States represented by politicians will contract only if they can thus maximise their political power and increase the probability of re-election: this is the 'political-support approach.'[125] The signing of a contract will be the result of the interaction between parties, but also the result of pressure exerted by interest groups who would also benefit from such a contract: this is the 'special groups approach.'[126] Politicians maximise their political function by undertaking regulation that is promoted by lobby groups who will in turn increase the probability of their re-election. As considered by Stigler[127] and Peltzam,[128] regulation (the signing of contracts) can be seen as payment for the contribution made by specific interest groups that increased the probability of winning elections. Their contributions are built on the approach proposed by Olson on collective action.[129] Stigler shows that collective action by organised groups results in regulation that benefits them.[130] While Stigler remains on the demand side, the contribution by Peltzman extends the approach to the supply side. He analyses regulation considering not only the 'winners' but also the 'losers' of the regulation process. Peltzman's theory is more balanced as it assumes that politicians develop their stances on any given regulation based on its marginal political costs and gains.[131]

Therefore, the signing of LSLI contracts can be framed as a political response to political utility-function maximisation. Politicians will only enter into LSLI contracts when they can maximise their own political function by doing so. At the domestic level this means that politicians promote specific laws to maximise their own political power.[132] By knowing the contractual motivation of economic actors, CT contributes to providing tools whose application will make it possible to create an adequate governance structure so that contractual goals can be met. This means that using the tools provided by CT, opportunistic behaviour can be tackled. Such tools may be applied to future and predictable events. Due to the limitations of contractual parties, they cannot regulate events that could happen but they do not have information about. In the next section we will explain how CT proceeds and how opportunistic behaviour can be avoided.

[125]For the application of this approach in trade-policies see: Scott and Stephan (2006), p. 64.

[126]A relevant work in this area: Hillman (1982), p. 675 and Rauser and Gérard (2010).

[127]Grossman and Helpman (2001).

[128]Stigler (1971), p. 3.

[129]Seminal work in: Peltzman (1976), p. 211.

[130]Ibid.

[131]Stigler (1971), p. 5.

[132]Peltzman (1976), pp. 211, 214.

4.5.2.3 Complete and Incomplete Contracts

CT works as a comparative tool. It firstly offers a standardised perfect normative model in which information asymmetries, bargaining power, and transaction costs are zero. This recalls the notion of a complete contingent contract. It proposes the positive analysis of a specific problem by integrating the different variables that shall be considered on a case-by-case basis. The notion of a complete contract is used as a tool to elaborate comparative analysis between the first optimal and the real contractual situation. Therefore, it helps to highlight in economic terms where the failures are and to determine to what extent contracts can be better designed to achieve political goals and more appropriate legal policies. This approach is based on the 'Pareto-efficient complete contingent contract' in an ideal and symmetric situation, without differences in information, without unforeseeable market failures, and with perfect enforcement capacity.[133] Complete contracts are able to foresee all future events that might affect the contractual relationship, they internalise all negative externalities they could produce, they solve problems between the parties associated with promises and their future fulfilment, they consider *ex ante* all possible future events, and regulate how parties will deal with them. Contracts are complete in the sense that they always prescribe a course of action and do not tolerate *ex post* discretion. They specify the efficient payoffs for every relevant action and the corresponding sanctions for non-performance.

Even when it is theoretically possible to model a complete contract using the aforementioned framework, in the real world there are some limitations to making a complete contract. Contracts can never be complete because it is not possible for the parties to foresee all scenarios that can arise during the entire course of the contractual relationship. Parties as rational actors draft the contract so that it can be considered the 'first best contractual approach'.[134] Negotiation is made under uncertain conditions, which arise from their cognitive limitations. This leads to bounded rationality due to transaction costs. Most contractual incompleteness is a consequence of uncertainty. Since uncertainty cannot be reduced to zero, contracts cannot be perfectly complete. However, there are some forms of incompleteness that are foreseeable and that can be avoided in order to better achieve the goals of the parties to the contract.

4.5.2.4 Incompleteness and Opportunism

Knowing that uncertainty arises because of the bounded rationality of the parties as well as transaction costs, and that uncertainty is the reason for incompleteness, we now consider it pertinent to analyse the kinds of incompleteness that exist so that we can consider to what extent they can be avoided or minimised. In fact, L&E academics have investigated this issue and proposed a number of different classifications for incompleteness. While Shavell only mentions two causes of incompleteness,

[133] Olson (1965).

[134] Shavell (1980), p. 467.

efficiency and verifiable reasons,[135] Shropp offers a more rigorous taxonomy which divides incompleteness into two groups, namely inadvertent and foreseeable incompleteness. The former group is composed of incompleteness arising out of ignorance and accidents; it supposes that the parties are not able to foresee the events and therefore contracts are incomplete. The latter group is composed of foreseeable incompleteness. Although the parties are aware that the contract is incomplete to some extent, they do not act to remedy this for reasons of strategy, efficiency, necessity, or unavoidability.[136] Dunoff and Trachtman posit that three different types of incompleteness exist which are made up of inadequate knowledge of the future, rational cost-benefit deliberations, and asymmetrical information.[137] Schwartz considers five sources of incompleteness which can be traced to ambiguous language, non-deliberate omissions, efficiency reasons, asymmetric information, and adverse selection.[138] All authors agree that incompleteness in general terms arises from the incapacity of the parties to foresee it—unpredictability—or because informational asymmetries make it possible. CT can only be applied when incompleteness arises from informational asymmetries and unforeseen contingencies.

When parties are negotiating, they try to guarantee their expected profit to as great an extent as possible. However, since they do not and cannot have complete information, all intentions to regulate future events increase the costs they have to internalise while negotiating. Therefore, reducing incompleteness in contracts makes it possible to solve future difficulties arising from this uncertainty. However, parties will not always opt to decrease the incompleteness of a contract to the minimum level because it generates costs that at some point will affect the willingness of parties to engage in this behaviour. As a consequence, parties accept some degree of uncertainty about the occurrence of opportunistic behaviour. By minimising incompleteness, parties can maximise their expected gains.

Incompleteness is relevant because its potential detrimental effects allow at least one of the parties to behave opportunistically. These problems are associated with moral hazard and adverse selection. It is to be expected that under certain circumstances, one party will follow their individual interests rather than seeking to increase overall social welfare. If one considers actors to be rational, one might expect this behaviour to not be rare. As a result, incompleteness can represent an important problem for contractual relationships. In our case, incompleteness can lead to HRs violations and the incorrect interpretations of contracts, which results in increased enforcement costs. Additionally, incompleteness of LSLI contracts can lead to third party interpretation failing to follow the original intentions of the parties. Since the third party (a judge or arbitrators) is also rational, the maximisation of their own welfare function will prevail over the social one—which in this case would be represented by the intentions of the parties.

---

[135]Ibid.

[136]Furubotn and Richter (2008), p. 202.

[137]Shavell (1980), p. 468.

[138]Schropp (2009), p. 63.

Furthermore, incompleteness creates rigid barriers to obtaining essential information for determining the existence of opportunistic behaviour. This is the case because under some circumstances, it will not be possible for the victims to (1) detect, (2) verify, and (3) quantify the effects of opportunistic behaviour. This legal shadow can be used in favour of one party to create benefits for themselves while producing negative side effects for the contractual party and other legal subjects. When negotiations are carried out between locals and investors, the huge informational and bargaining asymmetries between the parties, in addition to the local institutional environment, may lead to a situation where unfulfilled promises that result in HRs violations remain unenforceable. In relationships between states and investors, incompleteness leads to the generation of uncontrolled negative externalities that give rise to HRs violations. Incompleteness may also create opportunities for rent seeking. The reason for this is that contracts do not contain appropriate regulations to resolve uncertainty *ex ante,* leading to scenarios that are not provided for in the contract. In some cases this incompleteness will not be perceived by the victims in the short run; and when opportunism is acted upon, victims are not always able to enforce their rights due to a lack of appropriate institutions, or because the law forecloses this possibility. This is what happens in LDCs, where local institutions often fall short and investor-state contracts are governed by IIL, which restricts the access of victims to judicial remedies.

Therefore, when parties are contracting it is important that they find a balance and agree on the creation of mechanisms to enforce the commitments entered into by both sides. Flexibility mechanisms may permit *ex post* inefficiencies to occur. Events that parties ignore *ex ante* will 'increase performance costs (at least to one party) for the completion of a promised investment to exceed the value that the counterparty expected to generate from the contract'.[139] As a consequence of incompleteness, it may come to pass that 'once a party undertakes an investment, she is vulnerable to exploitation if her contracting partner fails to reciprocate fully'.[140] If the contractual relationship has been planned for a long time, as often happens in the agricultural sector, this problem becomes even more acute, as parties will have to consider the possibility of restructuring the contract to respond to changing circumstances. However, in some cases tribunals have considered the duration of the contract to be decisive in case of contractual breach.[141]

---

[139]Schwartz (1992), pp. 271, 278.

[140]Dunoff and Trachtman (1999), pp. 1, 34.

[141]There are two relevant cases that are frequently quoted in the IIL literature in reference to long-term contracts. This is due to the considerations the tribunals made based on time periods provided for in contracts, which formed part of their decision. The first case is: Scott (2006), pp. 279, 280 in para. 95 the tribunal states that sovereignty rights may not be waived for such a long time (60 years). It held that: 'with reference to every long-term contract, especially such as those that involve an important investment, there must necessarily be economic calculations, and the weighing up of rights and obligations, of chances and risks, constituting the contractual equilibrium' . . . 'it is in this fundamental equilibrium that the very essence of the contract consists.' (para. 148). The second case is: *The Government of the State of Kuwait v The American Independent Oil Company* (1982) Award, 21 ILM 976 (Ad hoc Arbitral Tribunal) in which it was stated that in economic and legal terms 35 years cannot be considered a 'relatively limited period'.

Even more complicated is the uncertainty in contracts involving states. This is because of the associated administrative processes and the inherent uncertainty of the political climate in some countries, e.g. to the possibility of an abrupt change of government, which is of particular relevance in LDCs.

4.5.3 Applying Contract Theory in LSLIs

The analytical approach offered by CT allows parties to design the best contract for their needs, in our case LSLI contracts. The best contract is the contract that is closest to the complete contract model presented above. As it approaches the contractual relationship from an *ex ante* point of view, the negotiation process can be framed with some degree of precision if we exclude the types of incompleteness CT cannot deal with. When designing the contracts, contractual actors recognise their own cognitive limitations and negotiate the contract knowing that they do not have complete information. By doing so, contractual parties will design as complete a contract as possible. CT also offers *ex post* solutions since it can analytically determine when and how a contract can be breached efficiently from a rational point of view.[142] The problem of uncertainty exists in all kinds of contracts, but only becomes acute in long-term contracts. However, mechanisms for avoiding incompleteness, which are based on specifications of clauses and the disclosure of information, make contractual negotiations more costly. While a rational investor may want to avoid renegotiation clauses in the medium-term (due to the high initial investment needed for most agricultural activities), states are incentivised to include renegotiation clauses to allow rectification of an unfavourable situation or to include new elements in the contractual relationship that may only be possible to address after the signing of the contract, e.g. new regulations on environmental issues and tax regulations. Additionally, states will try to include elements indirectly associated with the contractual relationship to achieve internal political goals. These goals will probably affect investment activity and investors will not have an interest in such clauses due to the costs they represent.

Thus, parties have to create norms that are as flexible or robust as necessary so that *ex post* disclosure of information can be expected and *ex post* opportunism is avoided or at least minimised. The limits of flexibility in our case are those that are intra-contractual and that are stipulated by the law of a specific jurisdiction. Accordingly, we consider it a given that parties operate within the scope of law while negotiating contracts. This flexibility is considered intra-legal as it is included

[142]The specialised literature refers to efficient breach contracts in such cases in which at least one of the parties deviate from contractual arrangements, since circumstances arise that make it less favourable for one of the parties to follow through with the pre-established contractual obligations. *Amoco Finance Corporation v Islamic Republic of Iran* (1988), pp. 1314–1405 (Iran - United States Claims Tribunal). Regarding the mechanisms to encourage efficient performance see: Schwartz and Sykes (2002), as well as Posner (1973), chapter IV.

in the contractual design. This is in contrast to cases of 'efficient breach', which involves parties going outside of what is legally permissible. Nonetheless, parties opt for 'efficient breach' because it promises a greater benefit than remaining in the contract. In order to achieve the desired economic goals through the contract, parties have to find a balance. This balance can be achieved by: '(1) securing a high level of cooperation *ex ante*, (2) distinguishing between (desired) flexibility in relation to new circumstances on the one hand and cases of purely opportunistic breach of the contract *ex post* on the other hand, and (3) providing adequate compensation for the victim.'[143]

Parties frame the 'scope of action' during the performance phase by including flexibility mechanisms. These mechanisms are useful in identifying whether a party is behaving opportunistically. Flexibility mechanisms can be balanced by the inclusion of conditions that create or remove an obligation. Contingency measures are used to describe permissible behaviour under specific conditions.[144] While they specify certain situations under which the party can act differently than has been agreed upon in the contract, it may be difficult for the parties to determine whether the requirements for these conditions have been fulfilled and as such, contingency measures are difficult to operationalise. For example, if farmers have to apply pesticides or products that affect the final product and therefore cause losses, insurance companies would ideally be able to make sure that the farmers applied the product correctly and at the correct moment. This kind of detail would be costly for the insurance company to determine. In such cases difficulty arises from the impossibility of observance. The same situation would apply if contracting parties regulated what a government can do during food shortages to satisfy internal demand. Some of the risks associated with these contingency measures are the potential costs they represent for contracting parties, whose willingness to contract decreases as the process of drafting and codifying more and more of these measures becomes increasingly lengthy. The literature recommends the use of contingency measures if these events are highly probable and have a sizeable impact.[145] Default rules are also considered a flexibility mechanism. In contrast to contingency measures, they are more abstract and can be applied in many situations so that parties can limit their discretional behaviour during the performance phase. The L&E literature defines default rules as unspecified provisions of entitlement protection apt for resolving any issues that have not been explicitly addressed in the contract.[146] In this sense they might facilitate the negotiation of an agreement and will set general rules regarding distribution. These rules are important in transitions that are naturally dominated by high transaction costs.

[143] Shavell (1980), p. 466.

[144] van Aaken (2014a), p. 827, 5.

[145] Ibid.

[146] For a law economic approach on default rules see: Schropp (2009), p. 92. As well as ibid; Gertner (1989).

Parties can reduce incompleteness and avoid opportunism by '*endogenously* strengthening trust and cooperation of the relationship.'[147] This means that parties can use the information available to them to minimise the likelihood of entering into disadvantageous contractual obligations.[148] Additionally, comprehensible language should be employed so that parties clearly understand what they are agreeing to. If they have to delegate competence of interpretation to a third party, they must apply the law in the way that was previously agreed upon by the parties. International adjudication institutions become more relevant from this point forward as parties can now make use of diverse ways to solve future legal conflicts. More specifically, parties can concretely define what behaviour shall be considered opportunistic and also include a sanctioning mechanism. In cases like ours involving states, such measures contribute to the fulfilment of pre-existing obligations. Parties can delegate the task of contractual interpretation to a reliable institution or court. The contracting parties can also delegate to a reliable third party the competence to determine the meaning of a provision over which the parties are in disagreement after the contract has been signed. The courts will come to a decision based on the provisions of the contract signed by the parties. If the court does not find any contractual principle to be applicable, it will usually apply general principles of law.[149] The court will make its decision after considering the interests of the parties and concluding what is in their best interest and if they can continue to perform the contract. The parties can delegate interpretative competence to a tribunal or create commissions to provide information to the tribunal to determine to what extent the contractual party can be considered opportunistic. The inclusion of such commissions may be a source of information that could influence the decision of the tribunal.[150]

4.5.3.1 Actors in LSLIs

States as sovereign entities are represented by politicians, ministries, or policymakers (these terms will be used interchangeably) in the negotiations of contracts for LSLIs. The other party to the agreement is the foreign investor. In most cases investment contracts are protected by IIAs that create an investor-friendly institutional framework so that investors are incentivised to invest where otherwise they may have been unwilling to do so. The main argument against signing LSLI contracts is based on development issues, which include economic

[147] Ware (1999).

[148] Dunoff and Trachtman (1999), pp. 1, 35.

[149] At the national level constitutional principles will be applied. At the international level in PIL, the Vienna Convention on the Law of the Treaties and the ILC's Draft Articles on State Responsibility are the compendium of general norms that will apply.

[150] See for example the following paper in which the inclusion of experts commissions in IIAs is permitted: Loomes and Sugden (1982), p. 805.

and social aspects as well as an increase in food production and the fight against poverty. LDCs have great incentives to attract FDI, given the potential it has to help them achieve their development goals. The problem of credibility is solved by signing IIAs and by LDCs creating special conditions for investments in agriculture in the areas of taxation, low prices for land, and long-term contracts. Beyond the idea of development being related to new agrarian policies, we include both politicians and investors in the assumptions of CT but consider them through the lens of political economy. The implication of these assumptions is that politicians, rather than negotiating to fulfil promises, see negotiations as a way to maximise their own utility function, which in this case means that these contracts enable them to remain in power. On the other side of the investment equation, investors who are profit maximisers and contribute towards the realisation of politicians' projects get access to land under generous conditions. These conditions may include more favourable treatment than that given by the state to its own nationals.

Therefore, in light of these assumptions, the benevolent face of states and their intention to promote development and reduce poverty appears in a different light. Instead, there appears an incongruity between what is argued in political discourse and the real interest of the state. Whether the self-interest of politicians can be complemented by development and poverty-reduction goals is another question. In this sense, LSLIs are undertaken not only to achieve development-oriented goals but also political ones, which emerge from the necessity of satisfying interest groups in order to maximise the political power of individuals. As a result negotiations have to be more politically efficient than economically efficient. The contribution to the welfare of the host country is marginal and cannot be considered the rationale for the investment. Parties will take into consideration the negative externalities of the contracts only if these externalities can affect their contractual gains. This means that parties will only care about environmental issues, HRs, and sustainable development if these measures contribute to the achievement of their goals in the short run. Contractual gains are influenced by the institutional framework that constrains the parties from internalising these externalities. The potential contribution of investors to host states may be marginal. Politicians gain popularity in local communities—at least in the short run—by promoting investments like these and introducing them as a tool designed to achieve development goals. This is a way for them to stay in power longer, and hence rent-seeking behaviour exists. In well-functioning states the institutional environment created by the law and also by informal institutions should provide sufficient incentives to maximise personal utility functions and thus prevent detrimental effects for individuals.

4.5.3.2 Contractual Motivation

In CT the question of contractual intention is formulated under the premise of the necessary cooperation and credible commitments that are achieved through the regulatory function of contracts. CT assumes that parties contract because it represents the best way to achieve their goals, or they would use less costly informal institutions. We explain how motivations for signing LSLI contracts are substantially grounded in a political context. Even though the literature develops different approaches to explain why countries cooperate to promote FDI, the results are not identical. Theories have tried to explain the propagation of IIAs. Even though LSLI contracts are not IIAs, we will use these studies as a basis to approach the proliferation of LSLI contracts since the motivation of parties is comparable. If one compares the results of the empirical literature examining the effects of FDI and the results of the literature analysing the benefits of IIAs to the host country, one might conclude that states are not acting in a benevolent manner by signing IIAs. IIAs do not necessarily contribute to an increase in FDI, and FDI does not necessarily improve the domestic institutional framework. Realising this, benevolent states should be reluctant to sign IIAs. However, they continue to do so.

The discussion in the literature follows at least two different strands. The first strand tries to understand why countries enter into BITs and why these investments are so widespread[151]; the second seeks to understand whether IIAs really work in the way they are supposed to.[152] We will draw on this research to figure out whether the rapid increase of LSLIs in agriculture is linked to previous signings of IIAs whose principal aim was the promotion of FDI, and whether the motivation for signing LSLI deals has something to do with the intention of politicians to partake in IIAs. While Guzman (1998) acknowledges that countries compete for capital, he is also sceptical about the effects of such a proliferation.

Guzman (1998) analyses why LDCs enter into BITs even when, as stated by himself, these treaties can be harmful to them.[153] The theoretical case for arguing that BITs hurt LDCs is that the cost of compensating investors if BITs are breached is higher than the gains for countries incentivising FDI. On the one hand Guzman affirms that BITs are instruments that contribute to attracting FDI with their credible commitments and enforcement mechanisms. On the other hand BITs solve an inconsistency problem which is commonly found in LDCs. By solving this problem, host countries create incentives to promote FDI. However, the potential harm of BITs lies in the fact that they do not *per se* create incentives for national actors to invest. However, Guzman shows that even though the country is more attractive to foreign investors and probably will receive more investment, they could increase their gains even more if they created the same FDI incentives without BITs. The reason is that for the host country, the gains will most likely be outweighed by the losses they will suffer as they bid against one another to attract investment. Therefore, increasing cooperation between LDCs and promoting FDI in blocks could help them to achieve more gains from investments. However, since coordination costs cannot be internalised by LDCs, they enter into the BIT game alone and potentially pay a very high cost. Elkins et al. (2006) empirically tested the

[151] Schropp (2009), p. 98; van Aaken and Lehmann (2011).

[152] Elkins et al. (2006), p. 811; Hallward-Driemeier (2003), Poulsen (2010a), Poulsen (2010b), p. 101; Salacuse and Sullivan (2005), p. 67.

[153] Sasse (2011).

different possibilities for explaining the proliferation of BITs and sought to understand why parties decided to enter into BITs in such high volume.[154] They tested different mechanisms in order to explain the phenomenon, namely: competition, culture, emulation, learning, and coercion. They found that the competitive explanation has strong theoretical foundations and is most consistently supported by their data. They also tested it in three different 'competitive spaces': export market, export product, and workforce/infrastructural quality. Although they found statistically high correlations with competence, they were not able to predict the effects of these treaties because of their potential redistributive effects. Montts critiques the approach of Elkins et al. (2006). He applies network theory to consider an evolutionary game characterised by network effects.[155] He explains the proliferation of BITs by arguing that it occurred as a result of a collective dilemma in which receptor countries developed a network of investment contracts seeking to attract more and more foreign investments. Network effects describe events in those markets where the utility derived from the consumption of a good or service increases as more users consume the same good or service. Network benefits are assumed to be higher than the net benefits associated with any extra FDI costs.[156] Montts concludes that the proliferation of BITs is justified by the standardised treaty structure of BITs. However, if one considers that IIAs are an instrument to achieve not only economic development but also social development, and one recalls their contribution to the promotion, protection, and fulfilment of HRs (including the right to property and food), then one would assume IIAs to take a different face. In light of this, the notion of a well-intentioned or benevolent state cannot be maintained in this context.[157] In the following paragraphs we will present some of the results obtained in the literature that tries to demonstrate the contributions of BITs to host states.

Hallward-Driemeier (2003) studied whether or not BITs realise their goal of bringing economic development to developing countries.[158] This was the first relevant empirical study showing that the function of BITs is complementary to the institutional improvement in developing countries. Her findings are relevant because it shows that it is easier for developing countries to create a special environment for foreign investors than to increase the quality of national institutions.[159] Neumayer and Spess (2005) tested the effect of BITs on developing countries and concluded that signing more BITs with developed countries leads to more FDI inflows for developing countries.[160] They did not test whether it has

[154]Guzman (1998), p. 639.

[155]Elkins et al. (2006), p. 811.

[156]Montt (2007), p. 150.

[157]For a similar analysis but in the issue of the promotion Sustainable Development through IIAs see: ibid.

[158]Ibid.

[159]Hallward-Driemeier (2003).

[160]Ibid.

any influence on domestic institutional demand but affirmed that those countries with particularly poor domestic institutional quality possibly stand to gain the most from BITs. These authors could not test how strong the effect of BITs on FDI was. However, they confirmed that '[w]e do know that BITs fulfil their purpose, and those developing countries that have signed more BITs with major capital exporting developed countries are likely to have received more FDI in return.'[161] Having changed elements of Neumayer and Spess' work, Hallward-Driemeier proves that only very little is known about the effects of BITs. Further, Hallward-Driemeier's basic replication results suggest an opposite conditional relationship where BITs are statistically significant predictors of FDI share for low-risk countries only, and the magnitude of that effect increases as risk decreases. Poulsen (2010a)[162] and Sasse (2011) do not find any strong effects of BITs on host countries.[163] However, Sasse (2011) concludes that even when BITs do not present strong effects, the small effects were of a negative tendency.

The literature is relatively inconsistent in determining whether BITs matter and if yes, how. Nonetheless, the empirical evidence provided by some studies convinces us that BITs could or should contribute even more than they currently do. Land investments are promoted in a weak institutional environment where policymakers overestimate opportunity costs associated with LSLIs to achieve domestic goals. In this sense, the access to national land markets is facilitated by contractual arrangements that offer much more credibility vis-à-vis national institutions. The ease of attracting investors might hasten the progress of negotiations by decreasing transaction costs and increasing political power in the short run. Such incentives may be a way to overcome a market that is relatively saturated with BITs.

LSLIs are contracts that are too incomplete, and the performance of new agrarian policies generates unexpected consequences for some groups of actors who are indirectly involved. These groups are not necessarily relevant to the policymaker's rational behaviour or the potentially opportunistic contractual party. Hence, the fact that the policymaker does not care about actors who may be affected means that these actors are not politically significant. Consequently, neither politicians nor investors would be interested in signing contracts under terms different than those in the current ones: rather than dealing with the possibility of asymmetric information in incomplete contracts, the problem might shift to economically misallocated incentives. In this case we observe that even though politicians can use BITs to attract investors up to a point, BITs do not necessarily lead to the improvement of national institutions when domestic interest groups lack bargaining power. Bargaining power has been approached twice so far in this research project. In the first chapter we approached it to explain property rights policies in sub-Saharan Africa and in the second chapter to analyse principal-agent

[161]Neumayer and Spess (2005), p. 1567.

[162]Ibid.

[163]Poulsen (2010a).

problems. Now we return to a discussion of bargaining power by stating that the combination of lack of incentives and a weak domestic institutional framework lead to a situation where politicians and investors sign contracts that are too incomplete and *de facto* allow investors to behave opportunistically.

Since most investments are made between developed countries and LDCs,[164] we now extend our approach to consider whether emissary states or investors' home states would contribute to the promotion of LSLIs and whether knowledge of the detrimental effects of such an investment might influence their decision. This consideration arises from the fact that it is widely accepted that states have a duty to contribute to the fulfilment of HRs obligations even outside of their own borders.[165] As such one might presume that countries would be concerned about the behaviour of their investors abroad. Therefore, we now extend our approach to the country of origin of the foreign investor. On this side of the equation, the rationale for promoting FDI is to contribute to an increase in the welfare of recipient countries through agricultural FDI. We now consider whether this would really happen in the investment environment we are dealing with. Rational and profit-maximising politicians in the investors' home countries would support investments abroad if they contribute to the maximisation of their own utility function. Our analysis considers two scenarios which are not exhaustive, but demonstrative. If the product produced abroad were a substitute product (meaning the product produced abroad is a substitute for a product produced in the country of origin), the overproduction abroad would bring about a decrease in national production because the production abroad is less costly than the production in the home country. This also assumes that investors are producing abroad to introduce the products in their own local markets, which commonly happens with LSLI contracts. Such a situation would be counterproductive for the national producers and lead to a loss of political power for the government. However, if the product produced abroad is a complementary product (for example, raw materials to be further transformed in the country of origin), the emissary country will support it more readily because allocation in the internal market of the product produced abroad will directly benefit a specific industrial sector, e.g. through the creation of jobs. Consequently, this sector will support the political agenda and thus help politicians and interest groups to maximise their profit. Politicians as profit maximisers would only intervene in investment abroad when their negative externalities affect their chances of their being re-elected.

Investors maximise their own utility function and also help to maximise the utility functions of politicians in the home and host countries. Investors are

---

164 Even though south-south investment relationships have increased in volume in recent years, north-south relationships still represent over 50% of investment. Sasse (2011), p. 196 ff.

165 Based on this approach, in the next chapter of this research we will take the discussion a step further by analysing to what extent emissary countries would contribute to the further development of the principle of extraterritoriality in HRL. We suggest that applying this principle would make it possible to create judicial incentives to initiate judicial procedures against enterprises that commit wrongful acts abroad that are considered as violations of human rights.

incentivised to produce abroad through subsidies, price guarantees, and the guarantee that products will be allocated in domestic markets.[166] In recipient countries, investors are incentivised through the legal protection offered by BITs and other incentives already described, e.g. tax preferences, low land prices, and a guarantee of protection against expropriation. Our theoretical approach suggests that rather than considering the implementation of agrarian policies as a way to achieve development, reduce poverty, and fulfil HRs obligations, the individual interest of politicians plays a more relevant role. Politicians are motivated to enter into negotiations to increase their chances of re-election, or the probability of remaining in power by supporting specific interest groups, namely investors. The domestic institutional environment must create incentives so that the investment goals which were initially aimed for can be achieved.

4.5.3.3 Incompleteness in LSLIs

Having analysed the motives of parties for entering into contractual activity, and following our political economic approach which suggests that politicians seek to increase the probability of their remaining in power by signing certain contracts, the next step is to assume that the contract will be structured in a manner that is as complete as necessary to achieve political goals. This means that the contract, in addition to being incomplete due to the cognitive limitations of contractual parties, will also be strategically incomplete. This does not mean that information between the parties is completely symmetric, but that there are some asymmetries unrelated to the cognitive limitations of the parties that could be avoided. However, since incentives are missing, parties strategically leave them in the contract.

Considering that the parties usually negotiate LSLIs in a highly discrete or secretive environment, the parties will share information and be aware of contractual deficits. However, they will have enough incentives to leave gaps in the contract if these gaps contribute to maximising their political function. Hence, parties strategically decide to leave the contracts incomplete. Nevertheless, in order to achieve specific political goals, parties agree to leave them in the contract. For instance, this happens in the case of the protection of the right to food and property. Our statement is accompanied by an increasing literature on agricultural investments that refers to what we call contractual incompleteness, or to the lack of contractual mechanisms to maximise economic benefits for the host country (e.g. through public revenues or a well-designed fiscal regime); gaps in the management of social and environmental risks (e.g. through necessitating impact

[166] See for example the research made by GRAIN. United Nations Conference on Trade and Development, World Investment Report 2013 (World Investment Report 2013, 2014) 36 ff. Additionally See: GRAIN, 'Land Grabbing for Biofuels Must Stop: EU Biofuel Policies are Displacing Communities and Starving the Planet' <http://www.grain.org/article/entries/4653-land-grabbing-for-biofuels-must-stop> accessed 10. 07. 2014, and an even more precise study has been run by the Land Matrix Stigler (1971), p. 6.

assessment statements, the protection of local property rights, socially oriented investment programmes, or effective compensation mechanisms for affected communities); and gaps in contractual revision or renegotiations that would be highly desirable in long-term contracts and could create incentives to place a greater emphasis on sustainable development and HRs violations. A balanced conflict resolution mechanism in which affected locals can enforce violated rights can also be a contractual gap, as well as the reluctance to include clauses contributing to transparency during the performance of the contract. As we have shown, the structure of investment contracts has allowed us to affirm that incompleteness has a strategic background and is used to achieve political goals. Such incompleteness affects the host state more than the investor. This is the case because investment law offers investors higher levels of protection, resulting in them having the power to interfere with domestic judicial decisions which affect them.

Since such incompleteness is *ex ante* unobservable for third-party neutral individuals (in our case the local population, NGOs, and other interest groups), decision makers can bring about immediate political success. The results of this will be palpable during the performance phase of the contract in the form of uncompensated expropriations or increased food insecurity. By leaving contractual gaps, parties increase the uncertainty over the effects of overly incomplete contracts, namely social revolts, protests, political unrest, and social distortions in general.[167]

4.5.3.4 Tackling Opportunism Through Contract Theory

The previous analysis has shown that there are two separate issues: contractual incompleteness and incentives to avoid them. Rational parties can hardly be expected to sign more complete contracts and thus increase social welfare if they are not incentivised to do so. LSLI contracts might well be the second best solution to politicians' utility maximisation goals, but not the second best solution to achieving food security and domestic institutional development goals.

Enforcement mechanisms are the most relevant element available to parties to get the desired payoffs of contractual activity and avoid opportunism.[168] Efficient enforcement mechanisms create incentives for the parties to perform the contract as was agreed during the negotiation phase; it brings about mutual commitments and deters defection. In order to judicially enforce the contract, the party needs to fulfil the substantive requirements regarding the *locus standi,* which is given by the law. To enforce the contract, infringement has to be observable, verifiable, and quantifiable. These are three elements for the decision maker (in this case the delegate designated to decide on the controversy, i.e. the judge or arbitrator) to decide on liability. The decision must be enforceable to make the contract effective.

[167] See for example the case of Madagascar at Sect. 2.3.

[168] This can be the most relevant argument also for International Land Coalition (2011).

In addition to the enforcement mechanisms designed by the parties, (intra-contractual) legal systems offer more general rules that do not lead to a disproportionate increase in negotiation and transaction costs. These provisions constitute the institutional environment described by Williamson and were previously referred to in this investigation.[169] They are legal mechanisms that control negative externalities in contractual relationships such as environmental damage and HRs violations. Such provisions create a baseline for entering into negotiations. They concede active legitimation to third parties to interfere in the negotiation phase when sensitive issues are raised. In most domestic jurisdictions, affected third parties can go to court if the performance of the contract produces damages. These incentives created by national legislation are essential to protecting the public order and minimising potential *ex post* opportunism. They motivate contractual parties to be mindful of the potential costs of negative externalities. These institutional arrangements frame the institutional environment in which the contractual activity will be carried out. In IIL access to the court for third parties is not given.

To avoid incompleteness and thus tackle opportunistic behaviour, there is a need for incentives in the political sphere to increase cooperation between politicians, investors, and additional interest groups. In order to maximise their utility function, politicians will only consider the requirements of those groups they can influence politically. The participation of interest groups acting on behalf of the local population would create incentives and potentially lead to more complete contracts. This means that policymakers as rational political actors will negotiate in favour of a certain contractual agreement that reflects the requirements of specific interest groups. Therefore, contractual parties will not only care about the potential repercussions of contractual activity if the affected populations are minority groups, small farmers, indigenous people, and nomadic communities that do not influence the political power of politicians. If national law provides judicial mechanisms to intervene in the contractual relationship, the question that arises concerns the accessibility and reliability of judicial systems in LDCs. These groups must be politically relevant to participate in the negotiation process. Although we have stated that the coordination costs of collective action are high due to the concrete situation in LDCs, it is almost impossible to expect non-organised or weakly organised groups to be taken into account during the negotiation process. Considering politicians under the model hitherto applied, more complete contracts are primarily achieved by increasing the bargaining power of potentially affected economic actors so that different interests are represented and contracts are drafted in such a way that avoidable and foreseeable incompleteness is prevented.

The contractual structure between investors and policymakers, in addition to the institutional framework—this includes the domestic framework and the higher level of protection that IIL offers to investors—in which these investments take place will increase the potential enforcement costs for affected third party actors to the point where affected individuals will not have any incentives to initiate judicial

[169]See in this research Sect. 1.2.

proceedings. Contractual actors can behave opportunistically and violate third parties' rights. Investors can behave opportunistically because LSLI contracts are incomplete and IIL offers them more protection. Investors may also behave opportunistically towards the state because contracts do not include credible enforcement mechanisms on the state's side. To put it another way, this means that the incentives for the state not to behave opportunistically are much more efficient since the investor is usually the only active party that can initiate the arbitration process. Such incentives are present if the host and home states have agreed on IIAs, which constitutes the huge majority of the cases. Incentives might be allocated to secure a high level of cooperation *ex ante*, to achieve a desirable level of contractual specificity and flexibility mechanisms, and to bring about appropriate compensation measures. In the political economic context such incentives emanate from interest groups that will maximise the utility function of politicians. In the next section we will analyse to what extent international legal strategies can lead to the creation of incentives so that incompleteness can be reduced, opportunistic behaviour can be avoided, and the proposed aim of LSLI policies can be achieved.

4.6 Intermediate Result: Control Mechanisms to Tackle Opportunism Are Needed

Having analysed the legal mechanisms in IL protecting the right to property and the right to food of locals, and having analysed the exertions that locals have to endure to enforce their rights due to the institutional environment and legal limitations, this chapter elaborated an economic analysis of LSLI contracts. Considering what we learnt about the international protection of the right to food and property, the two previous chapters modelled LSLIs by applying PAT and CT through the lens of political economy in order to examine what is needed to avoid opportunistic behaviour. We approached opportunistic behaviour by technically subsuming the violation of the right to property and the right to food to elaborate our functional analysis. The infringements of these two rights were taken as the condition for considering actors opportunistic; therefore, we posited that by solving the problem of opportunism we would also tackle the violation of HRs. We not only proved the existence of opportunistic behaviour but also found its source. Following this in-depth approach, the theories allow us to go further and now consider policy-oriented measures that open a window to the alleviation of the effects of agrarian reforms that are implicit in LSLI contracts. As proposed in this theoretical approach, control mechanisms discouraging opportunistic behaviour are needed. It is remarkable that we not only know which elements might be considered in the drafting of pertinent strategies, but also which incentives are required to realise these strategies. Well-organised groups can and do influence political decisions and can contribute to an increase in social welfare. Therefore, in the next chapter we must evaluate what needs to be brought into the anatomy of LSLI contracts to avoid them being too incomplete. We will also provide a coherent explanation of how to achieve the most complete contract scenario considering the pre-existing institutional environment in LDCs. Enforcement mechanisms will play a central role in the formation of our strategies.

References

Amoco Finance Corporation v Islamic Republic of Iran [1988] International Legal Materials, vol 27, No 5, pp 1314–1405 (Iran - United States Claims Tribunal).

Andrianirina-Ratsialonana, R., Ramarojohn, L., Burnod, P., & Teyssier, A. (2011). *After Daewoo? Current status and perspectives of large-scale land acquisition in Madagascar*. Commercial Pressures on Land.

Arrow, K. (1971). *Essays in the theory of risk bearing* (first published 1971, 2nd ed.). North-Holland.

Atwood, D. (n.d.). Land registration in Africa: The impact on agricultural production. *World Development, 18*, 659.

Bardhan, P. (1987). Alternative approaches to the theory of institutions in economic development. Working Paper 8761, http://escholarship.org/uc/4t97z6v6.

Bardhan, P. (1989). *The economic theory of Agrarian institutions*. Oxford University Press.

Bhandari, J. S., & Sykes, A. O. (1998). *Economic dimensions in international law: Comparative and empirical perspectives*. Cambridge, UK: Cambridge University Press.

Binswanger, H., & Rosenzweig, M. (1986). Behavioural and material determinants of production relations in agriculture. *Journal of Development Studies, 22*, 503.

Braverman, A., & Stiglitz, J. (1982). Sharecropping and the interlinking of Agrarian markets. *American Economic Review, 72*, 695.

Brobbey, S. A. (2008). *The law of chieftaincy in Ghana: Incorporating customary arbitration, contempt of court, judicial review*. Advanced Legal Publications.

Brousseau, É., & Glachant, J.-M. (Eds.). (2002). *The economics of contracts*. Cambridge University Press.

Calabresi, G. (2016). *Future of law and economics: Essays in reform and recollection*. Yale University Press.

Calabresi, G., & Melamed, D. (1972). Property rules, liability rules, and inalienability: One view of the Cathedral. *Harvard Law Review, 85*, 1089.

Cashore, B. W., Auld, G., & Newsom, D. (2004). *Governing through markets: Forest certification and the emergence of non-state authority*. Yale University Press.

Chayes, A., & Chayes, A. (1993). On compliance. *International Organization, 47*, 175.

Coase, R. (1937). The nature of the firm. *Economica, 4*(16), 386.

Coase, R. (1988). *The firm, the market, and the law*. The University Chicago Press.

Cooter, R., & Ulen, T. (2012). In D. Battista (Ed.), *Law & economics* (6th ed.). Pearson Adison Wesley.

Cotula, L. (2015). *Land rights and investment treaties: Exploring the interface*. International Institute for Environment and Development.

Davis, J. H., Schoorman, F. D., & Donaldson, L. (1997). Toward a stewardship theory of management. *Academy of Management Review, 22*, 20.

Deininger, K., Ayalew, D., Holden, S., & Zevenbergen, J. (2008). Rural land certification in Ethiopia: Process, initial impact, and implications for other African countries. *World Development, 36*, 1786.

Dunoff, J., & Trachtman, J. (1999). Economic analysis of international law. *Yale Journal of International Law, 24*, 1.

Eisenhardt, K. (1989). Agency theory: An assessment and review. *Academy of Management Review, 14*, 57.

Elkins, Z., Guzman, A. T., & Simmons, B. (2006). Competing for capital: The diffusion of bilateral investment treaties, 1960–2000. *International Organization, 60*, 811.

Feld, L., & Voigt, S. (2003). Economic growth and judicial independence: Cross-country evidence using a new set of indicators. *European Journal of Political Economy, 19*, 497.

Franck, S. (2005). The legitimacy crisis in investment treaty arbitration: Privatizing public international law through inconsistent decisions. *Fordham Law Review, 73*, 1521.

Fudenberg, D., & Tirole, J. (1990). Moral hazard and renegotiation in agency contracts. *Econometrica, 58*.

Furubotn, E., & Richter, R. (2008). *Institutions & economic theory*. The University of Michigan Press.

Gazal-Ayal, O. (2007). Economic analysis of "Law & Economics". *Capital University Law Review, 35*, 3.

Gertner, R. (1989). *Filling gaps in incomplete contracts: An economic theory of default rules*. Yale Law School Faculty Scholarship Series Paper 1545.

Goldstein, M., & Udry, C. (2008). The profits of power: Land rights and agricultural investment in Ghana. *Journal of Political Economy*, 981.

Grossman, G., & Helpman, E. (2001). *Special interest politics*. Cambridge.

Guzman, A. T. (1998). Why LDCs sign treaties that hurt them: Explaining the popularity of bilateral investment treaties. *Virginia Journal of International Law, 38*, 639.

Guzman, A. T. (2008). *How international law works: A rational choice theory*. Oxford University Press.

Hallward-Driemeier, M. (2003). Do bilateral investment treaties attract FDI? Only a bit and they could bite. World Bank Policy Research Working Paper No. WPS 312, http://wdsbeta.worldbank.org/external/default/WDSContentServer/IW3P/IB/2003/09/23/000094946_03091104060047/Rendered/PDF/multi0page.pdf. Accessed 14 April 2014.

Harriss, J., Hunter, J., & Lewis, C. (1997). *The new institutional economics and third world development*. Routledge.

Hermalin, B., Katz, A., & Craswell, R. (2007). Contract law. In A. M. Polinsky & S. Shavell (Eds.), *Handbook of law and economics* (Vol. 1). Elsevier.

Hillman, A. (1982). Declining industries and political support protectionist motives. *American Economic Review, 72*, 675.

International Land Coalition. (2011). *The land matrix. Beta version 2.0. International Land Coalition*. ILC, http://www.landmatrix.org/en/about/. Accessed 3 April 2015.

Jensen, M., & Meckling, W. (1976). Theory of the firm: Managerial behavior, agency costs and ownership structure. *Journal of Financial Economics, 3*, 305.

Kherallah, M., & Kirsten, J. (2002). The new institutional economics: Applications for agricultural policy research in developing countries. *Agrekon, 41*, 110.

Kirsten, J., Karaan, M., & Andrew, D. (2009). Introduction to the economics of institutions. In F. K. Johann, et al. (Eds.), *Institutional economics perspectives on African agricultural development*. International Food Policy Research Institute.

Komoremos, B. (2005). Contracting around international uncertainty. *American Political Science Review, 99*, 49.

Lipsey, R. G., & Lancaster, K. (1956). The general theory of second best. *Review of Economic Studies, 24*.

Loomes, G., & Sugden, R. (1982). Regret theory: An alternative theory of rational choice under uncertainty. *Economic Journal, 92*, 805.

Mahoney, P. (1999). Contract remedies: General. *EncL&E*.

Mannathukkaren, N. (2011). Redistribution and recognition: Land reforms in Kerala and the limits of culturalism. *Journal of Peasant Studies, 38*, 379.

Menrad, C., & Shirley, M. (Eds.). (2005). *Handbook of new institutional economics* (1. Aufl. ed.). Springer-Verlag.

Milgrom, P., & Roberts, J. (1992). *Economics, organization and management*. Prentice Hall.

Miller, G. (2008). Solutions to principal-agent problems in firms. In C. Ménard & M. Shirley (Eds.), *Handbook of new institutional economics*. Springer Verlag.

Montt, S. (2007). The BIT generations emergence as a collective action problem: Prisoners dilemma or network effects? *Latin American Caribbean Journal of Legal Studies, 2*, 150.

Mueller, D. (2008). *Public choice III*. Cambridge University Press.

Neumayer, E., & Spess, L. (2005). Do bilateral investment treaties increase foreign direct investment to developing countries? *World Development, 33*, 1567.

North, D. (1990). *Institutions, institutional change and economic performance*. Cambridge University Press.

Olson, M. (1965). *The logic of collective action*. Harvard University Press.

Ostrom, E. (1998). Institutional analysis and development approach. In E. T. Loeman & D. M. Kligour (Eds.), *Designing institutions for environment and natural resource management*. Edward Elgar.

Ostrom, E. (2005a). Doing institutional analysis: Digging depper than markets and hierarchies. In C. Ménard & M. Shirley (Eds.), *Handbook of new institutional economics*. Springer.

Ostrom, E. (2005b). *Governing the commons: The evolution of institutions for collective action* (17. print. ed.). Cambridge University Press.

Paul, B., & Stephan, I. (2002). Courts, tribunals, and legal unification - The agency problem. *Chicago Journal of International Law, 3*.

Peltzman, S. (1976). Toward a more general theory of regulation. *Journal of Law and Economics, 19*, 211.

Posner, E. A., & Sykes, A. O. (n.d.). An economic analysis of state and individual responsibility under international law. *American Law and Economics Review, 9*, 72134.

Posner, R. (1993a). The new institutional economics meets law and economics. *Journal of Institutional and Theoretical Economics, 149*, 73.

Posner, R. (1993b). What do judges and justices maximize? (The same thing everybody else does). *Supreme Court Economic Review, 3*, 1.

Posner, R. A. (1973). *Economic analysis of law* (1st ed.). Little, Brown and Company.

Poulsen, L. S. (2010a). The importance of BITs for foreign direct investment and political risk insurance: Revisiting the evidence. In K. Sauvant (Ed.), *Yearbook on international investment law and policy 2009/2010*. Oxford University Press.

Poulsen, L. S. (2010b). The significance of south-south BITs for the international investment regime: A quantitative analysis. *Northwestern Journal of International Law and Business, 30*, 101.

Rauser, G., & Gérard, R. (2010). Special interests versus the public interest in policy determination. In K. Anderson (Ed.), *The political economy of agricultural price distortions*. Cambridge University Press.

Reinier, K., et al. (Eds.). (2009). *The anatomy of corporate law: A comparative and functional approach* (2nd ed.). Oxford University Press.

Ross, S. (1973). The economic theory of agency: The principal's problem. *American Economic Association, 63*, 134.

Salacuse, J., & Sullivan, N. (2005). Do BITs really work? An evaluation of bilateral investment treaties and their grand bargain. *Harvard International Law Journal, 46*, 67.

Sasse, J. (2011). *An economic analysis of bilateral investment treaties* (1st ed.). Gabler.

Schlanger, E., & Ostrom, E. (1992). Property-rights regimes and natural resources: A conceptual analysis. *University of Wisconsin Press, 68*, 249.

Schropp, S. (2009). *Trade policy flexibility and enforcement in the World Trade Organization: A law and economics analysis*. Cambridge University Press.

Schwartz, A. (1992). Relational contracts in the courts: An analysis of incomplete agreements and judicial strategies. *Journal of Law and Economics, 21*, 271.

Schwartz, W. F., & Sykes, A. O. (2002). *The economic structure of renegotiation and dispute resolution in the WTO/GATT system*. John M Olin Law & Economics Working Paper No. 143. http://papers.ssrn.com/paper.taf?abstract_id=302813. Accessed 28 August 2015.

Scott, R. The law and economics of incomplete contracts. (2006) 2 Annual Review of Law and Social Science 279

Scott, R., & Stephan, P. (2006). *The limits of Leviathan. Contract theory and the enforcement of international law*. Cambridge University Press.

Shavell, S. (1980). Damage measures for breach of contract. *Bell Journal of Economics, 11*.

Shavell, S. (2004). *Foundations of economic analysis of law*. Belknap Press of Harvard University Press.

Shelton, D. (2002). Decision regarding communication 155/96 (Social and Economic Rights Action Center/Center for Economic and Social Rights v. Nigeria). Case No. ACHPR/COMM/A044/1. *American Society of International Law, 96*, 937.

Simon, H. A. (1957). *Models of man*. Wiley.

Stigler, G. (1971). The theory of economic regulation. *Bell Journal of Economics and Management Science, 2*.

The Government of the State of Kuwait v The American Independent Oil Company [1982] Award, 21 ILM 976 (Ad hoc Arbitral Tribunal).

Trachtman, J. (2008). *The economic structure of international law*. Harvard University Press.

van Aaken, A. (2003). *"Rational Choice" in der Rechtswissenschaft: Zum Stellenwert der Ökonomischen Theorie im Recht*. Nomos.

van Aaken, A. (2005). *Making international human rights protection more effective: A rational-choice approach to the effectiveness of Ius Standi provisions*. Preprints of the Max Planck Institute for Research on Collective Goods 2005/16 1.

van Aaken, A. (2006). Fragmentation of international law: The case of international investment law. In J. Klabbers & K. Creutz (Eds.), *Finnish yearbook of international law* (Vol. 17). Martinus Nijhoff Publishers.

van Aaken, A. (2008). How to do constitutional law and economics: A methodological proposal. In T. Eger, et al. (Eds.), *Internationalisierung des Rechts und seine Ökonomische Analyse* (1st ed.). Gabler.

van Aaken, A. (2009a). Defragmentation of public international law through interpretation: A methodological proposal. *Indiana Journal of Global Legal Studies, 16*, 483.

van Aaken, A. (2009b). International investment law between commitment and flexibility: A contract theory analysis. *Journal of International Economic Law, 12*, 507.

van Aaken, A. (2010). Primary and secondary remedies in international investment law and national state liability: A functional and comparative view. In S. Schill (Ed.), *International investment law and comparative public law*. Oxford.

van Aaken, A. (2013). Die vielen Wege zur Effektuierung des Völkerrechts. *Zeitschrift für rechtswissenschaftliche Forschung, 3*, 227.

van Aaken, A. (2014a). Smart flexibility clauses in international investment treaties and sustainable development: A functional view. *Journal of World Investment and Trade, 15*, 827.

van Aaken, A. (2014b). Delegating interpretative authority in investment treaties: The case of joint commissions. *Transnational Dispute Management, 1*.

van Aaken, A., & Lehmann, T. (2011). International investment law and sustainable development: Developing a new conceptual framework. In R. Echandi & P. Sauvé (Eds.), *Prospects in international investment law policy*. Cambridge.

Voigt, S. (2009). *Institutionenökonomik* (2., durchges. Aufl. ed.). Fink.

Voigt, S., & Hazo, B. (2007). Explaining de facto judicial independence. *International Review of Law and Economics, 27*, 269.

Volker, B. (1995). Aussagefähigkeit Agencytheoretischer Ansätze im Hinblick auf die Verhaltenssteuerung von Entscheidungsträgern. *ZFBF*, 821.

Ware, S. (1999). Default rules from mandatory rules: Privatizing law through arbitration. *Minnesota Law Review, 83*.

Wathne, K. H., & Heide, J. B. (2000). Opportunism in interfirm relationships: Forms, outcomes, and solutions. *Journal of Marketing, 64*, 36.
Williamson, O. (1979). Transaction-cost economics: The governance of contractual relations. *Journal of Law and Economics, 22*, 233.
Williamson, O. (1985). *The economic institutions of capitalism: Firms, markets, relational contracting*. Collier Macmillan Publishers.
Williamson, O. (1989). The firm, the market, and the law by R. H. Coase. *California Law Review, 77*, 223.
Williamson, O. (1993). Opportunism and its critics. *Managerial Decision Economics, 14*, 97.
Williamson, O. (1996). *The mechanisms of governance*. Oxford University Press.
Williamson, O. E. (2000). The new institutional economics: Taking stock, looking ahead. *Journal of Economic Literature, 38*, 595.
Wilson, R. (1968). On the theory of syndicates. *Econometrica, 36*.
Wu, S. (2006). Contract theory and agricultural policy analysis: A discussion and survey of recent developments. *Australian Journal of Agricultural and Resource Economics, 50*, 490.

Chapter 5
Tackling Opportunism in LSLIs

5.1 Overview

In Chap. 4, we showed that NIE could highlight the sources of opportunism and offered two approaches to tackle it. These approaches were modelled with PAT and CT. We know that control mechanisms are needed to decrease agency costs and to create incentives for parties to draft more complete contracts. We learnt about the institutional structures and the environment in which LSLIs take place, as well as the specific institutional areas in which incentives should be allocated to decrease agency costs. We showed the causal relationship between principal-agent problems and incomplete contracts in LSLIs. We argued that one way to justify why incomplete contracts are signed is pre-existing principal-agent problems. Contracts are incomplete and fail to incentivise parties to behave as required to achieve pre-determined goals and to fulfil IL obligations. Furthermore, we showed why and how violations of HRs to property and to food occur. In Chap. 3 we analysed the mechanisms in IL to protect the rights of affected individuals and investors. We elucidated which obstacles exist in IL from asymmetric levels of protection and how they lead to opportunistic behaviour. For this reason, incentives are allocated asymmetrically and lead to non-compliance and a higher cost for the enforcement of HRL. The opposite is the case in IIL, where correctly allocated incentives effectively protect the rights of investors.

Further, we showed that IL has diverse mechanisms to enforce the rights to food and to property. In order to comprehensively classify these mechanisms, we followed the approach developed by Born (2012) which distinguishes between a first and second generation of enforcement mechanisms. The first generation lacks judicial incentives to implement protected rights, while the second generation guarantees a high degree of enforcement of these protected rights through institutional involvement. We therefore analysed the mechanisms available to this first generation to enforce HRs. Here, the state and its willingness to comply play a central role in effectuating HRs. The second generation of enforcement

L.T. Montilla Fernández, *Large-Scale Land Investments in Least Developed Countries*, International Law and Economics, DOI 10.1007/978-3-319-65280-1_5

Table 5.1 Findings of previous chapters

Chapter	Results
1	We introduced the topic and analysed legal mechanisms of third-party enforcement at the national and the international level.
2	We justified why LSLIs can—under some circumstances—lead to HRs violations. We established a relationship between the infringement of the right to property and the right to food in LDCs.
3	We showed that the asymmetric level of protection governing different areas of IL leads to opportunistic behaviour
4	Applying NIE, we developed a model that explains why opportunism arises, we highlighted its sources, and we suggested a theoretical approach to tackle it.

Source: Prepared by the author

mechanisms is different because the existence of tribunals might guarantee the enforcement of protected rights. This is the case because the protection offered to investors by IIL is higher than that offered by HRL—as we showed in Chap. 2. In Chap. 1, apart from introducing the topic, we compared the mechanisms of third-party enforcement at the national and international level. Before we enter into the details of the next chapter, Table 5.1 offers a concise overview of the previous chapters and the results of the analysis.

In this chapter we will consider the possibility of enforcing rights of the first generation through IIL. In fact, IIAs are held to be strict legal instruments that are easy to enforce. We suggest that IIAs are effective controllers of state behaviour vis-à-vis foreign investors. The expectation to fulfil HRs obligations might increase considerably if they were incorporated into IIAs. There might occur cross-fertilisation between the two regimes because IIL would offer the benefits of its enforcement mechanisms to uphold HRs. In this chapter we aim to offer control mechanisms that incorporate HRs into IIAs and LSLIs. The idea of linking rights from diverse regimes is not new. It was proposed by recognised scholars and IOs as a way to improve compliance with HRs obligations and to promote the defragmentation of IL. The question of whether there are legal barriers to introducing HRs into IIL has been treated and answered. Therefore, it is not discussed in this study.[1] Previous studies concluded that no legal limitation to introducing HRL into IIL exists.[2] To the contrary, such an approach is broadly deemed a solution to the conflicts arising from the asymmetric level of protection for foreign investors vis-à-vis individuals, in particular because of the lack of positive law imposing direct HRs obligations on transnational corporations and the relevance of such organisations in weak states. It seems, however, that rather than being a normative problem, the issue is actually a lack of legal policies incentivising the promotion and protection of HRs through IIL. One might acknowledge that the broad scope, independence, and compliance costs of HRL can lead to some reluctance to include

[1]The most obvious example is the study by the ILC: International Land Coalition (2011).

[2]ILC (2006).

it in investment contracts.[3] In addition, an amendment of existing IIAs and thus the incorporation of control and monitoring mechanisms aiming to increase contractual governance are required. Such a process is not free of costs. Renegotiation of contracts can lead to high costs and risks for the parties that may threaten the level of protection already offered to investments through IIAs.[4] However, contractual design or redesign might well be the most pertinent measure to incentivise compliance (IL offers some alternative mechanisms, also). These are also considered in the next section.

In this chapter it is our goal to outline and evaluate the control mechanisms in IL which can be used to promote compliance with HRs obligations. We will apply the theoretical insights already gained in order to provide an answer to our main research question. Therefore, considerations of enforceability and incentives cannot be ignored. We will not empirically test which of the control mechanisms are the best solution in these situations. We will show a set of possibilities in IL available to contractual parties in scenarios of institutional weakness to tackle opportunistic behaviour. We will not only focus on mechanisms available in IIAs, but also on those available in LSLI. We will consider those situations in which a state *de facto* breaches an existent LSLI within IIAs in order to prevent further HRs violations in a food crisis and state of necessity.

The present chapter is structured as follows: after this overview (Sect. 5.1), Sect. 5.2 will discuss unilateral control mechanisms to tackle opportunism that can be introduced by states (Sect. 5.2.1) and by investors (Sect. 5.2.2). In the case of states we will focus on substantive legal measures and procedural law. In the case of investors we will consider the mechanisms that can be incorporated by specific industrial sectors, multi-stakeholder mechanisms, and individual mechanisms. We will then proceed to analyse the scope of such mechanisms. In Sect. 5.3 we will consider contract-based control mechanisms. In Sect. 5.4 we will discuss to what extent arbitrators can function as control mechanisms. In Sect. 5.5 we will analyse the role of external international actors as control mechanisms. In this section we will consider judicial (hard and soft law) and extra-judicial (market) mechanisms that can also be used to create and correctly allocate incentives so that contractual actors do not behave opportunistically.

---

[3]Ruggie (2008), p. 9. In the case of the right to food see: The World Conference on Human Rights on Human Rights; Vienna Declaration and Programme of Action [1993] available at http://www.ohchr.org/en/professionalinterest/pages/vienna.aspx. Accessed 11 November 2014.

[4]An economic approach explaining the costs of renegotiating long-term contracts is offered by: Vidar (2005). An economic paper applying the cost of renegotiation in agency contracts is offered by: Hart and Moore (1988).

5.2 Unilateral Control Mechanisms

5.2.1 By States

Unilateral mechanisms are measures that can be imposed by home or host states which produce effects on investments. They are regulatory measures that aim to control foreign investments through entry policies or by adjusting economic activity after an investment. They can be used to reform areas of trade law, competition law, investment law, export or import conditions, currency exchange law, and others. In these scenarios the existence of IIAs and the requirement to exhaust national jurisdictions are relevant in order to have access either to national or international courts. If the exhaustion of national jurisdiction is a pre-established contractual requirement, national courts play a vital role because they will be the first institution to decide on the legitimacy and legality of entry policies.[5] IIAs are relevant because of the restrictions they impose on the regulatory capacity of states. Depending on the flexibility of IIAs, host states can consider new policies based, for example, on public interest, health, or environmental issues. In some cases these policies can be seen as a contractual breach that could entitle the investor to compensation. Thus, in order for a state to consider unilateral control mechanisms, the restrictions included in IIAs and their interpretation by adjudicators play a relevant role.[6] Surveying the different positions taken by investment tribunals, we will aim to analyse to what extent entry policies can be considered control mechanisms. We will examine whether these mechanisms are able to create and properly allocate incentives to tackle opportunistic behaviour in the presence of LSLIs.

5.2.1.1 Adjusting Entry Policies

There is no doubt that sovereign states have the power to introduce laws controlling land markets in order to improve governance. The introduction of new and stronger land laws may affect foreign investors and create reluctance on their side to enter into a specific jurisdiction. Finding a balance between incentivising investors to enter into a specific jurisdiction and making sure that the host state receives net gains from such investments would mean, firstly, that states must offer an environment to investors in which they can make a profit, and, secondly, that regulations stabilise local land markets and produce sustainable outcomes so that governments can achieve national policy goals. In order to achieve such goals, governments need to identify strategic priorities and link them to regulations. This process would guarantee further consideration of whether the investment proposal is, in fact, in alignment with the state's priorities. As part of this process, states may improve

[5]See the applicable law at Sect. 1.2.2 of this study.

[6]The referred restrictions are given by the standards of protection IIAs offers. See Sect. 3.6 of this research.

their land governance and natural resources regulations. These regulations must respect local rights and ensure free access to economic actors. Furthermore, the negotiations and the adopted procedures to acquire the land must be auditable (i.e. states have to be able to audit the process and the contractual arrangements). Regulations might also contribute to the creation of incentives which promote development by building institutional capacity and by improving procedures to manage the process. This means that new legislation is introduced in states with institutional weaknesses, which make the introduction of appropriate legal policies challenging.

The adjustment of entry policies has been a widely used strategy since LSLIs skyrocketed in 2008. By employing FDI as a mechanism to promote economic growth, some states have created conditions for foreign investors to enter into their domestic jurisdiction and to make contact with local markets. In some states investors can only own a minority share in agribusiness companies. Some countries have adopted even stronger policies. These consist of blocking the entrance of new investors by forbidding the acquisition of land. In addition, some jurisdictions have restricted the parameters for signing LSLIs which arrange for land to be sold.

In post-independence African countries, as it was pointed out in Chap. 1, many jurisdictions have restricted the acquisition of land and real estate to nationals. However, some of these countries introduced new laws allowing foreign investors to enter into specific domestic markets as part of a wider liberalisation reform package. Today, some jurisdictions are reverting back to limiting not only the acquisition of land, but are also stipulating conditions for long-term lease contracts. This can be seen as a result of the externalities arising from the accelerated increase of LSLIs. The limitations created by the law have effects not only on investor-state relationships but also on the relationships between private parties. Such measures allow domestic institutions to monitor investments more closely.

By adjusting entry policies, states have to consider the limitations arising not only from LSLIs but also IIAs. Standards of protection, which apply through most favoured nation (MFN) clauses that are frequently included in IIAs, lead to a restriction of the regulatory capacity of states even before the investor arrives. The experience of Latin American countries over the past 5 years shows how such measures can be progressively incorporated to maintain low performance costs. Brazil as well as Argentina have taken regulatory measures that do not completely prohibit land acquisitions by foreigners, but that limit the amount of land that may be held by multinational enterprises (and even national companies). Two different approaches have been applied. On the one hand Argentina passed a law (Regime for Protection of National Domain over Ownership, Possession or Tenure of Rural Land) that limits foreign ownership of rural land to a maximum of 15% of all national productive land.[7] Moreover, nationals of one state are not allowed to own more than 30% of that amount. Furthermore, in areas classified as highly productive, nationals have an ownership restriction of 1000 ha. This amount can increase

[7]Fudenberg and Tirole (1990).

in areas classified as less productive.[8] On the other hand Brazil, instead of passing a new law, issued a binding legal interpretation of the existing law stating that some restrictions apply. Land rights in Brazil have been regulated by Federal Statute No. 5,709 since 1971.[9] In this act the federal government restricted the size of rural land that foreign-controlled Brazilian-based legal entities were entitled to acquire.[10] In this law, the government used two definitions of foreign investors for the purpose of land acquisitions: foreign investors *per se,* and Brazilian companies controlled by a foreign legal entity. After the adoption of the new constitution in 1988, the Brazilian Attorney General interpreted the differential treatment of other Brazilian-based legal entities to be unconstitutional and unenforceable. The Attorney General came to this decision because the constitution reads that no distinction shall be made between legal entities regarding the nationality of their capital and their equity holders, with only a few exceptions. This interpretation led to a land market liberalisation in which foreign investors were allowed to own rural land. The specific aspect that was considered unconstitutional concerned the definition of foreign investors. Under the new ruling, Brazilian companies controlled by foreign investors were considered domestic investors. In 2010 a new interpretation imposed restrictions on foreign investors and brought about the return of the *status quo* of 1971. Currently the Brazilian government is discussing a new law to regulate land investments. Other examples of land right reforms can be found in Paraguay, Bolivia, and Uruguay, where new laws to create restrictive mechanisms to control the entry of foreign investors into the national land market are being discussed.

Latin American countries were joined by other countries following similar or even stronger approaches. Algeria, the Democratic Republic of the Congo, and Benin have taken a more restrictive approach by prohibiting foreigners the ownership of rural land.[11] Foreign legal and natural persons are allowed to lease rural land for agricultural purposes. The new law in Algeria allows foreign investors to register joint ventures as minority shareholders (up to 40% of the capital) with local companies. The Democratic Republic of the Congo passed a similar law in 2012. It allows only nationals to hold land and foreigners may only be minority shareholders in companies. The new provisions apply to exploitation, agricultural training, research, commercialisation of agricultural commodities, protection of the environment; and taxation regimes. The implementation of this law has been widely discussed at a domestic level because of the complexities arising from its retroactive character. Unlike Argentina or Brazil, the Democratic Republic of the

---

[8]República de Argentina Régimen de Protección al Dominio Nacional sobre la Propiedad, Posesión o Tenencia de las Tierras Rurales Law N° 26.737 2011.

[9]Ibid.

[10]Lei No. 5.709 Regula a Aquisição de Imóvel Rural por Estrangeiro Residente no País ou Pessoa Jurídica Estrangeira Autorizada a Funcionar no Brasil, e dá outras Providências [1971].

[11]Ibid; République Démocratique du Congo Loi N° 11/022 du 24 Décembre 2011 Portant Principes Fondamentaux Relatifs a l'Agriculture 2011; Republique Algerienne Democratique et Populaire. Ministere de l'Agriculture et du Developpment Rural. Instruction Interministerielle 196 [2013] Journal Officiel 48.

Congo is applying the law retroactively with the consequence that already established investments now have to run restructuring processes to adapt to the new legislation.

The legislation passed by the Béninese government allows foreign investors to lease land for a maximum of 50 years. The contract is non-renewable and the size of acquisition is restricted to a maximum of 1000 ha per investor.[12] The most relevant aspect of this law is its aim to support local communities in the use, administration, and disposition of land. It lays out land use requirements to help fight speculation and promote sustainable development. Land investments must be linked to development projects that respect ecological balances and contribute to the protection of the environment and local food security. In addition, the law delegates the competence to monitor and report land activities to local authorities.

Tanzania has opted for an administrative approach rather than creating new laws. The Tanzanian Investment Centre was required in 2013 to design guidelines applicable to foreign investors. Previously, the government established a ceiling for sugar and rice of 10,000 ha and 5000 ha, respectively, for foreigners and nationals alike.[13]

Notwithstanding the impression that the different measures taken by states are creating incentives for economic actors to tackle opportunistic behaviour, restrictive measures cannot be seen as a panacea. Strategically designed domestic regulation might be accompanied by an institutional framework oriented to achieving the proposed goals. This could constitute a threat for LDCs because weak institutions would rapidly lead to transforming even well-intentioned legislation into paternalistic or protectionist measures that are unlikely to produce positive effects.[14] Regulating land markets is a necessary step to increase the chances of maximising net gains from land policies.

In the next section we will consider the possibility of states having to introduce domestic regulation post-establishment of investments.

5.2.1.2 Regulation Post-Establishment of Investments

We will now consider the regulatory power of states *ex-post* over the establishment of investors. Having previously discussed the effects of investment contracts and IIAs on the regulatory power of states, we will analyse in this part whether *ex-post* regulation could function as a control mechanism to tackle negative effects of

---

[12]Loi N° 2013-01 Portant Code Foncier et Domanial en République du Bénin [2013] available at http://actualites.visages-du-benin.com/wp-content/uploads/2013/02/DSL-LOI-PORTANT-CODE-FONCIER-I1.pdf. Accessed 14 September 2014. For a comment of Benin's land policies see: ibid.

[13]Source: GRAIN, 'Land Ceilings: Reining in Land Grabbers or Dumbing Down the Debate?' https://www.grain.org/article/entries/4655-land-ceilings-reining-in-land-grabbers-or-dumbing-down-the-debate. Accessed 17 August 2015.

[14]These have been the main arguments that investors made with regard to the land reform in Zimbabwe. The case of Zimbabwe approached at Sect. 3.6.2.

LSLIs. Comparing this control mechanism to the one we explained earlier, one can see that the costs are allocated in the performance phase of the contract, while the control mechanism we explained before allocates no costs in the negotiation process at all (since the regulation is passed before the investors arrives). However, it might influence the willingness of investors to enter into negotiations.

States can follow at least two different approaches in the introduction of regulation after the investment has been established. Applying the law retroactively would mean that all existent foreign investments would be affected and a restructuration process might be initiated. In cases like this it is highly probable that investors will have to be compensated if a breach of IIAs exists. Such a measure could lead to discrimination or unfair treatment. If the law does not apply retroactively, only future investments would be affected. As long as states do not discriminate, such decisions would be in line with IIAs. We turn to Argentina to illustrate our statement, which can be considered investor friendly as it does not apply the law retroactively. A contrary example is the case of Zimbabwe, where a 1992 agrarian reform aimed to solve a historic social conflict stretching back to independence (most of the arable land remained in the hands of nationals of the former colonial power).[15] The new law initiated the redistribution of land, which affected already existing investments. However, the implementation of this agenda has produced enormous costs for Zimbabweans. The main problem Zimbabwe faces is the lack of institutional infrastructure to perform the proposed agenda in the terms set in 1992. Specifically, these institutional weaknesses refer to corruption and missing capabilities for legal prosecution that could curtail governmental arbitrariness and populist measures under the banner of 'change the unjust land ownership in favour of the masses of Zimbabwe.'[16] Such an agenda has made Zimbabwe even more dependent on international food aid, and it has reduced agricultural production by 73% from 2000 to 2008. Some reports put the cost of this land reform at USD 2.8 billion in international food aid, nearly USD 12 billion in agricultural production over 10 years, and a potential USD 5 billion in compensations.[17] The case of Zimbabwe reflects the difficulties a state faces when it introduces new policies. It also shows that weak states struggle with continuous inconsistencies between what has been agreed upon and what is being performed. It is, however, a latent problem that most LDCs have to deal with.

In IIL, states can reduce risks by increasing the legitimacy of their measures. This can be achieved by improving transparency and participation in policy design, by providing proof of the public interest of the new regulation, and by demonstrating the relationship between the regulation and the fulfilment of a pre-existent non-investment obligation. The main problem in the framework of IIL is that there

[15]An analysis of the Situation in Zimbabwe see: Tanzania Investment Centre (2015); Coltart (2008).

[16]This are argued by Zimbabwe in the following case: Richardson (2005), p. 1.

[17]The most emblematic case related to the reforms is: *Bernardus Henricus Funnekotter and Others v Zimbabwe [2009] Award ARB/05/6 (ICSID) at para 55.*

is no system to apply and thus determine the legality of states' measures. In addition, IIAs do not traditionally include norms allowing the state to maintain its regulatory power in specific sensible areas. However, increasing the legitimacy of land policies could reduce the risk of having to compensate investors. The techniques of interpretation applied by the tribunal are decisive for evaluating the behaviour of the host state.

Even though investment tribunals are not bound by previous decisions, they can contribute—in a limited way—to forecasting the legal effects of regulatory land policies. It has to be highlighted, however, that such precedents can only illustrate previous decisions of tribunals. Again, they are not binding for future decisions. It means that tribunals are, from a legal perspective, free to take different approaches in identical cases and thus come to different conclusions. The legal fundament supporting the non-precedent in IIL can be found in Article 53 (1) of the ICSID Convention which expressly considers the applicability of the principle of binding precedent to successive ICSID cases. It only states that the award shall be binding '*on*' the parties. Additionally, Article 59 of the Statute of the ICJ is very clear in asserting that its decisions are not binding for future cases. Although the articles of the statute are very precise, none of them create a prohibition for tribunals. Both articles permit the tribunal to look at previous decisions in case it considers such a measure necessary. Parties may also require the tribunal to apply principles or frameworks chosen in previous decisions.

In case law, claims by investors affected by the regulatory policies of host states often centre on discrimination and unfair and inequitable treatment.[18] In *SD Myers v Canada* the tribunal examined a potential infringement of the minimum international standard of treatment as conceived under NAFTA in Article 1105(1).[19] The motivation of the case was a new law passed by Canada banning the transboundary shipment of toxic waste to the United States for processing purposes. The tribunal tested the potential conflict between the obligations imposed by NAFTA and those imposed by the Basel Convention and the Transboundary Agreement on Hazardous Waste. The Basel Convention deals with international traffic of polychlorinated biphenyl (PCB).[20] The Transboundary Agreement on Hazardous Waste contemplates the possibility of cross-border activity, recognising that the long common border between the United States and Canada engenders opportunities for a generator of hazardous waste to benefit from using the nearest appropriate disposal facility. The problem for the investor arose when the border between Canada and the United States was closed for cross-border movement of PCBs over a period of 10 months.[21] This closure was the strongest measure taken thus far by the Canadian

---

[18]See Sect. 3.6.2.3 of this study.

[19]Article 1105(1) NAFTA reads: 'Minimum Standard of Treatment: 1. Each Party shall accord to investments of investors of another Party treatment in accordance with international law, including FET and full protection and security.' Cross (2012).

[20]North American Free Trade Agreement [1993] 32 I.L.M. 289 and 605.

[21]Basel Convention on the Control of Transboundary Movements of Hazardous Wastes and Their Disposal [1998] 1673 UNTS 126; 28 ILM 657.

government and was preceded by regulations on the destruction of PCB. According to these new regulations, this process should be carried out within Canadian borders as much as possible.[22] The investor argued discriminatory treatment because the Canadian authorities stated 'that the handling of PCB should be done in Canada by Canadians', apparently following the requirements of the Basel Convention which prohibits the transit of PCB to non-signatory states like the United States.[23] The defence focused on the impossibility of fulfilling the requirements of both international norms simultaneously, namely free trade and the prohibition of PCB export. The tribunal proceeded to examine the arguments made by Canada and tested the potential contradictions between NAFTA and the other international treaties. The tribunal considered previous treaties signed by Canada and the United States in which they bilaterally coordinate the management of hazardous waste between both countries. In addition, it noted that the Basel Convention allows for bilateral agreements to coordinate cross-border transport of waste.[24] The tribunal refused Canada's defence. The tribunal advised that a state seeking to implement measures in order to promote certain values should consider an alternative that does not significantly impact the consistency of open trade.[25]

The approach followed in *SD Myers v Canada* was contradicted by an ICSID tribunal in *Parkerings-Compagniet AS v Lithuania*.[26] In this case it was stated that the host state may enact, modify, and cancel a law by exercise of its sovereign legislative power.[27] The tribunal highlighted that investors have to consider that laws evolve over time. Such a process has negative consequences for a state if it behaves unfairly, unreasonably, or inequitably in the exercise of its legislative power.[28] The tribunal determined that the regulatory capacity of a state is limited by the legitimate expectation of the investors, which might be provided with due diligence and depending on circumstances.[29] The tribunal thus appeared to limit the scope of IIAs vis-à-vis the regulatory power remaining with the states. This not only highlights the power of a state, also the precaution investors must take into account when planning the investment. In *Methanex v United States*[30]—in its final award—the tribunal challenged a ban on the manufacture of an environmentally harmful gasoline additive.[31] The state government of California imposed the ban. *Methanex*

[22] *S.D. Myers, Inc. (Claimant) v Government of Canada (Respondent) [2000] First Partial Award 40 ILM 1408 at para 103.*

[23] Ibid.

[24] Ibid.

[25] Ibid

[26] Ibid.

[27] *Parkerings-Compagniet AS v Lithuania* [2007] Award ARB/05/8 (ICSID).

[28] *S.D. Myers, Inc. (Claimant) v Government of Canada (Respondent) [2000] First Partial Award 40 ILM 1408 at para 221.*

[29] *Parkerings-Compagniet AS v Lithuania [2007] Award ARB/05/8 (ICSID) at para 332.*

[30] Ibid.

[31] *Methanex Corporation v United States [2005] Final Award (Ad hoc UNICTRAL).*

alleged that the measure was not imposed to avoid harm but to protect United States methanol producers and to harm foreign methanol producers. The tribunal came to the conclusion that the public purpose and the non-discriminatory element must be met before exempting states from compensating investors, unless the investors' legitimate expectations are frustrated by the measure.[32] Even when it seems to follow legal logic that sovereign states are allowed to introduce regulatory policies with public purpose, there are also instances of neglect of public purpose. The tribunal in *Metalclad v Mexico*[33] found public purpose to be fully irrelevant to the question of compensation, with the consequence that the calculation of compensation was not impacted by the illegitimate or arbitrary action of a state.[34] The background of this decision was a decree passed by the government establishing an ecological reserve affecting the investors' property. Mexico had to pay USD 16 million in compensation.[35] The tribunal in *Vivendi v Argentina* took a similar approach by holding the element of public interest to be irrelevant and declaring the expropriation unlawful.

The legal uncertainty created by irreconcilable decisions in IIL has led to state reluctance in pursuing new legal policies because they fear prohibitively high costs. From this point of view, the current 'regulatory chill' might be incentivised by the large amounts of money involved in investment cases. UNCTAD reported that USD 114 billion have been claimed by investors. The case *Occidental v Ecuador* produced the highest compensation ruling in history by far with USD 1.77 billion.[36] If one considers the repercussions of such an amount on the economy of LDCs it is quite obvious that states will show some reluctance to introduce new regulatory measures, even well-intentioned ones. In addition, statistics show that sensible sectors in need of regulation were indeed producing the most cases during the year 2012 due to the conflicts with other positive obligations of states. These sectors include gas, nuclear energy, marketing of gold, measures relating to the revocation of mining licenses, telecommunications, and tourism. Other cases include irregularities in public tenders, withdrawals of previously granted subsidies, and expropriations.[37]

The *status quo* today is dominated by legal uncertainty for states because they lack information to determine the scope of application of IIAs. Under these circumstances this kind of unilateral control mechanism constitutes a risk for states. One way to mitigate this is to increase local participation in policy design and to perform legal policies comprehensively and congruently. States might align legal

---

[32] *Parkerings-Compagniet AS v Lithuania [2007] Award ARB/05/8 (ICSID) at para 333* Chapter D page 4 para 7.

[33] *Methanex Corporation v United States [2005] Final Award (Ad hoc UNICTRAL) Part IV.*

[34] *Metalclad Corporation v The United Mexican States* [1997] Award ARB(AF)/97/1 (ICSID).

[35] *Methanex Corporation v United States [2005] Final Award (Ad hoc UNICTRAL) at para 119.*

[36] *Metalclad Corporation v The United Mexican States [*1997*] Award ARB(AF)/97/1 (ICSID) para 111.*

[37] *Occidental Exploration and Production Company v Ecuador [2004] Final Award UN3467 (LCIA).*

policies with more general public international legal norms and simultaneously highlight their relevance to achieving state goals. The protection offered by CIL and *jus cogens* might be invoked by states as a motivation for introducing legal policies that would allow them to achieve pre-established development goals. The main challenge faced by LDCs is to coherently apply these unilateral mechanisms in the presence of weak institutions. Problems associated with weak democracies, corruption, and populism might strongly perturb the legitimacy of these kinds of control mechanisms.

Having analysed the unilateral control mechanisms that can be implemented by states, in the following section we will analyse whether foreign investors can also make use of unilateral mechanisms to tackle opportunistic behaviour. Thereafter, we will consider the mechanisms that can be included in investment contracts to tackle opportunism.

5.2.2 By Investors

Not only states but also investors can create control mechanisms. These control mechanisms can contribute to improving the state of the art by increasing transparency, providing information that can be used in the judicial process, and maintaining a good reputation. Control mechanisms can be used by transnational companies to incentivise managers to adhere to domestic and international laws if the structure or size of the company prohibits frequent supervision or monitoring of local managerial decisions. In this regard, the notion of responsible investors gains relevance. Responsible investors are those who are aware that performing an economic activity constitutes an opportunity but also address the risks involved in such economic activity. The main limitation of these mechanisms is their voluntarily character.[38]

Even though large-scale agricultural investors have not developed private control mechanisms, examples in other areas exist. They include set-ups for specific industrial sectors and multi-stakeholders as well as individually developed mechanisms. They often take the form of standards and have been increasing in number over the last years. These regulations have progressively pervaded both domestic business and international trade. The FAO classifies these mechanisms by their functions as standard-setting adoption, implementation, conformity assessment, and enforcement.[39] Depending on the nature and structure of the mechanism or standard, they can be carried out either by public or private entities. However, rather than going into the FAO's technical classification, we will group the mechanisms by focussing on the typology of actors that can design them.

---

[38]United Nations Conference on Trade and Development, World Investment Report 2013 (World Investment Report 2013, 2014), p. 111.

[39]World Bank and United Nations Conference on Trade and Development (2014), p. 12.

5.2.2.1 Specific Industrial Sector Mechanisms

Specific mechanisms developed by industrial sectors have standardised business practices in the major areas of commercial activity at the domestic and international levels. These mechanisms take the form of a code through which companies address the social impact of supply chains, international operations, and other activities that can adversely affect local populations. In many cases IOs and NGOs contribute to the elaboration of codes in specific industrial sectors. This represents an advantage for large corporations because these organisations possess significant expertise in policy design as well as far-reaching knowledge of the application of IL.

These initiatives are based on national and international soft law. They were developed in different areas of soft law, for example the Electronic Industry Code of Conduct,[40] that include not only production but corruption, as in the UN Global Compact or the OECD Convention. The financial sector developed the Equator Principles that regulate bank activities and also includes ILO fundamental labour standards, HRs, and environmental issues.[41]

The International Chamber of Commerce developed the ICC Business Charter for Sustainable Development and the ICC Rules of Conduct to Combat Extortion and Bribery.[42] The International Mining and Metals Council acts as a catalyst for environmental and social performance improvement in the mining and metal industry.[43] Also, the Principles for Sustainable Development Performance, which integrate the UN Global Compact, the Rio Declaration, ILO Conventions, OECD Guidelines, and the OECD Convention on Combating Bribery, include the aim to respect HRs, labour practices, and the environment, and to fight bribery.[44]

---

[40] FAO (2009) at para 4.

[41] See Sect. 3.5.3 of this study.

[42] Electronic Industry Citizenship Coalition Code of Conduct, available at http://www.eiccoalition.org/media/docs/EICCCodeofConduct4_English.pdf. Accessed on 14 September 14.

[43] The ICMM's Council bases it activities on ten principles: Implement and maintain ethical business practices and sound systems of corporate governance; integrate sustainable development considerations within the corporate decision-making process; uphold fundamental human rights and respect cultures, customs and values in dealings with employees and others who are affected by our activities; implement risk management strategies based on valid data and sound science; seek continual improvement of our health and safety performance; seek continual improvement of our environmental performance; contribute to conservation of biodiversity and integrated approaches to land use planning; facilitate and encourage responsible product design, use, re-use, recycling and disposal of our products; contribute to the social, economic and institutional development of the communities in which we operate; implement effective and transparent engagement, communication and independently verified reporting arrangements with our stakeholders. Source: International Chamber of Commerce Combating Extortion and Bribery International available at http://www.iccwbo.org/Advocacy-Codes-and-Rules/Document-centre/2005/ICC-Rules-of-Conduct-and-Recommendations-to-Combat-Extortion-and-Bribery-(2005-Edition). Accessed 14 September 2014.

[44] International Council on Mining & Metals (2014).

5.2.2.2 Multi-Stakeholder Mechanisms

Some economic sectors have developed multi-stakeholder mechanisms. They group economic actors in order to address, in a standardised manner, methods of production that are monitored by external actors. These control mechanisms enable access to specific publicly accessible information and create competency between economic actors. They group producers, members of society, business, labour, consumers, and research institutions in order to determine best practices in the production and commercialisation of specific products.[45] These kinds of mechanisms can take different faces. There are mechanisms that are elaborated mainly for individual companies. There are other mechanisms that provide a certification of compliance with specific standards. Multi-stakeholder mechanisms address a broad range of issues, including HRs and labour rights, community development, consumer rights, the use of security forces, bribery and corruption, health and safety issues, and environmental standards. They involve cooperation of varying degree between many social partners, including companies, worker and employer organisations, NGOs, governments, or some combination thereof.

Most multi-stakeholder mechanisms are built on the normative framework of international and national soft law. The International Organization for Standardization (ISO) is the leading organisation promoting standardisation. They are an NGO that sets standards in a broad spectrum of activities around the world. ISO is represented at state level by national standard-setting bodies that are based in different countries. One of its most relevant contributions over the last years was the ISO 26000 concerned with Social Responsibility. The ISO is an international organisation that could be expected to have the expertise and knowledge to develop applicable standards for economic activities in LSLIs and further agricultural issues. There are, however, other initiatives that are closely related to LSLIs. These initiatives focus on specific agricultural commodities rather than on land itself. The Roundtable on Sustainable Biofuels (RSB) and the Roundtable on Sustainable Palm Oil (RSPO) are just two examples of multi-stakeholder standards that can be implemented as control mechanisms by private actors.[46] They are built on the pillars of relevant UN and ILO treaties and declarations concerning HRs, labour practices, and the environment.

[45]See the following report that was made as a part of the mandate of the G20 in Toronto 2010. It focuses on measures to promote economic growth and resilience, a development agenda and multi-year and action plans: ibid.

[46]See: Inter-Agency Working Group on the Private Investment and Job Creation Pillar of the G20 Multi-Year Action on Development (2011), p. 8 and Roundtable on Sustainable Biomaterials (2014).

5.2.2.3 Individual Mechanisms

Another option available to investors or states to implement control mechanisms is to create individual instruments leading to the disclosure of information about the mechanisms of production and the value chain. These kinds of mechanisms have quite a broad spectrum since they include legislative measures states can undertake as well as the creation of new entities whose business activity is closely related to generating social benefits.

Individual mechanisms have proliferated in many industrial sectors due to their reputational effects and the way in which they promote transparency. An UNCTAD study on Investment and Enterprise Responsibility reported that around 86% of multinational enterprises have developed policies on environmental and social responsibility.[47] Individual mechanisms have the advantage that investors can adapt the instruments to their own necessities and set a baseline as a starting point. Since they are promoted and also implemented by a single company or industrial sector, these same promoters will internalise the costs (investors will assume the costs of involving external actors as auditors in order to promote compliance). They are common across most industries.[48] Individual mechanisms are absent in areas related to LSLIs and their coverage of human rights issues is marginal. Most of these mechanisms were developed in the framework of corporate social responsibility as a response to the criticism of the effects of foreign investment in developing countries and LDCs.[49] Private standards involve a process at different levels that includes standard-setting adoption, implementation, conformity, assessment, and enforcement.[50]

These kinds of mechanisms can also be oriented towards creating incentives to make the investor comply and to influence their reputation. This must not necessarily occur in the host country but could also happen in countries in which their products are sold or the native country of the investor. In this case investors must be progressively incentivised to achieve higher levels of compliance. Responding to such incentives, investors can voluntarily undertake measures to maintain a good reputation. These incentives are inspired by extra-judicial rather than judicial mechanisms.[51] They are frequently combined with monitoring mechanisms in the form of periodical reports. Certification processes or the labelling of products are suitable instruments to provide information to consumers about the origin of products as well as the production process.[52] In the food sector, the focus has

[47] Roundtable on Sustainable Palm Oil (2014).

[48] For some examples we recommend: ibid and United Nations Conference on Trade and Development (2008), p. 18.

[49] For an analysis on the development of the corporate social responsibility agenda see: Inter-Agency Working Group on the Private Investment and Job Creation Pillar of the G20 Multi-Year Action on Development (2011).

[50] Organisation for Economic Co-operation and Development (2009).

[51] See e.g.: FAO (2009) at 5 and ff. and also Utting (2008), pp. 959, 960.

[52] We recommend the following study that deals with the question on the scope and economic implications of labelling being promoted from states. FAO (2009).

been on food security and food quality. Further progress has been made in the textile sector in value chain and processing.[53]

In the United States there is a new juridical form for corporations that is oriented not only towards capital but also towards social benefits. We refer here to the so-called 'benefit corporation'. This is an individual control mechanism because the investor unilaterally decides to change the structure of the entity that will be obliged to fulfil socially oriented requirements. A structural change of the company's anatomy takes place. This innovative form of corporation is already available in sixteen states of the United States.[54] On the one hand their aim is to promote profit-oriented activities, while on the other hand they allow managers to take decisions which are environmentally friendly and support HRs. This kind of entity demonstrates how incentives can be set to the benefit of the public. They seek to maximise positive externalities. Their performance is measured through the social, environmental, and financial measures the entity takes.

5.3 Contract-based Control Mechanisms

5.3.1 Introduction

Contracts are a pillar in the relationship between economic actors. From an economic point of view, they are a device for resource allocation. Contracts can efficiently move goods to whichever user values this service most highly and ensure that each step in the allocation process is a Pareto improvement.[55] The contractual freedom enjoyed by parties allows them to create their own law. Law created by the parties is the most relevant control mechanism because it regulates their economic activity. It expresses concrete preferences. It is the primary source of law to be taken into account if a contractual interpretation is needed, but it can also be used to limit the power of interpretation. Furthermore, contracts can be used to limit the power conceded by parties to the tribunal. We are thus interested in mechanisms allocated at two different levels, namely at the state-state level through IIAs, and at the investor-state level through LSLI contracts. While the control mechanisms anchored in IIAs encompass all investments between IIA signatory states, LSLIs control the specific economic activity in state-investor relationships. Some of the control mechanisms that we will map in the following section can be applied equally at both levels. There are other mechanisms that are more specific, making their inclusion more desirable at the investor-state level than at the state-state level.

[53]See Inter-Agency Working Group on the Private Investment and Job Creation Pillar of the G20 Multi-Year Action on Development (2011).

[54]For an overview on so called B-Corporations that also includes some criticisms we recommend: Crespi and Marette (2003).

[55]Reiser (2011), p. 591.

We will group them in order to provide a useful catalogue that can be employed to design future LSLIs and IIAs. Even though the inclusion of a specific control mechanism may be most appropriate at the state-state level, IIAs would make these highly costly due to the costs of a renegotiation. However, parties can include some of these mechanisms in investor-state contracts, which means that such control would apply only to this specific kind of investment. Although umbrella clauses are almost omnipresent in IIAs, there is the view that IIL tribunals have jurisdiction only if IIAs are breached.[56] This means that if LSLI contractual parties wish to include specific contractual mechanisms, these might be aligned with the standards of protection in IIAs. Parties can thus use the investment contract as a way to clarify the meaning of standards of protection in IIAs.[57]

In this section we will firstly illustrate the general aspects of contractual-based control mechanisms. Secondly, we will explain a set of control mechanisms that should be considered in LSLI contracts.

5.3.2 Preliminary Considerations

Approaches describing contracts as control mechanisms and managerial instruments have a well-established tradition in economics and in the L&E school of thought.[58] There has also been a relevant contribution in the field of L&E with a specific focus on IIL. van Aaken (2014b) analyses control mechanisms available to parties designing IIAs. We will discuss her approach and adapt it to our research agenda.[59]

From an L&E point of view contractual-based control mechanisms can take the form of rules or standards.[60] There are two ways to distribute the rights and duties among parties.[61] While rules are concrete in nature and regulate a specific behaviour, standards are more abstract.[62] They provide information to the tribunal about the preferences of the parties by framing the treaty, and also furnish information to the parties about how to behave in an unexpected event. States can make use of rules to function alongside their constitutional law, pre-existent obligations, and the investment treaty.[63] Although standards and rules are verifiable, the former are

---

[56]This as stated by: Sweet and Mathews (2008), pp. 68, 76.

[57]About IILs' Standards see Chap. 2.

[58]See *supra* footnote: 109 in Chap. 4.

[59]*Compañía de Aguas del Aconquija SA and Vivendi Universal SA v Argentina* [2005] Decision on Jurisdiction ARB/97/3 (ICSID) at para 95.

[60]Probably the most influential paper on this: van Aaken (2014b). See also: Kaplow (1992), p. 557 and applied in IIL see: Scott and Stephan (2006), p. 72 ff.

[61]van Aaken (2014b), p. 12.

[62]Ibid.

[63]Ibid.

costlier to verify than the latter due to their level of precision. Standards are more abstract and tend to change over time since their meaning is not static, i.e. the meaning of discrimination or indirect expropriation will shift over the course of decades. Rules provide more concrete information to the arbitrators to determinate contractual breach; for instance, they allow parties to identify if there was less production than expected or fewer jobs created than agreed in the contract. The costs implicit in rules and standards will be included in the negotiators' equation in different places. While rules make the negotiation process costlier, standards affect the enforcement phase more strongly since their application takes place in this phase. In fact, parties need to be able to internalise the costs associated with the inclusion of both, but since their costs are allocated at different times, they are eventually balanced because the cost of designing and the cost of performing the contract are split. During the negotiation, rules create more costs because of the level of specificity required to design them. This process can include, for instance, the consultancy of experts to gather information about specific issues. The costs of standards will be palpable *ex post* when they need to be interpreted. Some previous information about the scope of standards is contained in the jurisprudence and *opinio juris*.[64] Nevertheless, the specific meaning of a standard could change over time because it depends on factors including the preferences of the adjudicators and the interpretative techniques they apply.[65]

By designing contracts based on control mechanisms, negotiators will have to consider flexibility measures based on their own countries' constitutional law.[66] In addition, there are guidelines and principles developed by IOs and NGOs that are specifically designed to achieve some level of discipline in LSLIs. One example is the Principles for Responsible Agricultural Investment that Respect Rights, Livelihoods and Resources developed by the FAO, IFAD, UNCTAD, and the World Bank.[67] This document contains a core of principles that can be applied to promote LSLIs including economic, social, environmental, and HRs considerations. HRs are, however, only treated marginally. This means that there are some principles, like the observance of local land rights, as well as the principle on the promotion of food security, that inevitably touch on the subject of HRs. A specific consideration of these rights is missing. In 2012 the FAO published the Voluntary Guidelines on the Governance of Tenure which promote responsible governance of land tenure, fisheries, and forests, with respect to all forms of tenure, i.e. public, private, communal, indigenous, customary, and informal.[68] This instrument HRs in the

[64]It will contribute determinate the predictability of success in litigation. It means that economic actors will used available information—judicial decisions—to anticipate the tribunals' outcomes.

[65]It has been also stated that the stability of the standards in specific contractual relationship might be more volatile than the rules because is will easer to consider a standard up-to-date. Kaplow (1992), pp. 557, 586 ff.

[66]van Aaken (2014b), p. 14.

[67]Ibid.

[68]Ruggie (2008), p. 14.

context of property rights protection and focuses on the mandate of Article 11 UDHR. The most recently published instrument is the Practice of Responsible Investment Principles in Larger-Scale Agricultural Investments.[69] It has been promoted by the World Bank and by UNCTAD, and is developed in seven chapters that address different aspects of the land business. It includes responsibilities in the pre-investment phase, financial aspects, socio-economic aspects, issues of land access, and environmental impact. This instrument and the principles published in 2010 do not explicitly include the protection of HRs. All these instruments seeking to create discipline and homogenise LSLI contracts fail because they ignore legal aspects regarding enforcement mechanisms that need to be explicitly included in contracts. These instruments repeatedly declare that states have to ensure that specific standards are fulfilled, but lack the necessary legal policies to comply with these principles.

LDCs face the challenge of achieving development-oriented goals when they enter into LSLIs. The success of investment policies will depend on the institutional arrangements available to states to align their endowments, as well as on their capacity to design sustainable policies. In order to achieve such goals, states need to recognise their comparative advantage (for instance, a wealth of natural resources). Indeed, investors are probably only interested in the land to use it as a production resource. That is where states are in a better position to negotiate. States also need to map strategic priorities and achievable goals. Another challenge to the state is to set parameters and rules in order to make net gains perceivable. States could for instance require the investors to fulfil certain quotas of creating jobs and contributing to local food security. Moreover, as we will explain in the next paragraphs, in order to achieve proposed development goals, contracts should require the active participation of potentially affected stakeholders, create the obligation of regular audit procedures, reduce risks of local capitalisation, and create concrete sanctions in case of a violation of pre-existent obligations.

To recapitulate: contracts are attractive for investors only when the realisation of the economic activity through a contract is less costly than in the absence of a contract. As we already saw in the previous chapter, politicians enter into LSLI negotiations only when they allow them to achieve the maximisation of their own utility function. As profit maximisers, parties will try to decrease transaction or performance costs during the entire life cycle of the contract. Such costs can decrease over time because of access to information and better technology and know-how. At the same time contracts create incentives to avoid non-performance, making it possible to realise constitutional principles and to fulfil pre-existent HRs obligations. Well-designed contracts are an effective way to coordinate and promote production. The main challenge for states where LSLIs are propagated is to design appropriate contracts despite the huge inequalities between the parties. These inequalities mostly appear as asymmetries in bargaining power and information, as well as manipulation of the land

[69] Voluntary Guidelines on the Responsible Governance of Tenure of Land, Fisheries and Forests in the Context of National Food Security [2013] CL 144/9 C 2013/20, p. 8.

market in which rules to enter or exit are not clear.[70] The investment contract itself is the most appropriate control mechanism available to parties because they can design it to express their preferences.

In the next segment we will map relevant aspects that states need to take into consideration when negotiating LSLIs. If they adhere to these aspects, states can be expected to comply with pre-existent HRs obligations and will realise their constitutional mandate. These relevant aspects might also be seen as control mechanisms that create incentives for contractual performance over time, especially in LSLI contracts that are characterised by their longevity.

5.3.3 Types of Contractual-based Control Mechanisms

5.3.3.1 Definition of Applicable Law

States have the power to distribute rights and obligations and to regulate means to solve future conflicts by negotiating IIAs. It is yet to be verified to what extent LSLIs are protected under IIAs. The source is the IIAs themselves. If so, as in most of the cases, relevant aspects to consider include the applicability and interpretation of the law. These two mechanisms enable parties to retain control over the enforcement of the contract. Parties reduce the power of tribunals *ex ante* by defining applicable law and thus applying their own approach. Therefore, their success in case of conflict can be predicted more precisely. Whereas parties sometimes agree to apply either the law of the home, host country, or IL, in other cases eclectic alternatives can be considered.[71] By doing so, parties combine domestic with IL. As we have previously explained, parties have to define investments in the framework of IIAs in order to delimit the applicable law. This is the case because the ICSID Convention protects investments. However, it does not define what an investment is. Since the definition of investments is drafted in broad terms, the exclusion of land investments should be expressly considered. This means that due to the imprecise definition of investments in IIAs, LSLIs will be protected by IIAs in most cases.

Even though IIAs are investor oriented and do not contain obligations for investors in most cases, IIAs can impose sanctions if the state is able to prove that opportunistic behaviour by the investor has caused damage to third parties. If this occurs, IIAs will impact the investor at the moment in which damages are calculated, or when they oblige the tribunal to decline the jurisdiction. From the point of view of legal technique, the delimitation of applicable law creates a roadmap for the tribunal to follow in the case of an event. It is our interest to investigate what would happen if the applicability of the law were not

[70]See Sect. 1.4.

[71]Principles for Responsible Agricultural Investment that Respects Rights, Livehoods and Resources [2010] available http://siteresources.worldbank.org/INTARD/214574-1111138388661/22453321/Principles_Extended.pdf. Accessed 25 December 2013, p. 11.

pre-established. If the parties do not include dispositions regarding the applicable law in IIA, diverse regimes in IIL exist. ICSID and UNCITRAL differ on how to proceed. In the ICSID regime, Convention Article 42 (1) identifies the treaty as the primary applicable law. If parties do not agree on applicable law, the tribunal shall apply the law of the contracting state party to the dispute and those rules of IL that may be applicable. This means that if parties do not specify the applicable law, the tribunal has some discretion to consider the application of IL instruments. The risk in this approach is that the law selected by the tribunal is probably less adequate to solving the case than the host or even the home state's domestic law would be. In a world of rational arbitrators, the gains for a state or for investors from a decision might be marginal.[72] In UNCITRAL rules the tribunal can freely decide what law is the most appropriate for cases in which parties do not specify the applicable law. The applicable law as conceived by UNCITRAL in Article 35 lacks hierarchy and tasks the tribunal with applying the law it considers most appropriate.[73] Including clauses determining the governing law gives parties legal control over the exercise of the contract and thus limits the capacity of the tribunal. This translates to more legal security for contractual parties. The most rational position for contracting parties is to prevent the tribunal from deciding which IL to apply as much as possible.

Clauses determining the applicable law indeed create a kind of legal hierarchy which is, in principle, almost non-existent in the formal structure of IL.[74] Host states can make use of specific legal dispositions to solve tensions between norms that arise in IIL and HRL. From the economic point of view, parties abide by these clauses by disclosing information to the tribunal *ex ante* on the procedure to be followed in case of future conflicts. They allow a more precise prediction of outcomes of state measures taken in response to unforeseen events. This means that they can legitimise state behaviour.[75] Even though this is not a new approach at the international level, these clauses rarely exist in the framework of IIL. One commonly cited example in the literature is the hierarchy established in the UN Charter regarding its application. It states that if there is a conflict of norms, the application of the UN Charter prevails.[76] In the framework of IIL at the regional level, we found a normative hierarchy in which the laws protecting environmental issues prevail over the other rights, for instance Article 103 ff. of NAFTA. It could

[72]This statement goes back to the general assumptions of this research project. See Sect. 1.5.

[73]Art. 35 UNCITRAL gives parties the power to instruct the tribunal on the applicable law. It states: '1. The arbitral tribunal shall apply the rules of law designated by the parties as applicable to the substance of the dispute. Failing such designation by the parties, the arbitral tribunal shall apply the law which it determines to be appropriate.' Dolzer and Schreuer (2008), p. 265.

[74]United Nations General Assembly Resolution 65/22 UNCITRAL Arbitration Rules as Revised in 2010 [1976] A/RES/31/98 15 ILM 701 art 35.

[75]For similar approach see: Koskenniemi (1997), p. 566.

[76]Art 103 UN Charter states that: In the event of a conflict between the obligations of the Members of the United Nations under the present Charter and their obligations under any other international agreement, their obligations under the present Charter shall prevail.

be argued that the introduction of specific clauses leading to the application of domestic law would in some circumstances reduce the level of protection offered by IIAs. However, this may not always be the case because they only increase the level of protection in other legal areas, i.e. environmental law or HRL. What would happen is that these clauses would create control mechanisms that incentivise the tribunal to consider existent obligations whose application might prevail in specific cases and whose inobservance would lead to a further limitation of power. In order to avoid contractual weakness leading to misinterpretations and ultimately the wrong application, it is necessary for states to specify what law shall prevail and in which circumstances.

Now we will consider when and how states decide to exclude LSLIs from the protection of IIAs. In these cases one might assume that states need to individually create parallel investment incentives to be attractive to foreign investors. This statement is based on the controversial hypothesis that IIAs matter.[77] If this is the case, LDCs might not have an incentive to exclude LSLIs from the protection of IIAs. However, since there is no convincing approach affirming that IIAs lead to increased levels of agricultural FDI, one could consider the possibility of exclusion. This would mean that states create a parallel system protecting LSLI activities performed by foreign investors. States can either provide a specific and exclusionary rule as a component of IIAs or introduce new domestic laws. This kind of exclusion can also be made at the domestic level as part of a national investment law, seen for example in Argentina. The special law regulating land investments establishes in section 11 that,

> for the purposes of the law and according to the Bilateral Investment Treaties underwritten by the Republic of Argentina that are in force at the time this law becomes valid, the acquisition of rural land shall not be considered an investment as it is a non-renewable natural resource provided by the host country.[78]

This rule, nevertheless, leaves open the possibility of treating Argentine investments as FDI abroad. Such an option would not be available if the exclusion were made through an IIA.

A further implication of excluding the protection of LSLIs from IIAs is that the cost of negotiating investment contracts could increase. The reason for this can be explained as follows: if IIAs do not stimulate agricultural FDI, they still offer a set of institutions that increase the level of protection of investors vis-à-vis the protection offered by domestic jurisdictions. This means that the investment contract will have to implement at least some standards included in IIAs. It might lead to higher costs for the host state due to the number of actors, their particular preferences, and the high volume of investment contracts to negotiate. In addition, LDCs might negotiate with investors with considerably higher negotiation power. This shift of negotiation costs represents a challenge for LDCs because it is expected that investors will propose more attractive contractual conditions. However, it

[77] See Sect. 3.6.1.

[78] Neumann (2002), p. 72.

constitutes a considerable opportunity to promote the development of agricultural markets and to maximise the gains from agricultural FDI.

5.3.3.2 Definition of Legal Interpretative Techniques

By drawing up contracts, parties can interpret their meaning in a particular fashion.[79] Parties can also require the tribunal to take non-investment obligations into consideration in order to fill gaps in IIAs. This means that parties can *ex ante* inform arbitrators how to interpret the law. The VCLT takes a relevant role in this regard.[80] In Articles 31 and 32 it states the general and the supplementary rules of interpretation, respectively. These apply in accordance with the contract which is the primary source of law. Even though the VCLT lists the interpretation techniques that must be applied by the tribunal, it leaves open a broad spectrum of alternative interpretations whose application could, in some cases, fail to meet the preferences of the contractual parties at the moment of signing the contract. The aim is that the provisions designed by the parties are sufficiently clear with regard to their intentions and their preferences at the moment of interpretation.[81] International tribunals have recognised that the process of interpretation is 'an integrated operation, where interpretative rules and principles must be understood and applied as connected and mutually reinforcing components of a holistic exercise.'[82] The challenge to the parties is to include appropriate dispositions in the contract so that arbitrators, if necessary, are informed about how to apply the law in order to guarantee the fulfilment of the contract's purpose. In this sense we need to find a way to allow parties to design the contract so that at the moment of interpretation—following the structure of Article 31 VCLT—parties reduce the risks of an undesirable outcome. Although Articles 31 and 32 list different techniques of interpretation, there is no consensus on any hierarchy of application of a general rule. The 'ordinary meaning' as stated in Article 31 shall not be interpreted in an abstract way.[83] 'Ordinary' should be understood in the context of the treaty and in light of its object and purpose.[84] In this regard, parties should increase the level of specification in the treaty so that its content can be understood *ex post* by the tribunal.

A more complex issue is the purpose of the treaty as a rule of interpreting a treaty.[85] It not only requires looking at the text but also the consideration of other

---

[79]See i.e. the comments by: Ley 26.737 Régimen de Protección al Dominio Nacional Sobre la Propiedad, Posesión o Tenencia de las Tierras Rurales [2011] art 11.

[80]Roberts (2013), pp. 45, 85.

[81]United Nations, Vienna Convention on the Law of Treaties [1969] United Nations, Treaty Series, vol. 1155, p. 331.

[82]Roberts (2013), pp. 45, 85.

[83]*China – Measures Affecting Trading Rights and Distribution Services for Certain Publications and Audiovisual Entertainment Products* [2009] WT/DS363/AB/R (WTO Appellate Body) at para 399.

[84]Waibel (2011), p. 33.

[85]Dörr and Schmalenbach (2012), p. 541.

agreements and instruments that are connected to the conclusion of the treaty. This is complex because arbitrators are required to look at several different instruments that, even when connected, probably were not included intentionally. It requires, in consequence, that parties be specific on issues that usually remain abstract. If contracting parties provide the tribunal with a precise explanation of the aims of the contract, arbitrators will have to interpret the contract in order for this purpose to be achieved. Such information is usually included in the preamble of the contract which, however, does not tend to be very detailed. Nevertheless, it can be strategically designed to inform the tribunal about the concrete goals of the treaty. In this manner teleological interpretation can arise from the preamble.[86] The teleological interpretation of the contract will benefit the parties if they can link the purpose of the contract to specific issues arising from concrete problems during the performance phase.[87] The purpose of the treaty cannot be considered separately from the contract in an isolated manner. It is not an independent element. To the contrary, it is intrinsic to the text of the contract rather than a foreign concept imposed onto the treaty.[88] Parties should factor in the possibility that the tribunal is not bound to following a specific definition of common sense. For this reason negotiators should define their aims as precisely as possible in the contract so that the tribunal can refer back to them when interpretation is required.

Parties can require the interpretation of the contract from tribunals using methods not included in Article 31 VCLT. This article allows the collection of objective evidence to deduce the meaning of the contract through the practice of the parties.[89] It can also refer to a treaty that is in the process of interpretation or to other international treaties parties are signatories to.

The so-called systemic approach defined in Article 31(3)(c) VCLT allows the tribunal to treat the international legal system as part of the context of every treaty concluded under IL. Thereby, it lays the foundation for the treaty interpretation.[90] From the point of view of the tribunal, this article provides access to relevant international instruments so that the tribunal can take a decision on the conflict between the parties. This article poses a risk for the parties because the tribunal has the discretional authority to consider all relevant international treaties for its decisions. Moreover, the tribunal can only consider those treaties both states are part of. However, this technique is, as all techniques of interpretation are, driven by

[86] van Aaken (2014b), p. 17.

[87] Some examples are the US model BIT 2004 and Swiss BITs mention in the preamble their aim to promote development of the parties. Most of IIAs the purpose of the treaties is seen by economic cooperation, economic development or mutual prosperity. See ibid.

[88] This as considered in: Salacuse (2010), p. 114.

[89] See for example the jurisprudence of the ICJ that states: 'If there were any ambiguity, the Court might, for the purpose of arriving at the meaning, consider the action which has been taken under the treaty.' PCIJ Competence of the ILO (N 28) 39. Cf also Brazilian Loans (n 22) 93, 199; ICJ Corfu Channel Case (n 40) 25 that also states 'The subsequent attitude of the Parties shows [...].'

[90] *Federal Reserve Bank of New York v Bank Markazi* [2000] n 19 (Iran-U.S. Claims Tribunal) at para 58; MacLachlan, Dörr and Schmalenbach (2012), p. 560.

the principle of good faith, as affirmed at the beginning of Article 31 VCLT. This means that there is no guarantee that the tribunal will consider those instruments whose application can maximise the profit of the parties. It might be the case that the tribunal fails to look at the most appropriate or at the most relevant treaty to solve the issue at hand. The literature has extensively discussed the application of article 31(3)(c) as a channel to promote defragmentation of IL because treaty interpretation can link different sub-areas of IL. Nonetheless, tribunals are not necessarily incentivised to take into consideration the defragmentation of IL. In Chap. 2 we laid out the reasoning for this. At the least there is no hard law instrument obliging tribunals to follow techniques of interpretation in a specific way so that defragmentation can be promoted. Therefore, instead of shifting the focus to what tribunals can do, one might consider instead what parties can do to properly incentivise arbitrators. Negotiators can make use of their power during the negotiation phase to achieve a level of contractual specificity by setting clear rules on treaty interpretation and, if needed, which relevant international treaties might be taken into account.

Furthermore, parties should require the tribunal to apply measures in a proportional way so that compliance with non-investment obligations can be also achieved. Ensuring that the tribunal applies a balanced approach when interpreting the contract allows states to introduce non-investment policies that can affect investment activities.[91] Even though tribunals have sometimes taken into consideration the use of the principle of proportionality—as the *Termed* tribunal did[92]—the challenge to the parties is to incentivise the tribunals to apply this principle rather than leaving the possibility open of applying it or not.

This mechanism will contribute, on the one hand, to informing the arbitrators about the preferences of the parties and, on the other hand, to the tribunal's limitation of power by deciding how to interpret the law. The power of the tribunal is limited by the requirement that it has to follow the will of the parties in the contract. A further limitation of power is the consequence of inobservance of the rules pre-established by the parties. However, the discretional power of arbitrators will depend on the level of specification made by the contractual parties. The more abstract the parties remain in their design of this mechanism, the higher the risk that the arbitrators will not interpret the contract according to their preferences. It is a way for states to induce arbitrators to consider the protection of HRs by deciding on investment issues. Of course, states may also make use of their sovereign power to adapt their national policies to new requirements.

---

[91]We develop basic notions about the proportionality principle at Sect. 5.4.3.

[92]Mclachlan (2008), p. 280.

5.3.3.3 Delegation of Activities to Experts

Parties can delegate specific activities to experts. So far this measure has been underused in IIL. If the parties choose to make use of this mechanism, the investment contracts and their interaction with IIAs play a relevant role by increasing the level of protection and legal security. The main function of this mechanism is to exclude the possibility that arbitrators approach issues they do not have sufficient knowledge about. Some examples of this are the calculation of damages, as well as the generation of information needed to corroborate the fulfilment of specific contractual obligations.

The experience in IIL has frequently shown that tribunals are not the best suited to decide on technical facts that led to litigation. In fact, while they have the authority to decide, in some cases they have neither the legal option to get any information about the facts under consideration, nor the capacity, nor the appropriate incentives. Although the guarantees in IIL with regard to enforceability are indisputable, the inconsistency of tribunals may lead to reluctance on behalf of some economic actors to participate in the system because it appears to be more costly than being outside of IAA protection.[93] This reluctance has led some actors to consider renegotiations or to signal an exit from the contract. As discussed in previous section of this text, a poignant example of such tribunal weakness could be observed in the Argentina cases. In *CMS v Argentina* the tribunal lacked technical arguments to reject the existence of economic crisis.[94] It is quite normal that the tribunal is not to able to take a comprehensive approach with regard to the award. The problem is not the application or interpretation of the law. Instead the problem is the lack of information to subsume the facts into the law. Based on these facts, parties can prevent and avoid such failures by delegating the competence of deciding specific issues to professional guilds or experts.[95]

A precedent in IIL can be found in the 2012 US Model BIT.[96] This treaty delegates competence to a commission of experts in the investor's home state to determine whether a financial measure taken by the host state could be considered prudential and whether it complies with financial regulations.[97] Parties delegate authority to an expert body that has the necessary resources to determine to what

[93]On the problem of inconsistency we highly recommend: *Técnicas Medioambientales Tecmed SA v Mexico [*2003*] Award ARB(AF)/00/2 (ICSID) at para 122*; Schultz (2014).

[94]Gehne (2011) deduces that the short conclusion of the tribunal demonstrated that it failed to give sufficient reasons for its conclusion.

[95]The delegation of authorities at domestic level but also in international law is not a new phenomenon. About the rationale behind delegating this authority see: Foster (2009), p. 391.

[96]*CMS Gas Transmission Company v Argentina [*2005*] Award ARB/01/8 (ICSID).*

[97]Art 20 (3) (b): 'The competent financial authorities of both Parties shall make themselves available for consultations with each other and shall attempt in good faith to make a determination as described in subparagraph (a). Any such determination shall be transmitted promptly to the disputing parties and, if constituted, to the tribunal. The determination shall be binding on the tribunal.'

extent the measure taken by the contracting party is acceptable or not. The result of this consultancy must be observed in future judicial procedures. Such a commission legitimates governmental activity. While it helps to prevent opportunistic behaviour by disclosing information, states maintain control of legislative measures. Also, the experts' revision can be considered a kind of legitimisation.[98] In this sense the outsourcer as provider of information lacks the capacity to enforce any measures. They are limited to the role of a consultancy body. They contribute to decreasing uncertainty by providing reliable information, nonetheless. This means that they can *ex ante* guarantee efficiency by providing verifiable information and thus help reduce uncertainty. It might also reduce ambiguity and any *ex post* opportunism can *ex ante* be avoided.[99]

Weak states frequently lack the adequate institutional infrastructure and expertise to make appropriate assessments of food security in their own country. At the international level, some organisations are constantly producing data and are warning states that could be affected by food shortages. These sources of information could be linked in LSLI contracts so that future governmental measures can be substantiated and implemented. Information from independent experts can be used to justify and legitimate measures taken by states.[100] There might be different international bodies for different sectors. In the food sector, the United Nations World Food Programme (UNWFP) plays a relevant role since it collects global data on the state of food production and food security with a high level of precision.

5.3.3.4 Investment Procedures at the National Level

National procedures can play a relevant role as a control mechanism to tackle opportunistic behaviour. They can be considered at the state-state level. On the one hand judicial decisions at the national level on specific issues, e.g. indigenous peoples' property rights and peasants' rights, can contribute to increasing transparency throughout the investment process. On the other hand national institutions can be required to apply national remedies or administrative procedures before acceding to international jurisdiction. Even though most IIAs do not require the exhaustion of national remedies to access international jurisdiction, national controls can also apply outside the judicial

[98]See for a similar approach: U.S. Model Bilateral Investment Treaty [2012] available at http://www.state.gov/r/pa/prs/ps/2012/04/188199.htm. Accessed 12 July 2015.

[99]In general terms will the outsourcers provide information so that uncertainty in the contractual relationship decreases. As we have shown in previous chapters of this book uncertainty is one of the most relevant problems parties have to deal with by contractual process. See more details *supra* Sect. 4.5.2.

[100]By independent experts is meant that the commissioned do not depend of the contractual parties to produce relevant data. Or course in the very narrow sense, it won't happen since it is needed that experts are allowed to collect such information, but what is meant is that they expertise is not influenced by local governments.

system.[101] In principle, the ICSID Convention states in Article 26 that parties have the right to require the exhaustion of local administrative or judicial remedies as a condition for their consent to arbitration under the Convention. The so-called *fork-on-the-road* clauses included in some BITs give parties the choice to submit disputes either at the domestic level or the IIL level, but the access to one is premised on the exhaustion of the other. States can also include a national procedure to declare the economic activity an FDI, which would allow them to *ex ante* control access to IIL.

5.3.3.5 Guaranteeing Information Flows

By applying NIE, we showed that one of the main elements leading to detrimental effects and to opportunistic behaviour is the asymmetry of information between contracting parties. The need to guarantee informational flows cannot be limited to the disclosure of information during the negotiation process but should apply throughout the contractual performance. The challenge states face when contracting is to maximise access to information that will permit an audit of the investment project. Before using the flow of information as an incentive, states need to pre-establish goals regarding both the expected production goals and the additional development-oriented policies that will be performed by foreign investors. It has often been reported that lack of regular monitoring during the performance of the project leads to the inefficient allocation of the investors' resources, with the result that the region where investments take place remains underdeveloped. Promises of new roads, schools, and local infrastructure remain unfulfilled. The clear pre-establishment of goals and well-designed enforcement mechanisms make it possible that the contract remains enforceable over time. The duty to report, in combination with specific enforceable mechanisms that will be explained in the next paragraphs, might create incentives not to breach pre-established commitments. Furthermore, socio-economic goals including the protection of HRs will be more easily achieved by focussing on the creation of direct employment, improvement of food security, better access to markets, technological transfer, and capacity building.

5.3.3.6 Respect and Recognition of Pre-Existent Rights

The recognition of pre-existent rights and obligations between the state and its citizens are extremely sensitive and need to be systematically controlled and regulated by standards in LSLI contracts. In most LDCs legal pluralism exists at the ground level. These regimes are traditional land tenure systems that vary from region to region. Respecting and recognising pre-existent rights is relevant on the one hand because of the social costs that could arise by ignoring such rights, and on the other hand because

[101] U.S. Model Bilateral Investment Treaty [2012] available at http://www.state.gov/r/pa/prs/ps/2012/04/188199.htm. Accessed 12 July 2015.

of the detrimental consequences that—from the legal and reputational point of view—can impact states and investors. Previous studies have shown that one of the most relevant aspects for investors to consider in LDCs is the weak institutional framework at the domestic level facilitating the investment process. As such, investors might easily acquire land without the state recognising pre-existent rights. States have not elucidated whether the recognition of pre-existent rights should play a role when they negotiate LSLI contracts for economic and legal reasons. This is because, firstly, they can shift the costs of land acquisition or redistribution of property rights to the investors. Secondly, this course of action increases the probability of success for the new land policy implemented through LSLIs.

Over the past decades IOs have designed mechanisms to provide LDCs with tools to regulate land tenure. In many cases these projects did not work. Today a new wave of reports and publications recommend the implementation or activation of a cadastre system to register land and record land transactions. The main problem of such a demarcation policy is the institutional requirements that are needed to make it sustainable. The performance of such measures, for instance those being proposed by the World Bank, cannot be deemed realistic in the short run. One of the main challenges is the high agency costs at the local level. Political power held by elites at the local level might hinder the demarcation of land since its value to locals exceeds monetary compensation. The reason is that land in LDCs not only has economic connotations; it is part of the culture, the social status, and the political power.

If states were to build a legal framework and institutional support for landowners and were to promote a land market in which the free negotiation and reduction of informational asymmetries could be guaranteed, economic actors would freely enter into negotiations. In this case the performance of investment projects would accomplish expected benefits.

Respect and recognition of pre-existing rights do not preclude the displacement of the population or expropriations. If necessary, public scrutiny as well as prompt and fair compensation might be the guarantors of transmission. It is in the interest of investors to have information about the process of expropriation and about the means employed by the government to make the land accessible. Since most LSLIs are financed by multinational financial institutions, it might be relevant for investors to be able to demonstrate the proper use of resources to comply with specific standards of international financial institutions.[102]

Incentives are allocated correctly if states can enforce pre-existent rights over time. This control mechanism shall not only apply the moment the investor takes possession of the land. It must be a dynamic protection that is enforceable over time. Experiences in the United States, Europe, and Africa have shown that changes to the land system without recognising pre-existent rights produce a 'clash of law and cultures' that can lead, and has led, to violence and civil wars.[103]

---

[102]Some of these standards are explained *infra* at Chap. 3.

[103]*Malaysian Historical Salvors Sdn Bhd v Malaysia* [2007] Award on Jurisdiction ARB/05/10 (ICSID *Salini Costruttori S.p.A. and Italstrade S.p.A. v Kingdom of Morocco* [2001] Award on

5.3.3.7 Active Participation of Locals

The participation and consultation of locals is a control mechanism that contributes to the legitimisation of investments not only during the negotiation process but also during the performance of the contract. It provides relevant information, records reservations and decisions, and develops an agreed-upon approach to monitoring and remedies.[104] Taking locals into consideration in the decision-making process makes it possible to ensure the realisation of the interests of all parties involved. Moreover, participation contributes to making the investment sustainable over time, makes it possible to audit the project during the performance phase, and should have effects on transparency. It might play a singular role when the rural population has to be displaced to offer the land to investors. As we have seen in previous sections, a majority of people living in LDCs' rural areas are subsistence producers depending on the land and their production to survive. In this sense, participation contributes to carving out strategies, mitigating exacerbated damages, and avoiding social and economic negative impacts. Rather than being a voluntary act of the states, including locals in the negotiation process is an obligation for states to balance the asymmetric bargaining power between investors and the local population.

Participation of locals is effective if, firstly, the representation of the affected locals is legitimate, secondly, affected people can be integrated in the project and, thirdly, locals are allowed to monitor the investment project.[105]

Participation is effective because it can guarantee legitimisation. It is achieved by winning the consent of locals as they freely recognise their representation and also their decisions. Being part of the investment project means, under expected conditions, that locals will be better off than if they continued in the economic activity they were in before. Incentives are properly allocated if the non-participation of locals would mean an increase in social costs that cannot be internalised by the investor, and which would ultimately frustrate the project. Further, locals have the power to evaluate the performance of the project. This

---

Jurisdiction ARB/00/4 (ICSID *Kardassopoulos v Georgia* [2007] Decision on jurisdiction ARB/05/18 (ICSID Agreement Between the Government of Sweden and the Government of Malaysia Concerning the Mutual Protection of Investments (Sweden-Malaysia) [1979] SÖ 1979:17 available at: http://investmentpolicyhub.unctad.org/IIA/country/202/treaty/2484. Accessed 17 September 201 *Gruslin v Malaysia* [2000] Award ARB/99/3 (ICSID *Malaysian Historical Salvors Sdn Bhd v Malaysia [2007] Award on Jurisdiction ARB/05/10 (ICSID Salini Costruttori S.p.A. and Italstrade S.p.A. v Kingdom of Morocco [2001] Award on Jurisdiction ARB/00/4 (ICSID Kardassopoulos v Georgia [2007] Decision on jurisdiction ARB/05/18 (ICSID* Agreement Between the Government of Sweden and the Government of Malaysia Concerning the Mutual Protection of Investments (Sweden-Malaysia) [1979] SÖ 1979:17 available at: http://investmentpolicyhub.unctad.org/IIA/country/202/treaty/2484. Accessed 17 September 201 *Gruslin v Malaysia [2000] Award ARB/99/3 (ICSID).*

[104]Deininger et al. (2011), p. xliii.

[105]Principles for Responsible Agricultural Investment that Respects Rights, Livehoods and Resources [2010] available http://siteresources.worldbank.org/INTARD/214574-1111138388661/22453321/Principles_Extended.pdf. Accessed 25 December 2013, p. 11; Rabah et al. (2011), p. 5.

means they are also a monitoring mechanism of sorts. For locals, monitoring means that they have the resources to get information about the project. This information can be used to evaluate contractual compliance which in turn will create incentives for investors to fulfil contractual commitments. In case of a breach, participation can create incentives to enforce the contract either judicially or extra-judicially.

The legitimacy of local representatives is a keystone of their participation. In this particular example, as we demonstrated in our property rights approach, representatives are not elected democratically. They are political leaders whose opinion might be relevant for the negotiation.[106] The legitimisation of these actors is highly relevant because it will decrease the probability of future conflicts, enable the integration of the project into the community, and contribute to protecting sensitive issues associated with culture, religion, and the environment. Since they are supported by the government, local representatives will care about the nature of transferred rights, the size of transferred land, and the enforcement mechanisms they can apply. The participation of locals in the negotiation process might not be limited to cases in which locals are *de jure* owners but also to tenants and nomad communities.

Notwithstanding the widespread consensus on the relevance of including all potentially affected sectors in the negotiation process, field studies, though limited in number, show that communities are only rarely involved in the decision-making process.[107] In some Mexican regions, as well as in the Ukraine and Uruguay, most successful LSLIs actively involve the local population in project design and management.[108]

Fulfilling standards of local participation should be a condition for enforcing LSLIs in IIL jurisdiction. Investors should be able to submit evidence of the participation and consent of the local population to the investment project through pre-established assessments.[109]

5.3.3.8 Economic Maximization

From the point of view of public policy, states' priorities might be the technical feasibility of the project. Furthermore, economic maximisation is achieved not only by achieving high net revenues but also by maximizing the profit of all other goals outlined in the contract. Rules should be included in the contract to specify what is needed to achieve the proposed goals.

Since it is impossible to avoid that the implementation of public policies produces damages in certain areas, these damages should be shifted to areas not

[106]See Sect. 4.4 ff of this study.

[107]One experience from Ghana has been documented by: Sulle and Nelson (2009), p. 36.

[108]Simmons (2009), p. 24.

[109]The following country-based studies highlight the relevance and the effects of participation of locals: Sulle and Nelson (2009) and Nhantumbo and Salomão (2010).

compromising HRs as much as possible. The fact that some costs that need to be internalised by involved economic actors include irreversible actions demonstrates the high levels of precaution required to maximise economic gains. For example, the destruction of cultural goods might generate costs that cannot be liquidated and might produce social costs that will be hard to internalise. Accordingly, the maximisation of economic gains might include the recognition of the delicate nature of some elements that are part of the deal. It requires the disclosure of endogenous elements of the investment activity rather than formal aspects. This requires that such information is made available by the investor. However, the state must have the capacity to evaluate the quality of the information provided by the investor so that it can, to some extent, calculate its expected gains.

An additional requirement that states need to meet in order to economically maximize the project is to compare the offers of a number of different investors. To do so, competition, tender, or auctions can contribute to elaborating a cost-benefit approach and to selecting the most appropriate business model. This might be consistent with national goals and the development agenda, might fulfil financial requirements for an effective performance, and adhere to social standards.

5.3.3.9 Securing Transparency

A pervasive lack of transparency in the contracting process is one of the biggest obstacles to achieving proposed goals and to guaranteeing the proper allocation of development resources.[110] Transparency requires standards that promote the exchange of information and has direct implications on the negotiation process, the contractual performance, and therefore on the calculation of remedies. It functions as a control mechanism by increasing governance and accountability, which are translated into access to information, clear and correct allocation of incentives, and the improvement of the institutional environment.[111] While the role of transparency is to disclose information, additional legal institutions are needed to enforce infringed rights if a wrongful act needs to be determined. Accordingly, transparency might generate reluctance on behalf of investors because it increases not only the negotiation but also performance costs. For the World Bank and UNCTAD,[112] transparency is highly important because it decreases uncertainty about the intentions of the investor and wards off adverse consequences for the investment at the ground level.[113] Ethiopia is a poignant example of a country promoting transparency in LSLI contracts. It follows two policies to promote

[110]Principles for Responsible Agricultural Investment that Respects Rights, Livehoods and Resources [2010] available http://siteresources.worldbank.org/INTARD/214574-1111138388661/22453321/Principles_Extended.pdf. Accessed 25 December 2013, p. 12.

[111]Anseeuw et al. (2012), p. 59.

[112]See i.e. World Bank and United Nations Conference on Trade and Development (2014), p. 11.

[113]Johnson (2014).

transparency: it introduced a model agreement to negotiate LSLI contracts and the government makes all the signed contracts publicly available.

Rational parties need incentives to achieve a certain level of transparency. The reason is that it increases negotiation costs and negotiators will be reluctant to internalise such costs. This seems to be the idea behind a statement made by the IMF in the Guide on Resource Revenue Transparency, which highlights the fact that the non-disclosure of contracts may be advantageous since it can 'strengthen the hand of governments.'[114] Following this statement, it should not be expected that the entire process will be completely public. A higher level of discretion may be necessary during some initial phases to enter into negotiations more easily. The argument can be defended by considering that, on the one hand, investors will demand at least the same conditions under which states negotiated with previous investors and, on the other hand, if IIAs apply, a MFN clause requiring equal treatment for the investors will be applied in favour of these investors. Therefore, the increment of transparency will be limited over time.

Even though there might be commercial reasons to consider an elevated level of discretion when negotiating investment contracts, the fact is that LSLIs are public policy measures and local people must be informed. From this point of view the considerations regarding the improvement of transparency for decision-making shall play a relevant role. Our argument, which is contrary to the one made by the IMF with regard to contracts involving natural resources, is also the argument made by other IOs. Furthermore, it has been demonstrated that in many cases a lack of transparency worked against the investor. A study by the World Bank and UNCTAD showed that some investors were frustrated by the negative perception of the local population toward the investment.[115] This perception created a controversial atmosphere surrounding agricultural investments. In these cases the cost of contractual performance increases and thus hinders the realisation of the investment project.[116] To avoid such a situation, which affects not only the state but also the investor, an improvement of transparency in the negotiation of the contract is needed. Transparency decreases informational asymmetries between actors and makes it possible to calculate expected gains in a realistic way. It also contributes to the maximisation of productivity and to the fulfilment of contractual promises. It might also lead to a better understanding by the community of the investment process and of their rights. Governments might become more attracted to long-term and sustainable investments, and transparency might stimulate the direct communication and negotiation between investors and potentially affected people.

If investment agendas are seen as policies that are not planned in the short term, the cost generated by increasing the level of transparency can be internalised by the states. Placing the investment on a timeline, the cost generated by transparency is high when it is first implemented because the negotiation will become more

---

[114]International Monetary Fund (2007) para 11.

[115]World Bank and United Nations Conference on Trade and Development (2014), p. xiv.

[116]Ibid.

complicated. Over time, these costs will decrease because transparency requirements to closing investment contracts in a specific country will have become standardised. In addition, the costs parties have to internalise by increasing transparency are not only favourable to the host state. They are also favourable to the investor because of the positive reputational effects. Although transparency promises advantages for the contracting parties, the fact that these advantages will mostly be perceived in the long run will create some animosity.

5.3.3.10 Human Rights: Explicit Liability

Although the main argument against the implementation of new policies in the form of LSLI contracts is associated with the fulfilment of HRs obligations, we have shown that the fulfilment of these obligations is only of marginal concern to some investors. The argument can be explained in brief. If one sees contracts as coordination instruments describing the rights and duties of investors, then they might be considered a guarantor of governance. If these instruments do not contain specific regulations oriented towards protecting HRs, it is unlikely that investors will care. Even well-intentioned investors will not refrain from violating HRs if they are not incentivised to do so. In the short run, there is neither any economic nor legal reason to respect HRs if liability does not exist. In the long run, disregard for HRs may affect the investor's reputation and thus result in an increment of costs because their products must be reallocated on the global market. Since investors as well as policymakers are rational actors (albeit with different preferences), at least with regard to HRs protection, the investment contract as an instrument performing public policy shall expressly protect HRs and include enforceable sanctions in case of violation. The inclusion of concrete sanction mechanisms in LSLI contracts in cases of HRs violations would represent the ideal scenario for a state that subrogates its obligations to private actors. To counter this proposal one could argue that HRs are part of the national legislation, thus reducing the urgency to invest resources in negotiating those clauses in investor-state or state-state contracts. However, if we reconsider the arguments made in Chap. 2 of this text and consider the costs that have to be internalised to enforce HRs, and if one compares these costs to the amount that would be needed to enforce a bilateral investment contract, the conclusion would be that enforcing the investment contract is more plausible for a weak state because of the incentives that already exist from IIA protection. On the one hand states are incentivised through investment contracts to enforce HRs, while on the other hand IIAs are control mechanisms protecting the investor in case the state makes use of such mechanisms to harm investors.

The proposal to include HRs in investment contracts is not a novel issue. In practice it is almost non-existent. Although the success of this mechanism is unlikely given the institutional framework of host states, the efforts made in other places have produced some effects. For example, in the mining sector (where the inclusion of HRs in contracts has a long tradition), there is strong support from the International Bar Association to incentivise firms to undertake activities in a manner consistent with the standards established by the International Finance Corporation in which the right to property of indigenous people is protected.[117]

5.3.3.11 Exiting the Contract

Exit from and amendments to the contract are considered the eighth control mechanism. States can signal their desire to exit or renegotiate the treaties to incentivise cooperation. While in some cases of unilateral exit the protection extends to 10 years, if the contract is mutually terminated the effect is still unclear.[118] The amendment of the treaty by the parties leads to the closure of pre-existent gaps through readjustment of the treaty to current exigencies.[119]

The most severe decision that states can take is the termination of an investment contract. We will now show how under some circumstances, states could make use of such measures to perform a national HRs agenda. Unilateral terminations of contract that have led to investment disputes have frequently shown the negative consequences investors have to face when issues of corruption are at stake. Therefore, one can see that on the one hand investors could implement prophylactic mechanisms to avoid involvement in irregularities during the negotiation phase, but on the other hand states can also create incentives (by terminating investment contracts) for the investors to avoid irregularities. The reason why investors should care is because in case of a legal dispute, the tribunal itself could deny its jurisdiction if it can be proven that investors obtained benefits from the host state through corruption or violation of HRs. In other scenarios compensation could be lower or the state could unilaterally terminate the investment contract.[120] IIL jurisprudence has already dealt with these kinds of issues and these cases can be used as a reference by host states to design legal policies. Accordingly, some investment tribunals have been confronted with questions regarding malign conduct of investors.[121] This includes corruption, fraud, misrepresentation, undue influence, or abuse of power. In the next paragraphs we will go through some cases in which the aforementioned irregularities led to negative consequences for investors. We suggest that host states could make use of them in the context of LSLI.

Azinian v Mexico was a pioneer case in dealing with this question.[122] The US Company was given a concession for waste collection and disposal in a Mexican

---

[117]Cotula and Tienhaara (2013), p. 299.

[118]van Aaken (2013b).

[119]van Aaken (2014b), p. 30.

[120]For paper analysing the issue of corruption in International Investment Law see: Raeschke-Kessler and Gottwald (2008); Muchlinski (2006), pp. 527, 530.

[121]Some relevant examples are: *Fraport AG Frankfurt Airport Services Worldwide v The Republic of the Philippines* [2007] Award ARB/03/25 (ICSID) and *Metal-Tech Ltd. v Republic of Uzbekistan* [2010] Award ARB/10/03 (ICSID); *World Duty Free Co. Ltd. v Republic of Kenya* [2006] Award ARB/00/7 (ICSID).

[122]*Robert Azinian and others v Mexico* [1999] Award ARB(AF)/97/2 (ICSID) at para 13.

city. The claimants described damages resulting from the annulment by the local government. The annulment had been declared on the grounds that the concession was either void due to misrepresentation or rescindable for failure of performance. In total the government listed twenty-seven irregularities as a reason for cancelling the concession. These irregularities led local authorities to consider the behaviour of the investor unconscionable. Among others, the company's claim of having four decades of experience in the market could not be proved.[123] In addition, information about the investor that was required by the local government was not disclosed. In this case, the tribunal held that the non-disclosure of information was unconscionable and that the termination of the contract by Mexican authorities was justified.[124]

In *Genin v Estonia*[125] and *Plama Consortium Limited v Bulgaria*,[126] tribunals supported government decisions affecting investments after basing their argument on the investor's lack of transparency. In the first case the Bank of Estonia revoked the license of an American investor who had failed to disclose information regarding the parent company of which the investor was the ultimate shareholder. In the second case the Plama Consortium made a disclosure regarding limited resources after the major companies of a group (of which Plama was a part) withdrew and Plama proceeded with the investment alone. It has been stated by tribunals, for instance in *Azinian v Mexico*, that even though IIAs offer protection of investments, they cannot be considered insurance policies.[127] This relates to issues of performance and management, the quality of which was discussed in different cases in order to determine whether the losses suffered by the investor were in fact attributable to regulatory measures of the host state or to a lack of management.[128] Unilateral control mechanisms run by investors can lead to more realistic risk assessments and to an improved management of the company

Although neither the issue of transparency nor of corruption was raised in connection to HRs infringements in investment disputes, the aforementioned cases show how tribunals tend to recognise states' willingness to protect their regulatory power if either the negotiation of investment contracts or their performance was irregular.

After having mapped the control mechanisms that can be considered in investment law, we will now address some approaches to make IIAs more complete.

---

[123]Ibid.

[124]Ibid.

[125]*Genin and others v Estonia [*2001*] Award ARB/99/2 (ICSID).*

[126]*Plama Consortium Limited v Republic of Bulgaria* [2003] ARB/03/24 (ICSID).

[127]*Robert Azinian and others v Mexico [*1999*] Award ARB(AF)/97/2 (ICSID) para 114.*

[128]This has been stated in some cases by tribunals. Some examples: *Noble Ventures Incorporated v Romania [*2005*] Award ARB/01/11 (ICSID)*; *Biwater Gauff (Tanzania) Ltd v Tanzania [*2008*] Award and Concurring and Dissenting Opinion ARB/05/22 (ICSID) para 486*; *Methanex Corporation v United States [*2005*] Final Award (Ad hoc UNICTRAL) para 9.*

5.4 Arbitrators as Control Mechanisms

5.4.1 Introduction

Arbitrators can allocate incentives so that contractual parties do not behave opportunistically, meaning that they function as control mechanisms. In this section we will consider how arbitrators can contribute and to what extent they are incentivised to do so. It is also relevant for us to consider the role of the parties in drafting contracts in a way that will reduce their uncertainty about the outcomes of the arbitration process. We will also consider how this would promote the defragmentation of IL. The specialised literature has focussed more on the role of arbitrators when drafting contracts than on the role of contractual parties. Considering that there are no binding rules for the adjudicator to produce a defragmented ruling, we will evaluate how parties can play a decisive role by creating incentives through contract design to systematically integrate different IL regimes and oblige the arbitrators to take a more balanced approach in decision-making processes.

During the contractual negotiation, parties delegate to arbitrators the power to decide whether an event is considered a contractual breach and whether the other party has to be compensated.[129] In IIL, this power is usually given to arbitrators and, as we already saw in Chap. 2, their decisions are binding and enforceable. Consequently, arbitrators can incentivise parties to behave in a manner consistent with stipulations in the treaty. Looking to the treaty as the primary source of law, arbitrators should interpret and apply it while considering the preferences of the contractual parties at the moment of signing the treaty or contract. In order to do so, arbitrators need to be informed about the preferences of the parties, and their power to apply different interpretative approaches must be reduced.

If arbitrators are considered rational, then contractual parties must design the contract in a way that incentivises arbitrators to follow the parties' preferences. One has to bear in mind that 'panels usually dispose of a large margin of discretion.'[130] Therefore, in order to allow arbitrators to fulfil the expectations of contractual parties, incentives have to be placed. If parties do not clearly express their preferences, arbitrators will apply more general rules of interpretation that open up the possibility of misinterpretation.

Therefore, our argument is that in order to appraise arbitrators as effective control mechanisms, parties have to limit the discretionary power of arbitrators by deciding which interpretation technique should be applied.[131] They have to compel arbitrators to interpret the contract according to the parties' preferences at

---

[129] On delegation in IIL see Roberts (2010), pp. 179, 187.

[130] *Wena Hotels Limited v Arab Republic of Egypt [*2002*] Decision on Annulment ARB/98/4 (ICSID) at para 96.*

[131] For a similar approach see: World Bank and United Nations Conference on Trade and Development (2014), p. 9; Posner (1993), pp. 1, 25.

the moment of the contractual negotiation. In order to do so, contractual parties have to specify the contractual details.

5.4.2 The Need to Limit Arbitrators' Discretional Power

5.4.2.1 Understanding How Arbitrators Make Decisions

In order to maximise the effectiveness of an arbitration process, meaning that arbitrators fulfil the expectations of the parties by coming to a decision, contracting parties are required to design a proper framework that clearly signals their preferences. If parties fail to do so, they have to assume the risk that arbitrators misinterpret the law and apply it incorrectly.[132] Whether arbitrators in fact apply the law as expected by the parties will depend on the capacity of the parties to express their preferences in IIAs and investment contracts. Parties have to keep in mind that arbitrators as rational actors will maximise their own utility function when making their decision. Whether parties also maximise their utility function through the arbitrators' decision is—from the arbitrators' point of view—a marginal consideration. This constitutes a scenario proposed by PAT in which contractual parties are principals and arbitrators are agents. Parties need to make sure that the agency costs remain low. This means that parties have to design the contract in a way that arbitrators are not incentivised to behave opportunistically. Parties should increase the level of specification of IIAs and investment contracts since the preferences of arbitrators will impact the arbitration process.

There is an increasing literature on the role of arbitrators in mitigating jurisdictional conflicts between IIL, HRL, and environmental law.[133] These texts mostly agree that arbitrators are obliged to apply the law in investment decisions in a way that is mindful of other legal areas and the pre-existent obligations of states. Although the literature tends to state that arbitrators should take such aspects into account in the moment of making their decision, the reasons why arbitrators should care as rational actors are still up for investigation. Of course, it is clear that when IIAs started to proliferate it was not possible to predict judicial outcomes, but nowadays, when states have already gained some experience about how arbitrators take decisions, the power of arbitrators should be limited. Although there are enough reasons to think that such an approach might be beneficial for the further evolution of public IL in the long term (production of public goods or public order reasons), arbitrators, even when obliged, are not incentivised to do so. Notwithstanding, it is desirable in the long run to maintain the unity of IL

[132]In this context wrongly does not mean that arbitrators are violating any law. It does mean that arbitrators will probably fail by applying the proper law, as it would need to be applied so that parties' preferences can be realised.

[133]As a manner of example we mention: Dolzer (2005), p. 953; Calamita (2013); Meckenstock (2010).

while in the short term, rational actors only focus on maximising their gains. This does not mean that arbitrators' decisions are incompatible with HRs protection. In fact, there might be a scenario in which arbitrators support HRs policies that affect investors. However, this is not the case because arbitrators are incentivised to promote HRs but because arbitrators maximise their own utility function. For this reason the problem for contractual parties is the legal insecurity produced by the uncertainty regarding the arbitrators' decision. The effect of this uncertainty has been discussed in the legal literature as the 'chill out' effect produced by IIAs. This effect is simply the inhibition of states to introduce new well-intentioned regulatory policies to fulfil non-investment obligations.

5.4.2.2 Justifying Parties' Measures

To understand why parties should care about the power of arbitrators to interpret a contract, we have to acknowledge Article 31(1) VCLT. This article requires that in order for the interpretation of the contract to be in good faith, the interpretation must be in accordance with the ordinary meaning that was given to the contract, to the terms of the treaty in their context, and with its objects and purposes. The rules of interpretation in Article 31(1) do not seem to be hierarchical. This means that decision makers acting in good faith can decide how to interpret the contract. This room for interpretation should be limited by the parties. Even though article 31 (1) states that arbitrators shall heed the context and purpose of the contract, it also leaves open additional possibilities for arbitrators. Ergo, parties can decrease uncertainty by compelling arbitrators to consider specific instruments and techniques to interpret the law. In addition to that, parties contribute to the defragmentation of IL by narrowing the discretional power of arbitrators.

The law governing the interpretative techniques is broad and its application can be easily influenced by the subjective considerations of arbitrators. If arbitrators' preferences are the protection of HRs, then the interpretation mechanisms to elaborate these kinds of arguments are certainly available.[134] However, there are other methods—as has been demonstrated in the case law—that can be applied by arbitrators if their preferences are not HRs protection. Accordingly, one has to differentiate between the obligations of arbitrators and their discretional power. If parties do not clearly express their preferences regarding the protection of HRs, arbitrators could make legitimate use of their discretional power to protect HRs. If parties clearly express their preferences, arbitrators are obliged to follow them. This aspect will have different implications for the decision and its further effects. In the first case, arbitrators are authorised to protect HRs but are not obliged to do so. In this case arbitrators will care only if the protection of HRs leads to the maximisation of their own utility function. In the second case, if arbitrators ignore the preferences of the contractual parties, a further limitation of power of the tribunal takes place

[134] See i.e. the following approaches: Roberts (2013), p. 45; Dumberry and Dumas-Aubin (2013).

which leads to the nullity of the decision, as stated in Article 52.b ICSID Convention.[135] By achieving a level of contractual specification, parties create incentives for arbitrators to follow their preferences. As stated in Article 42.1 ICSID Convention, arbitrators shall primarily come to a decision by applying the law as agreed by the parties. If the parties have omitted or insufficiently specified how the law is to be applied, arbitrators may follow more general rules applicable in IIL (Article 42.2 ICSID Convention). These rules do not necessarily guarantee that the arbitrators' application of the law is aligned with the preferences of the parties when drafting the contract. The Convention establishes that if such an agreement is lacking, arbitrators shall apply the law of the contracting state party. However, there is no legal guarantee that the specific legal provision applied by the arbitrators is in accordance with the specific preferences of the parties. Roberts elaborates on this subject:

> By increasing the specificity of their treaty commitments *ex ante* and providing interpretations or mechanisms for the interpretation of their treaty commitments *ex post*, treaty parties can enlarge their own interpretative role and thereby reduce the breadth of interpretative authority delegated to arbitral tribunals. In doing so, they will diminish opportunities for tribunals to draw on analogies with which they are familiar. They will also increase the prospects for their own lawyers to draw on analogies which are familiar to them or favourable to states.[136]

As a result, parties should care because if they *ex ante* inform the arbitrators about their preferences (i.e. protecting HRs, environmental law, and sustainable development), the uncertainty over whether they can achieve a desirable outcome from a decision will decrease. In the opposite case arbitrators can discretionally apply the law they consider most convenient. Parties will perceive the gains of such decisions only marginally.

5.4.3 Limiting Arbitrators' Power

As our approach suggests, in order for arbitrators to function as an effective control mechanism, a specific level of contractual precision is required. We shall consider certain legal mechanisms that can ensure that arbitrators behave as expected by contracting parties. In order to do so, the autonomy of contractual parties is needed. We already know that the interpretative requirements established in the ICSID Convention are insufficient to incentivise arbitrators to follow the preferences of contracting parties. Further, we need to make use of the power of parties during the negotiation phase to include specific clauses able to incentivise the arbitrators to behave as expected by the parties in the contract. In other words, parties need to retain their regulatory power.

[135] Simma (2011), p. 573.

[136] Roberts (2013), pp. 45, 80.

The literature has used a different starting point than ours to compel arbitrators to apply the law in a defragmented way. Commentators usually chose a starting point that is *ex post* to the signature of the contract, while in our case we are starting during the negotiation phase.[137] These approaches provide a subsidiary way to solving potential conflicts arising in already-signed contracts that can be broadly interpreted. Due to the fact that the time when parties can create incentives is during the negotiation phase, we consider this moment appropriate for the parties to delimit the discretional power of arbitrators.

In order to guarantee that investment tribunals take HRs into account, contractual parties shall go further than considering the primacy of *jus cogens* norms. Parties need to acknowledge the inconsistencies that might arise in concrete cases and specify the relationship between investors' rights and other states' obligations. Although this approach has been followed in diverse areas, there are still no contracts for topics concerning HRs that would be impacted by the introduction of LSLIs. At the regional level NAFTA Article 103 explicitly limits the power of the tribunal by stating that the parties express their intentions to interpret the treaty in a manner harmonious with GATT and other agreements.[138] These kinds of clauses are also included in the Energy Charter and some BITs.[139]

Following our approach, the uncertainty of parties with regard to the potential outcomes of the arbitration process is mitigated by Article 42 ICSID, whose infringement can be used to demand the annulment of a decision. In the next section we will specify relevant aspects that parties should consider to decrease risks concerning the outcomes of arbitration procedures.

5.4.3.1 Specifying the Method of Interpretation

In order to effectively use arbitrators as control mechanisms and to decrease uncertainty about the outcomes of the process, parties can oblige arbitrators to apply specific interpretation techniques. If parties prefer arbitrators to follow the ordinary meaning, then they can clarify contractual concepts by making use of rules.[140] Parties can also link the treaty or investment contracts by referring to treaties in which such specifications have previously been made.

---

[137] See for example the approaches made by: ibid; Hirsch (2006), p. 97.

[138] Article 103 NAFTA states: Relation to Other Agreements 1. The Parties affirm their existing rights and obligations with respect to each other under the General Agreement on Tariffs and Trade and other agreements to which such Parties are party. 2. In the event of any inconsistency between this Agreement and such other agreements, this Agreement shall prevail to the extent of the inconsistency, except as otherwise provided in this Agreement.

[139] Annexes III Canadian BIT Model, Art 13 and 16 US BIT Model.

[140] On the meaning and function of rules see Sect. 4.5 of this paper.

5.4.3.2 Drafting More Specific Preambles

The preamble defines, in general terms, the purposes and considerations that led the parties to conclude the treaty or the contract.[141] It is a kind of source of information, which could be seen as *indicia*, about the incentives of the parties to sign the treaty or the contract, and they are helpful for the interpretation of any ambiguities. Parties can provide the arbitrators with specific pieces of information in the form of principles or definitions about how to interpret the contract, their intentions in signing the contract, and extra-contractual obligations that should be observed when interpreting the contract.[142] While the preamble is the part of the contract in which parties can include more abstract terms expressing their intentions, it does not preclude the possibility of using the preamble to elaborate a teleological interpretation.[143] At the same time, the abstract nature of the preamble does not offer any legal guarantee that in a specific case of HRs violation, or at least in case of contractual breaches, the appropriate interpretation will be followed.[144] A narrower approach could be undertaken by listing specific goals in a separate clause.[145] Some models of IIAs have included words signalling the willingness of the parties to collaborate on non-investment areas. One of the most prominent examples in IIL is the preamble of the 2012 USA Model BIT in which the parties are 'desiring to achieve [...] the protection of health, safety, and the environment, and the promotion of internationally recognised labour rights.'[146] The new Indian Model BIT signals a clear intention to promote development and to hold investors accountable.[147]

The aforementioned examples show that negotiators are considering more specific preambles to some extent. It appears to be their intention to avoid achieving investment goals at the expense of health, the environment, labour standards, or civil rights. Today preambles are more concrete than they were in the past. In LSLI

[141]Mbengue, 'Preamble' Max Planck Encyclopedia of Public International Law, para 1, http://opil.ouplaw.com/view/10.1093/law:epil/9780199231690/law-9780199231690-e1456?prd=EPIL. Accessed 18 August 2015.

[142]Salacuse considers that a carefully reading of the preamble provides information on long-term contractual objectives. See: Salacuse (2010), p. 114.

[143]Black et al. (2006), p. 1175. One example in the jurisprudence making use of the preamble is the following case: *United States – Import Prohibition of Certain Shrimp and Shrimp Products* [1998] WT/DS58/AB/R (WTO Appellate Body) at § 12.

[144]As a manner or example In the case *SGS Société Générale de Surveillance SA v Philippines [2004] Decision on Objections to Jurisdiction and Separate Declaration ARB/02/6 (ICSID)* the tribunal used the wording of the preamble to decide in favour of the investment because the BIT was intended to 'maintain favourable conditions for investments.' For critics on this decision see: Waibel (2011).

[145]van Aaken (2014b), p. 17.

[146]Salacuse (2010), p. 227 ff.

[147]Model Text of the Indian Bilateral Investment Treaty, available at: https://mygov.in/sites/default/files/master_image/Model%20Text%20for%20the%20Indian%20Bilateral%20Investment%20Treaty.pdf. Accessed 17 August 2015.

contracts, as previously shown, the preambles include some aspects related to development but not directly related to pre-existent HRs obligations. It is unlikely that simply the inclusion of HRs language in the preamble of contracts would lead tribunals to decide in such terms, at least if only the term 'human rights' is included without further specification. Therefore, it is not our intention to recommend the inclusion of HRs clauses in the preambles, which would be limited to an abstract form in any case. This would leave some room for uncertainties which would increase the cost of contractual performance. In order to include HRs in IIAs or investment contracts, parties are required to define the rights they want to include or link to the HRs treaty or treaties they aim to consider. In this regard parties must include HRs treaties in IIAs of which both states are signatories. Moreover, in order to make HRs clauses more efficient parties should expressly recognise the interpretation and comments made by special rapporteurs and HRs committees. Through such an inclusion parties provide concrete information to the tribunal about their particular preferences.

5.4.3.3 Inducing Systemic Integration

In addition to the specifications made in the preamble, parties can formulate clauses in which they list the objectives of contracting. By specifying contractual objectives for the short and long term, parties can on the one hand balance the protection offered to investors, and on the other hand systematically integrate diverse IL areas.

Article 31(3)(c) VCLT requires the consideration of 'any relevant rules of international law applicable in the relations between the parties.' As interpreted by the ILC, Article 31(3)(C) refers to 'rules of international law', thus emphasising that the reference for interpretation must be rules of law, and not broader principles or considerations which may not be firmly established as rules. This article refers to rules of IL in general, including the source of the law, customs, general principles, and, where applicable, other treaties.[148] The ILC also deems the article to refer to applicable law in the relation between the parties.[149] The article might be seen as a baseline allowing arbitrators to integrate other instruments of IL in their decision-making process. Parties can, however, by increasing the level of contractual specificity, create more precise incentives for arbitrators to consider other IL instruments. Contractual parties can also demand a narrower integration of systems to achieve proposed goals, not only by requiring the observance of hard law but also by requiring of arbitrators to consider soft law instruments. Interdisciplinary analogies are not forbidden in IIL. As we have seen in previous chapters, a cross-fertilisation can be found between HRL and IIL. The literature has, however,

[148]North American Free Trade Agreement [1993] 32 I.L.M. 289 and 605 art. 102.2.

[149]United Nations, Vienna Convention on the Law of Treaties [1969] United Nations, Treaty Series, vol. 1155, p. 331 at art. 426.

highlighted that in some cases it is questionable whether the analogies applied by the tribunals are the proper answer to claims of contracting parties.[150]

One example of such a measure is Article 102 NAFTA in which parties agree on the promotion of fair competition. In the territories of the parties, this measure provides adequate and effective protection and enforcement of intellectual property rights, creates effective procedures for the implementation and application of the agreement, and establishes a framework for further trilateral, regional, and multilateral cooperation to expand and enhance the benefits of the Agreement.[151] In addition to the specification of objectives, Article 102 specifically requires that parties interpret and apply the provisions in light of its objectives and in accordance with applicable rules of IL.[152] To promote systemic integration in the framework of LSLIs, soft law instruments can also be employed. These instruments can be referred to as relevant rules helping to achieve LSLI-oriented goals. We wish to highlight the relevance of the Voluntary Guidelines on the Responsible Governance of Tenure of Land, Fisheries and Forests in the Context of National Food Security.[153] The Guidelines constitute a comprehensive approach that covers all the areas that should be considered in LSLI negotiations. Highly relevant are the aspects regarding the standards of governance and management of natural resources in different systems and national contexts.

5.4.3.4 Making Use of the Proportionality Principle

Proportionality is used as a balancing method in constitutional law. It originated in German law, proliferated in Europe, and today is included in almost all constitutional systems around the world. It is deeply accepted in IL.[154] It can be viewed as a meta-principle in public international law.[155] Alexy (2003) developed the principle of proportionality. His work has been catalogued as highly influential as well as the most important contribution to constitutional theory in the past decades.[156] The proportionality principle presupposes a decision-making procedure employed by judges to resolve tensions between constitutional 'values' and 'interests.'[157] As described by Sweet and Mathews (2008), the analysis of proportionality involves

[150]Roberts (2013), pp. 45, 52.

[151]North American Free Trade Agreement [1993] 32 I.L.M. 289 and 605 art 102.a-f.

[152]Roberts (2013), pp. 45, 80.

[153]Voluntary Guidelines on the Responsible Governance of Tenure of Land, Fisheries and Forests in the Context of National Food Security [2013] CL 144/9 C 2013/20.

[154]For different approaches seeking at balance the rights of states and investors see Cordero (2008); Hirsch (2009); Foster (2009), Kriebaum (2006), see also, however in German: Simma (2011), p. 573.

[155]Sweet and Mathews (2008), pp. 68, 77.

[156]Alexy (2003).

[157]van Aaken (2009a), pp. 483, 502.

four steps. The first step is to test the legitimacy of the government by taking a specific measure. The second analytical step refers to suitability. Suitability has to do with the rationale of states' policy. The third step analyses the necessity of the measure taken by the government. The fourth step examines 'balancing in the strict sense'; it applies if the other three criteria have been met. At this stage the judge applies a narrow approach to weigh the benefits of the act.[158] van Aaken (2009b) describes the approach developed by Alexy as a rational procedure in its main part and very close to the reasoning of optimisation (or cost-benefit analysis, Pareto optimality).[159] The approach developed by Alexy applies a methodology that judges can use at the moment of the decision in a procedure in which tensions between two or more rights exist.

Proportionality plays a central role in the discussion on defragmentation of IL because it supposes a balance between contractually protected rights and extra-contractual rights. It helps to harmonise norms, creates compatibility, and rather than testing the validity of the norm, the judges need to test the priority to be given to a specific norm.

In IIL the notion of proportionality has been used in *Tecmed v Mexico*. Here the tribunal stated that it shall consider whether in addition to the financial impact of the regulatory measure undertaken by the state, the measure was proportional to the public interest.[160] In a further decision in *LG&E v Argentina*, the tribunal also applied the proportionality test.[161] In this case it weighed the right of the state to adopt measures with a social or general welfare purpose. The tribunal decided that the measure must be accepted without any imposition of liability, except if the state's action is obviously disproportionate to the needs being addressed.[162] The tribunal explicitly applied the principle of proportionality to determine the legitimacy of the regulatory policy introduced by the Argentine government. Furthermore, the tribunal presumed that the impact of a regulatory measure on foreign investments should be taken into account as well. Contrary to *Tecmed*, the tribunal in the *LG&E* case ruled in favour of the investor.[163]

The problem we are dealing with at this stage is that, again, parties face uncertainty *ex ante* over whether arbitrators will apply the principle of proportionality to evaluate the measure taken by the state in favour of extra-contractual obligations. Neither the ICSID Convention nor the VCLT prescribe any obligations for judges to follow such an approach. Furthermore, the ILC study on the fragmentation of IL is not a binding document. Even if the tribunal had authority in the interpretation of contracts, its application would depend on the consent of the

---

158 Sweet and Mathews (2008), pp. 68, 76.

159 Ibid.

160 van Aaken (2009a), pp. 483, 504.

161 ILC (2006) at para 411.

162 *Técnicas Medioambientales Tecmed SA v Mexico [2003] Award ARB(AF)/00/2 (ICSID) at para 122.*

163 We refer to: *LG&E Energy Corporation and others v Argentina [2006a] Decision on Liability ARB/02/1 (ICSID) at para 195.*

arbitrators. In this sense, even in cases where arbitrators have tried to balance the rights of investors vis-à-vis states, arbitrators have not gone too far in their efforts to focus their decisions on particular HRs claims alleged by the parties during the process. As we have shown through this investigation, arbitrators have differed in their approaches to solve conflicts in a number of cases, as demonstrated in *Aguas del Tunari v Bolivia,*[164] *CMS v Argentina,*[165] and *Glamis Gold v United States.*[166] It has to be highlighted that contracting parties in IIAs may wish to fulfil their HRs obligations despite the fact that they do not expressly demonstrate these intentions in IIAs, which allows the tribunal to broadly interpret the treaty. Therefore, parties can incorporate a requirement for the tribunal to apply the principle of proportionality in the contract. It would allow the parties to evaluate state's measures and guard the sovereignty of states.[167]

5.5 External International Actors as Control Mechanisms

In this section we will turn to analysing control mechanisms that can be performed by external actors, e.g. IOs and NGOs, and evaluate whether these control mechanisms play a relevant role and are able to mitigate opportunistic behaviour in LSLIs. The aforementioned external actors can play a relevant role in achieving social justice in two different ways: judicially and extra-judicially.[168] In previous sections we analysed the opportunities for external actors to intervene as *amici curiae* in an investment process. In these cases the judicial intervention was limited by the legal capacity of the special law governing the investment activity (ICSID Convention). Now we will assess mechanisms available to these actors which can contribute to increased governance and the economic maximisation of the project. Additionally, we will analyse the mechanisms—namely commercial activity—that external international actors can apply to create incentives. Our approach will focus

[164]In this case the tribunal made an approach that has been catalogued as 'undesirable'. In order to interpret the treaty the tribunal applied a 'standard-desk-dictionary-approach'. The approach made by the tribunal can be found at: *Aguas del Tunari v Bolivia [2005] Decision on Respondent's Objections to Jurisdiction ARB/02/3 (ICSID) at para 227 ff.* For an analysis of the case see: Kurtz (2007).

[165]*LG&E Energy Corporation and others v Argentina [*2006a*] Decision on Liability ARB/02/1 (ICSID) at para 195.*

[166]*Glamis Gold Ltd v United States* [2009] Award IIC 380 (Ad Hoc Tribunal UNCITRAL).

[167]One example is the Indian BIT Model 2015 in which new measures are included in order to make interpret the law so that investor can also be accountable for wrongful acts. Such measures were almost inexistent in older BITs. See: Model Text of the Indian Bilateral Investment Treaty, available at: https://mygov.in/sites/default/files/master_image/Model%20Text%20for%20the%20Indian%20Bilateral%20Investment%20Treaty.pdf. Accessed 17 August 2015.

[168]On the role of NGOs in international law see: Cotula, 'Regulatory Takings, Stabilization Clauses and Sustainable Development' (The Policy Framework for Investment: The Social and Environmental Dimensions), p. 18.

on those instruments that can produce immediate effects on populations. We do recognise that other mechanisms exist, albeit more indirect ones. These indirect mechanisms can also be used as mechanisms to tackle opportunistic behaviour. Some of these are instruments developed by financial institutions that require the investors' and also the states' compliance, as well as the fulfilment of international standards protecting sensitive issues such as the environment, health, and HRs.

IOs and NGOs can be relevant control mechanisms because they can produce law and because they can create and allocate incentives to economic actors through their actions.[169] IOs and NGOs can also decrease the costs of balancing asymmetric information between contractual parties, increase institutional capacity, and develop infrastructure at the state level. They can create incentives for stakeholders by producing and disclosing information, and through their specialised knowledge and technical expertise. In addition, the power exercised by IOs and NGOs helps stakeholders to consider the inclusion of minimum standards and to follow guidelines and principles in the implementation of the investment project. They can also contribute by providing reliable data from their own empirical research. Studies have demonstrated the impact of evidence-based research on the design and social cost of policies.[170] At the global level it helps to identify proper policies for specific economic areas. Moreover, this information can be used to draw implications for investment policies, to predict effects on other economic sectors, and to provide expertise for other states to increase their productive performance.[171] From the host state perspective, the work contributed by external actors represents a means to balance the institutional weakness in these countries. It might be seen as an opportunity to start considering relevant stakeholders in investment projects and to properly design policies that build the necessary capacity to perform the investment activity and, furthermore, to achieve the expected level of development.

We have selected the most relevant instruments for the following section by parsing principle guidelines that were drafted by IOs in cooperation with regional organisations and NGOs in order to establish baselines to improve the effects of LSLIs. In all of these instruments, the need to improve transparency in order to achieve higher levels of contractual governance and consequentially achieve pre-established development goals is omnipresent.[172] Considering transparency an essential element to achieving the goals proposed by legal policies in LSLI projects, we aim to explore what mechanisms the different instruments developed by IOs have at their disposal to achieve the expected level of transparency. Additionally, we will consider elements that enable us to elucidate the effects

---

[169]For some contributions following this approach see: Boyle and Chinkin (2007); Cafaggi (2011), p. 20.

[170]Franck (2005), pp. 1521, 1586.

[171]Simmons (2009) in page 79 approaches the success of NGOs and IO based on the support such organisations get from powerful countries that at the same time can influence though coercion.

[172]On the correlation between transparency and governance see: Shepard and Anuradha (2011).

that such instruments could have on the economic actors involved. These aspects include:

1) the requirement of legality that encompasses the regulatory requirements considered by the guidelines,
2) the level of specification regarding their application,
3) the specific issues that are addressed,
4) the period of time considered for the implementation,
5) the scope,
6) and the role and involvement of stakeholders.

The role and involvement of stakeholders are considered by looking at the participation mechanisms in the guidelines. We will also briefly look at the monitoring mechanisms proposed by each of the instruments and the sanctions that are imposed on stakeholders if they fail to fulfil obligations pre-established either by the guidelines or by regional or international applicable treaties. Our main goal is to offer alternatives to policy makers that might contribute to achieving LSLI goals.

5.5.1 *Judicial Mechanisms*

Judicial mechanisms are those instruments that external actors can develop to promote compliance. These instruments are soft law and usually include a body of rules, practices, and processes. As we have seen in Chap. 3 of this book, the proliferation of these instruments in LSLIs has not been an exception. Indeed, many actors have drafted diverse regulatory instruments to achieve discipline in LSLIs. Although a wave of new investments was reported from 2008 onwards, the proliferation of soft law instruments began earlier. In 2003 the World Bank, as part of a policy aiming to stimulate investments in LDCs, drafted the Land Policy Framework for Growth and Poverty Reduction. In this instrument the main focus was the stimulation of land markets as a mechanism to reduce poverty and promote development in LDCs. This study approaches the most sensitive issues in land policy, including the relevance of the definition of property rights and the conduct of transactions to achieve socially desirable land use.[173] This policy measure focuses on the proposal of land reforms in those countries where domestic policies were introduced in a discriminatory way and manipulated market rules. The proposed reforms include ways to avoid land conflicts, create a system of land taxation, delimit the land owned by the state as well as the power of the state to coercively acquire land, and introduce effective regulation for the use of land. One of the most emphasised issues is the transferability of land through the high incidence of rental markets and the role of these markets in the development of

[173]Shepard and Anuradha (2011).

an off-farm sector.[174] The report by the World Bank did not establish a regulatory framework but seems to have inspired other IOs to further develop instruments regulating land policies. Some examples include the 2004 European Union Guidelines, the subsequently developed Principles for Responsible Investment drafted by the World Bank, the ICARRD Principles, the FAO's Voluntary Guidelines, the African Land Policy, the Guidelines and Principles drafted by the International Land Coalition, the Nairobi Action Plan on LSLIs, the Dakar Appeal against land grabs, the Declarations on Food Sovereignty, the Voluntary Guidelines of the FAO-CFS, and the practice of responsible investment principles in larger-scale agricultural investments.

The above-mentioned instruments are only some examples showing the broad development of soft law instruments that were produced in order to ameliorate opportunistic behaviour in LSLI contracts. We argue that their consideration at the moment of entering into contractual relationships would contribute to increased governance. Assuming that external actors are relevant actors during the negotiation process, one could expect that bargaining groups would promote the introduction of soft law instruments in LSLIs. By doing so, soft law would be transformed into binding law between the parties and its inobservance would be sanctioned.

The European Union Land Policy Guidelines, the World Bank Group Principles for Responsible Agricultural Investments, and the Voluntary Guidelines of the FAO-CFS are those soft law instruments that have been strongly promoted with the expectation of creating discipline in LSLIs.[175] The most promoted and criticised of these three is the Policy Guidelines developed by the European Union. The main criticism is their lack of consideration of HRs.[176] Despite of that, the instrument includes a broad spectrum of stakeholders and requires their involvement. The consideration of civil society is a pre-condition to the performance of the guidelines. The guidelines proposed by the World Bank Groups offer a more HRs-friendly approach but are overshadowed by the conflict of interest between diverse stakeholders which can arise because stakeholders are not assigned specific roles. Even though the guidelines include HRs-aspects, they fail to ensure higher levels of transparency and participation of stakeholders. These guidelines propagate a normative approach but fail to develop the legal policies to achieve their goals. The African Union guidelines are the most complete instrument, combining comprehensive policies with procedural descriptions based on previous historical and empirical studies. The FAO Voluntary Guidelines also present comprehensive mechanisms to effectively regulate agricultural FDI.

The main problem faced by all the instruments analysed above is their high enforcement cost, making it hard to consider their effects on policy implementation. Although they include some control and monitoring mechanisms that would help to improve compliance, these duties could remain unfulfilled if there are no additional

[174]Deininger and World Bank (2003).

[175]See Sect. 3.4.2 of this study.

[176]Shepard and Anuradha (2011).

components creating incentives for the involved parties to fulfil them. As we mentioned previously, the inclusion of such instruments in LSLIs would be a step towards achieving compliance goals. The reason for this is as follows: if we consider actors to be rational with presumably heterogenic preferences, the fact that soft law instruments do not create incentives to fulfil their requirements will limit their effectiveness. As reported by the UNCTAD and World Bank, some of the policies that have been implemented by states combine different aspects of the guidelines. However, in some cases countries are introducing land ceilings to limit the amount of land foreign investors can acquire.

5.5.2 Extra-Judicial Mechanisms

The role that non-state actors can play in ameliorating opportunistic behaviour and improving governance in LSLI contracts is not limited to judicial mechanisms. Apart from national and international litigation, there are other ways for private actors and entities to enforce HRs without requiring enforcement mechanisms provided by national or IL.[177] Market mechanisms can be designed to create and also properly allocate incentives to economic actors so that IL can be realised more effectively. We suggest that market mechanisms can be used to promote compliance in the presence of LSLIs. Some L&E studies have already suggested the use of market mechanisms to effectuate public IL.[178] We will discuss whether market mechanisms could contribute to tackling opportunism in LSLI contracts.

5.5.2.1 Recent Developments

Over the last decades, non-state actors have developed market-based mechanisms to promote compliance in different legal areas. The effects of market mechanisms have led to an increased interest in the investigation of the potential governance benefits they offer.[179] Market mechanisms have been approached from different angles. The most developed mechanism has been used to address issues including environmental standards.[180] Market mechanisms have also contributed to increased scrutiny from transnational actors and IL.[181]

The initiatives implemented through market mechanisms have also increased in response to augmented interest from the international community in social and environmental issues. Interest groups continuously disclose information about

[177] On the increase of non-state actors promoting governance see: Deininger et al. (2011), p. 140.

[178] Keck and Sikkink (1999), p. 89; van Aaken (2009b), p. 33; van Aaken (2010).

[179] van Aaken (2013a), p. 227; Cashore et al. (2004).

[180] Tladi (2007); Berger 1996.

[181] Cashore et al. (2004), p. 10.

deforestation in sensitive parts of the world, contamination of water, the violation of HRs, or irregular acquisitions of land.[182] This information can be easily accessed by consumers and can rapidly produce reactions that are detrimental to the reputation of investors. Well-functioning market mechanisms can thus contribute to fulfilling regulatory gaps that hard law instruments cannot achieve.

5.5.2.2 Market Mechanisms

5.5.2.2.1 General Aspects

Market mechanisms can be seen as regulatory strategies that are designed for those areas where international adjudicatory mechanisms are absent and the ultimate addressees of the law are private actors. They have been catalogued as the most important means for corporations and other economic actors to engage in preferred activities, by creating links between groups, nations, and regions.[183] These strategies are underused, but new movements have developed modern mechanisms that supplement or alternate with traditional approaches. They were promoted more heavily in developed countries than in developing countries in an attempt to avoid increasingly ambitious regulatory goals. Market mechanisms are expected to create incentives for the investors to comply with the law. These mechanisms are able to alter the market structure, shift the preferences of consumers, and oblige producers to adapt their products to the preferences of consumers. From the legal point of view, market mechanisms are informal because they lack the law-making process required in IL. They are neither negotiated nor ratified by IL subjects and their enforcement does not require adjudicators.[184]

Market mechanisms create and allocate incentives for economic actors to adapt their economic activity to external requirements—created by private economic actors—that enable the further performance of the contract and the maximisation of their gains. They can help in scenarios where the institutional environment is precarious because market mechanisms can verify information at a low cost They may entail lower enforcement costs because information comes from market transactions, punishment arises from participants, and non-compliance leads to exclusion. Since an event—i.e. non-compliance with specific standards—must not be verified to produce consequences in the market, parties can make promises observable and unverifiable.[185] Market mechanisms must not proceed through a formal process of ratification, but they can affect the reputation of producers and their

[182]One example in the are of LSLIs is the contribution of the Land Matrix: Keck and Sikkink (1999), p. 89.

[183]Seminal for our approach: International Land Coalition (2011); van Aaken (2014b).

[184]For the discussion on formal and in informal enforcement mechanisms see: Kohli et al. (2003), p. 13.

[185]van Aaken (2013a), p. 227.

inobservance can lead to prohibitive costs for producers.[186] These mechanisms are market oriented, meaning that they have the power to influence consumers so that producers are incentivised to care about external exigencies.

5.5.2.2.2 The Role of States

Although states are sometimes part of market mechanisms, they do not participate as a Westphalian sovereign authority, meaning that they do not develop rules to which societies adhere. This fact does not decrease the relevance of governments but puts them in a different position. Governments can be influential if they take part as interest groups and influence the design of a market-driven policy. They can also influence initiatives by introducing procurement policies and other economic actions that may impact market-driven dynamics. Governments also play an important role by creating new policies that affect property rights by providing expertise and resources.[187] The effect produced by well-functioning market mechanisms is that producers compete for legitimacy. In this case legitimacy means that producers fulfil the requirement for pre-established standards which at the same time represent the preferences of consumers.[188]

For the state this opens a way to solving an efficiency problem. The state allows private actors to effectuate obligations that were originally conceived for states. This makes market mechanisms even more attractive to those jurisdictions where institutional capacity is limited.[189]

Although these mechanisms tend to be not as efficient as formal IL mechanisms,[190] they bear fruit in diverse sectors including the environment, money laundering, corruption, and production of some raw materials. One of the most advantageous aspects of these mechanisms is that they can work independently of states and IOs as a parallel system of soft law in which a non-state-actor authority is created to effectuate hard law. Market mechanisms are an alternative to sovereign authority.[191] In the case of forests, it has been found that a 'certification process is a unique and innovative governance system that is composed of an array of evolving procedures and policies designed to address and encourage sustainable forestry management globally.'[192]

---

[186] Scott and Stephan (2006), p. 28.

[187] On the role of governments on market-driven policies see: van Aaken (2009b), pp. 33, 4.

[188] Scott and Stephan (2006), p. 98.

[189] On compliance involving private actors see Sect. 3.5 of this study and also ibid.

[190] Chayes and Chayes (1993), p. 175.

[191] Abbott and Snidal (2003), pp. 421, 423.

[192] Cashore et al. (2004), p. 20 ff.

5.5.2.2.3 Market Mechanisms Influence Consumer Preferences

The specialised literature describes market mechanisms as those mechanisms that are oriented towards influencing consumer preferences.

Market mechanisms can be used to generate and disclose specific information to consumers in order to enable them to better decide whether to buy a product or not. These mechanisms are helpful in domestic jurisdictions where IL is hard to enforce due to weak institutions.[193] They can also apply in private relationships, i.e. supply chain and environmental standards. These kinds of mechanisms work through the certification and standardisation of industrial processes that inform the consumer about specificities regarding the fabrication of the product. Certifications can inform about the kinds of raw materials used, the fulfilment of HRs obligations, or about environmental standards. This mechanism will produce positive effects if (1) they represent the preferences of the consumers, (2) if consumers have the power to influence the market, and (3) if the standards or certification processes are credible.[194] These conditions are even more relevant if the production is run in poor institutional environments.[195] Over the last decades, these kinds of market mechanisms have become more relevant in the form of labelling standards and certification. Some examples include standards guaranteeing food quality, environmental standards, and working conditions.

Probably the most successful initiative in this regard has been the Kimberley Process. This is a standardisation process that discloses information about the origin and production of diamonds from conflict regions. Even though the effectiveness of this process has been criticised, its contribution to curbing the trade of conflict diamonds has also been recognised.[196] This process was initiated by states, industry, and NGOs and consists of a set of rules and monitoring mechanisms to extract and commercialise diamonds. The Kimberley Process was initiated as a response to the HRs violations suffered by Africans in regions where diamonds are produced. This process positively contributes to solving a problem in which neither domestic governments nor the recommendations given by the UN had been able to tackle the negative effects of diamond extraction for years.[197] The process discloses information about the origin of the diamonds, the conditions of production, and trade.[198] By fulfilling

---

[193]Ibid.

[194]Cafaggi (2012), p. 1.

[195]Cashore et al. (2004), p. 219 ff.

[196]On evidence that leads to appreciate the relevance of this market mechanism is the Resolution adopted by the UN General Assembly that welcomes and support the initiative. See: ibid; see also: United Nations General Assembly Resolution 55/56 The Role of Diamonds in Fuelling Conflict: Breaking the Link Between the Illicit Transaction of Rough Diamonds and Armed Conflict as a Contribution to Prevention and Settlement of Conflicts [2001] A/RES/55/56.

[197]Amnesty International (2006).

[198]United Nations General Assembly Resolution 55/56 The Role of Diamonds in Fuelling Conflict: Breaking the Link Between the Illicit Transaction of Rough Diamonds and Armed Conflict as a Contribution to Prevention and Settlement of Conflicts [2001] A/RES/55/56.

minimum standards, a certification allows consumers to be sure that diamonds were produced in compliance with pre-established standards. The certification forbids the participants to trade diamonds produced by non-participants.[199] The process also includes strong monitoring mechanisms that are carried out by representatives of involved stakeholders. Peer reviews are carried out annually. In the case of non-fulfilment states are expelled from the scheme. By infringing the norms proposed by the mechanism, the costs of a state's exclusion are higher than the gains states achieve by defecting.

5.5.2.2.4 Market Mechanisms in LSLIs

So far, there is no initiative based on market mechanisms in the area of LSLIs. A development of initiatives, which would be welcomed, represents challenges for the stakeholders involved. This especially applies to foreign investors who need to be incentivised to consider the protection of a public good (HRs protection) to be in their own interest. In order to make it possible for rational investors to consider such an option, additional external incentives need to be allocated. Here, financial institutions, NGOs, and civil organisations could play a relevant role by requiring the fulfilment of specific standards or certifications from investors to make investment profitable. The main challenge for market mechanisms is to create discipline in land transactions. It arises because they only occur infrequently, although land transactions are in fact repeated games. Due to the singularities of land transactions it cannot be expected that sanctions would lead investors to consider high costs if standards are infringed, nor that they would not be able to internalise reputational costs since their reputation would be recovered after 99 years, the general maturity of lease contracts. These models could work with products that are transmitted through the market more quickly, i.e. cocoa, flower, or coffee.

Focussing on the application of market mechanisms, goods produced on land that has been acquired under dubious conditions are less valued in the market. Therefore, a dense network is needed to make such mechanisms effective since the required level of informational flow is high. It means that pleasing consumers with similar preferences who are willing only to buy products that were produced respecting HRs could be a difficult goal to achieve. The reason for this is a coordination problem. Some states might be able to influence the market and sell their products even when minimum standards have not been fulfilled. We face the problem of collective decision-making in which the high number of economic actors leads to the growth of coordination costs.

---

[199] Kimberly Process (2013).

5.6 Intermediate Result: Market Mechanisms as a Potential Starting Point

In the previous section we presented a set of control mechanisms that can be used either by negotiators or by external economic actors to tackle opportunistic behaviour in LSLIs. They represent diverse instruments to enforce IL. They also present an opportunity to balance the protection offered by IIL with the protection offered in HRL. Control mechanisms as they are presented in this investigation cannot offer a singular solution and none of them can be seen as a panacea. This is the reason why focusing on just one of them and proposing its implementation cannot prevent opportunistic behaviour in LSLIs. The better approach is to consider a set of options for policy-makers, negotiators, and affected locals that may have to be appraised on a case-by-case basis. These mechanisms can contribute to achieving constitutional goals at the national level and also fulfil HRs obligations.

The challenge at this stage arises from the institutional environment where LSLIs are performed. In addition, we have to remember that IIAs and LSLIs are concluded in the way they are because it is the best option for negotiators to maximise their own utility function.[200] Moreover, there are risks involved in the implementation of some mechanisms which might sometimes hinder their implementation. There are also coordination costs that stakeholders have to internalise in order to achieve desirable effects. Oftentimes the institutional weakness in LDCs, in addition to the limitations imposed through IIAs, prevent the inclusion of unilateral mechanisms by states. This happens because the willingness of states to fulfil their HRs obligations plays a relevant role.[201] Furthermore, these mechanisms could, in the presence of weak institutional environments, be seen as protectionist measures and lead to reluctance, in the short run, of investors to initiate business in a specific state.[202]

Our set of contractual-based control mechanisms covers a two-level approach which includes mechanisms in IIAs and investment contracts. These types of mechanism have been most thoroughly developed in the specialised LSLI literature. Most scholars recommend the reconfiguration of investment instruments at the state-state level and also at the state-investor level. The problem one can see at this stage is, again, that even when they are flexible (in the sense that they can be adapted on a case-by-case basis), contractual parties will only be willing to internalise such costs under specific conditions (maximisation of their own utility function). One of the most relevant aspects of discussions around IIAs is the limitation of power of arbitrators due to the legal uncertainty that has arisen over

---

[200]See Sect. 1.5 of this study.

[201]On the role of states realising human rights see Sect. 3.5.3 of this study.

[202]This is being happening not only in LDCs as for example in Zimbabwe (See: see Sect. 3.5.2 of this study) but also in industrialised countries as i.e. the case *Vattenfall v Germany*. In this case the Swedish Vattenffall that operates in Germany demanded compensation of 3.7. Billion Euros. The dispute arose after Germany decided to shut down nuclear power industries. The case is still pending.

the last years. At this level one could consider a proper definition of applicable law. States could consider some national laws in order to deal with sensible issues involved in land investments. Narrower norms defining legal interpretative techniques, the delegation of activities to experts, and explicit HRs liability are examples of control mechanisms that could also be included in IIAs. Issues that concern the investment itself could be controlled in investment contracts (LSLIs). Here, as we pointed out previously, the discussion focuses on specific conditions for the investments including their timeline, scope, forms of production, inclusion of HRs, guarantees of job creation, integration of local population, and so forth.[203] Control mechanisms would imply regular reporting from the investor to a specific national authority. These reports might contribute to economic maximisation and to gaining insights in the short run about the achievement of production goals that motivated the contract. Furthermore, an explicit obligation to include the local population and making the state-investor relationship more transparent are control mechanisms that could be considered at the LSLI contract level.

Following our methodological approach one could evaluate whether the potential set of solutions could exclude certain contractual parties in LSLIs. In the institutional environment where LSLI contracts are performed, incentives are often absent. Therefore, external economic actors might be involved to improve the *status quo*. The term 'external actors' includes economic actors not involved in LSLI negotiations, for example affected locals, final consumers, and altruistic organisations. These actors can build structures to alter the behaviour of LSLI parties. This means that they could incentivise investors to undertake individual mechanisms.[204] In this regard we have already seen the impact that non-state actors can have on the realisation of HRs. Now we will consider whether external actors can contribute to achieving social goals by also promoting private incentives. While judicial participation of external actors is limited to some special cases in IIL, their extra-judicial contribution might be substantial. They are able to influence market structures and the cost chain through the disclosure of information that in turn can increase the reputational costs of parties involved in LSLIs. Disclosing information to consumers can lead to a decline in sales of products that do not fulfil pre-established standards. Ergo, one could expect detrimental effects on prices, and producers would react. Although market mechanisms bring some coordination costs, they do not have to be internalised by affected locals because they can be enforced abroad.

External actors can incentivise LSLI actors in at least two ways: they can disclose information concerning production standards so that investors are pressured to improve compliance, and they can monitor the fulfilment of standards. The entire process can be briefly described as follows: external actors cannot only create law (soft law), they can also monitor compliance and enforce it. Although we are in an early phase of the LSLI research agenda, market mechanisms have

[203] See Sect. 2.2 of this study.

[204] See Sect. 1.5 of this study.

demonstrated high levels of success in other areas. Therefore, one could also see them as promising instruments to improve governance in LSLIs. NGOs and civil organisations have shown their influence by representing local populations on issues concerning land governance. To some extent these groups have wielded the most influence by disclosing information and promoting awareness and discussions on LSLIs. In addition, unilateral and contractual control mechanisms would help to tackle opportunistic behaviour.

We previously mentioned the case of India which published a model BIT in 2015 that is one of the most progressive so far. One important step concluded in this BIT is the inclusion of social and development goals, the possibility to hold foreign investors accountable, and the reinforcement of the state's discretion to regulate in the public interest. It also mandates more transparency in tribunal constitution, claims, proceedings, and awards. Notwithstanding this model demonstrating the states' intentions to respond to local-social claims, the results of the negotiations with the United States will show to what extent parties are willing to cooperate on atypical investment issues.

5.7 Important Case: State Emergency Under the Presence of LSLIs

5.7.1 Overview

Although food crises have not yet motivated cases in IIL, throughout this investigation we have seen that the recent developments in agricultural FDI present sufficient reason to think that in the near future IIL will have to deal with cases where, as a consequence of food crises, states take regulatory measures affecting foreign investors. One cannot ignore that over fifty-five countries met the conditions of a food emergency and a state of necessity in 2013.[205] We have already seen that states continue to sign IIAs.[206] Furthermore, previous economic crises have imposed important challenges on IIL, especially in Argentina. One might expect cases to be brought when countries feel the need to create domestic mechanisms to tackle emergencies of food shortages and famines. In this sense it is relevant to analyse the outcomes of arbitration cases. In these situations states would need to decide whether they are allowed to undertake measures which would negatively impact on the performance of LSLIs and on the realisation of HRs. Such measures could include a temporary limitation or derogation of the right to property. It would materialise in the prohibition of exports of specific crops. We refer here to those cases in which the standards of protection offered under IIAs and HRL regimes would be *de facto* infringed. It is our goal at this point to briefly analyse whether states can make use of IL institutions to legitimate those actions that in regular

[205] World Food Programme (2005), p. 3. See with regard to protracted food crises *infra* at: 5.7.3.
[206] See Chap. 1 of this paper.

situations would constitute an IL infringement. From the point of view of the state, what is needed is a measure that allows the state to alleviate the emergency and to remain compliant with the investment contract, IL, and HRL. An ideal scenario would be that the measure undertaken by the state does not incentivise foreign investors or other legal subjects to make a claim. The second-best scenario would be that the state fulfils the expectations of the investment tribunal with regard to 'necessity' so that compensation is not considered (in this scenario a wrongful act would not be performed). The worst scenario for a state would be that the tribunal does not recognise the measure to be IIL compliant and compensation has to be paid. However, states have at least the following ways to legitimate domestic measures that affect LSLIs, namely CIL and in many cases a defence based on non-precluded measures (NPM) provisions that are incorporated in IIAs. Furthermore, HRL also offers a set of possibilities that leads to the limitation or derogation of HRs. Articles 2 (1) and 4 ICESCR are considered a starting point. CIL is subsidiary to provisions in IIAs and HRL.

5.7.2 *Applicable Law*

5.7.2.1 Customary International Law

CIL is arguable in cases of 'force majeure', 'distress', and 'necessity'. These are part of ARSIWA.[207] The literature accepts that these circumstances reflect CIL.[208] Due to the relevance of 'necessity' in our approach, we will focus on this circumstance.

'Necessity' refers to exceptional cases in which an essential interest of the state is threatened by grave and imminent peril.[209] As a result a breach of international obligations is justified as the only way to safeguard essential interests.[210] Again, the state of necessity is recognised as customary IL.[211] In addition to the codification provided by the ILC, international practice and case law provide considerable authority as autonomous circumstances aiming to avoid wrongfulness under general IL.

[207] ILC (2001) Arts. 24, 25 and 26 respectively.

[208] With regard to the acceptance in the literature see: Sornarajah (2010), p. 464 and see also: ILC (2001). Dolzer and Schreuer (2008) at 183 ff. The Special Rapporteur of the International Law Commission on State Responsibility stated that: the concept of state of necessity is far too deeply rooted in the consciousness of the members of the international community and of individuals within States. If driven out of the door it would return through the window, if need be in other forms Arangio-Ruiz (2009).

[209] Tanzi, 'State of Necessity' Max Planck Encyclopedia of Public International Law, para 1, http://mpepil.com/ViewPdf/epil/entries/law-9780199231690-e786.pdf?stylesheet=EPIL-display-full.xsl. Accessed 20 August 2013; ibid.

[210] Article 25 ILC (2001).

[211] See references in footnotes: 208 and 209 in this chapter.

Article 25 ARSIWA finds a declaration of the state of necessity justified if (a) it is the only way for the state to safeguard an essential interest against a grave and imminent peril and (b) the declaration does not seriously impair an essential interest of the state or states towards which the obligation exists, or of the international community as a whole.[212] The restrictive formulation of this article seeks to avoid abuses by states who would invoke necessity to bypass international obligations, which would certainly be contrary to the stability and predictability of the law. This restrictive approach has been commonly applied either in opinions or in judicial cases.[213]

Necessity applies only if the 'essential interest' of states cannot be guaranteed in any other way, and is determined on a case-by-case basis.[214] The state of necessity is not prejudiced towards the obligation of compliance once the factual circumstance is concluded and wrongfulness has ceased to exist.[215]

5.7.2.2 International Investment Law

In this section we will analyse the possibilities that IIL offers to states to derogate from enforceable law.

5.7.2.2.1 Non-precluded Measures (NPM) Provision

NPM provisions limit the applicability of investor protections under the IIA in exceptional circumstances.[216] They allow states to take measures that under normal

---

[212]For similar approach see: Tanzi, 'State of Necessity' Max Planck Encyclopedia of Public International Law, para 1, http://mpepil.com/ViewPdf/epil/entries/law-9780199231690-e786.pdf?stylesheet=EPIL-display-full.xsl. Accessed 20 August 2013.

[213]The ICJ confirmed the restrictive approach in the case *Gabcíkovo – Nagymaros* the restrictive approach in which the character of exceptionality was considered. In Isreali Wall Advisory Opinion the ICJ rejected the argument made by Israel of the need to protect the life of its citizens as an essential interest of the State.

[214]In *CMS Gas Transmission Company v Argentina*, the tribunal elaborated the argument in which it recognises 'Necesity' as CIL but did not consider that Argentina fullfiled the requirements of Article 25 to declare it. For an academic comment on this case see: ILC (2001) comment to para 25 An interesting contribution has been written by: *CMS Gas Transmission Company v Argentina [*2005*] Award ARB/01/8 (ICSID) at paras. 315 ff.* See also: Reinisch (2006).

[215]Thjoernelund Hoelck (2008), p. 436.

[216]Here some examples of BIT that include NPM provisions: *CMS Gas Transmission Company v Argentina [*2005*] Award ARB/01/8 (ICSID) see at para 358*; Burke-White and Von Staden (2007), p. 311; Model BIT Canada available [2004] at http://www.italaw.com/documents/Canadian2004-FIPA-model-en.pdf. Accessed 14 September 2014; Model Text of the Indian Bilateral Investment Treaty, available at: https://mygov.in/sites/default/files/master_image/Model%20Text%20for%20the%20Indian%20Bilateral%20Investment%20Treaty.pdf. Accessed 17 August 2015.

circumstances would be inconsistent with the IIA.[217] Some examples are the protection of essential security, the maintenance of public order, the response to a public health emergency, and probably a response to famines, too.

NPM provisions can be classified as non-self-judging and self-judging provisions.

The scope of non-self-judging provisions is not delimited in IIAs. Parties do not determine how much deference is given to a state's determination.[218] Theoretically, their interpretation should correspond with the IIA, its context, and its aims. Tribunals have interpreted these clauses in a contradictory fashion. In some cases the arbitrators equated the IIA's clause with the meaning of 'necessity' in the framework of CIL.[219] Other tribunals disagreed and annulled cases.[220] The annulments were substantiated with a manifest excess of power.[221]

Self-judging NPM clauses limit the arbitrators' scope of review.[222] These clauses require the measure to be judged by the host state.[223] It does not mean that a tribunal review is not required. It means that the tribunal will only test whether the notion of necessity as expressed in the IIA can be subsumed into the real facts that led the state to take a decision. These clauses have also been called 'explicitly purpose-restricted self-judging clauses' since they constitute a flexibility mechanism that is restricted to 'certain rather clearly defined purposes'. Some scholars have argued that a good-faith

---

[217] Agreement Between the Government of the Government of the Republic of India and the Government of the Republic of Ghana for the Reciprocal Promotion and Protection of Investments (India-Ghana) [2000] available at http://investmentpolicyhub.unctad.org/IIA/country/79/treaty/1785. Accessed 16 September 2015.

[218] Nowadays BITs include more self-judging NPM Clauses. As manner of example: the US Model BIT 2004 and 1012 in Art. 18 state that: 'Nothing in this Treaty shall be construed... to preclude a Party from applying measures that it considers necessary for the...'.

[219] Nolan and Sourgens (2012), pp. 408 and 417. Two relevant cases are: Burke-White and Von Staden (2007), p. 371; *CMS Gas Transmission Company v Argentina [2005] Award ARB/01/8 (ICSID).*

[220] *Enron Corporation and Ponderosa Assets, L.P v The Argentine Republic* [2007] Award ARB/01/3 (ICSID), *Sempra Energy International v Argentine Republic [2007] Award ARB/02/16 (ICSID)*; *LG&E Energy Corporation and others v Argentina [2006a] Decision on Liability ARB/02/1 (ICSID)see para 245*; *Continental Casualty Company v The Argentine Republic* [2008] Award ARB/03/9 (ICSID) at paras 221 et seq; *El Paso Energy International Company v Argentina [2006] Decision on Jurisdiction ARB/03/15 (ICSID) at para 552.*

[221] *CMS Gas Transmission Company v Argentina [2007] Decision on Application for Annulment ARB/01/8 (ICSID) para 128 ff.*

[222] *Sempra Energy International v Argentina* [2010] Decision on Argentina's Application for Annulment of the Award ARB/02/16 (ICSID) at para 199.

[223] As a manner of example, the U.S BIT Modell from 2012 includes the following self-judging NPM provision: 'Nothing in this Treaty shall be construed: (1) to require a Party to furnish or allow access to any information the disclosure of which it determines to be contrary to its essential security interests; or (2) to preclude a Party from applying measures that it considers necessary for the fulfillment of its obligations with respect to the maintenance or restoration of international peace or security, or the protection of its own essential security interests'. Burke-White and Von Staden (2007), p. 376.

review[224] should be undertaken to force states to internalise and justify the balancing of rights between the state and the investors.[225]

5.7.2.2.2 NPM Provisions in Practice

The use of NPM provisions as a defence mechanism in IIL arbitration procedures increased after the Argentina crisis in 2001.[226] Not only did the government consider the situation in Argentina to justify taking measures that affected foreign investors, but this opinion was also supported by international financial organisations like the IMF.[227] For our purposes the Argentine cases are relevant for the development of IIL because they highlight the problem of inconsistency, which could also affect food emergencies. Although Argentine cases made NPM clauses relevant, it was not the first time IIL had to deal with states of emergency. The Asia crisis in which Malaysia was severely affected was also relevant for IIL. However, the way in which Malaysia dealt with the crisis turned out to be different from the Argentine reaction.[228] In Malaysia currency controls were used as a regulatory mechanism and even though international investors suffered significant damages, the fact that investments were not 'approved' made the tribunal unable to recognise its jurisdiction.

The issue in the Argentine cases goes back to the ability of the tribunals to analyse whether Argentina did or did not fulfil the requirements to be able to introduce special measures to solve economic problems during the state of necessity when it made use of self-judging NPM clauses anchored in BITs.[229] Argentina argued in all cases that there was no wrongful act and hence no compensation owed to investors. Argentina also invoked the self-judging character of the clause subject only to good faith review.[230] The main problem was the failure of the tribunals to establish whether the existence of a crisis can be subjectively determined, and if yes, when.[231] From the few cases that

---

[224]U.S. Model Bilateral Investment Treaty [2012] available at http://www.state.gov/r/pa/prs/ps/2012/04/188199.htm. Accessed 12 July 2015.

[225]van Aaken (2014a), pp. 827, 843 et seqq.

[226]A very well summarised article that explains the Argentinean crisis: Burke-White and Von Staden (2007), p. 376. Nowadays there are more than forty cases are pending in which Argentina invoked NPM clauses.

[227]On the coordination problems between IFM's policies and BITs see: The Economist, 'Argentina's collapse A decline without parallel' http://www.economist.com/node/1010911/print. Accessed 12.05.2011.

[228]International Monetary Fund (2004).

[229]ILC (2001) at art 27.

[230]With regard to the use of 'good faith' as standard in the context of NPM clauses see: Treaty with Argentina concerning the reciprocal encouragement and protection of investment (USA-Argentina) [1991] available at http://2001-2009.state.gov/documents/organization/43475.pdf. Accessed 9 July 2016 Article XI.

[231]For a well elaborated comment on one Argentinian case see: *LG&E Energy Corporation and others v Argentina [*2006a*] Decision on Liability ARB/02/1 (ICSID) at paras 208 ff.*

have been decided, all had different substantive outcomes because the tribunals' understanding of NPM clauses was so divergent. This uncertainty arises because, although the clause in the BIT could be considered self-judging, the conditions for their performance were not clearly specified.

We now refer to three of the Argentine cases that we consider relevant for our purposes. They are *CMS,*[232] *Enron,*[233] and *Sempra,*[234] all against Argentina. In all three cases Argentina invoked the same defence, arguing that during its crisis, a state of necessity or emergency existed according to the BIT signed between Argentina and the United States. The problem goes back to the legislation introduced by Argentina in 2001/2002, which under regular circumstances would constitute a BIT breach. Some of the laws passed by Argentina led to the pesification of all financial obligations and the freezing of bank accounts through the so-called 'corralito'.[235] These measures were taken by the Argentine government to alleviate the effects of the worst financial crisis in its history.

The tribunals neglected the right of Argentina to self-enforce the clause in a situation of national emergency. In *Enron v Argentina,* for example, the tribunal ignored pre-existent contractual measures by ruling that the CIL rules regarding the case of necessity would apply, even though a different standard had been agreed between the parties that was not contrary to the CIL standard.[236] The tribunal equated 'necessity' with the requirements accepted as CIL. In *CMS v Argentina* the tribunal decided that even though Argentina experienced some 'economic difficulties', these were not sufficient to consider them in the framework of an emergency situation. The tribunal stated:

> The Treaty in this case is clearly designed to protect investments at a time of economic difficulties or other circumstances leading to the adoption of adverse measures by the Government. The question is, however, how grave these economic difficulties might be. A severe crisis cannot necessarily be equated with a situation of total collapse. And in the absence of such profoundly serious conditions it is plainly clear that the Treaty will prevail

[232]Reinisch (2006).

[233]*CMS Gas Transmission Company v Argentina [*2007*] Decision on Application for Annulment ARB/01/8 (ICSID).*

[234]*Enron Corporation and Ponderosa Assets, L.P v The Argentine Republic [*2005*] Decision on Jurisdiction ARB/01/3 (ICSID).*

[235]*Sempra Energy International v Argentine Republic [*2007*] Award ARB/02/16 (ICSID)* and also Emergencia Publica y Reforma del Regimen Cambiario. Ley de Convertibilidad 23928. Boletin Oficial 29.810, Página 1.

[236]In this regarding the Tribunal stated at para 339:

'As the Tribunal has found above that the crisis invoked does not meet the customary law requirements of Article 25 of the Articles on State Responsibility, thus concluding that necessity or emergency are not conducive to the preclusion of wrongfulness, there is no need to undertake a further judicial review under Article XI as this Article does not set out conditions different from customary law in this respect.' Decreto 1570/2001, 1 December 2001. Boletin Oficial 29.787. Página 1.

> over any plea of necessity. However, if such difficulties, without being catastrophic in and of themselves, nevertheless invite catastrophic conditions in terms of disruption and disintegration of society, or are likely to lead to a total breakdown of the economy, emergency and necessity might acquire a different meaning.[237]

Furthermore, the tribunal ruled that the argument made by Argentina concerning its constitutional HRs obligations could not be considered because the tribunal did not see any conflict between constitutional law, HRs obligations, and the obligations of the state to foreign investors.

In *LG&E v Argentina* the view of the tribunal was different.[238] It did recognise a difference between the definition of the state of necessity in CIL and in the contractual agreement between the parties. The tribunal recognised the temporary nature of the special situation. However, it determined the time period in which the crisis took place and exempted Argentina from responsibility. Later the case was decided in a similar fashion. For example, the tribunal in *Continental Casualty Company v Argentina* stated that the notion of an emergency situation applies in an economic crisis, as was the case in Argentina, in the case of HRs protection.[239] Reviewing these decisions, the inconsistency of the ICSID becomes apparent.

5.7.2.3 Human Rights Law

In the following section we will analyse the derogation from economic, social, and cultural rights in HRL. Starting points are Articles 2(1) and 4 ICESCR. Article 2 (1) obliges signatory states to 'take steps… to the maximum of its available resources, with a view to achieving progressively the full realisation of the rights recognised in the present Covenant [ICESCR] by all appropriate means…'.[240] In special situations, i.e. armed conflicts, natural disasters, economic difficulties, and other emergencies like famines, states are allowed to limit some rights according to Article 4 ICESCR.

[237]*Enron Corporation and Ponderosa Assets, L.P v The Argentine Republic [*2005*] Decision on Jurisdiction ARB/01/3 (ICSID) at para 339.*

[238]*CMS Gas Transmission Company v Argentina [*2005*] Award ARB/01/8 (ICSID) at para 115.*

[239]*LG&E Energy Corporation and others v Argentina [*2006a*] Decision on Liability ARB/02/1 (ICSID).*

[240]Article 4 CESCR states: 'The States Parties to the present Covenant recognise that, in the enjoyment of those rights provided by the State in conformity with the present Covenant, the State may subject such rights only to such limitations as are determined by law only in so far as this may be compatible with the nature of these rights and solely for the purpose of promoting the general welfare in a democratic society'.

5.7.2.3.1 Limitation of Rights

The fact that HRs can be limited demonstrates that not all of them are absolute or unconditional, and that there might be a balance between particular and general interest. This is the reason why some rights can, under some circumstances, be limited.[241] Limitations shall be 'determined by Law',[242] 'necessary',[243] or as qualified in some HRs treaties 'necessary in a democratic society'.[244] Necessity is linked to the principle of proportionality.[245] Limitations of HRs are always to be adapted to the circumstances under present conditions and modified along with the changing structures, values, and priorities of societies.[246] The literature states that limitations cannot be applied so as to eliminate a right.[247]

5.7.2.3.2 Derogation of Rights

Derogation is the complete or partial elimination of aspects of an international obligation. The ICESCR does not include derogation clauses and its approach is unclear. The *travaux préparatoires* neither contain any discussion on derogations, nor the reasons why the clause is absent.[248] The opposite is the case in ICCPR. It states in Article 4 ICCPR that it applies in an emergency which 'threatens the life of

---

[241] As a manner of examples see: *Continental Casualty Company v The Argentine Republic [*2008*] Award ARB/03/9 (ICSID) at paras 181*, as well as General Assembly (UN) International Covenant on Economic, Social and Cultural Rights [1976] United Nations Treaty Series 993 available at http://www.refworld.org/docid/3ae6b36c0.html. Accessed 15 July 2015 Art. 2, Arts. 12, 18, 19, 21 of the General Assembly (UN) International Covenant on Civil and Political Rights [2001] CCPR/C/66/GUI/Rev.2.

[242] See for example Art. 8 General Assembly (UN) International Covenant on Economic, Social and Cultural Rights [1976] United Nations Treaty Series 993 available at http://www.refworld.org/docid/3ae6b36c0.html. Accessed 15 July 2015. Arts. 12(3), 18(3), 19(3), 21 and 22 of the General Assembly (UN) International Covenant on Civil and Political Rights [2001] CCPR/C/66/GUI/Rev.2.

[243] See i.e. Arts. 4 and 8 General Assembly (UN) International Covenant on Economic, Social and Cultural Rights [1976] United Nations Treaty Series 993 available at http://www.refworld.org/docid/3ae6b36c0.html. Accessed 15 July 2015 and Arts. 11, 12(2) and 14 African Charter on Human and Peoples' Rights (Banjul Charter) [1986] OAU Doc. CAB/LEG/67/3 rev. 5, 21 I.L.M. 58.

[244] See i.e. Arts. 12(3), 18(3) and 19(3) of the General Assembly (UN) International Covenant on Civil and Political Rights [2001] CCPR/C/66/GUI/Rev.2 and Art. 11 African Charter on Human and Peoples' Rights (Banjul Charter) [1986] OAU Doc. CAB/LEG/67/3 rev. 5, 21 I.L.M. 58.

[245] See *supra* in Sect. 5.4.3.

[246] Arts. 14(1), 21 and 22(2) of the General Assembly (UN) International Covenant on Civil and Political Rights [2001] CCPR/C/66/GUI/Rev.2.

[247] Art. 8 General Assembly (UN) International Covenant on Economic, Social and Cultural Rights [1976] United Nations Treaty Series 993 available at http://www.refworld.org/docid/3ae6b36c0.html. Accessed 15 July 2015.

[248] As can be read from the *travaux préparatoires* some delegations opposed the inclusion of a general limitation clause since it was considered as unnecessary. Even more unnecessary could be considered the inclusion of a derogation clause. See: Müller (2009), pp. 557, 561.

the nation'.[249] The standards for derogation take a similar tone in ICCPR.[250] The provisions regulating emergency situations list the situations in which states are allowed to take specific measures, as well as the kinds of rights that are derogable and non-derogable.[251]

The Banjul Charter does not contain any articles regarding emergency situations. However, the ACHPR has stated that a derogation from any articles of the Banjul Charter in emergencies is not possible.[252] The fact that states derogate from some obligations in a situation of emergency does not mean that they are allowed to violate other international obligations they previously agreed upon. In addition to the regional treaties, the interpretation adopted by the HRs Committee—a supervisory body of ICCPR—in Comment 29 is a subsidiary source to consider emergencies.[253]

Although ICESCR does not mention the derogation of protected rights, there is an open discussion about the permission to derogate and its legal basis. The main argument in favour of potential derogations arises from decisions of the ILO[254] and the academic literature.[255] To briefly summarise, they equate the state of necessity to CIL; it is an exception to the principle of *pacta sunt servanda* found in Articles

[249] Art. 4 ICCPR reads: 'In time of public emergency which threatens the life of the nation and the existence of which is officially proclaimed, the States Parties to the present Covenant may take measures derogating from their obligations under the present Covenant to the extent strictly required by the exigencies of the situation, provided that such measures are not inconsistent with their other obligations under international law and do not involve discrimination solely on the ground of race, colour, sex, language, religion or social origin'. Commission on Human Rights (1948).

[250] Although the wording might differ the principles as such can be considered as the same as the ones we considered previously.

[251] No derogation from articles 6, 7, 8 (paragraphs 1 and 2), 11, 15, 16 and 18 may be made under this provision.

[252] General Assembly (UN) International Covenant on Civil and Political Rights [2001] CCPR/C/66/GUI/Rev.2 and (Commission Nationale de Droits de l'Homme et des Libertés v Chad; Malawi African Association and others v Mauritania; Media Rights Agenda v Nigeria). The commision has reiterately stated that: 'contrary to other human rights instruments, the African Charter does not allow for derogation from obligations due to emergency situations. Thus, even a situation of civil war [...] cannot be cited as justification for the violation by the State or its authority to violate the African Charter' ibid; General Comment No. 29. States of Emergency (Article 4) CCPR/C/21/Rev.1/Add.11 at para 1.

[253] *Malawi African Association and Others v Mauritania, African Commission on Human and Peoples' Rights* [2000] Comm Nos 54/91, 61/91, 98/93, 164/97 à 196/97 and 210/98 (ACHPR) at para 84.

[254] One prominent example for this position was the decision of the ILO Commission that based on the 'circumstances of extreme gravity' and the limitation in scope and duration, considered strictly necessary the derogation of the right contented in the following Conventions: *Commission Nationale de Droits de l'Homme et des Libertes v Chad* [1992] 74/92 (ACHPR) at para 21; and General Comment No. 29. States of Emergency (Article 4) CCPR/C/21/Rev.1/Add.11.

[255] For an overview of the discussion see: Freedom of Association and Protection of the Right to Organise Convention, 1948 (No. 87) (adopted 09 July 1948) San Francisco, 31st ILC session (09 Jul 1948).

54–64 of the VCLT[256] together with arguments that go back to ARSIWA. The approach of the CESRC and the African Commission on Human and Peoples' Rights runs counter to this argument by not including any provision that allows derogation of rights.[257] It has been suggested that the flexibility of ICESCR Article 4 is sufficient for signatory states to respond to emergency situations.[258] Another point of view is to consider as non-derogable a minimum core of obligations protecting basic subsistence rights like, for example, the right to be free from hunger.[259] A further approach deems it unrealistic that in an emergency situation states would, at least *de facto*, avoid derogation of protected rights.[260]

All in all there is no fixed position on whether to permit the derogation of rights in the framework of ICESCR. The literature indicates, however, a palpable tendency to support the derogation of the right to work and deny derogation of all other rights in the ICESCR.[261] The aspect of flexibility under Article 4 ICESCR concerning the progressive realisation of economic rights has been noted, alongside the Covenant's insistence that the suspension of most rights can hardly ever be necessary for the protection or restoration of public order. Ergo, states can take measures to respond to emergencies without derogating rights contained in ICESCR.[262] A further argument against the permission of derogation would be that in addition to the flexibility contained in ICESCR, humanitarian law also has mechanisms that can be activated before derogating economic, social, or political rights.[263] This variable is not considered in our analysis, nonetheless.

[256]Right to Organise and Collective Bargaining Convention, 1949 (No. 98) (adopted 01 Jul 1949) Geneva, 32nd ILC session (entry into force: 18 July 1951).

[257]See footnote: 253 in this chapter.

[258]In addition, as reaffirmed by CESCR: 'First, because core obligations are non-derogable, they continue to exist in situations of conflict, emergency and natural disaster'. Müller (2009), pp. 557, 594 et seqq.

[259]United Nations, Vienna Convention on the Law of Treaties [1969] United Nations, Treaty Series, vol. 1155, p. 331. See also: Rosas and Sandvik-Nylund (2001).

[260]Müller (2009), pp. 557, 599.

[261]An overview of the discussion can be read in: Economic and Social Council, *Substantive Issues Arising in the Implementation of the International Covenant on Economic, Social and Cultural Rights: Poverty and the International Covenant on Economic, Social and Cultural Rights* (E/CN12/2001/10, 19) para 18.

[262]Müller (2009), pp. 557, 593 see also footnote 48 in Chap. 2.

[263]In the framework of humanitarian law the notion of food emergencies has been broadly developed. See: ibid.

5.7.3 *Intermediate Result: Potential Judicial Outcomes if Famines are Hardly Foreseeable*

The previous analysis of the norms available to states as defence in case of famines does not indicate a clear pathway that could be followed to guarantee success. On the one hand, tribunals have been inconsistent in their decisions in similar emergency cases, while on the other hand, the contribution of HRL law in judicial cases seems to be even less promising. As a result, it is important to think about the mechanisms that could be employed to minimise legal insecurity arising from NPM provisions in food emergencies.

Considering exceptions to state responsibility in food emergencies, conflicts might arise depending on their magnitude. The impact on state structure has to be considered equally along with geographical aspects. The experience gained through certain emergencies, for example economic crises, show that these events affect the totality of the state and that they produce distortions and relevant negative effects in a very short time. They can cause detrimental effects like unemployment, poverty, and social violence. The scenario is different yet again in some food crises, which oftentimes emerge in specific regions and produce even worse effects. Famines occur more frequently in rural than in urban areas of LDCs.[264] Moreover, in food emergencies humanitarian law could play a relevant role by interfering and applying measures to confront these emergencies before a state collapses.[265] Furthermore, the Paris Minimum Standards of Human Rights Norms in a State of Emergency proposes restricting the territorial applicability of a state of emergency if the threat to life is contained in specific geographical areas.[266]

A further particularity of food emergencies is their longevity.[267] Necessity in CIL is viewed as a temporary event, as it is in most IIAs. This element has also been considered in tribunal decisions.[268] It thus might be variable in food emergencies. On the one hand some LDCs are almost in permanent crisis, while on the other hand protracted food crises have increased.[269] Protracted crises produce continuous national emergencies like in Somalia, Sudan, and Afghanistan, and they have elements of longevity and repetition.[270] In the three aforementioned countries,

[264]See first chapter at page: 22.

[265]For a similar viewpoint regarding the role of humanitarian law see: Müller (2009), pp. 557, 598.

[266]World Food Programme (2005), p. 3.

[267]Müller (2009), pp. 557, 598; Lillich (1985), p. 1072, at Article 4.

[268]Komoremos (2005), pp. 49, 561 the tribunal recognised that: '. . .from 1 December 2001 until 26 April 2003, Argentina was in a period of crisis during which it was necessary to enact measures to maintain public order and protect its essential security interests'.

[269]Protracted crisis are defined by the FAO as: 'Those environments in which a significant proportion of the population is acutely vulnerable to death, disease and disruption of livelihoods over a prolonged period of time. The governance of these environments is usually very weak, with the state having a limited capacity to respond to, and mitigate, the threats to the population, or provides adequate levels of protection.' Despouy (1999) paras 69 ff.

[270]*LG&E Energy Corporation and others v Argentina* [2006b] Award ARB/02/1 (ICSID) at para 226.

protracted crises have produced emergency situations over more than two decades.[271] Whether the most stable moment in a period of time can be considered a reference is a question that could come up in investment procedures. Having pointed out relevant characteristics of food emergencies, we will now consider the concrete options of governments to deal with them.

From the HRs perspective, considering the limitation of derogations under the ICESCR and ACHPR regimes in addition to the prohibition of derogation in the ACHPR,[272] one could expect either the limitation of some rights to protect the right to food, or the activation of humanitarian law.[273] Of these options, LDC governments would most likely prefer to shift the costs of food emergency to an external party, in this case humanitarian law. The decision to activate humanitarian law would be based not only on the political but also the financial costs of limitating HRs for the government.[274]

In situations without an IIA investment contract, CIL applies.[275] If an investment contract is in place, it will be the first source of law to determine whether the measure taken by the state can be subsumed under the notion of necessity.[276] If an IIA is in place it will be the first source of law for an investment tribunal deciding on the measure taken by the host state.[277]

The IIAs themselves will determine whether the specific situation under consideration can be subsumed under the meaning of necessity in the IIA.[278] If IIAs set a different standard of protection than the one provided by CIL, the applicable law will be what parties agree upon. CIL should apply only in those cases in which the adjudicator cannot deduce the intentions of the parties from the contract. Even here the interpretation following the language of the treaty would be expected to precede the application of CIL. Case law in IIL shows a different reality, nonetheless. In *Enron Corporation and Ponderosa Assets L.P. v Argentina* the tribunal did not recognise the intention of the parties to decrease—IIA vis-à-vis CIL—the standard of protection to declare a state of necessity. The consequence (of what in this case can be called misuse of CIL) is that the tribunal applied a law that was not agreed upon by the parties when they designed the contract. While Article 25 ARSIWA requires the state not to have been involved in the situation that produced the emergency in order to rightfully declare state of necessity, the BIT between Argentina and the United States does not include this condition.

[271]Food and Agriculture Organization of the United Nations (2010), p. 1.

[272]See footnote: 253 in this chapter.

[273]See footnote: 266 in this chapter.

[274]In a separate contribution we will offer a deep analysis about the possibilities IIL offers to require host states the activation of humanitarian law before undertaking measures affecting foreign investors in case of state of emergencies caused by famines.

[275]See page: 155 of this study.

[276]See page: 157 of this study.

[277]See page: 157 of this study.

[278]This following Article 31 Food and Agriculture Organization of the United Nations (2010), p. 1.

There is quite a broad spectrum of scenarios that could arise depending on each individual IIA. First of all, a lack of jurisdiction might be expected if there is no legal nexus between investment contract and IIA, but also if parties delegate such a competence to a different forum.[279] In these kinds of cases an umbrella clause and its effects must be considered by the tribunal.[280] If the investment tribunal fulfils the jurisdictional requirements, the scope and nexus of NPM clauses will increase in relevance.[281] Self-judging clauses should provide the tribunal with the minimum of information to test whether the food emergency can be considered a necessity in the framework of the IIA. In cases involving non-self-judging provisions, the tribunal will need to interpret to what extent the measure taken by the state can be subsumed under the terms agreed by the parties in the IAA. In order to make NPM clauses work properly, the tribunal should be able learn about the preferences of the parties during the negotiation of the IIA, and it might be incentivised to decide according to such preferences.

The praxis in the Argentine cases shows that the aforementioned questions can be highly challenging for investment tribunals.[282] Following our CT approach, we can consider the presence of incomplete contracts[283] that allow arbitrators to take decisions that are not expected by the parties, or at least that do not align with the purpose that parties negotiated in the clauses. In some cases where agency costs become too high in principal-agent relationships, such behaviour by arbitrators can lead to an extra limitation of powers.[284] Notwithstanding that the ICSID regime allows the initiation of annulment procedures,[285] parties might have some strategies available to avoid them. Annulment procedures are usually avoided due to the additional (potentially exorbitant) costs that can arise from the tribunal decision.[286]

The legal uncertainty for investors and host states over whether tribunals can freely apply IL correctly or not was demonstrated in the Argentine cases through the apparent inability of the host state to prove the state of necessity. Even the

---

[279]See page: 169 of this paper.

[280]See in page 169 the reference made concerning the case Food and Agriculture Organization of the United Nations (2010), p. 19.

[281]This as considered by tribunal in: *Enron Corporation and Ponderosa Assets, L.P v The Argentine Republic [*2005*] Decision on Jurisdiction ARB/01/3 (ICSID) at para 339.*

[282]See Sect. 5.7.2 of this study.

[283]Herewith are IIA referred. The word contract is used to maintain a concordance with the technical vocabulary.

[284]See Sect. 1.4 of this study.

[285]*Bureau Veritas, Inspection, Valuation, Assessment and Control BIVAC B.V. v The Republic of Paraguay [*2009*] Award ARB/07/9 (ICSID).*

[286]As a manner of example one can mention the potential liability from the cases that Argentina has could be greater than U.S.D 8 billion, which is higher than the entire financial reserves of Argentina in 2002. Burke-White and Von Staden (2007), p. 330. An additional well known case is Arts. 50 et seqq. Convention on the Settlement of Investment Disputes Between States and Nationals of Other States [1965] 17 UST 1270 TIAS 6090 575 UNTS 159. In this case Occidental awarded damages reached US$1.77 billion (US$2.3 billion with interest applied).

information and reports provided by the IMF were not deemed sufficient to demonstrate the magnitude of the emergency in at least three procedures.[287] Yet in food emergencies it could be expected that the information provided by the FAO—which is the IO with the competence to have information about the status of food production in the world—would probably have the same effect. These experiences show us that in the future, parties have to increase the level of specification in the treaties. Treaties need to be designed so that tribunals have a narrower scope to decide, can better follow what the parties agreed, and only in exceptional cases apply more general rules. Tribunals have to be incentivised to correctly follow the rules to interpret treaties.[288]

A case-by-case review might be needed in order to minimise risks arising from too-incomplete NPM provisions. The reason for this is the individualised character of the interpretation of the clauses. Argentine cases have shown the significant consequences that 'too' incomplete clauses have with regard to the costs they can generate. Some potential solutions can, however, be considered and gleaned from chapters preceding this section.[289] At the IIA level a contractual renegotiation involving increased specificity of NPMs could be proposed. This would help to better allocate risks during the performance of the investment project because NPM provisions reallocate risks to investors. Ergo, more precise or more narrowly drafted NPM provisions would increase legal security and make legitimate expectations more realistic. A natural consequence of a narrower drafting of NPM provisions would be a better definition of legal interpretative techniques and a limitation of arbitrators' power to interpret the contract.[290] The main aim of inducing specific interpretative techniques is that parties could make sure that arbitrators would balance HRs and investment issues.[291] By doing so, one could foresee that states increase the costs of capital to burden investors. This should decrease over time if the application of NPM provisions is consistent.[292] This means that states would be able to offer reasoned argumentations and consider governing rules in IIL and HRL when the application of NPM needs to be considered.[293]

---

[287] See Sect. 5.7 of this study.

[288] See Sect. 1.4 of this study.

[289] See Chap. 5.

[290] See Sect. 5.7 of this study.

[291] Some scholars have also recommended the incorporation of a 'margin of appreciation' approach as developed in the European Convention on Human Rights and Fundamental Freedoms. Burke-White and Von Staden (2007), at footnote 13 in Chap. 1.

[292] As stated in the literature: 'with respect to the U.S. BIT program, however, the U.S. interpretation of NPM clauses as self-judging has been so consistent, open, and notorious since 1984, that any investor expectations that such clauses were not self-judging cannot be legitimate and should not be given significant weight by arbitral tribunals'. *Occidental Exploration and Production Company v Ecuador [*2004*] Final Award UN3467 (LCIA).*

[293] About internalisation of norms in HRL see: Burke-White and Von Staden (2007), p. 370.

Further to the possibility drafted in the previous paragraph, IIAs could also involve commissions of experts to provide an opinion whether a particular situation could be catalogued as the state of necessity so that a state of emergency can be declared and special measures can be undertaken. In a food emergency this opinion could be introduced in order to allow the state to legitimise its decision.[294] All in all, programmes developed by IOs in the framework of humanitarian law have the proven expertise and technology to help in real time during famines in LDCs.[295] The use of such information can affect the derogation of rights and state responsibility, discriminatory measures, and the proof of wrongful acts in general. Such a collection of data covers health and epidemiologic issues, food prices, food accessibility, capital flows, and more.[296] In the area of humanitarian aid, for example, modern mechanisms exist to alert responders to potential crises and also to allow them to react in unexpected events.[297] This information can contribute in at least three ways: it can determine the compliance and progress of states in the realisation of the right to food and evaluate food security in risk countries, it can provide precise information about food shortages, and it can help in protracted crises that lead to food emergencies. Since the information produced by IOs is reliable but legally irrelevant, states should rely on it through contractual agreements either at the state-state or the investor-state level. This information can contribute in two ways: it can establish state responsibility in dispute settlements (in this case to legitimise state behaviour) and promote the implementation of food programmes at the national level with HRs obligations (in this case to evaluate the necessity and proportionality of the measure).

To sum up our analysis, we argued that the challenge to IIL regarding food emergencies is twofold because it has to consider the specific situation of the country and apply investment rules to the extent that HRs obligations are not

---

[294]See page 313 of this study.

[295]To have a notion about the scope of the data collection made by IOs consult: Burke-White and Von Staden (2007), p. 406. For more concrete issues see the data base elaborated by the World Food Program: Goodman and Jinks (2004), p. 620.

As manner of example, the World Food Programme need to be mentioned: The WPF is a unique network of food security analysts that works closely with national governments, UN partners and more than 2000 national and international NGOs. It is an autonomous programme, with juridical personality. It is a subsidiary of the UN the FAO. The main goal is to inform about the policies and programmes that WFP and its parents adopt in order to fight hunger in different circumstances. The programme has the most advanced technology which includes satellite imagery, geographic information system (GIS) and mobile data collection platforms. The activities of the programme are divided into a range of assessments that allow the identification of famines around the globe. The programme has developed fast reaction policies for cases of emergencies as well as alert assessments that allow the anticipation of the of proper food distribution plans. See: Nunn and Qian (2010); The World Bank (2016) and Shaw (2011), p. xxiii.

[296]To have a notion about the scope of the data collection made by IOs consult: Art. VIII World Food Program General Regulations and Rules available at http://one.wfp.org/aboutwfp/how_run/GeneralRegulations_E.pdf [accessed 11.13.2013]. For more concrete issues see the data base elaborated by the World Food Program: Shaw (2011), p. 4.

[297]Source: Nunn and Qian (2010).

infringed. The second challenge is to beware of potential wrongful acts camouflaged as emergency situations to legitimise protectionist government policies. Investment law has the instruments to apply, pertinently decide, and balance the protection offered under IIL and HRL. Under the current conditions incentives to act properly appear to be lacking, nevertheless. This leads us to believe that the outcomes of investment tribunals in food emergencies can hardly be foreseen.

References

Abbott, K., & Snidal, D. (2003). Hard and soft law in international governance. *International Organization, 54*, 421.

African Charter on Human and Peoples' Rights (Banjul Charter) [1986] OAU Doc. CAB/LEG/67/3 rev. 5, 21 I.L.M. 58.

Agreement Between the Government of Sweden and the Government of Malaysia Concerning the Mutual Protection of Investments (Sweden-Malaysia) [1979] SÖ 1979:17 available at: http://investmentpolicyhub.unctad.org/IIA/country/202/treaty/2484. Accessed 17 September 2015.

Agreement Between the Government of the Government of the Republic of India and the Government of the Republic of Ghana for the Reciprocal Promotion and Protection of Investments (India-Ghana) [2000] available at http://investmentpolicyhub.unctad.org/IIA/country/79/treaty/1785. Accessed 16 September 2015.

Aguas del Tunari v Bolivia [2005] Decision on Respondent's Objections to Jurisdiction ARB/02/3 (ICSID).

Alexy, R. (2003). On balancing and subsumption. A structural comparison. *Ratio Juris, 16*.

Amnesty International. (2006). Kimberley process: An amnesty international position paper. Recommendations to the Kimberley process participants in order to effectively strengthen the Kimberley process certification scheme. Amnesty International, http://www.amnestyusa.org/document.php?lang=e&id=ENGPOL300242006. Accessed 7 July 2014.

Anseeuw, W., Boche, M., Breu, T., Giger, M., Lay, J., Messerli, P., et al. (2012). *Transnational land deals for agriculture in the Global South. Analytical report based on the land matrix database*. CDE/CIRAD/GIGA Bern/Montpellier/Hamburg.

Arangio-Ruiz, G. (2009). *Third report on state responsibility* (A/CN4/440 and Add1).

Bardhan, P. (1997). Corruption and development: A review of issues. *American Economic Association, 35*, 1320.

Basel Convention on the Control of Transboundary Movements of Hazardous Wastes and Their Disposal [1998] 1673 UNTS 126; 28 ILM 657.

Bernardus Henricus Funnekotter and Others v Zimbabwe [2009] Award ARB/05/6 (ICSID).

Biwater Gauff (Tanzania) Ltd v Tanzania [2008] Award and Concurring and Dissenting Opinion ARB/05/22 (ICSID).

Black, H. C., Nolan, J. R., & Nolan-Haley, J. M. (2006). *Black's dictionary*. West Publishing Company.

Born, G. (2012). A new generation of international adjudication. *Duke Law Journal, 61*, 775.

Borras, S., Hall, R., Scoones, I., Ben, W., & Wendy, W. (2011). Towards a better understanding of global land grabbing: An editorial introduction. *Journal of Peasant Studies, 37*, 209.

Boyle, A., & Chinkin, C. (2007). *The making of international law*. Oxford University Press.

Bureau Veritas, Inspection, Valuation, Assessment and Control BIVAC B.V. v The Republic of Paraguay [2009] Award ARB/07/9 (ICSID).

Burke-White, W., & Von Staden, A. (2007). Investment protection in extraordinary times: The interpretation and application of non-precluded measures provisions in bilateral investment treaties. *Virginia Journal of International Law, 48*.

Cafaggi, F. (2011). New foundations of transnational private regulation. *Journal of Law and Society, 38*, 20.
Cafaggi, F. (2012). Introduction: The transformation of transnational private regulation: Enforcement gaps and governance design. In F. Cafaggi (Ed.), *Enforcement of transnational regulation*. Edward Elgar.
Calamita, J. (2013). In F. Baetens (Ed.), *International human rights and the interpretation of international investment treaties – Constitutional considerations*. Cambridge University Press.
Cashore, B. W., Auld, G., & Newsom, D. (2004). *Governing through markets: Forest certification and the emergence of non-state authority*. Yale University Press.
Chayes, A., & Chayes, A. (1993). On compliance. *International Organization, 47*, 175.
China - Measures Affecting Trading Rights and Distribution Services for Certain Publications and Audiovisual Entertainment Products [2009] WT/DS363/AB/R (WTO Appellate Body).
CMS Gas Transmission Company v Argentina [2005] Award ARB/01/8 (ICSID).
CMS Gas Transmission Company v Argentina [2007] Decision on Application for Annulment ARB/01/8 (ICSID).
Coltart, D. (2008). A decade of suffering in Zimbabwe: Economic collapse and political repression under Robert Mugabe. *Policy Analysis, 5*.
Commission Nationale de Droits de l'Homme et des Libertes v Chad [1992] 74/92 (ACHPR).
Commission on Human Rights. (1948). *Summary Record of the 308th Meeting* (E/CN4/SR308).
Compañía de Aguas del Aconquija SA and Vivendi Universal SA v Argentina [2005] Decision on Jurisdiction ARB/97/3 (ICSID).
Continental Casualty Company v The Argentine Republic [2008] Award ARB/03/9 (ICSID).
Convention on the Settlement of Investment Disputes Between States and Nationals of Other States [1965] 17 UST 1270 TIAS 6090 575 UNTS 159.
Cordero, G. (2008). Tribunal's power versus party autonomy. In P. Muchlinski, F. Ortino, & C. Schreuer (Eds.), *The Oxford handbook of international investment law*. Oxford University Press.
Cotula, L., & Tienhaara, K. (2013). Reconfiguring investment contracts to promote sustainable development. In K. Sauvant (Ed.), *Yearbook on international investment law & policy*. Editorial Staff Columbia University.
Crespi, J., & Marette, S. (2003). Some economic implications of public labeling. *Journal of Food Distribution Research, 34*.
Cross, E. (2012). *The cost of Zimbabwe's continuing farm invasions*. Cato Institute Economic Development No. 12.
Decreto 1570/2001, 1 December 2001. Boletin Oficial 29.787. Página 1.
Deininger, K., & World Bank. (2003). *Land policy framework for growth and poverty reduction*. Oxford University Press.
Deininger, K., Byerlee, D., Lindsay, J., Norton, A., & Selod, H. (2011). *Rising global interest in farmland. Can it yield sustainable equitable benefits?* World Bank.
Despouy, L. (1999). *Report by the UN Special Rapporteur, Mr. Leandro Despouy, on the question of Human Rights and State of Emergency*.
Dolzer, R. (2005). The impact of international investment treaties on domestic administrative law. *New York University Enviromental Law Journal*, 953.
Dolzer, R., & Schreuer, C. (2008). *Principles of international investment law*. Oxford University Press.
Dörr, O., & Schmalenbach, K. (Eds.). (2012). *Vienna Convention on the law of treaties*. Springer.
Dumberry, P. (2013). How to impose human rights obligations on corporations under investment treaties? Pragmatic guidelines for the amendment of BITs. In K. Sauvant (Ed.), *Yearbook on international investment law & policy 2011–2012*. Editorial Staff Columbia University.
El Paso Energy International Company v Argentina [2006] Decision on Jurisdiction ARB/03/15 (ICSID).
Emergencia Publica y Reforma del Regimen Cambiario. Ley de Convertibilidad 23928. Boletin Oficial 29.810, Página 1.

Enron Corporation and Ponderosa Assets, L.P v The Argentine Republic [2005] Decision on Jurisdiction ARB/01/3 (ICSID).

Enron Corporation and Ponderosa Assets, L.P v The Argentine Republic [2007] Award ARB/01/3 (ICSID).

FAO. (2009). *The impacts of private food safety standards on the food chain and on public standard-setting processes* (ALINORM 09/32/9D-Part II).

Federal Reserve Bank of New York v Bank Markazi [2000] n 19 (Iran-U.S. Claims Tribunal).

Food and Agriculture Organization of the United Nations. (2010). *Countries in protracted crisis: What are they and why do they deserve special attention?* FAO ed.

Foster, C. (2009). The consultation of independent experts by international courts and tribunals in health and environment cases. In J. Klabbers & K. Creutz (Eds.), *Finnish yearbook of international law* (Vol. 20). Martinus Nijhoff Publishers.

Franck, S. (2005). The legitimacy crisis in investment treaty arbitration: Privatizing public international law through inconsistent decisions. *Fordham Law Review, 73*, 1521.

Fraport AG Frankfurt Airport Services Worldwide v The Republic of the Philippines [2007] Award ARB/03/25 (ICSID).

Freedom of Association and Protection of the Right to Organise Convention, 1948 (No. 87) (adopted 09 July 1948) San Francisco, 31st ILC session (09 Jul 1948).

Fudenberg, D., & Tirole, J. (1990). Moral hazard and renegotiation in agency contracts. *Econometrica, 58*.

Gehne, K. (2011). Responsible investment through international investment law: Addressing rights asymmetries trough law interpretation remedies. In S. Heri, et al. (Eds.), *International instruments influencing the rigths of people facing investments in agricultural land.*

General Assembly (UN) International Covenant on Civil and Political Rights [2001] CCPR/C/66/ GUI/Rev.2.

General Assembly (UN) International Covenant on Economic, Social and Cultural Rights [1976] United Nations Treaty Series 993 available at http://www.refworld.org/docid/3ae6b36c0.html. Accessed 15 July 2015.

Genin and others v Estonia [2001] Award ARB/99/2 (ICSID).

Glamis Gold Ltd v United States [2009] Award IIC 380 (Ad Hoc Tribunal UNCITRAL).

Goodman, R., & Jinks, D. (2004). How to influence states: Socialization and international human rights law. *Duke Law Journal, 54*, 620.

GRAIN. Land ceilings: Reining in land grabbers or dumbing down the debate? http://www.grain.org/article/entries/4655-land-ceilings-reining-in-land-grabbers-or-dumbing-down-the-debate. Accessed 17 August 2015.

Gruslin v Malaysia [2000] Award ARB/99/3 (ICSID).

Hart, O., & Moore, J. (1988). Incomplete contracts and renegotiation. *Econometrica, 56*.

Hirsch, M. (2006). *Interactions between investment and non-investment obligations in international investment law.*

Hirsch, M. (2009). Investment tribunals and human rights: Divergent paths. In P.-M. Dupuy, F. Francioini, & E.-U. Petersmann (Eds.), *Human rights in international investment law and arbitration.* Oxford.

ILC. (2001). Draft articles on responsibility of states for internationally wrongful acts. In *Yearkbook of the International Law Commission* (Vol. II). United Nations.

ILC. (2006). *Fragmentation of international law: Difficulties arising from the diversification and expansion of international law* (A/CN4/L682).

Inter-Agency Working Group on the Private Investment and Job Creation Pillar of the G20 Multi-Year Action on Development. (2011). *Promoting standards for responsible investment in value chains.*

International Chamber of Commerce Combating Extortion and Bribery International. available at http://www.iccwbo.org/Advocacy-Codes-and-Rules/Document-centre/2005/ICC-Rules-of-Conduct-and-Recommendations-to-Combat-Extortion-and-Bribery-(2005-Edition). Accessed 14 September 2014.

International Council on Mining & Metals. (2014). *Sustainable development framework. 10 principles*. ICMM, http://www.icmm.com/our-work/sustainable-development-framework/10-principles. Accessed 14 September 2014.

International Land Coalition. (2011). *The land matrix. Beta version 2.0. International Land Coalition*. ILC, http://www.landmatrix.org/en/about/. Accessed 3 April 2015.

International Monetary Fund. (2004). *The IMF and Argentina, 1991–2001* (Evaluation Report 2004).

International Monetary Fund. (2007). *Guide on resource revenue transparency*. IMF.

Johnson, L. (2014). The transparency rules and transparency convention: A good start and model for broader reform in investor-state arbitration. *Columbia FDI Perspectives, 126*.

Kaplow, L. Rules versus standards: An economic analysis. (1992) 42 Duke Law Journal 557

Kardassopoulos v Georgia [2007] Decision on jurisdiction ARB/05/18 (ICSID).

Keck, M., & Sikkink, K. (1999). Transnational advocacy networks in international and regional politics. *International Social Science Journal, 51*, 89.

Kimberly Process. (2013). *The Kimberly Process*. KP, http://www.kimberleyprocess.com/en. Accessed 26 November 2013.

Kohli, A., Chung-in, M., & Sarensen, G. (Eds.). (2003). *States, markets, and just growth*. The United Nations System in the 21st Century.

Komoremos, B. (2005). Contracting around international uncertainty. *American Political Science Review, 99*, 49.

Koskenniemi, M. (1997). Hierarchy in international law: A sketch. *European Journal of International Law, 8*, 566.

Kriebaum, U. (2006). Privatizing human rights. The interface between international investment protection and human rights. *Transnational Dispute Management, 3*.

Kurtz, J. (2007). Aguas del Tunari v. Bolivia. *Transnational Dispute Management, 4*.

Ley 26.737 Régimen de Protección al Dominio Nacional Sobre la Propiedad, Posesión o Tenencia de las Tierras Rurales [2011].

LG&E Energy Corporation and others v Argentina [2006a] Decision on Liability ARB/02/1 (ICSID).

LG&E Energy Corporation and others v Argentina [2006b] Award ARB/02/1 (ICSID).

Lillich, R. B. (1985). The Paris minimum standards of human rights norms in a state of emergency. *American Journal of International Law, 79*, 1072.

Malawi African Association and Others v Mauritania, African Commission on Human and Peoples' Rights [2000] Comm Nos 54/91, 61/91, 98/93, 164/97 à 196/97 and 210/98 (ACHPR).

Malaysian Historical Salvors Sdn Bhd v Malaysia [2007] Award on Jurisdiction ARB/05/10 (ICSID).

Mbengue, M. *Preamble*. Max Planck Encyclopedia of Public International Law, http://opil.ouplaw.com/view/10.1093/law:epil/9780199231690/law-9780199231690-e1456?prd=EPIL. Accessed 18 August 2015.

Mclachlan, C. (2008). The principle of systemic integration and Article 31(3)(c) of the Vienna Convention. *International and Comparative Law Quarterly, 54*.

Meckenstock, C. A. (2010). *Investment protection and human rights regulation: Two aims in a relationship of solvable tension* (1st ed.). Nomos.

Metalclad Corporation v The United Mexican States [1997] Award ARB(AF)/97/1 (ICSID).

Metal-Tech Ltd. v Republic of Uzbekistan [2010] Award ARB/10/03 (ICSID).

Methanex Corporation v United States [2005] Final Award (Ad hoc UNICTRAL).

Model BIT Canada available [2004] at http://www.italaw.com/documents/Canadian2004-FIPA-model-en.pdf. Accessed 14 September 2014.

Model Text of the Indian Bilateral Investment Treaty., available at: https://mygov.in/sites/default/files/master_image/Model%20Text%20for%20the%20Indian%20Bilateral%20Investment%20Treaty.pdf. Accessed 17 August 2015.

Muchlinski, P. (2006). "Caveat Investor"? The relevance of the conduct of the investor under the fair and equitable treatment standard. *International and Comparative Law Quarterly, 55*, 527.

Müller, A. (2009). Limitations to and derogations from economic, social and cultural rights. *Human Rights Law Review, 9*, 557.
Neumann, J. (2002). *Die Koordination des WTO-Rechts mit anderen völkerrechtlichen Ordnungen. Konflikte des materiellen Rechts und Konkurrenzen der Streitbeilegung*. Berlin: Dunker & Humbolt.
Nhantumbo, I., & Salomão, A. (2010). *Biofuels, land access and rural livelihoods in Mozambique*. London: IIED.
Noble Ventures Incorporated v Romania [2005] Award ARB/01/11 (ICSID).
Nolan, M., & Sourgens, F. (2012). The limits of discretion? Self-judging emergency clauses in international investment agreements. In K. Sauvant (Ed.), *Yearbook on international investment law & policy 2010–2011*. Oxford University Press.
North American Free Trade Agreement [1993] 32 I.L.M. 289 and 605.
Nunn, N., & Qian, N. (2010). *The determinants of food aid provisions to Africa and the developing world*. National Bureau of Economic Research, Working Paper 16610, http://www.nber.org/papers/w16610. Accessed 30 September 2013.
Occidental Exploration and Production Company v Ecuador [2004] Final Award UN3467 (LCIA).
Organisation for Economic Co-operation and Development. (2009). *Overview of selected initiatives and instruments relevant to corporate social responsibility*.
Parkerings-Compagniet AS v Lithuania [2007] Award ARB/05/8 (ICSID).
Plama Consortium Limited v Republic of Bulgaria [2003] ARB/03/24 (ICSID).
Posner, R. (1993). What do judges and justices maximize? (The same thing everybody else does). *Supreme Court Economic Review, 3*, 1.
Principles for Responsible Agricultural Investment that Respects Rights, Livehoods and Resources [2010] available http://siteresources.worldbank.org/INTARD/214574-1111138388661/22453321/Principles_Extended.pdf. Accessed 25 December 2013.
Rabah, S., Klaus, D., & Harris, S. (2011). *What drives the global land rush?* The World Bank, Development Research Group, Agriculture and Rural Development Team Policy Research Working Paper 5864, http://elibrary.worldbank.org/content/workingpaper/10.1596/1813-9450-5864. Accessed 25 June 2012.
Raeschke-Kessler, H., & Gottwald, D. (2008). Corruption. In P. Muchlinski, F. Ortino, & C. Schreuer (Eds.), *The Oxford handbook of international investment law*. Oxford University Press.
Reinisch, A. (2006). Necessity in international investment arbitration - An unnecessary split of opinions in recent ICSID cases? Comments on CMS v. Argentina and LG&E v. Argentina. *Transnational Dispute Management, 3*.
Reiser, D. B. (2011). Benefit corporations - a sustainalbe form of organization? *Wake Forest Law Review, 46*, 591.
República de Argentina Régimen de Protección al Dominio Nacional sobre la Propiedad, Posesión o Tenencia de las Tierras Rurales Law N° 26.737 2011.
Republique Algerienne Democratique et Populaire. Ministere de l'Agriculture et du Developpment Rural. Instruction Interministerielle 196 [2013] Journal Officiel 48.
Richardson, C. (2005). How the loss of property rights caused Zimbabwe's collapse. *Economic Development Bulletin, 4*, 1.
Right to Organise and Collective Bargaining Convention, 1949 (No. 98) (adopted 01 Jul 1949) Geneva, 32nd ILC session (entry into force: 18 July 1951).
Robert Azinian and others v Mexico [1999] Award ARB(AF)/97/2 (ICSID).
Roberts, A. (2010). Power and persuasion in investment treaty interpretation: The dual role of states. *American Journal of International Law, 104*, 179.
Roberts, A. (2013). Clash of paradigms: Actors and analogies shaping the investment treaty system. *American Journal of International Law, 107*, 45.

Rosas, A., & Sandvik-Nylund, M. (2001). Armed conflicts. In A. Eide, C. Krause, & A. Rosas (Eds.), *Economic, social and cultural rights: A textbook*. Dordrecht: Martinus Nijhoff Publisher.

Roundtable on Sustainable Biomaterials. (2014). *Sustainability*. RSB, http://rsb.org. Accessed 12 July 2015.

Roundtable on Sustainable Palm Oil. (2014). *About sustainable palm oil*. RSPO, http://www.rspo.org/consumers/about-sustainable-palm-oil. Accessed 12 July 2015.

Ruggie, J. (2008). *International investment agreements, business and human rights: Key issues and opportunities*. International Institute for Sustainable Development.

S.D. Myers, Inc. (Claimant) v Government of Canada (Respondent) [2000] First Partial Award 40 ILM 1408.

Salacuse, J. (2010). *The law of investment treaties*. Oxford University Press.

Salini Costruttori S.p.A. and Italstrade S.p.A. v Kingdom of Morocco [2001] Award on Jurisdiction ARB/00/4 (ICSID).

Schultz, T. (2014). Against consistency in investment arbitration. In D. Zachary, J. Pauwelyn, & J. Viñuales (Eds.), *The foundations of international investment law: Bridging theory into practice*. Oxford University Press.

Scott, R., & Stephan, P. (2006). *The limits of Leviathan. Contract theory and the enforcement of international law*. Cambridge University Press.

Sempra Energy International v Argentina [2010] Decision on Argentina's Application for Annulment of the Award ARB/02/16 (ICSID).

Sempra Energy International v Argentine Republic [2007] Award ARB/02/16 (ICSID).

SGS Société Générale de Surveillance SA v Philippines [2004] Decision on Objections to Jurisdiction and Separate Declaration ARB/02/6 (ICSID).

Shaw, J. (2011). *The world's largest humanitarian agency*. Palgrave Macmillan.

Shepard, D., & Anuradha, M. (2011). *(Mis)Investment in agriculture: The role of the international finance corporation in global land grabs*. Oakland Institute.

Simma, B. (2011). Foreign investment arbitration: A place for human rights? *International and Comparative Law Quarterly, 60*, 573.

Simmons, B. A. (2009). *Mobilizing for human rights*. Cambridge.

Sornarajah, M. (2010). *The international law on foreign investment* (3rd ed.). Cambridge University Press.

Sulle, E., & Nelson, F. (2009). *Biofuels, land access and rural livelihoods in Tanzania*. London: IIED.

Sweet, A. S., & Mathews, J. (2008). Proportionality balancing and global constitutionalism. *Columbia Journal of Transnational Law, 47*, 68.

Tanzania Investment Centre. (2015). *Investment guide*. Ministry of Industry Trade and Investment, http://www.tic.co.tz/Team?l=en. Accessed 27 August 2015.

Tanzi, A. *State of necessity*. Max Planck Encyclopedia of Public International Law, http://mpepil.com/ViewPdf/epil/entries/law-9780199231690-e786.pdf?stylesheet=EPIL-display-full.xsl. Accessed 20 August 2013.

Técnicas Medioambientales Tecmed SA v Mexico [2003] Award ARB(AF)/00/2 (ICSID).

The World Bank. (2013). *Processing a request*. The World Bank, http://ewebapps.worldbank.org/apps/ip/Pages/Processing-a-Request.aspx. Accessed 12 July 2015.

The World Bank. (2016). *Working for a world free of poverty*. The World Bank, http://data.worldbank.org. Accessed 14 January 2016.

The World Conference on Human Rights on Human Rights; Vienna Declaration and Programme of Action [1993] available at http://www.ohchr.org/en/professionalinterest/pages/vienna.aspx. Accessed 11 November 2014.

Thjoernelund Hoelck, M. C. (2008). *State of necessity as an exemption from state responsibility for investments*.

Tladi, D. (2007). *Sustainable development in international law: An analysis of key enviro-economic instruments*. Pretoria University Law Press.

Treaty with Argentina concerning the reciprocal encouragement and protection of investment (USA-Argentina) [1991] available at http://2001-2009.state.gov/documents/organization/43475.pdf. Accessed 9 July 2016.

U.S. Model Bilateral Investment Treaty [2012] available at http://www.state.gov/r/pa/prs/ps/2012/04/188199.htm. Accessed 12 July 2015.

United Nations Conference on Trade. (2008). *Intellectual property provisions in international investment arrangements* (UNCTAD/WEB/ITE/IIA *2008 Review of the Implementation Status of Corporate Governance Disclosures: An Examination of Reporting Practices Among Large Enterprises in 10 Emerging Markets* (TD/B/CII/ISAR/CRP1).

United Nations Conference on Trade. *World investment report 2014*. World Investment Report 2014, 2015.

United Nations General Assembly Resolution 55/56 The Role of Diamonds in Fuelling Conflict: Breaking the Link Between the Illicit Transaction of Rough Diamonds and Armed Conflict as a Contribution to Prevention and Settlement of Conflicts [2001] A/RES/55/56.

United Nations General Assembly Resolution 65/22 UNCITRAL Arbitration Rules as Revised in 2010 [1976] A/RES/31/98 15 ILM 701.

United Nations, Vienna Convention on the Law of Treaties [1969] United Nations, Treaty Series, vol. 1155, p. 331.

United States - Import Prohibition of Certain Shrimp and Shrimp Products [1998] WT/DS58/AB/R (WTO Appellate Body).

Utting, P. (2008). The struggle for corporate accountability. *Development and Change, 39*, 959.

van Aaken, A. (2009a). Defragmentation of public international law through interpretation: A methodological proposal. *Indiana Journal of Global Legal Studies, 16*, 483.

van Aaken, A. (2009b). Effectuating public international law through market mechanisms. *Journal of Institutional and Theoretical Economics, 165*, 33.

van Aaken, A. (2010). *Trust, verify or incentivize? Effectuating public international law regulating public goods through market mechanisms*. University of St Gallen Law & Economics Working Paper, http://ssrn.com/abstract=1591404. Accessed 25 August 2015.

van Aaken, A. (2013a). Die vielen Wege zur Effektuierung des Völkerrechts. *Zeitschrift für rechtswissenschaftliche Forschung, 3*, 227.

van Aaken, A. (2013b). *Large scale agricultural investment and international investment law*. UNCTAD, http://investmentpolicyhub.unctad.org/Blog/Index/22 der. Accessed 12 July 2015.

van Aaken, A. (2014a). Smart flexibility clauses in international investment treaties and sustainable development: A functional view. *Journal of World Investment and Trade, 15*, 827.

van Aaken, A. (2014b). Control mechanisms in international investment law. In D. Zachary, J. Pauwelyn, & J.Viñuales (Eds.), *The foundations of international investment law: Bridging theory into practice*. Oxford University Press.

Vidar, M. (2005). The interrelationships between the right to food and other human rights. In W. B. Eide & U. Kracht (Eds.), *Food and human rights in development: Legal and institutional dimensions and selected topics* (Vol. I). Intersentia.

Voluntary Guidelines on the Responsible Governance of Tenure of Land, Fisheries and Forests in the Context of National Food Security [2013] CL 144/9 C 2013/20.

Waibel, M. (2011). International investment law and treaty interpretation. In R. Hofmann, et al. (Eds.), *From clinical isolation to systemic integration*. Nomos. Accessed 18 August 2015.

Wena Hotels Limited v Arab Republic of Egypt [2002] Decision on Annulment ARB/98/4 (ICSID).

World Bank and United Nations Conference on Trade and Development. (2014). *The practice of responsible investment principles in larger-scale agricultural investments*.

World Duty Free Co. Ltd. v Republic of Kenya [2006] Award ARB/00/7 (ICSID).

World Food Programme. (2005). *Definition of emergencies* (WFP/EB1/2005/4-A/Rev1).

Chapter 6
Concluding Remarks

This study analysed LSLIs made by foreign investors in sub-Saharan LDCs through an L&E framework that employed NIE. As a research problem, the investigation found that in certain countries, FDI could lead to HRs violations going unpunished due to institutional weaknesses. In order to approach the matter, the work investigated how to hold contractual parties accountable in cases of non-performance. We were able to identify certain mechanisms in IL that could be employed as a means to tackle contractual parties' opportunistic behaviour in LSLIs.

More specifically, the investigation noticed that agricultural policies in several LDCs could benefit from more FDI because these could trigger reforms to tackle very low levels of agricultural productivity, the rapid demographic development over the last decades, and the extreme poverty and undernourishment in LDCs. However, we argued that despite the positive effects of FDIs, the fact that local populations face forced limitation to the access and use, as well as the illegal transmission of their land, raises several legal questions about the consistency of LSLIs with domestic and international norms. In most cases, those affected include small-scale rural producers, indigenous peoples, and minority groups such as nomadic and landless communities. For all these groups, land possession represents more than an economic advantage, namely the ability to produce their own food and (in some cases) to trade the excess of produced commodities on the market in order to have access to a greater variety of goods. Land represents a social privilege and cultural heritage that, as we analysed, is broadly recognised at the national level through constitutional laws and at the international level by international law. It was confirmed that any attempt to produce a vertical integration of new illegitimate structures (as LSLIs do) might cause reactionary effects that can lead to prohibitive social costs and further infringements of HRs.

One of the major problems identified in this study relates to the manner in which LSLIs are performed in the weak institutional context that often characterises LDCs. Through the L&E framework, it could be argued that the bargaining power of international investors is disproportionately higher than that of local populations. Under these conditions, nothing will change for small farmers and

L.T. Montilla Fernández, *Large-Scale Land Investments in Least Developed Countries*, International Law and Economics, DOI 10.1007/978-3-319-65280-1_6

sub-Saharan African countries, whose resources have been used since the colonial era to satisfy the demand of external actors who at the same time have primary control over such resources. This is the reason why some scholars consider LSLIs a form of 'neo-colonialism'.[1] In their current form LSLIs inhibit the progressive realisation of pre-existing international legal obligations regarding the implementation of HRs standards pertaining to the right to property and the right to food. In such an environment, LSLIs first and foremost have a detrimental impact on local property rights and therefore food security systems. LSLIs might also lead to an increase in the dependence of affected people on governments, international aid programmes, and foreign investors.

While a discourse promoting global food security is used to stimulate liberalisation of agricultural markets and LSLIs, the negative effects on local food security in LDCs is a marginal and less considered effect. An aggravating factor is that, in addition to the weak institutional framework at the domestic level, LSLI contracts do not contain substantial specific provisions to achieve the goals that politicians mention to promote this investment policy. We have seen that under these circumstances, the international legal framework protecting the right to property and the right to food are insufficient to provide effective prophylactic mechanisms or legal remedies to ameliorate the produced effects. We have hitherto shown two contradictory scenarios: on the one hand LSLIs are intended to be the answer to food shortages in a world that produces plenty of food but distributes it poorly. On the other hand such investments have an exacerbating effect on costs because of their detrimental impact on and violation of the HRs to property and food.

Furthermore, this investigation provided a legal analysis of LSLI contracts. It confirmed that development goals, which LSLIs are aimed at, can only be achieved if investors act altruistically. LSLI contracts do not contain substantive provisions to promote or achieve the goals concerning development, poverty, and undernourishment. The poor wording of LSLI contracts shows that these instruments cannot support the achievement of the goals committed to by host states. Reasons include:

- their negotiation process lacks legitimacy because local stakeholders are not included in negotiations
- they lack mechanisms to hold investors accountable in case of non-compliance
- there is no balance between risks and benefits, neither at the local nor at the national level
- there is no provision concerning the duty to provide assessments of relevant issues like project funding, impact on national land policies, environment, food security, and HRs

Considering that national jurisdictions fail to enforce the right to property and the right to food, it was investigated whether local communities affected by FDI could seek protection at the international level. Two legal regimes exist in IL to protect the right to property: HRL and IIL. We ran a cross-jurisdictional analysis encompassing both

[1] See above at footnote 136 in Chap. 2.

regimes. It showed the different mechanisms of protection in both legal regimes available to affected locals to enforce infringed rights. We found that although most sub-Saharan countries have ratified HRs treaties, meaning that locals' rights should be protected, their enforcement is prohibitively costly in many of these cases. It is important to recall that the enforcement of HRs is state oriented. If state institutions fail, enforcement of HRs usually remains unfulfilled. This does not happen in IIL because IIAs effectively monitor and sanction wrongful acts and enforce investors' rights.

We showed that the asymmetric level of protection between different legal subjects (i.e. locals vis-à-vis investors) in IL goes back to the fact that IL is fragmented. Fragmentation makes it possible for justice administrators to apply interpretative techniques in a way that ignores the non-investment obligations of states. Furthermore, it leads to a considerable augmentation of legal insecurity that in some cases hinders states from passing even well-intentioned laws, given the effects that stabilisation clauses produce.

Taking the above into consideration, we discussed how IIAs can affect national agricultural policies. Our approach showed that although there is no legal impediment to including HRs considerations, arbitrators only narrowly make use of such an option when deciding investment issues. This leaves open the possibility that if contracts lack proper rules and standards, arbitrators could take decisions that produce detrimental effects for the contractual parties. We also showed how tribunals have dealt with issues likely to be encountered by LSLIs regarding complex land issues. These include neglecting jurisdiction if investors were involved in illegal issues (i.e. corruption, bribery) and valuating legitimate expectations of foreign investors in LDCs.

Having compared both regimes, we stated that infringements of the rights to property and food cannot be associated with a lack of substantive law at the international level. Instead, it is rather strongly linked to the institutional weakness of LDCs in enforcing HRs obligations, as well as a lack of incentives for arbitrators to consider HRs violations in IIL. For this reason we further investigated what other options are available to affected locals to individually or in groups incentivise actors involved in LSLIs to comply with HRs obligations.

We therefore mapped an NIE approach in which we assumed that HRs violations are a consequence of opportunistic behaviour of parties involved in LSLIs. Applying principal-agent theory and incomplete contract theory, we investigated the sources of opportunism and subsequently how to tackle it. We followed the classic NIE definition of opportunism and equated it to the infringement of the right to property and the right to food. Two sources of opportunism were found: (a) in stages previous to entering LSLIs and (b) in the contracts. The property rights approach indicated that in LSLIs, opportunism goes back to local institutional structures (weakly defined property rights) that allow individuals or elites to transmit property rights irregularly due to the presence of principal-agent problems. This conclusion was possible after applying a 'fragmented property rights approach' that elucidated how bundles of property rights are distributed and how economic actors interact. We were also able to understand hierarchical structures in common property rights systems.

These facts allow economic actors to behave opportunistically. It is almost impossible for landowners to undertake legal action leading to the enforcement of their rights and to the accountability of investors and politicians. Unenforceability is a consequence of limited access to national judicial systems, a lack of *standi* in IIL, a lack of judicial infrastructure with the competence to attend HRs cases, high procedural costs, as well as the omnipresent risk of personal reprisals. This institutional environment makes it possible that politicians negotiate contracts that generate benefits for special interest groups to the detriment of some locals. We further followed the methodological requirements of NIE and came to the conclusion that control mechanisms are needed to ameliorate the negative effects produced by LSLIs.

We developed a set of control mechanisms that, without being considered a panacea, are able to minimise negative effects produced by LSLIs and to increase compliance. These mechanisms show the possibilities in IL available to victims to effectuate HRs. By doing so, we demonstrated that even though judicial mechanisms fail to impart justice in LSLIs in LDCs, IL offers alternatives that can be activated as safeguards against arbitrary state conduct and abusive investor behaviour, and also to effectuate HRs in the presence of LSLIs. Thus, opportunistic behaviour can be tackled.

To tackle opportunistic behaviour in the presence of LSLIs we proposed the following control mechanisms:

- Unilateral mechanisms that can be considered either by states or by investors: these would be mechanisms focusing on regulatory measures to control the entry of investors into states' jurisdiction (proposed by states). Furthermore, we also considered mechanisms oriented towards the disclosure of information about investment processes and of their compliance with HRs standards (proposed by investors). However, this kind of mechanism can pose risks to states due to the protection that IIL offers to investors. Therefore, discriminatory measures could be in place and result in compensation. In addition, these mechanisms could easily turn into protectionist measures in weak states. Unilateral mechanisms appear to be promising. Effective coordination between states and investors should exist to lead to realistic effects.
- Contractual mechanisms that encompass a set of strategies that can be considered during the contractual negotiation process: the types of clauses included by negotiators are highly relevant because they will determine the flexibility mechanisms throughout the contract. Contractual mechanisms allow negotiators to design the contractual anatomy and therefore include elements that enable states to retain power. We showed that states can make use of such mechanisms to make known their preferences regarding applicable law, the interpretation techniques, and the allocation of some issues to the national jurisdiction. They can also employ these mechanisms to grant information flows through contractual performance, securing transparency, and considering explicit liability for HRs violations.
- The possibility that negotiators have to consider arbitrators as control mechanisms was also reviewed in this investigation. We proposed that contractual parties could restrict the power of arbitrators by drafting more specific preambles, inducing systemic integration, and requiring the use of the proportionality principle.

- External actors were also examined as control mechanisms. We made the case that non-state actors are entities able to create incentives by influencing the market segment where investors interact. In this context, IOs and NGOs can be helpful by disclosing information that further decreases the informational asymmetries between economic actors. In this regard non-state actors have demonstrated their expertise in influencing different markets or industries by disclosing information and promoting transparency for consumers whose behaviour would lead producers to reconsider their forms of production.

We highlighted that even though market mechanisms are relatively complex and costly, they offer a balance because implementation and enforcement costs are considerably low. In addition, one of the most relevant aspects is that these mechanisms can be designed without the participation of LSLI contracting parties. Moreover, they can have extra-territorial effects because they can impact final consumer markets.

Throughout this research we have showed that the challenges of LSLIs cannot be approached in a narrow way because the issues involved are multifaceted. Sub-Saharan LDCs need technical support to design land policies and to negotiate or renegotiate investment contracts in a way that expected development goals can be achieved. While in the short run market mechanisms can provide a temporary alleviation of the problem, further steps following the Voluntary Guidelines on the Responsible Governance Concerning Tenure of Land, Fisheries and Forests in the Context of National Food Security might be promoted not only in LDCs but also in developed countries. Addressing the issue of LSLIs requires further transformation and revision of national and international legal frameworks in which states and foreign investors are offered a balance of protection even in emergency and necessity cases. Both situations will very likely occur and will represent considerable challenges to IIL because most tribunals will have to interpret contracts that do not consider scenarios of food crises affecting the integrity of sovereign states.

Notwithstanding, we were able to show that IL has mechanisms that allow the effectuation of HRs even in cases where institutions are weak. This is particularly significant because today there is an increasing concern over the toleration of HRs violations in IIL. While most of the criticism from NGOs has been directed towards the TTIP and also EU-Canada Comprehensive Economic and Trade Agreement negotiations, their effects could be perceived in other IIAs. Their concern were over the lack of transparency in arbitration processes. It includes issues ranging from the election of arbitrators, which is limited to a small number of persons who are involved in the majority of the cases, to the public character that arbitration processes should have.[2] It is expected that the outcomes of these discussions will contribute to the implementation of international legal policies leading to a defragmented application of IL through the creation of an international centralised judicial organ with competence over investment issues.

---

[2]An empirical contribution on this regarding: Puig (2014), p. 387.

Some aspects covered in this investigation are still open and certain conflicts are still unresolved. They are mostly related to contractual design, transparency, and regimes' conflicts in IL that produce an imbalance between the different mechanisms of protection. The question in this context is to what extent mechanisms are able to improve the state of the art with regard to the implementation of LSLIs and how they should be developed. Both issues correspond to legal policy design and were thus beyond the scope of this study. However, the relevance of non-state actors in developing compliance mechanisms and their role in effectuating HRs has to be highlighted for further research. We are convinced that due to the relevance these issues are gaining, more legal studies should provide expertise to policy designers.

Reference

Puig, S. (2014). Social capital in the arbitration market. *European Journal of International Law, 25*, 387.

Printed by Printforce, the Netherlands